3D STUDIO MAX R3

f/x & Design

Jon A. Bell

with Ken Allen Robertson, Michael Spaw, and Scot Tumlin

Plug-ins by Tom Hudson and Johnny Ow

CORIOLIS

The Coriolis Group, LLC
14455 N. Hayden Road, Suite 220
Scottsdale, Arizona 85260

480/483-0192
FAX 480/483-0193
http://www.coriolis.com

Library of Congress Cataloging-In-Publication Data
Bell, Jon A. (Jon Allen), 1961-
    3D Studio MAX R3 f/x and Design / by Jon A. Bell.
      p. cm
    Includes index.
    ISBN 1-57610-423-0
    1. Computer animation. 2. 3D studio. 3. Cinematography--Special effects. I. Title. II. Title: Three D studio MAX R3 f/x and design
TR897.7.B472   1999
006.6'96'02855369--DC21   99-43078
                    CIP

Printed in the United States of America
10 9 8 7 6 5 4 3 2 1

President, CEO
Keith Weiskamp

Publisher
Steve Sayre

Acquisitions Editor
Mariann Hansen Barsolo

Marketing Specialist
Beth Kohler

Project Editor
Melissa D. Olson

Technical Reviewer
Scot Tumlin

Production Coordinator
Meg E. Turecek

Cover Design
Jody Winkler
additional art provided by Brandon Riza

Layout Design
April Nielsen

CD-ROM Developer
Robert Clarfield

Other Titles For The Creative Professional

ABOUT THE AUTHOR

Jon A. Bell is a writer and 3D computer graphics artist who has used 3D Studio since Version 1 (for MS-DOS). After working 10 years as an editor and writer in the computer magazine industry, Jon changed careers to concentrate full time on producing 3D computer graphics and animation for television, films, computer games, multimedia, and print. He provided 3D models and animation for the films *Exorcist III: Legion*, *Terminator 2: Judgment Day*, *Honey, I Blew Up the Kid*, *Soldier* and *Mighty Joe Young*. His video work includes the 1991, 1994, and 1997 SIGGRAPH reels for Autodesk/ Kinetix, their 1993 and 1996 National Association of Broadcasters (NAB) reels, and work for Digital Phenomena and Matte World Digital. His multimedia and game industry work includes architectural models and animation for Oracle Systems' Athenia CD-ROM, model designs and animation for LucasArts Entertainment's X-Wing and Rebel Assault, Sega of America's Jurassic Park and Wild Woody CD-ROMs, and Gametek's Robotech and Wheel of Fortune. In addition, he provides 3D graphics as a volunteer for Hawkes Ocean Technologies, Port Richmond, California, the builders of the experimental minisub *Deep Flight I*. (And if his wife will let him, he wants to pilot one of Graham's subs down to the bottom of the Marianas Trench some day.) You can reach Jon at **joanjon@sirius.com**.

ABOUT THE CONTRIBUTORS

Scot Tumlin is a San Francisco Bay-area 3D artist and animator with more than eight years of experience in creating digital content. Scot has worked with several game developers, including Acclaim Coin-Op Entertainment, Maxis, Sega of America, Spectrum Holobyte, and GameTek. He currently works for New Pencil, a digital content creation company in Sausalito, California. In his spare time, he writes how-to articles for *3D Magazine* and provides 3D graphics support for Hawkes Ocean Technologies. You can reach Scot at **scot@dnai.com**.

Michael Spaw is a 2D illustrator and 3D artist who currently works in the computer games industry, and he is a beta tester for various 3D Studio MAX-related plug-ins. Michael's projects include the content for Autodesk's Texture Universe CD-ROM, the Xeno-1 CD-ROM, and shots for Autodesk's 1995 SIGGRAPH reel and the Kinetix 1996 NAB reel. In addition, he has provided documentation for Digimation's Chameleon and Pandora plug-ins. You can reach Mike at **eclipse@scc.net**.

Ken Allen Robertson began his career as an actor and director for theater and film, and he has appeared in numerous productions. He's created graphics and animations for the 1996 Summer Olympics and for such companies as Mattel, Velocity, Intel, and AT&T. For the past four years, he's focused on next-generation, realtime 3D for gaming platforms and Internet environments. Ken holds a M.F.A. from the National Theatre Conservatory. Currently, he works in the computer games industry, teaches 3D Studio MAX special effects at the Computer Arts Institute in San Francisco, and also teaches cinematography at Pixar. You can reach Ken at **acellen@hooked.net**.

ACKNOWLEDGMENTS

I would like to thank a bunch of people who helped me create this, my third MAX book, either with literal help, moral support, or just some sort of mystical feel-good auras:

- My editors at The Coriolis Group: Melissa Olson and Mariann Barsolo; thanks for your patience; Michelle Stroup, for the last book; and Stephanie Wall, Robert Clarfield, Meg Turecek, April Nielsen, and Jody Winkler.

- Friends and fellow authors Andy and Stephanie Reese, for their friendship, editorial support and legal advice.

- Matte World Digital's Craig Barron and Krystyna Barron; Ben Barron, Morgan, Paul, Ken, Martin, Geoff, Brian, Brett, and Chris. Your visual effects advice was invaluable.

- The amazing folks at Hawkes Ocean Technologies: Graham, Karen, Oliver and Madeline Hawkes, Bob Whiteaker, Eric Hobson, and Howard Konvalin, the builders of the experimental minisub *Deep Flight*. Thanks for letting me be a part of your dream.

- The guys and gals of Digital Phenomena (**www.dph.com**): Jamie Clay, Jeanne O'lone, Kevin O'lone, Peter Clay, Karl, Jonah Loop, Kim, Lance, Laurel, and Walter. Thanks for your pointers and for letting me steal cycles from your rendering farm.

- Industrial Light + Magic Effects Supervisors John Knoll and Bill George, Model Shop Supervisor John Goodson, and *Star Trek* modelmaker extraordinaire Ed Miarecki, who've provided expert advice to me over the years on both CGI and traditional cinematic effects.

- Banned From The Ranch effects gurus Van Ling and Casey Cannon and storyboard artist/composer/"Professional Shatner Simulator" Daren Doctermann.

- Ron Cobb, an immensely talented artist and wonderful human being. Your work has inspired me for 20 years.

- Doug, Mary Ann, Regina, and Veronica Fake, and Jeff Johnson at Intrada, San Francisco. Thanks again for the friendship and the film music.

- The rest of the Intrada gang, who didn't get mentioned in the last book, here you go: Roger and Rebecca Feigelson, "George, George Champagne!" (no, that's not a typo; sing it to the end titles from Henry Mancini's score to *Lifeforce*), Rick Hauserman, Phyllis and Anton, and Larry Tate.

- Our fellow African adventurers Glenn and Trudie BonBernard, Frank Holmes, Marion Holmes, Paul and Pauline Raven, Jeff Barnard, and Thomas Gorowoto.

- Jim and Janet Curto, and Greystone, the best cat in the world.

- 3D Studio/DOS and 3D Studio MAX developers Gary Yost, Jack Powell, Tom Hudson, Dan Silva, Don Brittain, Rolf Berteig, and Eric and Audrey Peterson.

- Discreet's Phillip Miller, Frank Delise, Jo-Ann Panchak, Donell Willis, Cheryl Fromholzer, Alan Poore, Jeff Kowalski, Randy Clark, Peter Watje, Harry Denholm (**www.ishani.com**), and Norman Crafts.

- And, because they didn't get mentioned last time...thanks to Steve "SWD" Dailey, Kirk Wiseman, Dr. Lajos V. Kreinheld of the Joplin, Missouri, School of Minerals and Mine Engineering ("Go Moles!"), Freddy Franklin Fruegle, Joseph Kevin Flerk, and Klanky the Robot.

—Jon A. Bell

Contents At A Glance

TABLE OF CONTENTS

FOREWORD

As the cliché goes, the third time's the charm. During the first six months of 1996, I wrote my first book, *3D Studio MAX f/x: Creating Hollywood-Style Special Effects*. It was an amazingly difficult task—dictating, writing, and editing a 500-page MAX book, while simultaneously learning and testing the (then-beta) MAX Release 1 software—without a finished manual until the software shipped in April! On top of that, I had to create all the scene files, models, animations, and texture maps for the CD-ROM, as well as produce more than 200 still renderings, screen grabs, and the rendering for the book's cover. Nevertheless, I got it done, then went on a much-deserved vacation.

The book came out at the 1996 SIGGRAPH in New Orleans, and it was a success. I got a great deal of nice comments from people who enjoyed the sci-fi flavor of the effects techniques I presented. However, even though I enjoyed creating the book (and fulfilling my long-time dream of being a published book author), I wasn't anxious to repeat the job. Come to think of it, I vowed to whoever would listen, "I'm not doing this again!"

Okay, so I flip-flopped on this issue. After some arm-twisting from my publisher, Coriolis/Ventana, I wrote a second book, *3D Studio MAX R2.5 f/x and Design*, which was published in May 1998. For this book, I decided to cover more of the new features present in MAX R2.x. To aid me in this task, I enlisted several friends to help out. James Green did some technical editing and wrote a chapter on dynamics; Ken Robertson covered NURBS modeling; Mike Spaw contributed chapters on materials, lighting, and raytracing; and Scot Tumlin wrote about expressions and MAXScript. Their expertise in these areas broadened the scope of the book to the benefit of all the readers (including me).

However, even with all this help, writing and editing the book was a grueling, nine-month task that we all accomplished while holding down full-time jobs. After the second book, I vowed, "never again."

As you can see, I changed my mind (again), and here's another *3D Studio MAX f/x* book. There are so many great new features in 3D Studio MAX Release 3 that it was tough to contain myself during the alpha and beta-testing phase; I wanted to sit down again and share some of the cool techniques and tricks that I learned about the software. I hope you'll enjoy reading about them here, as you've seemed to enjoy the first two books.

Another flip-flop decision....Maybe I'll give up computer graphics and writing to become a politician.

—Jon A. Bell
Sonoma, California

INTRODUCTION

As my previous readers are probably aware, I spent the first half of 1996 writing *3D Studio MAX f/x: Creating Hollywood-Style Special Effects*. The emphasis of that book (my first) derived from my interests in outer space and underwater environments. These interests, in turn, came from a childhood spent watching 1960s television. Shows such as the original *Star Trek*, *Voyage to the Bottom of the Sea*, *The Time Tunnel*, and *Land of the Giants*, as well as *Wild Kingdom*, Jacques Cousteau specials, and shows about the Apollo space program, fueled my youthful imagination.

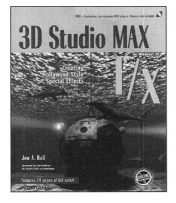

Figure I.1
My first 3D Studio MAX book, *3D Studio MAX f/x: Creating Hollywood-Style Special Effects*, described how to create a variety of outer space and underwater special effects.

My first MAX f/x book (see Figure I.1) introduced readers to techniques for creating Hollywood-style special visual effects using 3D Studio MAX Release 1 only—additional plug-ins weren't required. (No plug-ins existed for MAX at that time.) The book covered techniques for creating believable outer space and underwater environments and all of the elements therein, such as planets, laser beams, nebulas, force fields, explosions, solar flares, bubbles, plankton, water caustics, and so on. It also covered MAX's unique parametric Object Modifiers, its rendering features (such as environmental mapping, volumetric fog, and lighting), and advanced texture-mapping techniques.

Although the book was quite successful, by the time you read this, The Coriolis Group (taking over from the original Ventana imprint) has allowed the book to go out of print. That's fine by me; given the speed at which the computer industry evolves, the material in the book became more and more dated as new incarnations of MAX and new plug-ins were released (although some of the techniques described may still be useful, as I'll explain in a moment).

In the second half of 1997, as I began beta-testing 3D Studio MAX Release 2 (and soon thereafter 2.5), I decided to write a follow-up book to my first f/x work. The Coriolis Group released *3D Studio MAX R2.5 f/x and Design* in May 1998 (see Figure I.2), and it's been quite well-received, selling out its initial print run in its first two months. In the second book, I decided to present a grab bag of effects techniques that were feature related rather than genre related. In addition, I roped in several friends—all MAX beta testers and experienced MAX artists—to help cover some topics in which their particular 3D expertise was greater than mine. (It also helped lighten my workload, as the second book was 20 percent larger than the first.)

Figure I.2
3D Studio MAX R2.5 f/x and Design.

Among the subjects covered in *3D Studio MAX R2.5 f/x and Design* were creating complex surfaces using custom bitmaps; creating organic shapes with NURBS; using Release 2's Object- and World-Space Modifiers; particle systems; and raytracing, dynamics, expressions, and scripting.

In addition to material native to MAX R2.5, the book presented general 3D effects techniques, such as suggestions for improving your lighting and creating realistic materials. It also discussed how to augment your MAX work with third-party tools, such as Adobe Photoshop.

3D Studio MAX R3 f/x and Design: About This Book

And now, we come to this book. Because the time between the release of the R2.5 f/x book and this one is little more than one year, Coriolis and I decided that we didn't want all the previous book's information to go to waste. So, we've decided to create an amalgam of all-new techniques specific to 3D Studio MAX Release 3, mixed with some of the most highly regarded material from the previous book. However, wherever possible, I've updated these reprinted tutorials to reflect 3D Studio MAX Release 3's new features.

As with my previous two books, *3D Studio MAX R3 f/x and Design* will teach you how to create effects you may have seen in various Hollywood movies and TV shows, such as *Star Wars*, the *Star Trek* films and TV series, and *Babylon 5*. Therefore, this book is geared primarily toward MAX users who have an interest in special visual effects, particularly the unusual and otherworldly. It is not intended to be an exhaustive tutorial on every capability found in MAX. (For that, you can rely on MAX's own tutorials, online help from MAX users, and other MAX books, including The Coriolis Group's *3D Studio MAX R3 In Depth* by Rob Polevoi. These and other MAX resources are covered in the appendixes at the end of this book.) Nor is this book intended specifically for architects or forensic animators, although certain techniques discussed here may be useful to them.

This book is designed primarily for intermediate to advanced users of 3D Studio MAX who have experience dating (at least) from 3D Studio MAX Release 2. To get the most from this book, you need to complete the tutorials included with 3D Studio MAX R3 and have some solid experience with previous versions of MAX and its plug-ins.

Also, as with the previous two f/x books, in this book's color "MAX Studio," you'll see examples from the effects tutorials presented here in the form of screen captures, texture map examples, and sample renderings. You'll also see rendered artwork from myself and other MAX users—from talented students to professional 3D artists working on theatrical films, multimedia, and broadcast video.

Breaking It Down

3D Studio MAX R3 f/x and Design is divided into four sections, each covering different categories of MAX Release 3 features. The categories are as follows:

- An introduction to MAX Release 3, including primers on customizing MAX Release 3, lighting, basic materials creation, and MAX's new rendering features

- Materials

- Modeling and modifiers

- MAXScript and plug-ins

In each section, a series of rendered scenes illustrates the effects. Each chapter describes, step-by-step, how to create the various effects and presents suggestions to the reader for customizing the techniques.

This book concentrates on how to make the most of MAX Release 3's new features, such as the (very cool) Material Editor and Rendering settings, Surface Tools, MeshSmooth modeling techniques, and so on. Wherever possible, I concentrate on creating effects that you can produce entirely with MAX's core features or with plug-ins included on this book's companion CD-ROM.

On The Companion CD-ROM

In the back of this book is a CD-ROM, burned with the Joliet long file name system. This CD contains the MAX scene files, texture maps, material libraries, plug-ins, custom scripts, and other files used to create all of the special effects described here. Demonstration animations for the chapter tutorials are on the CD-ROM as AVI files rendered at 320-by-240 resolution. The files for the particular effects are in separate directories on the CD-ROM and correspond to each chapter of this book that contains tutorial how-to information.

CORE FEATURE TUTORIALS VS. PLUG-INS

Covering commercial (third-party) MAX plug-ins presents a vexing challenge from a book tutorial standpoint. MAX users who've purchased these plug-ins often want additional information and tips beyond those presented in the plug-in documentation. On the other hand, in discussions with MAX users, I've heard that many want to explore the interesting effects they can achieve by using just the core features of the program. Some 3D Studio/DOS and MAX tutorial books have been criticized by readers who are resentful of tutorials that require specific plug-ins. (In other words, you just spent $50 for a book that tells you that you need to spend a few hundred bucks more to make the book useful. Argh!)

So again, although it's impossible to please everyone, this book focuses on how you can create a wide variety of effects with just MAX Release 3's core feature set and the plug-ins included on this book's companion CD-ROM. You will *not* be required to buy any other plug-ins in order to create any effect described here.

Note: You do *not* need to install the MAX files from the companion CD-ROM onto your hard drive. If you load the MAX files directly into 3D Studio MAX, the program will look for the MAX file's maps not only in your designated map paths, but also in the directory from which it loaded the scene file. Due to the size of the demo animation files, however, you may want to copy them into your 3DSMAX\IMAGES directory and play them back from your hard drive to get better playback speed.

FREE TEXTURES!

The CD-ROM includes more than 300MB of original texture maps, distributed royalty-free and immediately available for your personal use. In addition, it contains various MAX scene and texture map files from both previous MAX f/x books.

Also on the CD-ROM is a large assortment of still and animated texture maps from my personal collection, as well as some maps provided by third-party vendors. Some of these maps are featured on the models used in this book, of course. Many of them started life as scanned photos of real-world industrial textures, which I then manipulated in Adobe Photoshop. I created many of the textures with an eye toward the industrial; they can serve to decorate your own spaceships, futuristic factory walls, robot bodies, and so on (even though the source material often originated from photos of Dumpsters and earth-moving equipment). Note that I've included the best texture maps from both my first book, *3D Studio MAX f/x: Creating Hollywood-Style Effects*, and the second book, *3D Studio MAX R2.5 f/x and Design* (both of these books are now out of print). In addition, the CD-ROM contains selected scene files from both books.

The majority of the textures are 24-bit color, lossless JPG files at 640-by-480-pixel resolution, although some are much larger; the textures also span a wide variety of colors. These images are designed to serve as a kit that you can alter and manipulate endlessly to create new materials. (For instance, if you wish to place a wide red stripe down the body of a spaceship, you might select a strip of the red CLEMBOX1.TGA material, which you then paste across ALUMINM6.TGA.) Other textures, including 8-bit flics and AVIs, GIF images, and CELs, have been included at varying resolutions and with varying color palettes, including grayscale. You can use many of these textures as Bump, Shininess (now called Glossiness), Opacity, and Reflection maps.

The texture maps are all found in the \MAPS directory; many of them are found in the respective CD-ROM chapter directories as well. Note that although you can use the textures in your own projects, you may not resell or distribute them.

Finally, the CD-ROM contains an updated version of Tom Hudson's popular Greeble plug-in, which appeared in *3D Studio MAX R2.5 f/x and Design*. The CD also includes Johnny Ow's Blur and Terrain plug-ins.

The CD-ROM Directories

The CD-ROM contains the following directories:

- \ARTBEATS contains 53 digitized explosion images, courtesy of Artbeats Software.

- \CHAP_01 through \CHAP_18 correspond to the tutorials presented in Chapters 1 through 18. They contain the MAX scene files, textures, and other files required for each chapter's tutorials.

- \COLOR GALLERY contains lossless JPG images of all the images (with the exclusion of four transparencies from Matte World Digital) used in this book's color "MAX Studio."

- \FX1 contains various scene files from the book *3D Studio MAX f/x: Creating Hollywood-Style Special Effects* (now out of print).

- \FX2 contains various scene files from the previous book *3D Studio MAX R2.5 f/x and Design.* By the time you read this, the 2.5 f/x book will go out of print, although you may still be able to find copies at your local bookstore or through the Web.

- \FX3 Extras contains some additional scene files, including a photorealistic spotlight, a full-body version of the cartoon dragon, an underwater scene, and a deep-space galaxy.

- \MAPS contains all the texture maps used in the book, along with many extra maps.

- \MATLIBS contains the custom *3D Studio MAX R3 f/x and Design* material library, featuring all the materials used on the various MAX scene files throughout this book.

- \PLUGINS contains Tom Hudson's Greeble 1.5 and Johnny Ow's Blur and Terrain plug-ins. (These plug-ins also are included in the \CHAP_18 directory.)

- \UI contains custom UI files for 3D Studio MAX Release 3, which you can load or customize to make your modeling and animating tasks easier.

Setting Up Your Map Paths

All of the maps you need for the tutorials are contained in their respective \CHAPTER directories as well as in the \MAPS directory of this book's companion CD-ROM.

To make sure you have access to all the maps on the CD-ROM, load 3D Studio MAX Release 3, select Customize|Configure Paths, and add the companion CD-ROM \MAPS directory manually to your map paths.

The Figures

Most of the tutorial screenshots presented in this book use the 3D Studio MAX R3 defaults that are present when you first install the program. You may notice that I have a custom floating menu called JonStuff, which contains icons for various program options, such as Render Scene, Material Editor, Track View, and Schematic View. (The JONSTUFF.CUI file is included in the \UI directory of this book's companion CD-ROM.) At the screen resolution required for this book's figures (1024 by 768), these icons aren't all visible on the top toolbar, hence my creation of this convenient floating toolbar.

If you have altered your keyboard hotkey assignments or other user-customizable features of the user interface, you may find that some of the

> **THE BOOK'S FIGURES: INCLUDED IN ELECTRONIC FORM**
>
> Various figures (rendered as lossless JPG files) from each chapter are included in the \FIGURES subdirectories within each \CHAPTER directory. As you follow along with the instructions in each chapter, you will be either viewing or loading pertinent images, mesh files, and/or scene files from the CD-ROM.

instructions presented here do not correspond precisely with your 3D Studio MAX Release 3 desktop layout. If you wish, you can change most of your default screen settings back by using the Customize|Preferences panel. See your MAX manuals for more information on configuring your program layout.

Getting The Most From This Book

Most of the special effects techniques in this book require only 3D Studio MAX Release 3 itself and the plug-ins included on the companion CD-ROM. To get the most out of this book, however, it's helpful to have a few other programs in your 3D toolbox.

For instance, virtually every 3D animator today owns a paint and/or image compositing program (many people have several different types) that produces 24-bit images with an added alpha channel. Programs such as Autodesk Animator Pro or Animator Studio (now both discontinued), Adobe Photoshop, Fractal Design Painter, Adobe After Effects, or Discreet's paint* and effect* are absolutely necessary for creating and retouching texture maps and manipulating final rendered 3D scenes. The layering features of these 24-bit programs are invaluable for compositing prerendered 3D imagery, especially for print. Although you can use 8-bit programs such as the venerable Autodesk Animator Pro to create simple maps, for photorealistic textures, 24-bit images are the way to go.

On the hardware side, because you're running 3D Studio MAX, you should also have the most powerful PC you can afford. For Release 3 of MAX, Discreet (formerly Kinetix) recommends the following:

- Microsoft Windows NT 4 or Windows 98. Service Pack 4 is required by Windows NT for year 2000 compliance. Network rendering is not supported on Windows 98.

- Intel-compatible processor at 200MHz minimum (full SMP support and dual Pentium III system recommended).

- 128MB RAM and 250MB swap space minimum (actual amount depends on scene complexity).

- Graphics card supporting 1024×768×16-bit colors minimum (1280×1024×24-bit colors recommended). OpenGL and Direct3D hardware acceleration supported.

- Windows-compliant pointing device (specific optimization for Microsoft Intellimouse).

- CD-ROM drive for installation and tutorials.

- Optional hardware includes 3D hardware graphics acceleration, network cabling (for network rendering), video input and output devices, a three-button mouse, sound card and speakers, joystick and MIDI instruments (for motion capture).

Of course, all versions of 3D Studio MAX after Release 1 (running under Windows NT 4 and above) take advantage of symmetric multiprocessing (SMP) via multithreading. That is, MAX can use multiple CPUs to perform its tasks. If you can afford a multiple-CPU computer or motherboard upgrade, you'll see a noticeable increase in both rendering speed and screen redraws in the user interface.

And, speaking of screen redraws, another nifty piece of hardware that MAX can use is a graphics accelerator card. Starting with MAX Release 2, you have a choice of using Autodesk's custom Heidi drivers as well as the industry-standard OpenGL. A large number of cards from such vendors as 3D Labs, Diamond Multimedia, and ELSA Technologies are available to speed up your MAX workflow so that it rivals that of high-end Unix workstations. For more information, see Appendix B, "3D Studio MAX Resources."

Moving On

Well, that's it for the introductions. Before you begin the tutorials, again, make sure you have this book's CD-ROM \MAP paths set up properly in MAX. Once you do, you can dive right in.

Finished? Good. As with the last f/x books, it's time to get started. In the next chapter, you'll get a brief introduction to the new features in MAX; then contributor Scot Tumlin will show you how to create your own customized MAX user interface (UI).

PART I

Introducing 3D Studio MAX Release 3

CUSTOMIZING 3D STUDIO MAX RELEASE 3 FOR YOUR NEEDS

BY
SCOT TUMLIN
AND
JON A. BELL

In this chapter, author Jon A. Bell presents a brief history of 3D Studio MAX and some of the software's changes from previous releases. Then, contributor and technical editor Scot Tumlin shows you how to customize MAX Release 3's flashy new user interface (UI) and tool sets for your own needs.

A Brief History Of MAX

In April 1996, at the National Association of Broadcasters (NAB) show in Las Vegas, the newly established Autodesk multimedia subsidiary, Kinetix, took the wraps off 3D Studio MAX Release 1 and changed the face of desktop 3D graphics once again. 3D Studio MAX was a radical departure from its predecessor, 3D Studio Release 4. 3D Studio MAX wasn't a port of its MS-DOS-based ancestor; instead, it was, and is, a completely reworked application that takes full advantage of its Windows NT environment. With its elegant GUI, open architecture, and core components technology, 3D Studio MAX has blazed a path that others—including its competitors—have been forced to follow.

In addition, every copy of MAX sold includes MAX source code and the software development kit (SDK), which has enabled MAX users with C++ programming expertise to develop their own plug-ins. During the first three years of MAX's existence, numerous professional software development companies and individual MAX users have written a large number of MAX plug-ins (from the release of 3D Studio MAX R1 to R3, more than 400 plug-ins have hit the market). These plug-ins have ranged from expensive surface deformation and character animation tools to shareware object modifiers and ready-to-run MAXScripts.

In October 1997, Kinetix shipped 3D Studio MAX Release 2, an upgrade with a massive number of new features, including non-uniform rational b-splines (NURBS), Raytraced maps and material types, enhanced particle systems, the MAXScript language, Lens Effects, and new modifiers and space warps. Then, in May 1998, Kinetix released 3D Studio MAX R2.5, an incremental upgrade that featured enhancements to its NURBS tools, enhancements to MAXScript, a Camera Tracking utility, and various other improvements.

In spring 1998, Autodesk purchased Discreet Logic, the makers of the acclaimed Flint and Flame compositing systems and the effect* and paint* software. The Kinetix Multimedia Division was folded into the new Discreet division, and both divisions' product lines were consolidated.

And now, Autodesk's new Discreet division has shipped 3D Studio MAX Release 3. Although this upgrade continues the tradition of providing better, more powerful tools for 3D artists and animators, MAX R3's enhancements have taken a different direction than the previous two upgrades took. Instead of fighting "the features war" with competing 3D programs, Autodesk's Discreet division has added a new level of maturity to 3D Studio MAX. You can see this maturity in the emphasis Discreet has placed on making the software more usable and powerful in production (for example, multiuser) settings.

MAX Release 3 provides a large number of obvious new features, which include:

- Dramatically improved rendering capabilities, including new antialiasing modes and new material types. All of these are implemented as plug-ins and can be modified and enhanced by other programmers.

- Improvements to MAXScript, allowing users to gain access (and control) many more parts of the program. The improvements include a macro feature that can record users' keystrokes and button clicks and turn them into scripts and buttons.

- A Schematic View, allowing users to more easily control and modify components of complex scenes.

- The X-Refs feature, which enables production houses to update parts of MAX scenes quickly.

- Easier-to-use polygonal editing tools for improved workflow.

- Fast organic modeling capabilities via new Surface Tools spline and patch technology.

- The inclusion of rendering effects previously confined to Video Post.

- "Tear-off" floating menus, new icons, and a customizable interface.

Release 3 also offers a wealth of other features, including a large number of unseen "under the hood" enhancements. These are improvements to the underlying architecture of the program to improve memory handling and speed up screen redraws, inverse kinematics (IK) solutions, modeling capabilities, and other features. Although many of these improvements aren't immediately apparent when you first begin using 3D Studio MAX R3, they become obvious as you work with the software.

Customizing MAX Release 3's User Interface

When you load MAX Release 3, the first thing you'll notice is how the UI has changed from MAX's Release 1 days. If you're using MAX's Large Icons UI setup, you'll see that MAX now includes tabbed panels festooned with high-color icons denoting the many different objects, shapes, modifier types, and space warps. You also notice the myriad features that fill the program, such as the new Schematic View, Tab panel, Transform Gizmo, and Mini Listener.

What may not be instantly apparent, however, is that this new, colorful UI is completely customizable. You can create your own floating panels with custom icon combinations; you can "dock" the panels at the top, bottom, or sides of your MAX desktop; you can even create your own icons to suit your fancy.

Customizing the user interface provides a number of benefits. You can reduce your desktop (or workspace) clutter by hiding the tools you don't need; this creates more space for the viewports. You can create user interfaces for specific tasks, such as an interface just for low-polygon games modeling, for example. Finally, you can create different user interfaces for individuals sharing the same 3D Studio MAX license.

In this chapter, you'll see several different ways you can customize MAX's desktop to suit your particular workflow. You'll take a look at each of these UI components and how you can modify them for your own needs.

The Tab Panel

The best way to start tweaking MAX's UI is by familiarizing yourself with the new interface elements.

Load MAX, and then take a look at your screen. The first thing you'll take a look at is the most important addition to the user interface—the Tab Panel, shown in Figure 1.1.

Before the introduction of the Tab Panel, you could (and still can) access a MAX tool via the drop-down menu, the Command panels, or a hotkey. All three of these methods have advantages, but they also have disadvantages: The drop-down menus temporarily obscure the viewports, the Command panels can take up valuable screen real estate, and unless you have the memory of an elephant, remembering dozens of hotkey combinations is difficult.

The Tab Panel provides all the benefits of the drop-down menus, Command panels, and hotkeys without the disadvantages. Unlike the drop-down menus and Command panels, the Tab Panel takes up little screen real estate. Unlike hotkeys, you can store and use only the tools you need, and no more. The Tab Panel also provides a nice balance between MAX's original default layout and the spare Expert mode.

Adding A New Tab To The Tab Panel

Before you modify the Tab Panel, you should save the current user interface (if a problem occurs you can always reload your original user interface). To add a new tab to the Tab Panel, follow these steps:

LOADING A SAVED USER INTERFACE

If you need to load the original MAX user interface, select Load Custom UI from the Customize menu. A window will appear listing UI files saved to your MAX \UI directory. Locate and select the DEFAULT.CUI file. The user interface is updated.

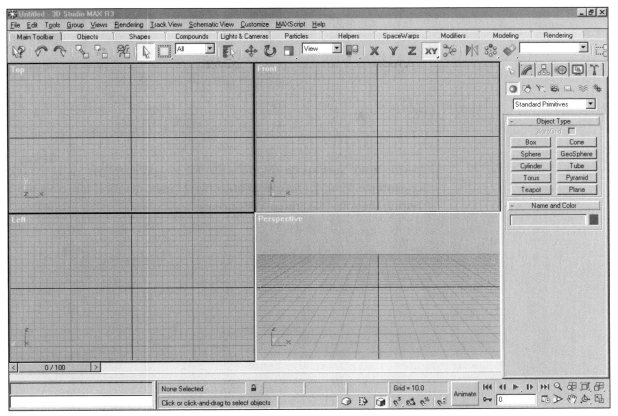

Figure 1.1
3D Studio MAX Release 3's user interface shows the new Tab panel at the top of the screen.

1. Select Save Custom UI As from the Customize menu. A Save UI File As window appears.

2. Type "Original" in the File Name field. Then, click on the Save button to complete the operation.

3. Now, you'll add a new tab to the Tab Panel. Place the mouse cursor over the Tab Panel and click-hold the right mouse button; as you do, a drop-down menu appears.

4. Select Add Tab from the menu. A window appears asking for the name of the new tab.

5. Type "Test" in the Tab name field and click on the Okay button. A new tab called Test appears at the end of the Tab Panel, as shown in Figure 1.2.

Moving A Tab On The Tab Panel

Once you've added your tabs, you'll want to reorder them to improve workflow. For example, it stands to reason that you're going to model

TABS AND YOUR SCREEN RESOLUTION

If your screen resolution is 1024 by 768 or less, you are limited to approximately 11 tabs when you use MAX's Large Icon format. This will make it difficult to see new tabs; if necessary, you may have to consolidate your tools into fewer tabs.

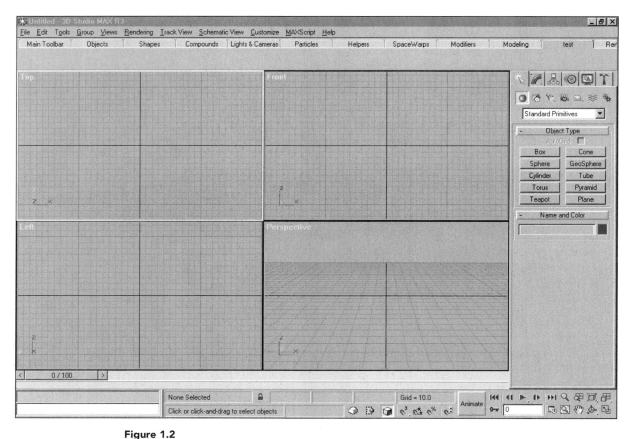

Figure 1.2

The new Test tab appears on the right side of the screen.

something and then animate it, so it makes sense to place the Model tab to the left of the Animate tab. Let's move the Test tab to the left side of the screen, just after the main Toolbar tab:

1. Place the mouse cursor over the Test tab. Click and hold the right mouse button; a drop-down menu appears.

2. Select Move Left from the menu; the Test menu moves to the left.

3. Repeat these steps until the Test tab is next to the main Toolbar tab, as shown in Figure 1.3.

Renaming A Tab On The Tab Panel

As you consolidate and organize your tabs, you may need to rename a tab so that its meaning is more immediately apparent. Let's rename the Test tab Misc.:

1. Place the mouse cursor over the Test tab again and click-hold the right mouse button; a drop-down menu appears.

2. Select Rename Tab from the menu. As you do, a window appears.

3. Type "Misc." in the Tab name field and click on the Okay button. The Test tab is renamed Misc., as shown in Figure 1.4.

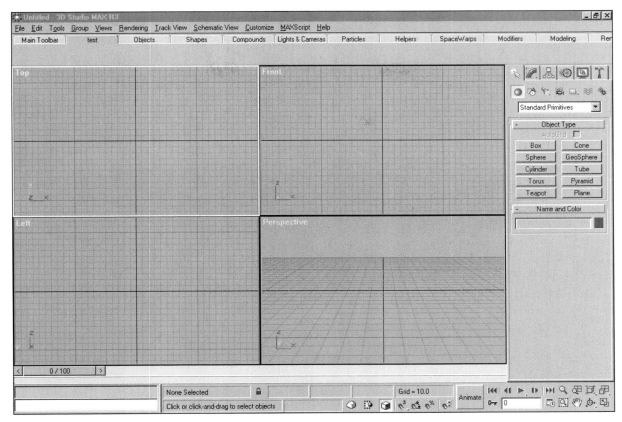

Figure 1.3
The Test tab next to the main
Toolbar tab.

Adding A Tool To The Tab Panel

A tab with no tools is a useless tab! So, let's add the Create Box tool to the
Misc. tab:

1. Click on the Misc. tab to bring it to the front of the Tab Panel. Note
   that the area under the Misc. tab is empty.

2. Place the mouse on the Misc. tab and click-hold the right mouse
   button; a drop-down menu appears.

3. Select Customize from the menu. A Customize User Interface window
   appears (see Figure 1.5).

   Let's take a moment and examine some of the items in the dialog
   box. Two buttons, Commands and Macro Scripts, appear at the top of
   the window. When you click on the Commands button, 3D Studio
   MAX commands that can appear in the Tab Panel are listed. When
   you click on the Macro Scripts button, macro scripts that can appear
   in the Tab Panel are listed. Generally speaking, a macro script is a tool
   you would find in the Command panel (the Bend modifier, for example). A command is a tool you would find in a drop-down menu
   and above or below the viewports (such as the Animate buttons).

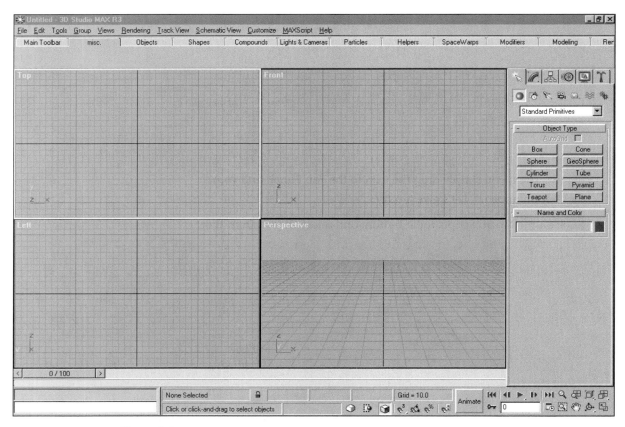

Figure 1.4

The Test tab renamed Misc. on your MAX desktop.

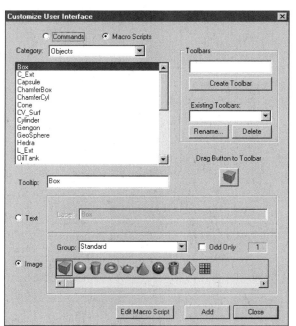

Figure 1.5

The Customize User Interface window.

When you click on the Macro Scripts button, the Category field is engaged, allowing you to sort the tools by category type. The Tool Tip field stores text messages that appear when the mouse moves over the tools. The text you place in the Tool Tip field will remind you of a tool's function. Your tools can appear as text or as icons. If you want a tool to appear in text format, click on the Text button and enter a description in the Text Label field. If you want a tool to appear as an icon, click on the Icon button and select an icon from the list. Then, you simply drag the icon to the Tab Panel, and your tool button appears. Let's give it a try.

4. Click on the Macro Scripts radio button, and select Objects from the Category field. The list changes to show only Object Macro scripts.

5. Click on Box, and then type "Creates a box" in the tool tip field.

6. Select Standard from the Group field; the Standard icons appear.

7. Click on the blue Box icon.

8. Drag the button under the Drag Button To Toolbar field to the Misc. Tab Panel. The Create Box tool appears in the Misc. Tab Panel, as shown in Figure 1.6.

Figure 1.6

A Create Box tool placed in the Misc. tab.

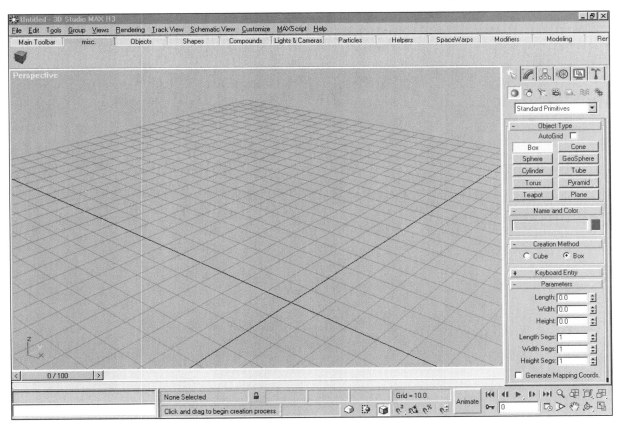

9. When you're finished, click on the Close button to close the window.

10. Now, let's test the Create Box tool. Click on the Create Box tool.

11. In the viewports, use the mouse to define the width, length, and height of the box.

Changing The Appearance Of A Tool On A Tab Panel

The best tool icons visually define the function of the tool. For the moment, let's ignore this concept and replace the box icon with the teapot icon:

1. Place the mouse cursor over the Create Box tool on the Misc. tab, and then press the right mouse button. A menu appears.

2. Select Edit Button Appearance from the menu; the Edit Macro Button window appears.

3. Select Standard from the Group field, then scroll through the list and locate the teapot icon.

4. Click on the teapot icon, then click on the Okay button. The box icon is replaced with the teapot icon.

Now, even though the icon is incorrect and misleading, the button functionality remains the same. Clicking on the teapot icon will still create a box.

Removing A Tool From The Tab Panel

During your customization of MAX Release 3's interface, you may duplicate a tool or realize a tool doesn't fit on the current tab. For example, you may decide that the Create Box tool doesn't really belong in the Misc. tab. So let's remove it:

1. Place the mouse cursor over the Create Box tool, then press the right mouse button. A menu appears.

2. Select Delete Button from the menu; a confirmation window appears.

3. Click on the Yes button to delete the Create Box tool from the Misc. tab.

Converting A Tab Into A Floating Toolbar And Back

Another nice feature of 3D Studio MAX Release 3's new interface is the ability to float a tab away from the Tab Panel. For example, say you have a tab called Poly Edit. Your Poly Edit tab contains the tools you use for manipulating vertices, faces, and edges. You can convert the Poly Edit tab into a floating toolbar. Once it's converted, you can place the toolbar right next to your model in a given viewport, which can speed up your workflow.

Here, let's convert the Misc. tab into a floating toolbar:

1. Using the steps shown earlier in "Adding A Tool To The Tab Panel," add Box, Sphere, and Cone tools to the Misc. tab, as shown in Figure 1.7. All three tools appear in the Macro Scripts/Objects section.

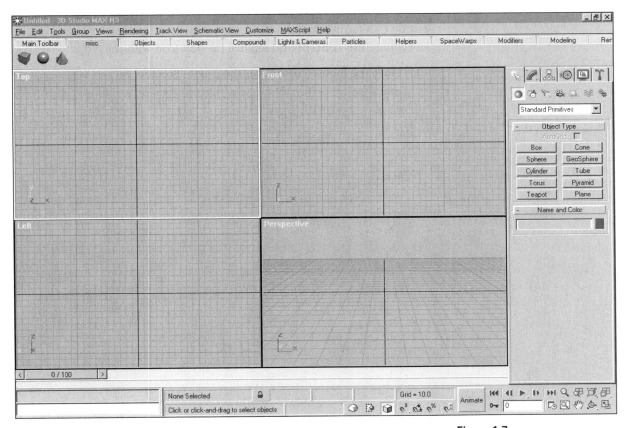

Figure 1.7

The Misc. Tab Panel with three object construction tools.

2. Place the mouse cursor over the Misc. tab and press the right mouse button. A menu appears.

3. From the menu, select Convert To Toolbar.

4. The Misc. tab changes into a floating toolbar, as shown in Figure 1.8.

    Now, you can move the Misc. toolbar anywhere on the screen, closer to your work. You can also dock a floating toolbar to the top, sides, or bottom of the screen. Let's dock the Misc. toolbar to the left side of the screen.

5. Place the mouse cursor over the Misc. floating toolbar and press the right mouse button; a menu appears.

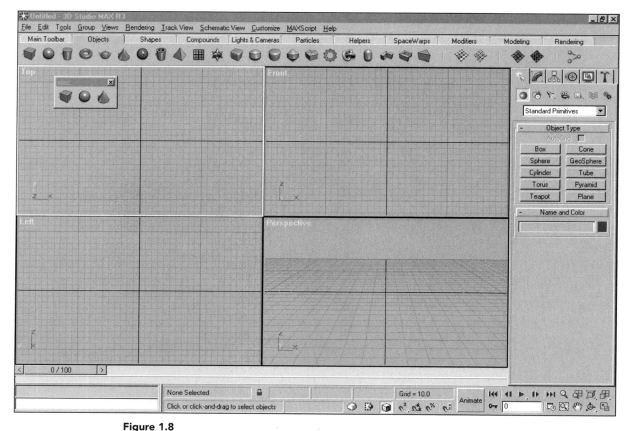

Figure 1.8

The Misc. tab converted into a floating toolbar.

6. From the menu, select Dock|Left.

7. The Misc. toolbar docks with the left side of the screen, as shown in Figure 1.9.

   Docking to the top, sides, and bottom of the screen offers another workflow advantage. Using docking, you could place tools (grouped within the same category) on one side of the screen. For example, you could dock all your modeling tools to the left side of your screen and your animation tools to the right side of the screen.

8. Now, let's put the Misc. tab back on the Tab Panel. Note the embossed horizontal line that appears above the Create Box tool. Place the mouse cursor over the horizontal line; the cursor changes from an arrow into two rectangles.

9. Press the right mouse button; a menu appears. From the menu, select Move To Tab Panel. The Misc. toolbar is converted into a tab and appears at the end of the Tab Panel.

10. Place the cursor over the Misc. tab, press the right mouse button, and select Move Left from the menu. The Misc. tab moves one space to the left.

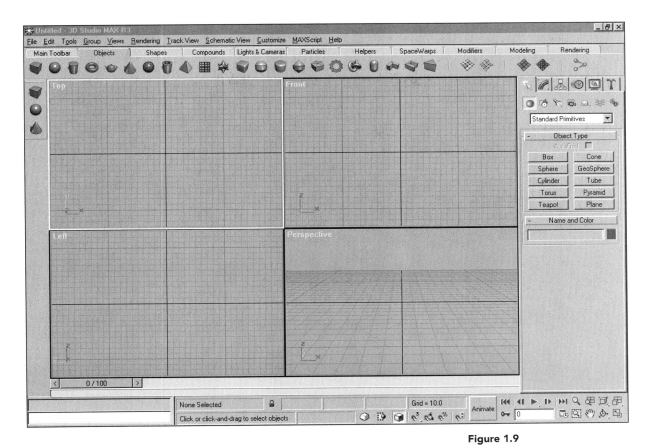

Figure 1.9

The Misc. toolbar docked to the left side of the screen.

11. Repeat until the Misc. tab is next to the Main Toolbar tab, as shown in Figure 1.10.

Hiding The Tab Panel

With the ability to dock tools, you can hide the Tab Panel and place your tools on the top, sides, or bottom of the screen. Let's try hiding and displaying the Tab Panel:

1. Place the mouse cursor over the Tab Panel and press the right mouse button. A menu appears. Note the checkmark before the Tab Panel menu item.

2. Select Tab Panel from the menu. This removes the checkmark and hides the Tab Panel, as shown in Figure 1.11.

3. Now, let's bring the Tab Panel back. Place the mouse cursor on the drop-down menu bar.

4. Press the right mouse button and select Tab Panel from the menu. The Tab Panel returns.

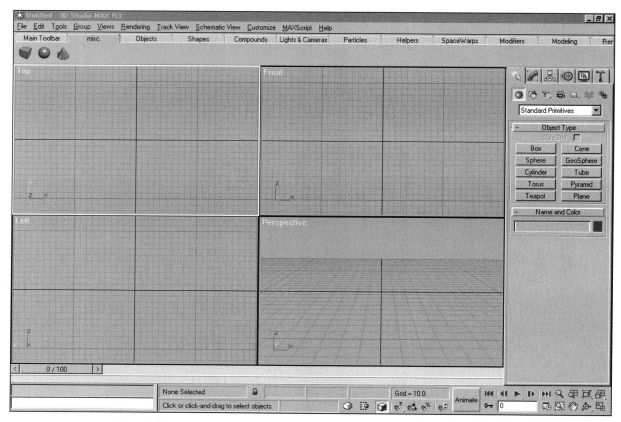

Figure 1.10

The Misc. tab, back on the Tab Panel where it belongs.

Saving And Loading Custom UI Files

Okay, so now you think your custom interface is perfect; you've got it tuned and tweaked to your heart's content. Now, you need to save it so you can use it later, like so:

1. If necessary, unhide the Tab Panel. From the Customize menu, select Save Custom UI As. A Save File window appears.

2. Type "Test" as the name of the file and click on the Save button. The interface is saved to your MAX \UI subdirectory.

3. Loading the saved interface is just as easy. From the Customize menu, select Load Custom UI. When the Load File window appears, select TEST.CUI. When you click on the Open button, your default MAX startup interface is replaced with the Test interface you just created.

This is all fine and dandy, but what if you don't want to load your custom interface every time you start 3D Studio MAX, or what if there are multiple people—each with his or her own customized MAX interfaces—sharing one or more MAX workstations? By copying all your custom CUI files to the \UI subdirectory of each

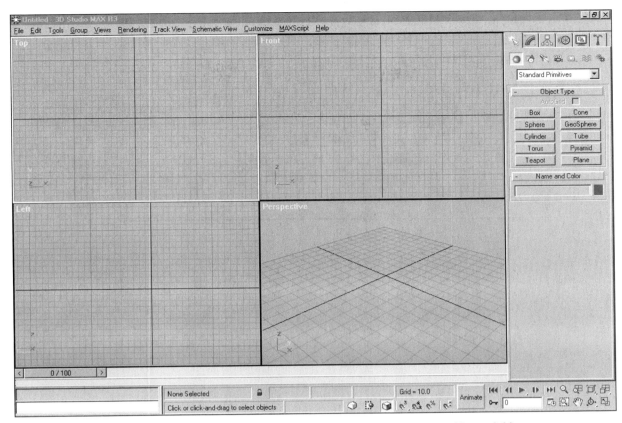

Figure 1.11

The Tab Panel hidden, providing more real estate for the viewports.

machine and then modifying the 3D Studio MAX desktop shortcut, you can start 3D Studio MAX with your custom interface. Here's how.

4. Load your custom interface and note the file name, for example, TEST.CUI.

5. Quit 3D Studio MAX, then right-click on your desktop to bring up the Properties menu. Select New|Shortcut. When the Create Shortcut dialog box appears, you'll see the Command Line field awaiting an MS-DOS command line that points to a specific executable file in a specific directory.

6. In the Command Line field, you'll need to add the name of the MAX directory in which Release 3 is located followed by the MAX executable, the value **-c**, and then the executable name and the name of the specific interface file. If you want to have a MAX session start with your TEST.CUI file when you click this new shortcut, you would enter:

```
D:\3DSMAX3\3dsmax.exe -c D:\3DSMAX3\UI\TEST.CUI
```

The **D:** denotes the drive where 3D Studio MAX is installed (you should change this to whatever letter represents the drive on which you have MAX Release 3 installed on your personal computer, of course). The value **-c** tells MAX which specific CUI file to use.

7. Next, click on the Apply button, then click on the Close button to complete the process. (You may want to rename this MAX shortcut to suit you, of course.)

8. If you double-click on the icon, MAX will start with your custom interface.

Although this may seem like a lot of work, you can quickly create a series of custom MAX setups on your desktop, both for your needs and for those of others who may be working on your system. (If you're working on various MAX-equipped systems in a production environment, again, you'll want to copy your custom CUI files to each local MAX \CUI directory.)

The Macro Recorder

In "Adding A Tool To The Tab Panel" earlier in this chapter, you added a Create Box tool to the Misc. tab. The Create Box tool executed a single task—it created a Box primitive. For situations where you need multiple tasks executed, possibly repeated often, MAX Release 3 includes a Macro Recorder feature. The Macro Recorder creates a MAXScript that duplicates your specific mouse clicks and produces the same end result.

Let's create a macro that combines the functions of the Create Box, Create Sphere, and Create Cone tools on the Misc. tab:

1. Select New from the File menu to start with a new MAX scene. If prompted to save the file, click on the No button. When prompted, select New All.

2. Make sure the Misc. tab appears in the Tab Panel. If necessary, load your TEST.CUI file to load your custom interface with the Misc. tab. Then, click on the Misc. tab; the Create Box, Create Sphere, and Create Cone tools appear, as shown in Figure 1.12.

3. Select Macro Recorder from the MAXScript menu. A checkmark appears in front of the Macro Recorder menu item. The Macro Recorder will record all user commands in a new MAXScript. The recording process ends when this menu item is selected again.

4. Click on the Box button on the Create tab, and create a box in the Top viewport. (For this example, the exact dimensions don't matter; just make sure you can see it easily in each of your viewports.) A box is added to the scene.

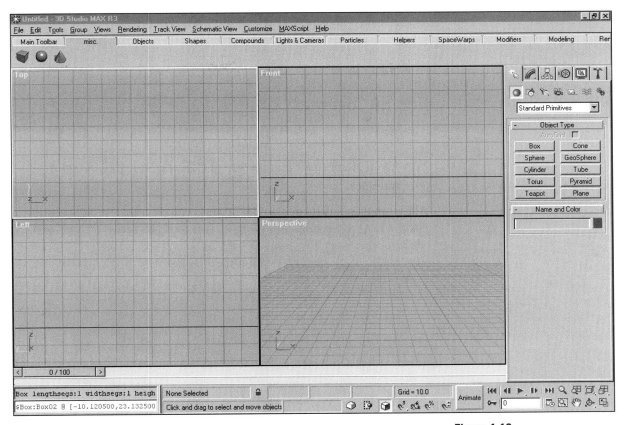

Figure 1.12

Your custom interface with the Misc. tab visible.

5. Click on the Sphere button on the Create tab, and create a sphere in the Top viewport. A sphere is added to the scene.

6. Click on the Cone button on the Create tab, and create a cone in the Top viewport. A cone is added to the scene. At this point, your scene should contain three objects—a box, a sphere, and a cone, as shown in Figure 1.13.

7. Next, select Macro Recorder again from the MAXScript menu. The Macro Recorder stops, and the recording process ends.

8. The lower-left corner of your MAX Release 3 screen contains a Mini Listener MAXScript window. Place the mouse cursor over the Mini Listener and click the right mouse button; a menu appears.

9. Select Open Listener Window from the menu; the MAXScript Listener window appears, as shown in Figure 1.14. The upper portion of the window contains the MAXScript commands that mirrored your mouse-clicking, function-picking actions. (Hey, that rhymed!) Now, note the three lines of code. The first creates a box object, the second line creates a sphere object, and the third—you got it— creates a cone object.

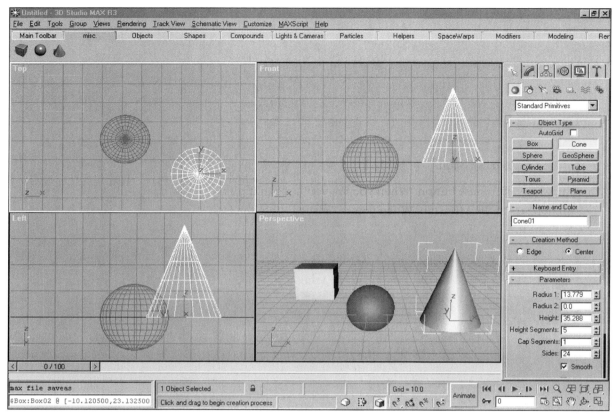

Figure 1.13

Your scene now contains Box, Sphere, and Cone primitives.

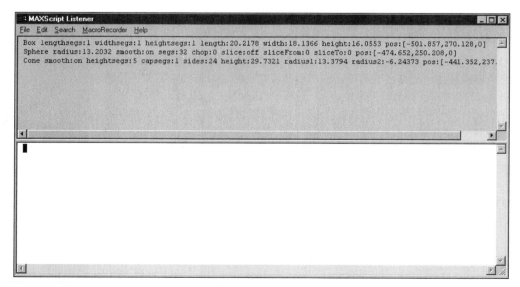

Figure 1.14

Your recorded actions converted into a MAXScript.

Converting The Macro To A Tab Tool

At this point, you could save the script and use it like any other MAXScript. A better option is to convert the three lines of code into a tool on the Tab Panel. Let's give it a try:

1. Press Ctrl+A to select and highlight the three lines of code, then place your mouse cursor over the highlighted code.

2. Left-click and drag this code to the Misc. tab; you'll see that the cursor changes to a plus sign.

3. Release the left mouse button. When you do, you'll see that a new icon appears in the Misc. tab. When you're finished, close the Listener window.

4. Next, select New from the File menu. When prompted to save the file, click on the No button. When prompted, select New All.

5. It's time to try out your new macro, so click on the new icon you just created. A box, sphere, and cone appear on your desktop.

Congratulations! You just created a macro that duplicates the work of the three buttons on the Misc. tab.

Of course, you don't need to create macros just for these simple object-building functions; you can create macros to automate highly repetitive tasks for custom effects.

Moving On

In this chapter, you learned how to customize the Tab Panel, load and save your custom interfaces, create a MAX Release 3 startup interface, and create macros. The Tab Panel reduces your dependency on the menu bar and Command panel, thus freeing more screen space for the viewports. Saving custom MAX Release 3 UIs can improve your workflow. You can tailor Release 3 interfaces for specific tasks (such as modeling) and reduce your visible desktop tool set to a manageable level. With startup interfaces customized to meet their individual needs, numerous artists can work with the same 3D Studio MAX license on a given machine. Finally, the new macros can increase productivity by converting a series of repetitive tasks into an easy-to-use tool button. (For homework, create a custom interface, taking your most-used tools and placing them on the Tab Panel. Then, try using 3D Studio MAX with the menus and Command panel hidden. For suggestions, take a look at the additional UI files included in the \UI directory of your copy of 3D Studio MAX Release 3.)

In the next two chapters, you'll take a breather from R3-specific work to refresh yourself with some basic lighting rules and realistic materials construction. You'll then explore MAX's new rendering enhancements and custom materials, maps, and shading types.

THE MACRO RECORDER AS A PROGRAMMING AID

You can use the Macro Recorder to help understand how MAXScript works. Not sure how to write code for a given task? Use the Macro Recorder to record the tasks. The Macro Recorder converts your actions into MAXScript. Paste the code created by the Macro Recorder into your own scripts and examine the results.

LIGHTING
BASICS
REVISITED

BY
MICHAEL SPAW
AND
JON A. BELL

In this chapter, you'll find some general thoughts on creating realistic lighting techniques for computer graphics (CG) scenes. You'll learn about some of the new lighting features found in MAX Release 3 and see some examples that show how you can build lighting from the ground up for different 3D scenes.

Lighting: A Primer

You may rarely think about how light works in the real world. Yet it often takes a great deal of thought and experimentation to achieve the look you want when you create lighting in the computer graphics world. Computer graphics offer nearly endless options for lighting a scene, without the constraints found in nature. Unfortunately, the freedom to create any type of lighting you can dream up can also make it difficult to produce a realistic look in your finished image. Although digital lighting provides you with new tools that are unavailable with traditional lighting design, you can improve your CG work dramatically if you know traditional techniques.

Light and its interaction in the real world is so complex that, because of the physics involved, any reasonable discussion of it would fill this book and several more volumes. Fortunately, we don't have to go to that level of detail here. Instead, you'll learn about some of the important attributes that light possesses and what you can do to re-create those attributes in MAX. Some of the concepts presented here may sound familiar, or even obvious, but it's often helpful to revert to the basics when you find it difficult to light a particular scene.

First, every time you're ready to light a MAX scene, you should ask yourself a few questions:

What kind of environment is this scene in?

One way to break this problem down is to try to fit your scene into one of three basic groups—natural lighting, artificial lighting, and a combination of the two.

Natural lighting typically refers to lighting from the sun, whether the scene is outdoors or in an enclosed environment that is solely illuminated by the sun from windows and other openings. There are several additional issues to consider when using natural lighting: What time of day is it? Is it bright or overcast? And how much light will be bouncing around in the environment?

Figure 2.1 depicts the far wall of the Great Zimbabwe Ruins in Zimbabwe, Africa. The long shadows indicate that the sun is low in the sky; Jon A. Bell took this photo in the late afternoon, October 1998. Due to the roughness of the rock, there are virtually no specular highlights showing; the rough stone scatters and diffuses the sunlight across the surfaces.

Artificial lighting can be almost anything. Any type of environment lit by electric light, firelight, or both can be considered artificial; a photo-studio light setup is a good example. Artificial lighting is probably the most common of the three types.

Once again, you need to consider where the light will come from and what its qualities are. If there are several sources, which one is the main source? With

Note: You'll take a look at creating realistic-looking rocky surfaces in Chapter 7.

Jon A. Bell

Figure 2.1
The Great Zimbabwe Ruins at dusk.

artificial light, it's also important to determine whether or not there will be a colorcast to the lights. Colorcast refers to the tint color of the light. Almost all light sources have a color tint instead of being pure white.

The last type of lighting is a combination of natural and artificial lighting. Even in brightly lit outdoor shots for films, the cameraman and lighting technicians may use reflectors or supplemental lights to mitigate harsh shadows.

What's the objective of the lighting?

In other words, what is the mood or atmosphere of the scene? Conveying a mood in the lighting can be critical to selling the overall look of the image. In some cases, the only goal is to see the object or objects clearly. More often than not, though, the goal is more complex.

Lighting can help convey an emotion or direct the viewer's eye to a particular point. It can also give greater depth and richness to a scene. Many of these considerations reflect the use of lighting as a storytelling element; this is particularly true in cinematic lighting. The use of pools of light in Figure 2.2 conveys a sense of mystery in the empty castle setting.

These same considerations are important when you are lighting a still image. Studio photographers can spend enormous amounts of time creating appropriate and captivating lighting. Consequently, when you are lighting a scene, you may ask yourself the following: What mood am I trying to convey? Is there a story to this scene, and does the lighting enhance it? (For further reference, check out books on stage, film, and studio lighting. There are hundreds of books on studio photography alone.)

Sergio Palacios

Figure 2.2
The pools of light in this otherwise dark castle courtyard help
create a sense of mystery
and loneliness.

*Are there special lighting effects that take place in the scene, and if so, should
they be created with lights or by other means?*

Besides the normal light types, MAX offers many additional effect possibilities in the form of glows, volume lights, lens flares, and special material
attributes. Although some are not strictly light types, they often add to the
appearance of visible light effects in the scene. A simple example of this is
a flare or glow from a visible light source. Because these effects are not
produced automatically in 3D (as they are in nature), you may need to
specifically include them in your renderings and adjust their look and promi-
nence. Lightning, beacons, neon, and other light-producing sources all have
their own special considerations.

You can also take into account the actual qualities of the objects that you
are "photographing," or rendering. Figure 2.3 shows a highly reflective sports
car in a futuristic garage; the glowing light panels in the garage convey the
overall lighting scheme. However, the reflections of the environment itself
(especially the ceiling light panels) help delineate the extremely reflective
vehicle surface.

Do I have reference material to draw from?

When you are creating realistic 3D lighting scenarios, it's helpful to get
into the habit of working from actual photo and film references. Clip-
pings from magazines and other sources can provide excellent visual
references. Likewise, good reference materials can provide subtle clues to
how certain objects and environments look at various times of day or
under specific conditions.

Johnny Ow

Figure 2.3
A shiny sports car is illuminated by practical scene lights and the reflections of the environment itself. This is a raytraced MAX Release 2 image.

By carefully analyzing the position of highlights and shadows in a photo, you can often reconstruct the basic position and intensities of the lights that contributed to the image. You can also learn a lot by using an existing source to re-create a lighting setup, because the artist who originally created it probably worked out some of the problems that you may otherwise encounter.

Quite often, you will have a general idea of how a scene should look, but without reference, you will be working solely from your visual memory. Sometimes, the end result will be less than you hoped for. Much like when you draw or paint, you can often accomplish a good lighting approximation for 3D scenes solely from memory, but the end result often turns out better when you can work from real life. This is especially true when you need to light a scene that is easily recognizable, but you can't quite remember what it really looks like.

Basic Light Types

After considering all of the questions in the preceding section, it's time to get to work lighting a MAX scene. Although the number and types of lights and their individual attributes will change from scene to scene, there's a general process you can follow that will give you better results than if you merely create several lights and adjust their parameters and positions in no particular order.

The first step in this process is to consider the type of lighting your scene requires. Then, you can begin to list the various light sources you'll need. Often, you'll find similarities from scene to scene in the basic number of lights and their relative positions. Unfortunately, there is no single lighting setup that will work for every scene, but there are three basic types of lights that reappear consistently and that you can use to start: a key light, a fill light, and a kicker, as shown in Figure 2.4.

Figure 2.4
A standard three-light setup showing a key light, a fill light, and a kicker.

The Key Light

The main light in a scene is often referred to as the *key light*. The key light is not necessarily just one light, but it is always the primary source of illumination. Likewise, the key light is not always localized like a spotlight; it can cover an extended area in a scene.

Even though the key light is often placed at a three-quarter position (usually, an angle of 45 degrees from the object's front and 45 degrees above the centerline), it doesn't have to be in this location. It could even come from behind or below the subject or from any other position. However, the key light is often the first light a photographer or 3D artist places, and he or she usually uses it to create preliminary light in the scene.

Although this initial placement provides a good way to see the object, the result is typically a flat, uninteresting image. If you use a key light alone, as shown in Figure 2.5, shadows are generally harsh and quite pronounced. Likewise, the scene will almost always appear too dark because there is no natural ambient light to brighten the shadow areas. This look can be useful in some occasions—a nighttime scene, for example—but it's rarely adequate for most scenes.

Figure 2.5
In this image, only the key light is used; it provides strong illumination from the three-quarter top and side angles.

The Fill Light

Fill lights round out the dark and shadow areas of the scene. The key light may be the most noticeable source in the scene, but it's up to fill lights to give the scene depth and a sense of reality.

Fill lights can be broken down into two groups. The first and most important group results from natural diffuse interreflections, or radiosity. This type of lighting is often called ambient light. Ambient light is light that, once emitted from the source, bounces around the scene until it is fully absorbed by the objects in the scene. This effect occurs automatically in nature, but it is one of the components that is missed the most when it comes to rendering in the CG world.

For a moment, take a good look around the room you're now in. Although some of the surfaces are directly illuminated by specific light sources, there are other surfaces that are indirectly illuminated. In fact, most environments contain a large number of surfaces that are not directly illuminated.

Unfortunately, most 3D rendering software (save specific radiosity rendering software, which I'll discuss later) ignores the contribution of indirect illumination. Part of the reason this type of light is so important is that it brings up the level of illumination throughout the scene, but it is not necessarily consistent across all objects. MAX's renderer, along with most other renderers, simulates the ambient component of fill light with a global ambient amount.

MAX's ambient light is applied uniformly throughout the scene with no apparent source. This additional "bump-up" in illumination decreases the overall darkness in a scene, but it tends to wash out the range of possible values. It also fails to provide any modeling of light and shadow on the objects it illuminates, which is the main reason a scene appears unrealistic.

Better Ambient Lighting Techniques

A better way to simulate ambient light is to place low-intensity spot and Omni lights in logical locations throughout your scene. Basically, your goal is to simulate the light that is bounced from the light's initial point of contact. This type of secondary illumination should decrease the shadow areas and provide some light to the underside and the corners not directly hit by the key light. If you set up fill lights with care, the whole scene can take on a radiosity-like quality.

In addition to the natural diffuse or ambient light in the scene, photographers use fill lights for both studio photography and cinema to brighten areas that are too dark or to emphasize some aspect of the scene. These additional sources sometimes come in the form of bounce cards (or reflectors) that merely reflect existing light from other sources. Bounce cards can be placed close to the base of objects to lighten the underside, or they can be placed opposite the key light to soften shadows.

In lighting for the CG environment, the difference between ambient light and other fill lights is vague because all secondary light is created by hand. What you need to determine is how much your lights will influence the scene and whether or not the additional fill lights will cast shadows. Typically, the natural diffuse/ambient light is soft enough that it will not cast a discernible shadow. Other fill lights from practical sources are often strong enough to cast shadows, as shown in Figure 2.6.

Figure 2.6
Through the use of a second spot placed to the front and opposite the key light, fill lighting gives some shading to the shadow areas.

The Kicker

In this case, *the kicker* isn't a football term; it's a light that provides backlighting to an object in the scene. Also known as *rim light* or *backlight*, the kicker's job is to help separate the target objects from the background by illuminating the object's edge (see Figure 2.7).

The kicker is often placed directly opposite the three-quarter key light. This works well if you want a stylized, studio photography look. However, this effect also happens in nature. Both sunrise and sunset have what's known as "a magic hour." It's during this time that the sun acts as a rim light and can produce an unreal glow around objects as you look toward the sun.

Backlighting also tends to catch edges of objects, causing small specular highlights. If the models in your 3D scene are constructed with small radiused edges, this highlighting can lend believability to the scene.

Other Types Of Lights

Practical lights are sources of illumination that actually appear in the scene. Table lamps, car headlights, lightning, and open flames are all potential light sources that can end up in your rendered frames.

When lights exist in the frame, they're quite often localized in effect. It's critical to use attenuation to simulate these types of lights. To the human observer and the camera, bright lights and surfaces also have the tendency to look as if they're flaring or blooming. In MAX Release 3, you can simulate these effects easily by using the Lens Effects filters Glow or Highlight, in the Rendering|Effects menu or in Video Post.

BACKLIGHTING ADDS TO REALISM

Bill George, effects art director at Industrial Light + Magic (*Star Trek: Generations, Star Trek: First Contact, Deep Impact*), recommends that CG artists remember a lighting rule for shooting miniature sets—when appropriate, try to backlight your miniature, or the models in your 3D scene. It tends to make the models look larger or more imposing and can heighten their realism. MAX's volumetric lighting effects, when projected from above and behind the central model in your scene, can particularly enhance your rendering.

Figure 2.7

When it's placed high and opposite the key light, the kicker helps to separate the objects from the background, as well as produce nice highlights along the edges.

PLACE YOUR
LIGHTS AWAY FROM
YOUR CAMERA!

One mistake 3D artists some-times make is to place their lights right behind their cam-era. Although this provides more even lighting, it also tends to flatten the rendering. The object of lighting is not only to illuminate the scene, but also to sculpt the objects with both light and shadow.

Sample Scenes: A Simple Three-Light Setup

Now that you know what the basic types of lights are, it's time to see them in action. To do this, you'll load a scene that has all three of the main light types and look at what each one does in turn:

1. Start 3D Studio MAX Release 3, or save your current work and reset the program.

2. Select File|Open, and load LIGHT_1.MAX from the \CHAP_02 directory of this book's companion CD-ROM.

   When the file opens, you'll see that it consists of basic studio-photography-style objects and lighting (it's the same scene you saw in the previous example images). Although this setup will not be exactly what you need for every MAX scene, it shows the three main types of lights that appear most often. At the moment, only the key light is turned on.

3. With the Camera view selected, render the scene.

   As you can see from the finished rendering, all of the light is cur-rently coming from the upper right. The overall image, including the shadow areas, is very dark. Likewise, the background sweep goes to black in the areas that the light misses.

   Now that you know what the key light looks like, it's time to move on to the fill light.

4. Press the *H* key to bring up the Select By Name menu, and select the Key light. Next, go to the Modify tab to bring up the Light attributes. At the top of the General Parameters section, uncheck the On button to turn the light off.

5. Bring up the Select By Name menu again, select the Fill light, and click on OK. Go back to the Modify tab, check the light on, and re-render the scene.

   The first thing you'll notice is that the fill light is very low in inten-sity and coming from the lower-left side. The main job of fill lights is to lessen the dark and shadow areas.

6. Using the Select By Name menu and the Modify panel, turn off the Fill light, select the Kicker light and turn it on, then render the scene again. This time you'll see that all the light is coming from above and opposite the key light. The kicker or backlight not only high-lights the top edges of the objects, it also separates the objects from the background sweep.

Figure 2.8
The finished image combines all the lights and reproduces a full studio-lighting setup.

7. Finally, turn on all three of the lights and render the scene. Your screen should look like Figure 2.8.

With all three lights in place, your scene now looks very much like a studio shot.

Although this is a good start, there's room for improvement. What's missing is the subtle bounce light found in reality. To produce it, you would create additional fill lights. You'll see how in the next example.

Lighting An Interior Environment

Many 3D scenes you create fall into the category of enclosed environments. When this is the case, it's critical that you pay close attention to the effects of radiosity or ambient lighting. As mentioned earlier, light will bounce around an environment until it is fully absorbed by the various surfaces. Unless you're using a true radiosity renderer, you need to give careful thought when re-creating these effects.

The following example demonstrates a more complex lighting arrangement. Here, I've created a total of eight lights to give this room a sunlit appearance with no practical lights visible. To help visualize the lighting process, the scene starts off with only the sun's contribution. To see the scene, follow these steps:

1. Start MAX, or save your current work and reset the program.

2. Select File|Open, and load ROOM_1.MAX from the \CHAP_02 directory of this book's companion CD-ROM. When the scene is

Figure 2.9
Only the strong directional lighting of the sun is produced, leaving no illumination in the rest of the room save for the amount of shading given by the global ambient light.

loaded, render the Camera01 viewport. Your screen should look like Figure 2.9.

At this point, you will see only the effect of the sun and the small amount of global ambient light. Although the light streaming through the windows looks okay, the rest of the room is lacking any directed bounce light. The little bit of the room that you see is the result of the global Ambient light setting in the Environment dialog box. If you increased the Ambient value, the room would be illuminated, but the result would be flat and unrealistic. You need to employ several carefully placed lights to simulate the room's diffuse light.

Note that the sun isn't the only source of light from outside this room. General bounce light from outdoors also contributes to the light coming in the windows. To simulate this bluish sky light, I created three additional lights for this scene. I set up one light for each of the windows and one at the far end of the hall. You can see an example of this in the next MAX scene:

1. Select File|Open, and load ROOM_2.MAX from the \CHAP_02 directory of the companion CD-ROM. Render the Camera01 view; your screen should look something like Figure 2.10.

   The three new light sources help lighten most of the surfaces in the room. Unlike the general ambient light, however, they don't illuminate every surface evenly. The corners of the room still provide shadow areas. Also, notice in your rendering the broad specular highlight on the floor with its blue tint.

2. Now that you've seen the two primary sources of illumination, it's time for the first set of bounce lights to be called into play. Select File|Open, load ROOM_3.MAX from the \CHAP_02 directory, and render the Camera01 viewport. Your screen should look like Figure 2.11.

ORDER OF OPERATIONS

One good method for setting up lights is to create and modify them in the order of least importance or brightness. When you first start, you may want to create the main key light, but before you get too comfortable with it, turn it off and decide which of the lights you need to create will have the most *subtle* influence. By doing so, you can clearly see the individual contributions of the various lights. This backward process can also help reduce the amount of time you'll spend going back and forth tweaking lights when you don't really know their net effect.

Figure 2.10
The widely scattered bluish light from the sky (in your color rendering) helps to bring up the overall level of illumination. It acts like a fill light and begins to provide shading to the walls, ceiling, and objects in the room.

Figure 2.11
Two spotlights placed below the room simulate the bounce light produced when the sunlight reflects off the floor. (In the final rendering and on your screen, both lights are a warm yellow.)

Take a close look at your rendering. When the sunlight from outside the room hits the floor, a portion of it will bounce up to illuminate the walls and ceiling.

To create this secondary light, I placed two additional spotlights below the floor and used MAX's Exclusion list to set them to exclude the floor. Both lights have a warm color to not only simulate the warmth of the sunlight, but also pick up the color of the floor.

This subtle attribute of radiosity is called *color bleeding*. Simply put, color bleeding takes place when light strikes a colored surface and then bounces to another surface. The first surface's color tends to influence the second surface's apparent color. The idea of color constancy in human perception works to counter this effect and is part of the reason you don't tend to notice color bleeding. Even though you may often not notice this effect in the real world, if it's missing from your 3D renderings, the final result may appear wrong.

3. In this scene, take a moment to select one of the secondary spot-lights. Then, click on the Modify tab and look over the light attributes. Although the light has a light yellow tint, its overall amount of illumination is low within the scene. The reason for this is that the light's Multiplier value is set to only 0.25, a quarter of the normal value. The Multiplier setting allows you to easily control the relative intensity of a light without changing its base color.

The final lighting attribute this scene needs is light that bounces from the ceiling back onto the floor and walls.

4. Load ROOM_4.MAX from the \CHAP_02 directory and render the Camera01 viewport. Your screen should look like Figure 2.12.

Figure 2.12
The last level of illumination comes from the light bouncing off the ceiling around the rest of the room. This is accomplished with two additional lights above the ceiling.

This time, I've placed two lights above the ceiling; I used the Exclusion list to exclude the ceiling so that only the walls and floors are lit.

5. Next, load ROOM_FNL.MAX from the \CHAP_02 directory and render the scene. Your screen should look like Figure 2.13.

Now that all of the lights have been turned on, you can see the final result. Notice that there is a great deal of subtlety in the luminance values of the walls and ceiling. These variations lend credibility to the scene and look like the variations generated by a radiosity solution, but without the long radiosity rendering times.

It's also worth noting that, even though there are eight lights in this scene, only one is a shadow-casting light, so the render time is not a problem. With the addition of some digitized texture maps and some fine-tuning, you can probably make this room rendering into a photorealistic representation.

Figure 2.13
The final rendered image (when shown in color) displays a richness in values and tonality similar to an image produced with a radiosity render.

6. For an additional exercise, try changing the lighting to re-create different times of day or atmospheric conditions. You could also try to change the mood of the scene or add a practical light, such as a floor lamp.

Note that you can use these same techniques for a variety of lighting situations. Although this scene differs in appearance from the studio example, it contains most of the same basic lighting types. In this case, the sun was the key light, and all the additional lights contributed to the effect of natural bounce light.

Lighting An *Anime*-Style Robot

As I mentioned previously, the goal of lighting is often not only to illuminate the object, but to lend focus to the scene or to create a particular mood.

In the next example, you'll load a complex scene featuring a Japanese *anime*-style robot built by author Jon A. Bell. This robot scene is a good example of how to use lighting to give a stylized look to the objects in the environment. To view the scene, follow these steps:

1. Load 3D Studio MAX R3, or save your current work and reset the program.

2. Select File|Open, and load ROBOTFX3.MAX from the \CHAP_02 directory of the companion CD-ROM.

   This scene consists of a custom-built giant robot model standing in a circular hanger bay. Jon created the spiked details and ribbing on the walls by duplicating the original cylindrical shape for the room and then applying MAX's Lattice modifier. Green industrial textures for the walls and custom robot textures (created from digitized photos and modified in Adobe Photoshop) complete this metallic behemoth.

ADDITIONAL LIGHTING CONTROL

MAX Release 3 gives you the ability to control lights so they don't affect the Diffuse or Specular components of the objects they illuminate. You can use this additional control to increase the realism of your scenes. In the room scene in this section, for example, you could turn off the Affect Specular option for all of the ambient bounce lights.

Because ambient light generally originates from a large source area, it typically doesn't display a specular highlight on the receiving objects. This can allow you to apply light from a variety of locations without quickly betraying their location. The Affect Specular option, although not commonly used, can be useful if you need to place a hotspot on the surface of an object (especially at a specific location) but not illuminate the rest of the object.

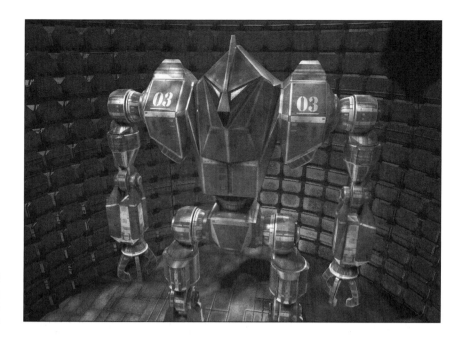

Figure 2.14
The varied lighting focuses on the robot and adds drama to the scene.

3. Render the Camera01 view. Your screen should look like Figure 2.14.

   Take a look at the effects of the colored lights in your rendering. Note how the colors give the robot a more menacing appearance. The lighting also pulls the robot out from the background.

   The choice of color is also important. Notice how the warm red and orange colors of the rim light and backlight contrast with the overall blue color of the robot. (Orange is also the complementary color of blue.) The color also could be a reference to off-camera "warning" lights, giving an additional story element to the scene. If you were to animate this scene, you might pan these lights or pulse their intensity or colors to impart a sense of danger or impending movement.

4. This scene also makes use of another not-so-evident lighting trick. Open the Select By Name menu and select Spot01. Go to the Modify panel and scroll down to the Spotlight Parameters rollup. Notice that there is a bitmap placed in the light and the Projector checkbox has been checked.

5. Select File|View File, select GRIDLITE.JPG from the \MAPS directory, and click on OK. The image is shown in Figure 2.15.

   As you can see, the GRIDLITE map is a simple black-and-white grid that acts as a *gobo* in the scene. In traditional studio and film photography, gobos are used to mask out portions of a light as well as provide additional shadow elements. These masks are sometimes

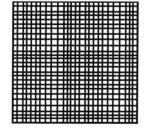

Figure 2.15
This simple grid bitmap, placed in a projector light, produces complex shadows within the scene and replicates a lighting effect known as a *gobo*.

simple cardboard cutouts mounted on an additional stand in front of the light. In other situations, camouflage netting or tree branches are used to simulate the shadow produced in outdoor conditions. The net result typically lends a more complex and interesting look to the lighting, without the need to create additional elements that sit in between the light and the receiving objects.

In the robot scene, the map takes the place of grating or an overhead gantry. In addition to making the lighting more interesting, gobos can give a sense of scale to the illuminated objects.

6. Take a moment and play with the lighting in the scene. If you look at the lights individually, you'll notice that most of them cast shadows and use exclusion lists. Excluding the background from the effects of the colored lights tends to isolate the robot from the background. Remove the exclusions and notice how the background becomes tied into the foreground elements. You could also apply attenuation to the lights to reach a compromise in these two looks.

7. Finally, you could also create your own gobo to insert in place of the GRIDLITE, or you could remove it altogether and see how this influences the scene.

Some Other Thoughts On Lighting

After you've set up lighting for your MAX scene, it's worthwhile to look back over your work and ask a few more questions:

Is my solution both simple and necessary?

Unlike lighting in reality, CG lighting requires overhead in terms of rendering time. Naturally, the more complex the lighting setup, the more time will be spent rendering and the more difficult the lighting management becomes. You should ask yourself if every light is necessary for the look that you are trying to achieve.

There's certainly a point of diminishing returns when it comes to adding lights. At some point, adding more lights will not add to the look of the scene, and it will become difficult to distinguish the worth of any additional light. If this becomes the case, try to look at each light independently to gauge its relative worth to the scene. If its contribution is questionable, get rid of it. If you follow the suggestion of creating the lighting based on the least noticeable light first and work your way up to the key light, you'll probably avoid creating redundancies.

Are the lights excluding objects that do not need to be lit? Are the lights using attenuation?

READY FOR
INVERSE KINEMATICS

Note that this robot model has linking already established on its joints and is suitable for animating with MAX's inverse kinematics (IK).

TINTED LIGHTS

Lights are almost never white. Both natural and artificial lights generally have some colorcast to them. We typically think of sunlight as being pure white light, but even it changes color with the time of day and the environment. Artificial lighting is also notorious for having a tint to it. Fluorescent lights generally have a green cast to them; halogen bulbs give off a blue-white light.

Truly color-corrected lighting environments are exceptionally rare. This fact should be used to your advantage when you are trying to reproduce specific lighting. You can add depth and richness to otherwise sterile-looking environments by giving slight variations to the color of lights in a scene. Tinting lights for artistic purposes can also be effective for conveying a specific mood or atmosphere. In most cases, subtlety is wise, but dramatic color in lighting can lead to refreshing but stylized-looking images.

Make sure you've checked all your lights and objects to see that their properties match your expectations. By simply excluding an object from some lights, you can save time when it comes to rendering.

The same is true for shadow casting. It's rare that every light in the scene needs to cast shadows. Casting shadows can be very render-intensive (especially in the case of raytraced shadows) and sometimes detrimental to the resultant image as well.

Have you simulated ambient light adequately?

As I pointed out earlier, using MAX's default ambient lighting is not the best way to simulate the subtle effects that diffuse lighting can provide. A little of the default ambient lighting may be okay, but it's worth the extra effort to place additional lights to compensate for ambient light's lack of contrast.

Can any of the lighting be simulated with mapping effects instead of actual lights?

Building lights, illuminated displays, and other small self-contained pools of light can sometimes be created with maps instead of actual light sources.

Other Options

One of the nicest aspects of MAX's design is its ability to accept plug-in components. This plug-in architecture extends not only into the realm of modeling and materials, but also into the renderer.

Several plug-ins make it possible for MAX's rendering and shading to look more photorealistic. Starting with Release 2, MAX included raytraced materials and map types, which can greatly enhance the look of your scenes. (These features have been optimized and enhanced for MAX Release 3.) There are several third-party plug-in renderers (such as RayMAX and RayGun) as well as MAXMan, Discreet's mental ray renderer, that provide additional raytracing options.

As I mentioned earlier, using radiosity is another way of producing photorealistic effects. Unlike the standard scanline render, a radiosity solution provides for diffuse light interaction in an environment. With radiosity, you do not need to cheat when you are trying to create the look of ambient light in a scene. Radiosity physically calculates the various bounces that light makes as it travels from the light source until all of the energy is absorbed in the environment. Although this type of rendering typically takes much more time to calculate than the standard MAX scanline render, it also easily re-creates one of the most difficult aspects of lighting.

Discreet's radiosity rendering program Lightscape gives MAX users this powerful rendering option. Whereas Lightscape is a standalone rendering engine, it imports MAX scenes and materials directly and can produce images of startling realism.

The other benefit of using a physically based rendering engine is that you can specify real-world luminaire light types in the scene. This allows architects and lighting designers to simulate actual lighting scenarios prior to construction and to visualize the finished look. Radiosity rendering is also finding its way into film usage because it can more accurately match lighting setups on location.

Radiosity solutions allow for very quick raytracing internally; once the light solution has been calculated, it's view independent, enabling realtime navigation through the environment. As the state of the art in rendering moves forward, radiosity will begin to play a greater role because it allows users to create more photorealistic lighting scenarios almost automatically.

Moving On

In this chapter, you explored some of the basic concepts of lighting design. You walked through several examples to get a better understanding of how to approach lighting a scene, and you learned the importance of fill and ambient lighting. Finally, you explored new lighting features in MAX Release 3. With these concepts under your belt, you should be able to improve the lighting in your 3D scenes, whether they're realistic or fantasy oriented.

In the next chapter, I'll discuss some of the general considerations for designing realistic materials, both organic and inorganic.

CREATING
REALISTIC
MATERIALS:
A PRIMER

BY
MICHAEL SPAW
AND
JON A. BELL

In this chapter, instead of re-creating specific materials by completing tutorials that take you step-by-step through the process, you'll learn a more generalized set of techniques that you can apply to many natural and man-made materials to make them realistic.

What Does Reality Look Like?

It can be tough to build believable natural materials that represent real-world surfaces. Not only do you need to have a keen eye and a reasonable understanding of how nature looks, but you also need a good deal of creativity. MAX's Material Editor enables you to create highly complex and convincing materials—if you have a clear idea of what you want to create and how to achieve a particular look.

The topics in this chapter include:

- The use of layered detail to produce dirt, grime, and natural weathering

- Determining the appropriate level of detail and realism

- Building maps from scratch with various paint programs

- Ways to modify existing maps for increased realism

- Materials for skin, eyes, and fur

For many 3D graphics artists, attaining photorealistic (or at least strongly believable) results is the Holy Grail of CG visualization. The exact look of reality can be elusive, and unfortunately, it's difficult to re-create, even with the most powerful 3D tools. Reality is inherently complex, and re-creating it in the 3D world can be expensive, in both creation time and rendering time.

Thankfully, we don't need to model at the subpixel level or write physically based reflectance shaders to create images that look stunningly real. The bulk of both realistic lighting and realistic shading currently relies on clever cheats. Even with the cheats, however, re-creating real-looking images can be difficult.

Part of the problem of re-creating reality comes from the fact that we, as observers, are immersed in visually complex environments our entire lives and can determine immediately if something doesn't look "right." A large portion of our visual perception system is designed to do just that—detect differences and irregularities in what we see. (In terms of pattern recognition, humans can blow the most sophisticated computer out of the water any day of the week.) When we see something that looks "wrong," it tends to be glaringly apparent.

The real problem in creating a realistic CG environment is not just one of knowing when something looks wrong, but of analyzing what the problem is and figuring out what modifications you need to correct the problem. As with most of the arts, success at re-creating reality requires practice and a keen eye. Understanding the attributes that most natural materials share is a good starting point for re-creating them in the 3D world.

Fortunately, 3D Studio MAX's Material Editor gives you a great deal of power in manipulating your material attributes. You can use additional maps (preferably real-world, digitized bitmap textures) in the various map channels or add modifications to the main Diffuse texture map. For any material, you can also use any of MAX's varied map channels. Although you may end up creating complex material "trees" composed of multiple layers of maps and masks, consider this the price you pay for added realism. You may literally spend days building your models and getting the details right. But when it's time to create the materials for the objects, you don't want to adopt a "hurry up and get it done" attitude. You need to spend as much time on your objects' "paint jobs" as you did creating the objects themselves.

Levels Of Complexity

To create the look of a particular material, all too often a 3D artist places a single texture map in the Diffuse channel, makes some modifications to its specular component, and proclaims it done. The result of this quick-and-dirty material creation resembles a sheet of contact paper that's been slapped on the object. Regardless of the quality of the texture map, the resulting material may lack the subtle complexities associated with most real-world surfaces.

The single most important quality of real objects and materials is that they are *complex*. Even a flat, white, painted wall will look complex when viewed at the right angle.

In 3D Studio MAX, select File|View File, and view the STUCCO.JPG image in the \CHAP_03 directory of this book's companion CD-ROM. This image is also shown in Figure 3.1.

The Diffuse component of a material is typically the first one noticed by the observer, but it's not the only one. To add to the material's verisimilitude,

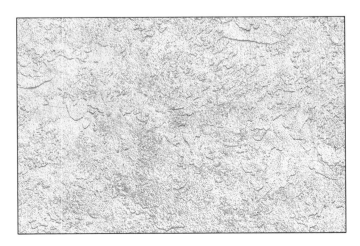

Figure 3.1
A digitized photo of a white stucco wall texture; you could not only use this on a wall as a Bump map, but as a Diffuse map as well. (Note that this bitmap is included in both the \CHAP_03 and \MAPS directories of this book's companion CD-ROM as STUCCO.JPG.)

you need to consider not just color, but also the amount of gloss, roughness, and wear and tear that most natural materials exhibit.

One of the best ways to create realistic materials for the objects in your scene is to consider their history. How old is the object in question? How often is it used and does that use impart a particular type of wear? How long has it been in its environment, and how has the environment affected it? Is it wet, dry, dusty, or cracked? This list could go on, but it's important to think of how the object has been affected so you can re-create the appropriate look. Once you know what the effects are, you need to consider their placement; most types of degradation are not omnipresent over the surface of objects. Finally, you need to find good visual research from which to work—don't guess at the look of a surface when you can work from real life.

Color And Saturation

Take a quick look around and study the objects that surround you. The first thing you'll probably notice is an object's overall color. Under good lighting, if you squint, you can get a pretty good feel for what that color is. This said, it's important to realize that color isn't nearly as constant as you might think. Lighting plays a critical role in a material's perceived color. When the lighting changes, so does the apparent color.

When you replicate a material, it's a good idea to view whatever source you are working from in conditions that are as close to daylight as possible. This ensures that no unwanted colorcast that alters the appearance of the base color is introduced. Usually, you'll want to build a material based upon this unmodified color. However, there may be situations in which you need to design a whole set of materials around a specific type of environmental lighting. You may want to create custom versions of materials for scenes with low-level lighting, add stylized or painterly effects to a material, or convey a particular mood.

Another common attribute of most natural, real-world materials is that they rarely contain highly saturated colors. This is especially important when creating materials that replicate environments. The sky, ground cover, soil, and rocky surfaces rarely exhibit saturated colors, especially when viewed from a distance.

In 3D Studio MAX, select File|View File, and view the ROCKS.JPG image in the \CHAP_03 directory of the companion CD-ROM. This image is also shown in Figure 3.2.

This digitized photo of a rocky surface shows clear earth tones and shading, but none of the colors is particularly vibrant in the image on your screen.

Note that there are exceptions to the saturated color rule in nature. For example, many animals utilize vibrant colors for defensive and display

ALWAYS USE A MAP!

It's best to always use a bitmap texture or a procedural map instead of a solid diffuse color when re-creating a natural or even an artificial surface. Even seemingly solid colors contain slight variations of hue, saturation, and value. These small color changes help break up otherwise static or obviously rendered surfaces.

Note: You'll see how to create the appearance of wet surfaces in Chapter 7.

Figure 3.2
A rocky surface.

purposes. Foliage, when viewed at close or medium range without much atmospheric attenuation, also can appear saturated. Wet surfaces also display increased saturation and overall darkening.

In 3D Studio MAX, select File|View File, and view the MUD_5.JPG image in the \CHAP_03 directory of the companion CD-ROM. This image is also shown in Figure 3.3.

Figure 3.3 shows a close-up of a wet, muddy surface taken near a parking lot after a hard rain. The bright sunlight accentuates shiny highlights in the mud. This texture is useful for (you guessed it) depicting a muddy, slimy surface, such as a wet field or even the bottom of the ocean.

It's often good practice to bring down the saturation of many materials to help blend them into their environment better. The real world is a dusty, dirty place, and dirt has a tendency to get on objects, which will naturally

Figure 3.3
A muddy patch of field after a rainstorm.

mute normally vibrant colors. Most texture maps that are either created from scanned images or acquired from a CD-ROM source can generally benefit from decreasing the saturation (using a paint package) 5 to 10 percent to help account for this.

A material's saturation can also suggest how new it is. Many materials' colors have a tendency to fade over time when exposed to sunlight. This bleaching effect is especially noticeable in man-made objects. Pigments often fade dramatically because of exposure to ultraviolet light. It's also important to note that all colors or pigments don't fade equally. Reds and yellows are notorious for fading. Printed material sitting in a store display window will probably be faded. Quite often, the only colors left are cyan and black. The magenta will have faded because of the bleaching action of the sun.

In 3D Studio MAX, select File|View File, and view the GRENELEC.JPG image in the \CHAP_03 directory of the companion CD-ROM. This image is also shown in Figure 3.4.

This is a picture of the front of an industrial electrical junction box. As it sits outside exposed to the sun and rain, its painted surface becomes bleached and faded.

Saturation also plays an important role when you create materials for poorly lit or nighttime scenes. The rods and cones in the human eye control overall perception of color. The cones are adapted to detect variations in color during normal levels of illumination. When the level of illumination falls, as in the case of a darkened room or at night, the rods begin to take over and color vision disappears. The rods sense light achromatically; that is, they can only detect changes in the value of a color. The net result is that in

Figure 3.4
An electrical junction box with a faded surface.

low illumination, colors appear to become desaturated. To help account for this, you may want to alter your standard maps for the various objects in a dim scene and create textures with far less saturation.

Dirt, Grime, And Other Weathering

Nothing stays clean very long. It may sound pessimistic, but it's a useful fact to consider when you're replicating a natural-materials look. Virtually everything you come into contact with (especially outdoors) eventually acquires some form of weathering as a result of general use and exposure to the sun and the elements.

The effects of weathering can take many forms—typically, variances in coloration, texture, and shininess. When you create these texture effects, you need to consider the object's environment and the types of weathering that would be appropriate. Keep all effects understated unless their purpose is to attract attention.

The degradation of an object's factory-new surface can be the result of one or more of the following: bleaching or fading due to the sun; abrasions, dents and scratches; stains due to splashes, dripping, and leaching; dust, soot, and other airborne particles; polishing due to wear; chipping, cracking, and peeling paint; and oxidizing and patination.

In 3D Studio MAX, select File|View File, and view the RUSTYCAR.JPG image in the \CHAP_03 directory of the companion CD-ROM. This image is also shown in Figure 3.5.

Figure 3.5
An old car door shows rust and paint cracks.

This image shows the door of an old junked car. Its paint has become cracked and is falling off; rust spreading over the metal underneath the paint is also accelerating the aging process. In the case of organic materials such as wood and leaves, surface changes may be the result of moss, mold, decomposition, and bacterial decay.

In the sections that follow, you'll find some of the approaches you might take to achieve various weathering effects on an object's surface.

Bleaching Or Fading

The simplest way to achieve the effect of bleaching or fading is to alter the saturation of the texture map in Photoshop or a similar program. Although it is not seen all the time, this modification to the basic material can help blend man-made objects into natural environments.

Look for areas on the object that may not have direct exposure to the sun—these areas could retain more of their original color and vibrancy. For example, a label or other object may cover a portion of the surface; the covered areas would most likely retain much of their original coloration.

Remember, not all colors fade equally. You could re-create this effect in Photoshop by utilizing the Curves function in the individual color channels of a bitmap to desaturate specific colors. As with all weathering effects, having a good reference is a must.

Abrasions, Dents, And Scratches

General wear and tear is apparent in almost every object that we come in contact with; thus, it's critical that objects in your 3D environment share these attributes.

The simplest way to achieve the effects of general wear and tear on a material is through the use of Bump and Glossiness maps. A library of premade maps for this purpose can be a great time-saver.

In 3D Studio MAX, select File|View File, and view the GENBUMP1.JPG image in the \CHAP_03 directory of the companion CD-ROM. This image is also shown in Figure 3.6. I created this Bump map in Photoshop to depict scratches for many different types of surfaces.

If you have a graphics tablet, it's simple to create a fairly large grayscale image and fill it lightly with scratchlike markings of various sizes and intensities. It's often helpful to create a number of marks, slightly blur them

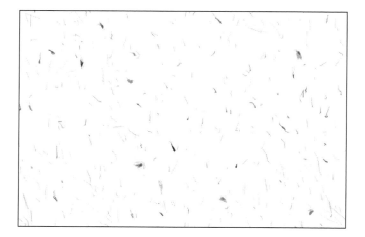

Figure 3.6
A subtle Bump map used for various surfaces.

using Gaussian Blur, and continue to make more. By repeating this process several times, you can create a layered look that matches the effect that real objects receive from continuous exposure to scratching and burnishing through contact with other objects.

If you have access to a flatbed scanner, you can create Bump maps via "analog" means. Just take a soft pencil or charcoal, draw marks on a sheet of plain white paper, and then scan it. You can smudge and soften these marks on the paper—or in a paint program after you've scanned them—to build up a complex layered appearance. In addition, charcoal rubbings from natural surfaces, such as brick and concrete, can provide all manner of textures that look pitted and abraded.

Stains: Splashes, Dripping, And Leaching

Any material that can absorb moisture has a tendency to become stained. These items include not only the obvious materials, such as fabrics, but also nonorganic porous surfaces, such as concrete and painted items. Parking lots and tabletops provide ample proof that relatively hard surfaces can also acquire stains.

The most straightforward way to create a stained look is, once again, via a paint program. In general, stains have a tendency to darken and saturate the receiving surface. By using airbrush tools, or Photoshop's Burn, Dodge, or Sponge tools, you can create the color changes that stains create. If the surface should appear wet or oily, you may also need to use the same Diffuse map you created as a Glossiness map. Of course, you can also start from a real-world texture.

In 3D Studio MAX, select File|View File, and view the GRYSTREK.JPG image in the \CHAP_03 directory of the companion CD-ROM. This image is also shown in Figure 3.7.

Stains usually occur because of contact with water or other liquids, so you should consider how and where the exposure will take place. Unless the receiving surface is flat and horizontal, liquids will flow, leave streaks, and concentrate in low spots. More viscous liquids, such as oil, will flow less and tend to pool.

Another result of exposure to moisture and dirt is an accumulation of these materials in the recesses of an object. This effect is so critical to the appearance of large man-made objects that traditional model-makers have created a special weathering technique called a *wash*. In traditional modeling, artists may dilute small amounts of dark brown, gray, or black paint with thinner and allow it to flow into the recesses and cracks on a model. When they wipe away the excess wash, some of it remains in corners and along seams and panel lines and gives an increased sense of depth to the model.

CREATING CUSTOM WEATHERING MAPS

You can save a huge amount of time by creating a library of grayscale weathering maps rather than creating everything each time from scratch. Many details—such as dents, smudges, and water spots—can be used repeatedly on several objects in a scene as long as they remain subtle and you place them carefully. Use a paint program (such as Fractal Design Painter or Adobe Photoshop) that allows you to layer several maps with varying degrees of blur and detail until you arrive at a result you like.

Figure 3.7
Water stains and streaks on a
painted surface.

You can simulate this effect in 3D with careful painting of object-specific maps. You can darken panel lines or recesses to re-create the accumulation of dirt, oil, and other grime. There are also third-party MAX plug-ins, such as REM Infografica's DirtyREYES, that can simulate this effect automatically. An example is shown in Figure 3.8.

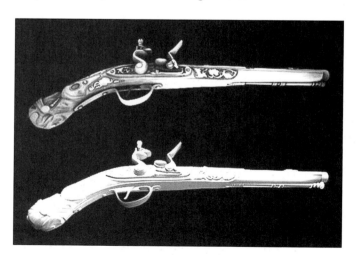

Figure 3.8
REM Infografica's DirtyREYES
plug-in applied to a 3D model.

Dust, Soot, And Airborne Particles

As you just learned, recesses are best accentuated with dark shading. Flat or top surfaces of objects can acquire an accumulation of dust and other airborne particulate matter, which generally dulls the surface and decreases its saturation.

To create dust-accumulation effects in MAX, you can use a Top/Bottom material. The Top material should contain a Blend material; the Bottom material represents the main material for the object. In the Blend material, Material1 should re-create the dust or particle covering. Material2 should be an Instance of the main body material that you used as the bottom material for the Top/Bottom. In the Mask: Map entry, you can use procedural Noise to simulate the collection and variation of dust covering.

To see an example of this technique, follow these steps:

1. Select File|Load, and load the DUSTY.MAX file from the \CHAP_03 directory of this book's companion CD-ROM.

2. Open the Material Editor and take a look at the Dusty Top/Bottom material settings. The Top material consists of a Blend material, with a grayish surface blended with a blue surface using a Noise map as the mask. The Bottom material consists of the same blue surface (as an Instance copy), with the Top/Bottom settings further blending among all these material components. (Note that this material is saved in your MAXFX3.MAT Material Library.)

3. Next, activate your Camera01 viewport and render a test image of this scene. As your rendering indicates, the top of the sphere looks as if it's accumulated a coating of dust, making its surface less shiny.

Polishing Caused By Wear

Objects that are handled often, or are subject to abrasion, exhibit either a shine or a dullness. These effects, which are critical to realism, show that the surface is not consistently smooth.

You can generate this look in MAX by using custom maps in the Glossiness and Specular Level map slots. The trick is in careful placement of the effects because they will most often appear only in certain areas. You can use simple grayscale maps to enhance the perceived complexity of the material. (In the next two chapters, you'll see how to create complex metal materials using these techniques.)

Chipping, Cracking, And Peeling

Through the processes of heat expansion and contraction, cracks tend to form in both solid and coated surfaces. You can create simple representations of the effects of chipping, cracking, and peeling with both Diffuse and Bump maps.

If your objects are going to be viewed up close, you may want to create more complex geometry so the surface will self-shadow correctly. MAX's Object Modifiers, such as Noise or Displace, can create random surface displacements or custom topology on your objects.

Oxidizing And Patination

Metals and surfaces that are chemically active oxidize when exposed to oxygen and moisture. In nature, the process is known as *oxidation*. When this effect is created for artistic purposes, it's called a *patina*.

The most common example of metal oxidation is reddish rust on iron surfaces, of course. However, copper, brass, and bronze also demonstrate the reaction to oxygen and moisture—they tend to develop a powdery, greenish blue coating of copper oxide when exposed to the elements. Bronze, if not fully oxidized, can take on a darker, mottled appearance with little or no green cast.

In 3D Studio MAX, select File|View File, and view the BRASS_1.JPG image in the \CHAP_03 directory of the companion CD-ROM. This image is also shown in Figure 3.9.

Figure 3.9
An image of a mottled brass metal surface with tarnished areas in the detail.

Aluminum also oxidizes, but to a lesser visual degree. You may represent this effect in MAX by softening your object's reflectivity and adding some dark gray or black specks to its Diffuse map to give it a dusty appearance. Silver blackens with oxidation, and other metals oxidize and acquire different appearances. Even when metal objects are polished frequently, the oxide tends to remain in recesses.

You can often re-create the look of many chemically active surfaces by acquiring existing digitized texture maps of metal materials via CD-ROM texture libraries such as Discreet's Texture Universe or Digimation's Xeno-1 collection. Check out the appendixes in this book for other sources.

Determining Levels Of Detail

Geometry and material detail go hand in hand. Sometimes it is difficult to separate what should be modeled and what can be accomplished through the use of well-constructed textures. One way to approach this problem is to divide a model's surface characteristics into three separate levels: the macro level, the material level, and the sub-pixel level.

The Macro Level

The *macro* level describes gross features that you can't create with either materials or shading and that you need to add during the modeling phase. Some 3D artists create their models with the same level of overall detail and don't add appropriate complexity in certain areas. Certainly, not allowing for enough faces on curved surfaces is a noticeable flaw when dealing with polygon-based geometry.

Less obvious is the lack of radiuses, or rounded-off edges, on your models. Few objects, other than knife or razor blades, have absolutely straight, sharp edges where two surfaces meet. Most have at least a small radius on the edge.

Sharp edges on natural and man-made objects tend to be worn down through general use and abrasion and thereby create radiuses. Conversely, many manufactured objects have radiused edges so they won't show wear and because radius edges are safer and more appealing to interact with.

In the CG world, adding radiused edges (even tiny ones) to your objects will increase their complexity (and possibly your rendering time), but the result is increased realism. In any object with a degree of shininess, specular high-lights will tend to show up on the radiused edges. The human visual system recognizes this, and we've come to expect that the highlights will be present.

Figure 3.10 shows two parametric MAX box objects. The left object has stan-dard sharp edges with no radius on them. The right one has a slight edge, created with the MeshSmooth modifier.

Figure 3.10
By adding radiused edges to objects, you can pick up specular highlights.

Notice how the box on the right has better specular highlights along its radiused edges. Tiny surface details like these, although subtle, can make your 3D objects much more aesthetically pleasing.

The Material Level

You control the next level of detail at the *material* level. When it comes to re-creating medium-scale texture, bump mapping is a must. Because few natural surfaces are as smooth as glass, very subtle bump mapping, using either procedural Noise or texture maps, lends to more interesting surfaces and takes away some of the flat or plastic look so prevalent in computer graphics imagery (CGI). You should also use scratches, dents, and other surface defects in conjunction with the regular surface to indicate wear. Although very small bumps will most likely be filtered out when rendered at a distance, they should be present if the object will appear close to the camera during an animation.

As with all map and geometry details, consider how much time they will appear in the scene and at what distance. If the object is moving and has motion blur, it may negate the need for more subtle details. Sometimes you may want to create multiple versions of the same maps with different resolutions (using the Image|Image Size features of Photoshop) depending on the needs of your scene.

The Subpixel Level

The final level of surface detail can be thought of as occurring on the *subpixel* level. Very flat surfaces reflect light with less scattering and tend to be shiny; perfectly flat surfaces act as a mirror. However, because real surfaces are rarely perfectly smooth, this micro-scale roughness causes light to bounce around a localized area, which tends to further illuminate the surface.

You can see this effect on materials like flat paint or chalk, where the shadow areas tend to be less pronounced. You can also see it if you take a look at the full moon some clear night; you'll notice how there's little in the way of shading, even though Luna is basically a sphere lit from one source—the sun.

When you're creating objects with very dull surfaces, consider how light may be scattered across them and adjust your texture maps and material parameters accordingly.

Creating Good Texture Maps: The Basics

With the advent of Photoshop and other 24-bit paint programs for the PC, you can create convincing MAX texture maps with relative ease if you know exactly what you're trying to reproduce. Once again, real-world photographic reference is critical. If you can go out and photograph the subject, do it. Otherwise, hit your local library or bookstore to find examples of the material. Magazines can provide excellent visual reference on myriad subjects. (You may find a use for those copies of *National Geographic* that you just can't throw away.) For relatively simple materials, try the following basic techniques:

• Once you know what the material should look like, start off by creating a new map at a larger resolution than its intended final size. It's always better to start larger than you think is necessary and crop it or scale it down later.

• Consider the type of mapping coordinates you're going to use with the map. If the mapping requires a particular aspect ratio, set the length and width of the bitmap appropriately. If you're using planar projection to apply the map, render an orthographic view of your geometry in MAX and use it to help determine the final aspect ratio.

• You should also determine if the map needs to be tilable. If so, you can use the Offset filter in Photoshop with the Wrap Around feature enabled. This will help you locate the map's seams and then paint them out.

Painting The Maps

If you have Photoshop or Fractal Painter, here are some quick steps to get you started on a plain Diffuse map for a MAX object:

1. Determine the base color of the map. If it's going to be an ivory-colored texture, you need to determine the correct RGB settings for the initial ivory color. You should then determine the RGB settings for lighter highlights and darker shadings of the ivory color.

2. In either Photoshop or Fractal Painter, create a new image of at least 640-by-480 resolution; then, fill the map with the most prominent base color.

   Note that very few materials are one solid, consistent color. Try to identify secondary colors within the material and create swatches for them in a palette or second file. By adding subtle color variations in the map, you can help remove a flat appearance, as shown in Figure 3.11. (You can also view this file in MAX or one of the paint programs; load IVORY.TGA from your \CHAP_03 or \MAPS directory.)

Figure 3.11
An ivory texture.

3. At this point, you may want to introduce some noise into the basic map. To produce some nice variations, apply Photoshop's Add Noise filter at a low amount with Monochromatic either checked or unchecked. (The latter depends on how much additional color variation you want to introduce into the original map.)

4. If the end result is too prominent, apply a small amount of Gaussian Blur over it. For a more layered look, you can repeat this combination several times, decreasing the amounts each time.

By using many filters in combination, you'll have a good starting point for complex bitmaps. This is especially true when creating Bump maps. It's also useful to make several copies of your base map in case you want to create variations.

Analyzing The Map

Once you've painted a basic texture, you need to analyze the main details and see if you should replicate particularly effective areas. If the features are large in scale, you may want to find a second map that has similar features and clone and blend them into your new map. You can also use cloning to add subtle amounts of a color to other areas of the map.

If you like the look of one feature, clone it several times and modify the copies to hide their repetition. For best results (especially for high-resolution still images), try to keep the features random unless you need to create a particular repeating pattern for the surface. Now, consider the extra details (such as dirt, dents, scuffs, and discoloration) you need to add to make the material convincing. One of Photoshop's most useful features (starting with version 4) is that it allows you to work in layers. Sometimes a modification of the base map can provide a starting point for the Bump or Glossiness maps. You can add dusty spots and general grime by airbrushing lightly on a transparent layer, which sits on top of the finished texture.

You will also be able to see the exact placement of details if you create the maps in a layered format. Once all the layers are complete, you can save them individually and place them in their respective map slots.

The Apple Scene

For an example of convincing hand-painted texture maps created with the layering techniques you learned in the preceding section, take a look at this apple scene:

1. In 3D Studio MAX, load APPLE.MAX from the \CHAP_03 directory of the companion CD-ROM. When the file loads, you'll see a simple scene consisting of an apple sitting on a tabletop.

2. Activate the Camera01 viewport and render the scene; your rendering should look like Figure 3.12. To create the apple's surface, I painted two textures—a Diffuse map and a Bump map—in Photoshop.

Figure 3.12
Hand-painted Diffuse and Bump maps help create this convincing apple image.

3. To see the bitmaps, open the Material Editor and examine the Apple texture's Diffuse and Bump map slots, or choose File|View File and view the APPLESKN.JPG and APPLEBMP.JPG images in the \CHAP_03 directory of the companion CD-ROM. These images are also shown in Figures 3.13 and 3.14.

Figure 3.13
The Diffuse map for the apple.

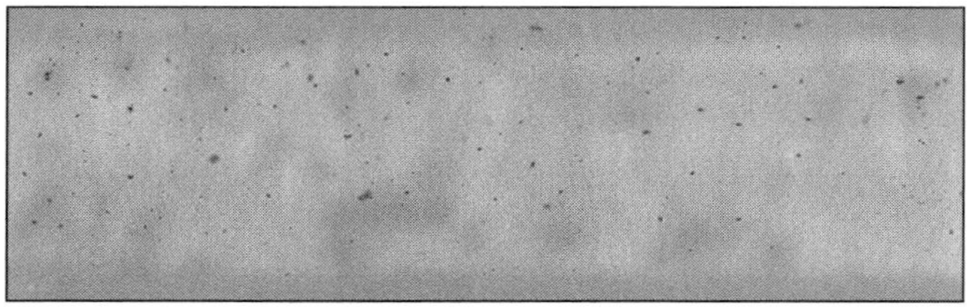

Figure 3.14
The Bump map for the apple.

Note: In Chapter 8, you'll see how you can pump up the apple's color saturation by using the RGB Multiply map to combine the APPLEBMP.JPG image with the APPLESKN.JPG Diffuse map.

Using Preexisting Textures

If you feel you don't have the art skills to paint your own realistic texture maps, you might want to use existing bitmaps for your scenes. If you do, however, you should ask yourself several questions:

Is the map of high enough photographic quality and resolution for its intended purpose?

Quite often, maps that come on texture CD-ROMs are fairly small. If this is the only problem, you can tile or retouch the map to increase its size. If the map is much too small, you may be better off finding a replacement or trying to paint one from scratch. To determine if the map's resolution is high enough for your rendering, ask yourself if the object that uses the map will be rendered, at any point, at a larger resolution than the map itself (for still images, this may often be the case).

Is the scale of the texture correct for the scale that will be represented?

When you photograph surfaces, it can be especially difficult to keep the lighting consistent over large areas. Consequently, the map you want to use may be the right material but at the wrong scale. You can tile maps if there are few macro features that will betray the repeats, but it's usually best to create a larger map that has had these features removed or rearranged.

Does the map have intrinsic lighting clues in it that will contradict the lighting in the scene?

Sometimes maps that come from photographs include shadows and highlights because of the lighting in their environment when they were shot. These lighting artifacts will rarely correspond with your scene's lighting. Your best bet is to use maps that are flatly lit or create your own. If you have to use a map with shadows and highlights already in it, you can sometimes minimize them by using the Dodge and Burn tools in Photoshop. By decreasing the variance in luminance, you can hide some of these artifacts.

Is there a colorcast to the map?

Photos from print film and scanned images sometimes acquire a colorcast that is caused by their original lighting. Use Photoshop's Curves tools to neutralize the colorcast if possible. Also, remember that overly saturated colors tend to be unrealistic.

Does the map need to be tilable?

Many of the better CD collections try to make their maps tile without visual discontinuities at the seams. If you are forced to make a map tile, use the Offset filter in Photoshop and be prepared to spend some time working on it. Retouching can take practice. This is especially true if the detail is macro or the seams are wildly different in content. Sometimes retouching isn't an option and the map is best replaced.

Will the map be used in more than one place in the scene?

If the answer is yes, consider making variations of the map. Slight variations of smudges, dents, stains, and so on, can make multiple instances of geometry appear more realistic. If you can't modify the map, consider changing its mapping to help conceal the repetition.

Organic Materials

Organic materials are some of the most difficult surfaces to reproduce faithfully with the current level of sophistication in CG. Often, these materials are not merely defined by their outermost surface.

Skin

Human skin in particular is difficult to reproduce because there are several layers to it and each layer has varying degrees of opacity, color, glossiness, and texture. When you try to paint the net results of these effects, you'll typically produce a flat unrealistic surface.

Some of the components to keep in mind when you paint skin textures are variations in skin tone, blemishes, bruises, large and small wrinkle textures, hairs, oiliness, and subsurface features such as veins. To create an excellent reference from which to paint or clone, try scanning or photographing a representational-size image of real skin. Although human skin remains a real challenge to reproduce, various animal skins have been replicated to appear photorealistic. Both on TV and in films such as *Jumanji*, animals including elephants, crocodiles, and dogs are showing up with greater regularity; a large part of their believability is due to accurate surface representation. Figure 3.15 shows a human skin example. Although

---

HIDING A REPEATING BITMAP PATTERN

Here's an excellent trick to hide tiling bitmaps. Use a Blend material in MAX with the exact same bitmap in both Material #1's and #2's Diffuse slots. However, change the UV tiling of the Diffuse map in Material #2—for example, if the first is UV tiling at 1/1, tile the second at 2/2 or 3/3. Then, load a procedural Noise texture as the mask between the maps. The subtle shades in the Noise will blend between the two textures and help extend the non-tiling areas of the maps.

Figure 3.15

The H_FLESH2.TGA map from the Xeno-1 texture CD is included on this book's companion CD-ROM in the \MAPS and CHAP_03 directories.

this image is fairly macro in scale, it should give you a good starting point to create object-specific skin maps.

Eyes

Eyes make up another area that deserves some attention in character-material creation. We tend to get a lot of information from the movement and appearance of a character's eyes. Consequently, it's important to put enough detail into the eyes so that they appear realistic.

If the creature remains at a far enough distance from the camera, you can often incorporate the eyes into the overall body texture maps. In most other cases, though, you'll want to create independent maps and geometry for the eyes.

As with everything else, working from a reference is a must when trying to replicate the fine detail within the eye. One problem with grabbing an eye image from an existing photo is that the extremely shiny, wet eye surface invariably produces unwanted highlights on the image. You can sometimes retouch these images to remove the lighting artifacts. Unfortunately, eye images are often too small; you must either find close-up images to retouch or paint maps from scratch.

To alleviate some of these problems, this book's companion CD-ROM includes several human, animal, and alien eye examples. You can use them in your own work or use them as reference for creating your own original eye texture maps. Figure 3.16 shows two sample eye maps from Digimation's Xeno-1 texture CD.

Corneal Distortion: Creating Realistic Eyes With Raytracing

To see an example of one of the textures from the Xeno-1 texture CD used in a MAX scene, follow these steps:

Digimation

Figure 3.16
Some sample eye images from the Xeno-1 texture CD.

1. In MAX, load EYE.MAX from the \CHAP_03 directory of the companion CD-ROM. When the file loads, you'll see two hemispheres sitting inside a boxy room.

2. The smaller hemisphere serves as a cornea over the main eye surface. Open the Material Editor and you'll see that it has a raytraced material applied to it. This provides a slight amount of spherical distortion to the eye bitmap and makes the final rendering more realistic.

3. To see an example of the spherical distortion, activate your Camera01 viewport and render the scene (it may take a few minutes because of the raytraced material). When the scene appears, your screen should look like Figure 3.17.

Figure 3.17
The SHEEP_Y.TGA eye map as applied to a hemisphere; a second hemisphere with a raytraced material provides spherical distortion.

Hair And Fur

In the last few years, there's been a lot of interest in the simulation of fur for CGI. As with most developments in the field, the first examples of fur and hair came out of the research community.

Not long after, proprietary software examples began to show up in both TV and film. Now, this same functionality has shown up on our desktops. Although MAX doesn't have a specific hair routine built into it, there are workarounds and new plug-ins that not only make the creation of fur and hair possible, but make them realistic looking as well.

One simple solution is to use MAX's Scatter compound object type to distribute simple hair geometry across the surface of your object. Figure 3.18 shows an example of how this technique was used by noted MAX artist Martin Foster.

Figure 3.18
On its nighttime feeding flight, a bat chases after a moth.

You can also use shareware or commercial MAX plug-ins to create hair or fur on your MAX creatures. MAX plug-in developer Peter Watje has created a particle-system-based hair that enables users to create long, dense hairs on their creatures and base the coloration on the object's original texture mapping. It also allows for secondary motion-based dynamics.

Digimation's Shag: Fur and Shag: Hair plug-ins produce ultrafast photorealistic fur and hair through the use of atmospheric shaders. Unlike the other options mentioned here, the Shag plug-ins produce no real geometry, which allows you to create super-dense coats of fur or hair with little problem. It also allows you to set almost all of its parameters via maps. This gives you solid visual control of where and how the fur will be created.

Regardless of which method you use, make sure to give some randomness to the hair and fur through various parameters. Variations in color and length will improve realism. Figure 3.19 shows an example created with the Shag: Fur plug-in.

Figure 3.19
An example created with
Digimation's Shag: Fur plug-in.

Moving On

In this chapter, you explored some of the most important aspects of realistic material design, including materials for both organic and inorganic surfaces. In the next few chapters, you'll continue exploring materials creation in MAX and see how Release 3's new material shading types and rendering filters enhance your final results.

MAX R3's New Rendering Options

Among the most noticeable—and appreciated—improvements in 3D Studio MAX Release 3 is the enhanced renderer. MAX's default scanline renderer has been improved in many different ways, ranging from the addition of a variety of antialiasing (AA) modes to improved materials supersampling. These improvements, when coupled with Release 3's new material shading types and lighting defaults, can help fledgling MAX artists create photorealistic scenes more quickly and easily.

BY JON A. BELL

Antialiasing And Supersampling

In this chapter, you'll take a quick look at MAX's various antialiasing (AA) filters, such as Area, Blackman, Catmull-Rom, Soften, and Video, and learn how to pick the right one for the right effect. You'll also see how the new supersampling filters in the Material Editor can enhance your final renderings and remove some of the jaggies from harsh Bump maps. To illustrate these features, you'll take a look at a complex sample scene and examine how the different AA and supersampling modes help address specific rendering issues in it.

The '60s Retro Set

Over the course of this chapter, you're going to see the term *AA* a lot—but it has nothing to do with 12-step rehabilitation programs. Instead, AA refers to antialiasing—the process whereby pixel jaggies on digital images are smoothed out. MAX Release 3's different antialiasing algorithms not only smooth out your final 3D renders, they can actually change the look of your scenes dramatically.

To show off the effects of these filters, you're going to load a complex sample scene and render portions of it using the different Release 3 AA filters to achieve different results, as so:

1. From the \CHAP_04 directory of this book's companion CD-ROM, load 60SRETRO.MAX. The file loads, and your screen should resemble Figure 4.1.

   I built the first version of this bizarre scene (in 3D Studio Release 4 for DOS) several years ago for a proposed multimedia project. The client, a large Silicon Valley technology company, wanted a funky, futuristic space, and I decided to build a 1960s-inspired, "future retro" room. (Much of my inspiration for the design came from the aesthetics of the classic cartoon *The Jetsons*.) During a design meeting with the client, I began to idly doodle on a piece of paper, and when the client considered the five-minute sketch (shown in Figure 4.2), he said, "Hey, how about that?!" Alas, after seeing the 3D renderings of the design, the client ultimately decided on something more conventional (which made little difference because the CD-ROM project ended up being cancelled). Since I retained rights to the design, I filed it away for future use.

   Later, as I was planning this chapter of the book, I decided that this wacky room might be a fun way to illustrate MAX Release 3's various AA and supersampling filters. So I located the model and its textures (long archived on an old CD-ROM), loaded it into MAX,

DESIGN IT ON PAPER FIRST!

Although it's fun to simply boot up MAX and start constructing your 3D models from scratch, it's often better to create some basic line drawings to work out aesthetic problems beforehand. You don't have to be an industrial engineer, a draftsman, or a professional sketch artist to find the usefulness of committing several ideas to paper before constructing them in 3D. Often, even a simple thumbnail sketch will help you work out object proportions and balance in your final 3D scene.

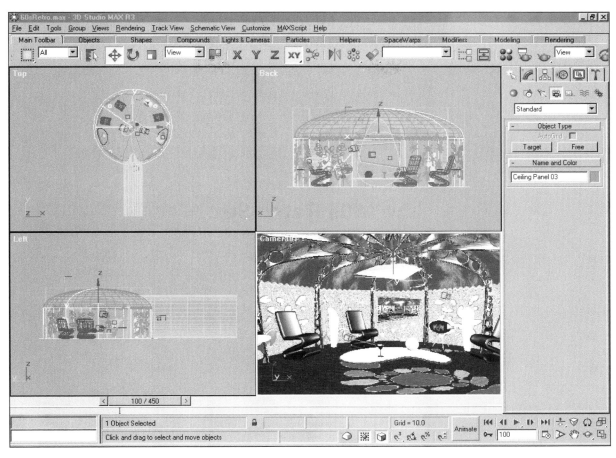

Figure 4.1

The 60SRETRO.MAX scene (note that the Camera01 viewport is showing Frame 100).

Figure 4.2

A rough, five-minute pencil sketch served as the basis for the final '60s retro room design.

THE '60s RETRO ANIMATION

If you want to see a 320-by-240 animation of this set, click on File|View File and select the 60SRETRO.AVI file from the \CHAP_04 directory of this book's companion CD-ROM.

and began tweaking and rebuilding it. In the years since I first constructed the model, I had improved my modeling and materials techniques, courtesy of MAX's advanced features. So for this book, I decided to update the room. I put in additional furniture (including an "antigravity" coffee table), put filleted edges on the ceiling beams, improved the lighting and textures, and so on. (It's a good thing you don't have to blow digital dust off of old 3D models when you load them up again years later.) A few shiny metal textures later and the room was ready for habitation by open-minded humans, or most robots.

2. To get a better look at this set, drag your Time Slider to frame 100, or highlight the frame number, type "100", and press Enter. (In the complete animation, Camera01 has a slow tracking move down the hall and through the doorway, and then it pans leisurely around the room.) Then, activate your Camera01 viewport and render an 800-by-600-pixel version of the scene; your rendering should look like Figure 4.3. Don't close your Camera Virtual Frame Buffer (VFB) window when you're finished; you'll want to save this rendering in a moment.

Figure 4.3
A rendering of the 60SRETRO scene, frame 100.

3. Your rendering should show clearly the, um, eclectic aesthetics of the scene. If you open the Material Editor and examine the materials, you'll see a variety of hot colors: pink stucco for the walls; bright red, green, and blue plastic wall decorations; an op-art carpet; and

"cowhide" chairs. The chair material is actually a procedural Noise map with the Thresholding adjusted to create the distinctive black/white patterning. In addition, you'll notice numerous shiny metallic surfaces. The various metal surfaces use MAX Release 3's Reflect/Refract map (loaded with cubic environment maps); the Reflect/Refract maps are then mixed using MAX Release 3's new Falloff map. (For more information on how to use Falloff to create convincing metal effects, see Chapter 6.)

To speed up rendering this complex scene, I opted to not use raytracing to create any of the metal reflections. (When I was finished with the overall model, I showed it to my wife and tried to convince her to let me decorate our house in exactly this manner. Her response was slightly more colorful than the '60s rendering itself.)

4. Close your Material Editor, but before you close the rendering, click on the Save Bitmap icon (the disk in the upper-left corner of your Camera01 VFB). Save this rendering to your \3DSMAX3\IMAGES directory as 60S_AREA.TIF. (In a few minutes, you'll be looking at this rendering again and comparing it with renderings that use different AA filters. The AA filter for this scene is the MAX Release 3 default Area filter.)

5. In addition to the outlandish material colors and textures used in this scene, I paid careful attention to lighting and lighting effects as well to create a stylized look. Click on Rendering|Video Post; in the Video Post queue, you'll see the Camera01 view and the Lens Effects Glow and Flare filters. Next, click on the Execute Sequence icon. When the Execute Video Post menu appears, under Time Output, check Single and set it for frame 100. (Your rendering resolution should be at least 640 by 480.) Then, click on Render. After a few minutes, the rendering appears, and your screen should look like Figure 4.4.

   In this rendering, you should see how the Lens Effects filters add hot, visible light sources to the scene and provide a reasonable rationale for the 3D lighting. They also draw your attention toward specific details, such as the "hall of mirrors" room portrait on the far wall and the two decorative tables and their assorted gewgaws.

6. Before you close your Video Post VFB window, you might take a quick look at a new MAX Release 3 VFB feature that enables you to examine various aspects of your rendering. In the middle of the window is a name field with a drop-down arrow next to it; in the

Figure 4.4

The Lens Effects Glow and Flare filters add bright highlights to the scene.

name field is the current RGB Alpha rendering. If you click on the drop-down arrow, you'll see a list of other components of this scene, such as Z (which shows Z-buffer, or camera depth, information), Material Effects (which shows materials in the scene that have Material Effects channels active), Object (G-buffer information), Normal (which shows face normals), and Non-Clamped Colors (which shows colors that are too hot for video rendering). Click through each one of them in turn and examine the results in your Video Post VFB.

7. When you're finished looking at the rendering, close your Camera01 VFB window (you don't need to save this image for later comparison) and your Video Post menu. For the rest of this chapter, you'll be doing your rendering tests without adding these specific post-processing optical effects.

Choosing The Right AA Filters For Your Scene

As you examined the Video Post rendering, you probably noticed that the overall contrast and colors in the scene are quite hot. This is true regardless of your screen display gamma, although if your MAX Gamma correction is turned off (in the Customize|Preferences|Gamma tab), the scene will appear with more contrast. The aesthetics of this scene are bright and cartoony.

Given the look of this scene, can you change—or enhance—its appearance and artistic direction simply by altering MAX Release 3's AA filter settings? Certainly—you'll do that right now.

1. Select Rendering|Render, then scroll down to the MAX Default
   Scanline A-Buffer rollout. (This assumes that you're using the default
   MAX Release 3 renderer; if you're using a third-party renderer, some
   or all of these filtering options may not be present.) Under Anti-
   Aliasing, you'll see several settings. Anti-Aliasing (AA) is checked
   On, of course; Filter Maps (for material textures, specifically
   bitmaps) is also checked.

2. In the middle of the rollout is a small name field with a down arrow
   icon to the right. The current filter (and MAX Release 3 default) is
   Area. This is an enhanced version of the default AA method used in
   previous versions of MAX; as its description in Table 4.1 says, it
   "computes antialiasing using a variable size filter." (To the right of
   the name field is a Filter Size field; the default pixel setting is 1.5.)

3. If you click on the down arrow, you'll see a list of 12 AA filters in all.
   Take a look at Table 4.1; it describes each filter, using terminology
   taken from MAX itself.

Whew! Table 4.1 offers a lot of interesting stuff, but what does it all mean
for your renderings?

Table 4.1 3D Studio MAX Release 3's antialiasing filters.

Filter Type	Description	Filter (Pixel) Size
Area	Computes antialiasing using a variable size filter.	1.0 to 20; default is 1.5.
Blackman	A 25-pixel filter that's sharp, but without edge enhancement (see Catmull-Rom).	N/A
Blend	Blend between sharp Area and coarse Soften filters.	1.0 to 20; default is 8.0 (Filter); Blend is 0.0 to 1.0; default is 0.3.
Catmull-Rom	A 25-pixel filter with pronounced edge enhancement effects.	N/A
Cook Variable	General-purpose filter. Values 1 to 2.5 are sharp; higher gives greater blur.	1.0 to 20; default is 2.5.
Cubic	A 25-pixel filter based on a blurring spline.	N/A
Mitchell-Netravali	A two-parameter filter: Trade off blurring, ringing, and anisotropy.	Blur and Ringing range from 0.0 to 1.0; default on both is 0.333. (Note: High Ringing values can result in nonopaque alpha, causing ghosting of your image. Adjust this filter carefully.)
Plate Match/MAX R2.5	MAX R2.5 method (with no map filtering) for Camera Mapping and MAX R2.5-style anti-aliasing. Recommended Size: 1.0 to 1.5.	1.0 to 20; default is 1.5.
Quadratic	A 9-pixel blurring filter based on a quadratic spline.	N/A
Sharp Quadratic	A sharp 9-pixel reconstruction filter, from Nelson Max.	N/A
Soften	Adjustable Gaussian softening filter. For mild blurring.	1.0 to 20; default is 6.0.
Video	A 25-pixel blurring filter optimized for NTSC and PAL video applications.	N/A

Well, you can relax—for MAX Release 3, Discreet decided to include all these AA filters to let users decide how they wanted their renderings to appear: from sharp to soft, for stills, video, or film. For most purposes, you might only use one or two of these filters for the majority of your scenes. (In MAX Release 3's software development kit (SDK) there are code examples of even more filters not shown here. If you're a C++ programmer, take a look at it on your MAX Release 3 CD-ROM.) In addition, filters that may not be particularly interesting for still renderings work wonders for eliminating jaggies and texture scintillation in MAX video renderings or for film.

The best way to see how these filters can alter the appearance of the 60SRETRO.MAX file is to simply select each one and re-render your scene, one at a time. You'll do that in a moment. Note that, for this tutorial, I'm not going to step through every single filter; I'll simply cover several representative ones that demonstrate the wide range of rendering effects you can produce. In addition, you'll also see how to use another new feature of MAX—the RAM Player—and how you can use it to compare your renderings.

Sharpening The Scene: The Blackman And Catmull-Rom Filters

The first two filters we'll take a look at are designed specifically to sharpen aspects of your scene. They do this by applying different image-filtering algorithms (which have results similar to Adobe Photoshop's Sharpen filters), to boost texture sharpness, edges, and/or contrast. (In addition, they bear the name of the programmer responsible for coming up with them; Edward Catmull, for instance, is one of the pioneering figures in computer graphics imagery and was a cofounder of Pixar.)

To see the AA differences, let's do another test rendering:

1. Your frame number should still be set to 100 (if it's not, drag the Time Slider back over to 100, or enter this frame value into the field). Your Rendering|Render menu should still be open; if not, open it again, and go down to the Anti-Aliasing Filters area. Click on the drop-down arrow and select Blackman. As Table 4.1 indicates, the Blackman filter sharpens your image (primarily in the appearance of bitmap textures), but it doesn't provide the edge enhancement of Catmull-Rom. Click on Render to render a 640-by-480 resolution image.

2. When the image appears, take a close look at it. Although the difference may be subtle, you should still see that the Blackman filter has punched up the apparent sharpness of the scene compared with the Area filter used earlier in this chapter.

3. To get a better idea of the differences, click on the Save Bitmap icon again and save this rendering to your \3DSMAX3\IMAGES directory as 60S_BLACKMAN.TIF. (In a moment, you'll load the various images in the RAM Player and compare them directly.)

4. Return to the Rendering menu, change the AA filter type to Catmull-Rom, and then re-render the scene. After a few minutes, the image appears, and you should notice a difference between the Blackman rendering and the new one. In addition to sharpening the edges of the objects in your scene, the Catmull-Rom filter has sharpened the object textures themselves.

Comparing The Renderings With The RAM Player

You can compare the different AA settings in the renderings more easily by using MAX Release 3's RAM Player feature. To use it, follow these steps:

1. Click on the Save Bitmap icon in your Camera VFB window and save this new image to your \IMAGES subdirectory as 60S_CATMULL.TIF.

2. Minimize or close your Rendering menu, then select Rendering|RAM Player. The RAM Player window appears. MAX Release 3's new RAM Player lets you load image sequences and play them back—even high-resolution sequences—depending on how much RAM is in your computer (a fast video card helps as well). In addition, the new RAM Player lets you "scratch" back and forth between two different images to make quick comparisons between subtle rendering effects. It's a good way to check out the differences in our AA filter settings.

3. Click on the Open Channel A icon (the open folder icon), and from your 3DSMAX3\IMAGES directory, select 60S_AREA.TIF. When the RAM Player Configuration menu appears, click on Okay to accept the 640-by-480 resolution image. The first AA rendering loads into the RAM Player.

4. Next, click on the Open Channel B icon and load the 60S_BLACKMAN.TIF file from your \IMAGES directory. Click on Okay again to accept the image. When it finishes loading, you should see both images sitting in the RAM Player with a scrollable dividing line running down the middle, as shown in Figure 4.5.

5. At the top and bottom of your RAM Player screen, you should see small triangular markers, or arrows, pointing at the scrolling dividing line. Place your mouse cursor on this line, then left-click, hold,

Figure 4.5

The '60s test images loaded into the RAM Player. (These images are rendered at 800 by 600 pixels for clarity.)

and drag the line back and forth across the two images. As you do, the RAM Player image changes back and forth between your two different AA renderings.

6. The differences between these two images (when rendered at 800 by 600 resolution) are *extremely* subtle. As you scroll back and forth (slowly), pay particular attention to the bottom edge of the floating coffee table and some of the tiny specular highlights along the edges of the metal ceiling beams and the ceiling light. The Blackman filter makes the textures in the scene a little more crisp, when compared to the Area filter.

7. Next, in the B Channel of your RAM Player, load the 60S_CATMULL.TIF image from your MAX \IMAGES directory; this will replace the 60S_BLACKMAN.TIF image. When the image loads, drag the line back and forth across the two images and note the differences.

The differences between the default Area filter (with a pixel size of 1.5) and the Catmull-Rom filter are more obvious. The Catmull-Rom filter appears to punch up the edges of the objects in your scene as well as punch up the overall contrast—at the expense of some slight aliasing. For very large still renderings (say, 2K-by-3K resolution, for print), the Catmull-Rom filter can make your rendering seem crystal-clear.

Softening Your Scene: Filters For Video Rendering

Now we'll test the two other extremes of MAX's new AA filters: the Soften and Video filters.

As Table 4.1 indicates, the Soften filter applies an adjustable Gaussian blur to your image; the default pixel size is 6.0. With it, you can give your images a soft, hazy look that's well-suited for misty, ethereal effects, for hot scenes (such as the volcano interior you'll see in Chapter 18), for atmospheres, and for underwater effects.

The Video filter is much the same: It applies a softening effect designed specifically to mitigate the effects of video "crawl." If you've looked at a lot of computer graphics renderings on television, you've probably seen examples of this. Rendered scenes that show slowly moving horizontal lines (which cross over the actual scanlines of your video or TV display) are the worst culprits. The Video filter can help smooth out these problems, creating a more filmlike appearance to your graphics.

To test the Soften and Video filters, follow these steps:

1. Your frame number should still be set to 100 (if it's not, drag the Time Slider back over to 100 or enter 100 into the field). Your Rendering|Render menu should still be open; if not, open it again and go down to the Anti-Aliasing Filters area. Click on the drop-down arrow and select Soften. Then, click on Render to render an 800-by-600-resolution image. After a few minutes, the image will appear on your screen.

   As you examine the image, you'll notice, of course, that it's much softer than before; the Gaussian blur that the Soften filter applies creates an ethereal, hazy effect over the scene.

2. Before you close this image, save it to your \IMAGES directory as 60S_SOFTEN.TIF.

3. Return to your Rendering menu, change the antialiasing filter to Video, and render another test image. Again, the Video filter is

designed specifically to soften your image and mitigate the "crawling" of slowly moving horizontal edges in your renderings.

4. When you're finished looking at this rendering, save it to your \IMAGES subdirectory as 60S_VIDEO.TIF. Then, as before, load both of these images, in turn, into the B Channel of your RAM Player and compare them with the original Area-filtered rendering. (If you want, you can then clear out the A Channel, load one of the sharper images done with the Blackman or Catmull-Rom filters, and see the striking differences between the sharp and soft extremes.)

Now, you may think, "I always want my CG renderings to be sharp, not fuzzy. Why should I use these filters that simply blur the image?" Again, it depends on whether you're rendering stills or video (or for film). For most animated sequences (done at least at NTSC resolution), what may look much too soft as a still image will look great when projected at 24 or 30 frames per second. The softness helps take the harsh CG/video edge off of your renderings.

The best way to really appreciate how these filters work is to examine a video-resolution scene being played back on a TV screen. If you have the opportunity (and/or the equipment) to render and dump your MAX animations to videotape, do some test sequences using some of the new softening filters instead of the default Area filter. If you see video renderings that use MAX Release 3's Video filter (rendered to fields, no less), you'll note that the results look surprisingly like film. There is a soft, "non-CGI look" to the animations, and edge aliasing and texture scintillation are virtually non-existent.

That's it for the specific AA filter tutorials. If you want, you can continue with the current 60SRETRO scene and try out the remaining antialiasing filters, or (when you finish the following tutorial) you can load up your favorite 3D scenes and use them to test MAX Release 3's new rendering capabilities.

A Look At The Supersampling Filters

To conclude this chapter, we're going to take a quick look at 3D Studio MAX Release 3's new Material supersampling options. By turning on supersampling, you can soften the appearance of high-contrast bitmaps. The supersampling options work particularly well in fixing aliased Bump maps, especially Bump maps that appear to "crawl" during video animations.

VIDEO VS. STILL IMAGES

Rendering to video presents a different set of considerations than simply rendering beautiful CG still images does. When doing video work, you have to be careful with Release 3's sharpening filters. Although you may like the look of the Catmull-Rom filter, you have to be careful that you don't create unnecessary texture scintillation and aliasing when rendering for video animations.

If you want, you can skip this section and simply continue your antialiasing filter tests with your favorite MAX scenes. If you want to test supersampling, do the following:

1. Make sure your 60SRETRO.MAX scene is still loaded (if it's not, load it again from the \CHAP_04 directory of this book's companion CD-ROM).

2. Activate the Camera01 viewport, place your mouse cursor in the viewport, and press *C* on your keyboard. The Camera menu should appear; select Camera02. (Don't worry about the specific frame number here; this camera is stationary.) As you do, you should see the Camera viewport change to a close-up of the decorative table on the right side of the room doorway.

3. Now, go ahead and render this scene; use the default Area filter for antialiasing. After a few minutes, the rendering should appear, and your screen should look like Figure 4.6.

Note: This short tutorial is resource-intensive. Turning on the supersampling options in your rendering can dramatically increase your rendering times; it depends on the number of materials in which you're using this feature.

Figure 4.6
A close-up of the right-hand decorative table, showing off the funky decorations.

Now, this rendering shows some obvious flaws that the more distant Camera01 renderings didn't reveal. First, there's a pretty ragged-looking Bump map on the brass kinetic sculpture; it shows ugly aliasing. The stucco Bump map on the walls is a little heavy, too. (The stone Shona abstract sculpture doesn't use a Bump map.)

4. There are a couple of things you can do to fix these. Open the Material Editor (if it's not already open) and take a look at the first two materials in the Editor. The first material is called Burnished Brass, the second is Pink Stucco, and both are used on the sculpture and walls, respectively.

5. Activate the Pink Stucco texture, go down to the Maps rollout, and open the Bump Map rollout (which shows the STUCCO.JPG image). Under Coordinates, take a look at the Blur and Blur Offset settings: Blur is set to 1.0, but Blur Offset is set to 0.0. When you're using high-contrast bitmaps in a Bump map slot, you should usually set Blur Offset above 0.0; this will help soften the map and mitigate aliasing in your rendering. However, the value usually can be fairly low; for our purposes, change Blur Offset to 0.001.

6. Activate the Burnished Brass material, go down to the Maps rollout, and open the Bump map slot (which shows the MTLBMP3.JPG image). Change its Blur Offset value to 0.001 as well. Then, activate your Camera01 viewport and render another test scene.

   As the rendering appears, note the differences between the look of the Bump maps compared with the preceding rendering. The stucco wall texture is okay, but the Bump map on the metal sculpture is still showing bad aliasing.

7. Return to the Material Editor and change the MTLBMP3.JPG Blur Offset setting to 0.01; then, reactivate your Camera01 viewport and re-render the scene.

   Now, we have a "Goldilocks and the Three Bears' porridge" problem: The first Blur Offset value was too low, and now this one is too high—the Bump map is so soft that we lose the distinct lines embedded in the sculpture surface.

8. Okay, as they say in the special effects industry, let's try splitting the difference. Go back to the Blur Offset field of the MTLBMP3.JPG Bump map, enter a value of 0.005, and then re-render the scene.

   Hmm. Well, this image has less aliasing, but are the etched lines distinctive enough? They still seem too soft. Well, you could try changing the Blur Offset setting to a lower value, such as 0.0025. However, what if you want to lessen aliasing in high-contrast Bump maps yet still have them be distinct and sharp edged? The answer may be to use MAX Release 3's new supersampling options.

9. Return to the Material Editor, change the Blur Offset value of the MTLBMP3.JPG image back to 0.0, then click on the Go To Parent icon to return to the main Material rollout. Open the Supersampling rollout. This short rollout shows three fields: Enable Sampler, Supersample Texture, and the name field for the type of supersampling used. In this case, the default is the MAX 2.5 Star sampler, introduced in Release 2 of 3D Studio MAX.

As MAX Release 3's Online Help says, "Supersampling is an optional additional step that provides a 'best guess' color for each rendered pixel.... [It] performs an additional antialiasing pass on the material. This requires more time but can improve image quality. Supersampling is especially helpful when you need to render very smooth specular highlights, subtle bump mapping, or high resolutions.

"As a rule, turn on supersampling only when you notice artifacts in your final renderings. For example, a thin Bump map might produce scintillating, jagged bumps that supersampling can correct. Supersampling requires considerably more time to render, although it does not necessarily require any additional RAM."

The different filters, along with their MAX Help descriptions, are shown in Table 4.2. (For more information on these filters and how they work, in MAX, select Help|Online Reference|Index and enter the word "supersampling.")

10. Well, if you don't mind spending a little extra time here, check the Enable Supersampling box to enable the default MAX R2.5 Star filter. Then activate your Camera01 viewport and re-render the scene. (Again, as stated earlier, this may take some time to render.)

Table 4.2   The 3D Studio MAX Release 3 supersampling filters.

Filter	Description
Adaptive Halton	Spaces samples along both X- and Y-axes according to a scattered, "quasi-random" pattern. Depending on the Quality setting, the number of samples can range from 4 to 40.
Adaptive Uniform	Spaces samples regularly, from a minimum quality of 4 samples to a maximum of 36. The pattern is not square, but skewed slightly to improve accuracy in the vertical and horizontal axes.
Hammersley	Spaces samples regularly along the X-axis, but along the Y-axis it spaces them according to a scattered, "quasi-random" pattern. Depending on the Quality setting, the number of samples can range from 4 to 40.
MAX 2.5 Star	The sample at the center of the pixel is averaged with 4 samples surrounding it. The pattern is like the fives on dice. This is the supersampling method that was available in 3DS MAX R2.5.

Note: All the materials used in this scene are included in the MAXFX3.MAT Material Library in the \MATLIBS directory of this book's companion CD-ROM.

Figure 4.7
The table decorations, with Supersampling enabled on the metal sculpture's Bump map.

SUPERSAMPLING AND RAYTRACING

As MAX Release 3's Online Help notes: "The Raytrace map and Raytrace material both perform their own supersampling. If you use the Raytrace map to create reflections or refractions, turning on this option significantly increases rendering time because the material is supersampled twice. In general, don't use Supersample with raytraced reflections or refractions unless you experience problems with aliasing, for example, in specular highlights or Bump maps."

When the Render menu appears, make sure the Disable All Samplers box under the Global Supersampling area is unchecked. Your rendering should look like Figure 4.7.

When the rendering appears, take a close look at the quality of the etched lines appearing in the Bump map. The Supersampling filter has lessened the effect of the jaggies while leaving the Bump map lines fairly sharp and distinctive.

11. If you have the time, again, you might want to try out the other supersampling filters and check their results, on this scene or other MAX scenes in which you've previously had rendering problems. Again, as before, you can save the images and use the RAM Player to compare the differences between the renderings.

Moving On

That's it for MAX's new AA Rendering filters and supersampling options. In the next few chapters, you'll see how to create complex metal materials using custom bitmaps, blending techniques, and MAX Release 3's improved Falloff map. (Note that as you experiment with the different metal texture effects in those chapters, you might apply the AA filter and supersampling lessons learned in this chapter to see how they affect your renderings there as well.) You'll then see how to combine the complex material techniques with Video Post optical effects to create glowing electricity, disintegrations, and explosions.

PART II

MATERIALS

MATERIALS I: PHONG, BLINN, AND METAL

BY JON A. BELL

Now that you've learned the basics of creating natural materials in MAX, you'll move on to duplicate industrial materials—specifically, you'll learn how to create refined metal textures.

Heavy Metal

In this chapter, you'll create a Standard Metal material in Release 3's Material Editor; then, you'll build on this material through a series of layering techniques. These techniques include using a variety of custom bitmaps and using Blend materials to mix between MAX's original Phong, Blinn, and Metal shaders to refine the results.

By employing a combination of maps, including Diffuse, Ambient, RGB Tint, Specular Color, Glossiness, Specular Level, and Reflection, you can create stunning metallic surfaces for your objects. These techniques are applicable to all sorts of objects, such as, for example, a present-day factory interior, a sleek sports car, or a futuristic space vehicle.

In Chapter 6, you'll continue looking at MAX's "standard" shaders, and you'll take a new look at the Falloff map, which has been substantially updated for MAX Release 3. The Falloff map can help you produce excellent reflective surfaces, iridescent and black light effects, and even X-ray imagery. In later chapters, you'll explore MAX Release 3's new material shaders, such as Multi-Layer, Anisotropic, and others.

For the first metal tutorial, you'll load a simple scene consisting of a sphere, a camera, and a couple of spotlights. You'll use the sphere as a test object for rendering the next few metallic textures. To set up the scene, follow these steps:

1. Load 3D Studio MAX Release 3, or else save your current work and reset the program.

2. From the \CHAP_05 directory of this book's companion CD-ROM, load the file METAL_1.MAX. The file loads, and your desktop should resemble Figure 5.1.

3. Now, it's time to create your first metal material. Select the sphere and then open the Material Editor. Rename Material #1 to Metal 1 Single, change the Shading option from Blinn to Phong, and then apply it to the sphere, either by dragging it over to the sphere or by clicking on the Assign Material To Selection button. (You can experiment with the Blinn shading type later, if you want, and examine the differences in the sphere's shading. The Blinn shader first made its appearance in 3D Studio MAX Release 2 and is named after Jim Blinn, one of the pioneers of modern computer graphics imagery. This shader is a variant of MAX's Phong shader, and Blinn's specular highlights tend to be softer than Phong.) For the tutorials in this chapter, you're going to use Phong to get somewhat sharper specular highlights. (For more information on this and the other new shading types, consult your Release 3 manuals or the online tutorials and Help file.)

FOR ADVANCED USERS...

If you're an advanced MAX user, you can load the various METAL.MAX scene files from the \CHAP_05 directory from the companion CD-ROM. You can then examine the Material Editor settings and reverse-engineer the techniques and materials described in this chapter.

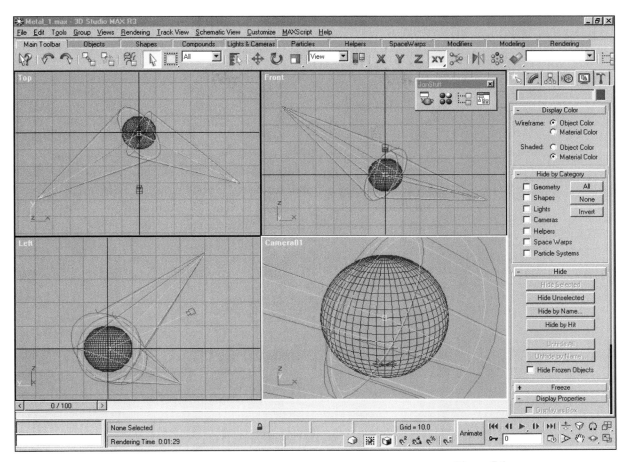

Figure 5.1

A simple test scene for creating your metal textures.

4. You'll construct your first metal texture from this Standard default material. First, you'll want to change the Ambient and Diffuse Colors, so change Ambient to RGB 8, 32, 48, or a dark, dusky blue.

5. Drag the Ambient Color swatch down to Diffuse to copy it; then, change the Diffuse value to 64, 255, 255, or a light cyan. Change Specular to pure white, or 255, 255, 255, and then change Glossiness to 0 and Specular Level to 100.

   You may be wondering about these last two attributes—why set Glossiness to 0, but Specular Level to 100 percent? As you can see, in the Material Editor, you currently have a cyan object with a giant diffused specular highlight. Don't worry about that for now—in a moment you'll apply some bitmaps that will clamp the highlight to specific areas yet still allow for glossiness (formerly shininess) all over your test sphere. These bitmaps will then pump up the shininess to create the proper specular highlight, even if the actual Glossiness value is low.

SHININESS OUT, GLOSSINESS IN

One of the many changes made to 3D Studio MAX Release 3 is the difference in terminology for certain Material Editor features. Previous versions of MAX (1.x and 2.x) used the terms *Shininess* and *Shininess Strength*; starting with Release 3, these have been changed to *Glossiness* and *Specular Level*. Likewise, *Ambient* and *Diffuse* are now *Ambient Color* and *Diffuse Color*.

6. Now, go down to the Maps section of the rollout, open it (if it's not already open), and make sure the Diffuse/Ambient Map Lock button is unchecked.

As I've mentioned in both of the previous MAX f/x books, it's usually better to not have these attributes locked when you want to create realistic materials. By unlocking them and adjusting the color settings and map levels individually, you can increase the contrast and realism inherent in your materials. If the Ambient swatch is not darker than the Diffuse one, shadows and dark areas lack depth.

For best results, you should always make sure your Ambient and Diffuse Color settings aren't identical. A good rule of thumb is to make the Ambient Color a much darker version of the Diffuse Color. Use the same Hue and Saturation—just a different Luminance value. (The RGB Tint map provides an easy way to darken or tint the bitmap; you'll use it a little later on in this chapter.) Note that for some special-case materials, the Ambient and Diffuse Color settings make little or no difference in the final material appearance. (For an interesting Maxfield Parrish effect, make the Ambient Color a complimentary color of the Diffuse Color.)

7. Click on the Ambient slot in the Maps rollout to bring up the Material/Map Browser. Under Browse From, select New, and then double-click on Bitmap. From the \CHAP_05 directory of the companion CD-ROM, select the file MTLGREEN.JPG, and click on View. The image is also shown here in Figure 5.2.

Figure 5.2
The MTLGREEN.JPG forms the basis for the primary Metal_1 texture.

The MTLGREEN.JPG image is an 800-by-400 bitmap of a mottled green metal surface. This texture began as a photograph of a large electrical junction box I found in a Silicon Valley industrial parking lot. The large metal box, once painted a uniform green, had irregular patterns where its hues had been bleached out by the sun. The accumulated scratches and scuff marks in its surface added to its usefulness as a realistic CGI texture map.

To create this texture, I digitized the photograph on a flatbed scanner and then began tweaking it in Adobe Photoshop. I cut and pasted parts of the image and used the Offset filter (with Wraparound) to make it seamlessly tilable. I then drew on various light panel lines and overlaid dark panel lines, which were derived from a separate Bump map (which you'll load in a moment). The 2:1 ratio of this bitmap makes it perfect for spherical mapping and, thus, our spherical test object.

8. Close the View window and click on the Open button to load the image into your Ambient Color bitmap slot. Under Tiling, change U and V to 2.0; then, click on the Go To Parent icon to return to the main Material Editor rollout. Drag this bitmap down to Diffuse Color and select Instance instead of Copy.

Making It From Scratch(es)

At the moment, the sample sphere in the Material Editor doesn't look like much—you still have to fix that glossiness problem. You'll do that now:

1. Click on the Map slot next to Specular Color; when the Material/ Map Browser appears, select RGB Tint. This map adjusts the value of the three color channels in an image. You'll use it to enhance the greenish tint of the specular highlights in the metal texture.

2. Click on the Red color swatch of the RGB Tint map; when the Color Selector appears, bring the Green color value up to 255 so the Red Tint is bright yellow instead of pure red. Now, click on the Green color swatch, and change the RGB settings to 0, 128, 0. Leave the Blue color swatch as it is. Then, close the Color Selector.

3. Click on the Map button, and select Bitmap from the Material/Map Browser. From the \CHAP_05 directory on the companion CD-ROM, select the file MTLSPEC.JPG and click on View.

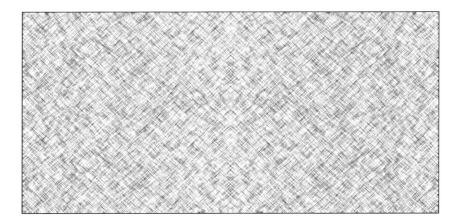

Figure 5.3
A crosshatched specular highlight pattern created in Adobe Photoshop.

The image shown on your screen and in Figure 5.3 is very simple: grayish, crisscrossing lines on a lighter background. I created this texture in Adobe Photoshop by applying a heavy layer of Noise to a new white background image. Next, I applied Motion Blur (approximately 25 pixels in length, at a 45-degree angle). This streaked the Noise pixels. I then copied the image, flipped it horizontally, and pasted the original image on top of the flipped one using Multiply. The result is a simple crosshatched pattern that resembles scratched metal. Close the View window and assign MTLSPEC.JPG as the bitmap for the RGB Tint map in the Specular slot.

4. Click on the Go To Parent icon twice to return to the main Material Editor rollout, and click on the Glossiness map name slot. Select Bitmap from the Material/Map Browser, and from the \CHAP_05 directory on the companion CD-ROM, select the file MTLSHNY3.JPG and view it.

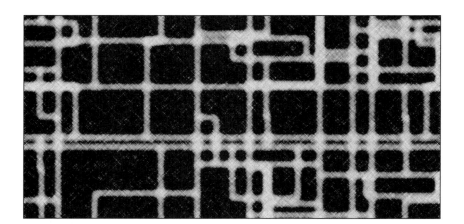

Figure 5.4
The MTLSHNY3.JPG image restricts the specular highlight to specific areas.

Figure 5.4 is a grayscale bitmap derived from the panel lines present in the MTLGREEN.JPG image. The thick white and gray lines and irregular specks against the dark background help clamp the specular highlights to specific areas.

To create these Glossiness/Specular Level textures, I inverted the MTLBMP.JPG Bump map image (which you'll load in a moment) in Photoshop. This produced white lines on a black background. I applied Gaussian Blur to the image, which created soft washes of gray along the original panel line areas. Then, I applied various other filters and added bitmaps on top of the image to produce several variants. (If you want, take a moment to use MAX's File|View File feature to examine the other MTL*.JPG bitmaps in the \MAPS directory of this book's companion CD-ROM.)

5. Close the VFB window, then change the U and V Tiling to 2.0 and return to the main Material Editor rollout. Change the Glossiness amount to 50 and then drag the MTLSHNY3.JPG map down to the Specular Level map slot. Make it a Copy instead of an Instance, but leave the Specular Level Map amount at 100.

6. Open the Maps button next to Bump, select Bitmap from the Material/Map Browser, and load MTLBMP.JPG into the Bump map slot. By viewing the file, you can see that it's a network of black panel lines that correspond to the lines present in the MTLGREEN.JPG bitmap.

I used the MTLBMP.JPG image shown in Figure 5.5 to create the panel lines on the first MTLGREEN.JPG image. By pasting the former image onto the latter using Adobe Photoshop's Multiply option, I darkened the areas of the Diffuse and Ambient textures where the

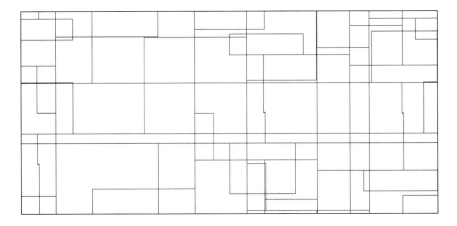

Figure 5.5
The MTLBMP.JPG Bump map.

Bump map would appear later. This emphasizes the recessed panel lines scribed into the metal surface.

7. Change both the U and V tiling to 2.0 so the Bump map panel lines correspond to the other maps. To mitigate Bump map aliasing in the final rendering, set the Blur Offset to 0.003, then return to the main Material Editor rollout.

8. Now, it's time to finally render this scene. Activate the Camera01 viewport and render a test image of at least 640-by-480 resolution. The image will appear on your screen, and it should look like Figure 5.6.

Figure 5.6
The custom bitmap textures create specular highlights confined near the panel lines of the object.

The final effect shows a green metallic sphere, looking vaguely reminiscent of the *Star Wars Deathstar* before all the windows were installed and it was painted in Evil Empire Gray. (It also looks kind of like Luke Skywalker's little training sphere that was zapping him aboard the *Millenium Falcon* during his Jedi lightsaber training.)

Anyway, back to your rendering: Notice how the bright green specular highlights run along the edges of the panel seams. Faint scratches also appear in the shiny areas—the specular highlights aren't simply shiny white patches. All these bitmaps, when combined, create the effect of scuffed or worn metal and suggest the illusion of bare metal showing through where the paint has worn off along the edges.

Anisotropic Specularity: Coming Soon To A Chapter Near You

The effect you're seeing in these metal renderings is similar to what's called *anisotropic specularity*, which describes nonuniform specular highlights in shiny materials where the surface tends to break up the highlight or even produce multiple highlights. With the release of the third version of 3D Studio MAX, we now have genuine anisotropic specularity (courtesy of a new shader in the Material Editor), as well as Anisotropic settings in the new Multi-Layer shader. In Chapters 7 and 8, you'll play around with these new shading types and see their effects. For now, though, you'll experiment with creating unusual metallic specular effects by using only custom bitmaps.

For a Phong (not Metal) shading type, the metal texture you've just created is pretty realistic. However, you can refine this effect further by using Blend materials to combine Phong/Blinn and Metal shaders. These hybrid materials will enable you to further adjust the shininess and reflective qualities of your materials. (You'll explore this later in this chapter.)

You can use this metal effect in numerous ways, of course. You can apply these techniques to objects—from fighter planes and spaceships to weathered pickup trucks or construction equipment. You could also use them to create realistic galvanized tin or the metal siding of buildings.

Blending The Shaders

Now, you'll improve this metal texture by creating a Blend material combining the attributes of the Phong shading type with the Metal shader. You'll create your new metal texture by expanding the existing Metal 1 Single material. To do so, follow these steps:

1. Return to the Material Editor. Under the Metal 1 Single material slot, click on the Standard button next to Type, and from the Material/ Map Browser, select Blend. (When the Replace Material alert box appears, make sure you select Keep Old Material As Sub-Material.) The original Metal 1 Single material now appears in the Material #1 slot.

2. Before you go further, it's a good idea to change the names of your various materials to eliminate confusion as you edit them. (It also helps to give specific names to your various maps, too, rather than simply Tex. #1 and the like. That way, if you're browsing from your scene or the Material Editor, you can more easily pick out a specific map that you want to duplicate in another slot.) Highlight the Metal 1 Single name in the Material Editor and change it to Metal 2 Blend.

MAX RELEASE 3'S NEW LIGHTING ATTRIBUTES AND DEFAULTS

For additional control over your metal materials, check out Studio MAX Release 3's new lighting attributes, such as Soften Diffuse Edge, Affect Diffuse, and Affect Specular. By setting different lights for the Diffuse and Specular components of your materials, you can produce striking results. In Chapter 7, I'll show you how to use multiple lights, set to affect Diffuse and Specular separately, to produce "wet" materials.

NAME YOUR MATERIALS!

When you're creating complex materials, give both the materials and each map within them specific names rather than the defaults. That way, if you are browsing for a new map or material from your scene or the Material Editor, you can more quickly pick out the items you need.

3. Next, click on the Name button for Material #1 and change its name to Metal 2 Phong. Go down to Ambient Color and change its settings to RGB 0, 64, 32, drag this color swatch down to Diffuse Color to copy it, and then change the Diffuse RGB settings to 0, 235, 128 (dragging the value up to around 235 will be close enough). Make sure Specular is set to pure white or RGB 255, 255, 255.

4. Right-click on the Glossiness and Specular Level spinners to set them to 0; then, go to the Maps rollout. Click on the Ambient Color button to go to the Ambient map level and then click on Type: Bitmap to bring up the Material/Map Browser. Double-click on RGB Tint, and when the alert box appears, select Keep Old Map As Sub-Map. Click on the Red color swatch under Tint Parameters and change its parameters to RGB 64, 0, 0. Click on the Green color swatch and change it to RGB 0, 128, 0. Leave Blue as it is, and close the Color Selector.

5. Click on the Go To Parent icon to return to the Metal 2 Phong rollout; then, click on the Go To Parent icon again to return to the Metal 2 Blend level of the material. Drag the Metal 1 Single material down to the Material #2 slot; in the Instance Material dialog box under Method, make sure Copy is checked rather than Instance. Then, open this new material and change its name to Metal 2 Metal (which sounds like a new headbanger rock band).

6. Next, you need to change Material #2 not just in word but in deed, so select Metal under Shading Type. When you do, you'll see the Specular component of the Maps become grayed out. (You'll use the Diffuse attribute to provide the specular for the Metal material.) Change Ambient to RGB 0, 64, 0 and change Diffuse to pure white, or RGB 255, 255, 255. Change Glossiness to 75 and Specular Level to 100.

7. Go to the Maps section, and drag the MTLGREEN.JPG Diffuse Color map up to Ambient Color to replace the existing RGB Tint map. (You can make this an Instance instead of a Copy.) Change the Ambient Color amount to 25 and the Diffuse Color amount to 50.

8. Click in the Specular Level and Glossiness map checkboxes to turn them off—for this Blend material, you don't need the custom bitmaps as part of the Metal shader. Then, click on the Go To Parent icon to return to the Metal 2 Blend material level.

Masked Marvels

You now have a material that allows you to blend between a Phong and a Metal shading type, each with its own particular specular attributes.

Next, you'll apply the Metal 2 Blend material to the sphere and adjust the Blend between the two components:

1. If you want to see what each material looks like individually, apply this new Metal 2 Blend texture to the Sphere01 object and adjust the Mix Amount setting. (If you set it to 0, only the Metal 2 Phong material shows up, of course.) For a new test rendering, crank it all the way up to 100 (so just the Metal 2 Metal material is present) and then activate your Camera01 viewport and render the object.

   The image on your screen and in Figure 5.7 shows the effects of a pure Metal shader. Unfortunately, it's not particularly interesting; the large specular highlight and the extremely dark surface tend to drown out the Ambient Color and Diffuse Color map details. Here, it looks somewhat like a dark green, metallic soccer ball.

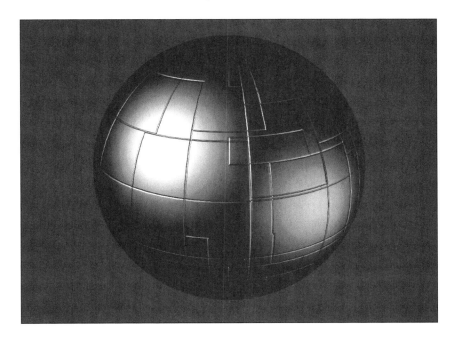

Figure 5.7
The Metal shader component of the Metal 2 Blend material shown at 100 percent.

2. Adjust the Mix Amount setting to 50 so you're seeing a half-and-half blend of the Phong and Metal shading types, and re-render the scene.

   As your rendering shows, this is a more interesting effect. The Phong shading of the first material provides an overall glossiness, yet you can begin to see the faint specular areas of the Metal shader.

3. Change the Mix Amount setting to 25 and re-render the scene.

As a straight blend, this is a better compromise between the two materials. The Phong provides more Diffuse and Ambient detail, and you can still see Metal shading delineation.

Here's one final thing to try for this particular metal texture. Instead of simply mixing between the two materials, you'll load another custom bitmap as a mask to blend between the two.

4. Click on the Mask Name button to bring up the Material/Map Browser, select Bitmap, and from the \CHAP_05 directory on the companion CD-ROM, click on MTLSHNY6.JPG and View it.

The MTLSHNY6.JPG image, shown in Figure 5.8, is another bitmap derived from the Bump map you're using in the scene. As with the Glossiness and Specular Level textures, I inverted the Bump map values in Adobe Photoshop and applied Gaussian Blur. I then combined this image with another inverted Bump map modified in good old Autodesk Animator Pro using Jumble ink. This broke up the white panel lines into a dusting of scattered pixels.

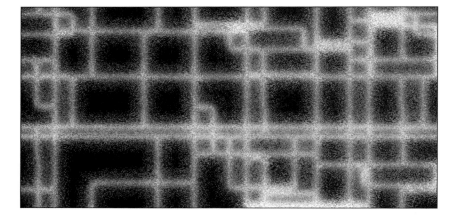

Figure 5.8
The MTLSHNY6.JPG image used as a mask between the Phong and Metal materials.

5. Click on OK to load it into the Material Editor; then, activate your Camera01 viewport again and render the scene; it should look like Figure 5.9.

Take a close look at the rendering on your screen. As you can see, the MTLSHNY6.JPG mask allows the Metal material to show through the Phong material only along the panel lines, with scratches and flecks fading out to the middle of each panel.

Also, note the appearance of the bright specular areas along the bump-mapped panel lines as contrasted with the matte appearance of the overall sphere. It looks as if the object started out with a satin painted finish (the

Figure 5.9
The final Metal Blend material.

Diffuse and Ambient maps of the Phong material). However, due to wear and tear, the edges of the panel appear as bare, scuffed metal. The combined qualities of the respective materials provide a better effect than the same materials used separately.

Variations On A Theme

If you like this effect, here are some variations to try:

- Change the UV tiling of all the bitmaps on one of the Blend materials (either the Phong or the Metal). Keep one set at 2.0 and change the others back to 1.0, 3.0, or whatever appeals to you.

- Experiment with different Specular Color, Glossiness, and Specular Level settings and bitmaps. (Explore the \CHAP_05 and the \MAPS directories of the companion CD-ROM for other textures.)

- Use procedural textures, such as Noise, as masks between the two materials. (For a really odd effect, you might even try animating the mask.)

- Use 3D Studio MAX Release 3's Raytrace map type for any of the map channels.

Note that two versions of this scene are saved in the \CHAP_05 directory of the companion CD-ROM as METAL_1.MAX and METAL_2.MAX. The materials described here are also included in the MAXFX3.MAT material library on the companion CD-ROM.

Moving On

In this chapter, you learned how to create good-looking metal textures using custom bitmaps and Blend materials. By applying multiple layers of bitmaps (or even procedural textures) in MAX's powerful Material Editor, you can produce texture effects that are both subtle and striking.

In the next chapter, you'll see how to refine your metal textures using Reflection maps and MAX Release 3's improved Falloff map. In addition, you'll see how you can use Falloff to create iridescent or pearlescent effects, an interesting retro-computer-graphics look, or even an X-ray look.

MATERIALS II: FALLOFF AND REFLECTION MAPS

6

BY JON A. BELL

In Chapter 5, you learned how to use custom bitmaps and blend materials to create refined metal textures. In this chapter, you'll expand on the techniques you used previously.

Testing Your Metal Mettle

This chapter focuses on how to create metal textures using Reflection maps and MAX Release 3's new and improved Falloff map. You can use these techniques for any metallic objects in your scenes, whether they're space-ships, factory walls, or '57 Chevy's. You'll also see how you can use Falloff to create iridescent or pearlescent effects, a retro-computer-graphics look, or even an X-rayed object.

In the first part of this tutorial, you won't use a simple test sphere as you did in Chapter 5. Instead, you'll load an existing model from this book's companion CD-ROM and experiment with the new metal textures on it. Follow these steps:

1. Reset MAX, then load the THRUST_1.MAX file from the \CHAP_06 directory of the companion CD-ROM. The file loads, and your screen should look like Figure 6.1.

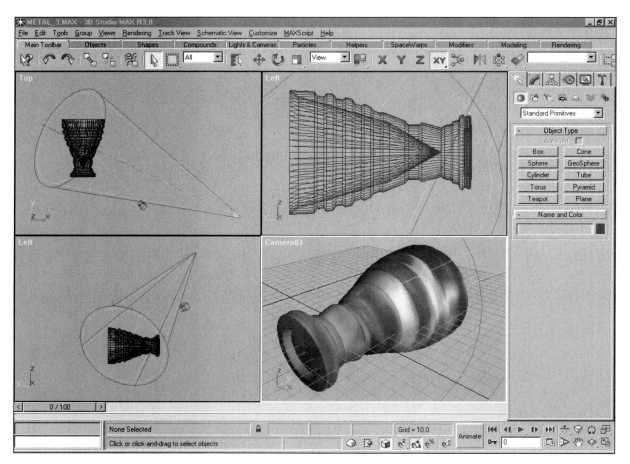

Figure 6.1

The test model for the Metal Reflection Blend/Falloff material type.

This simple model is designed to resemble a NASA rocket thruster. In a moment, you'll load some variations of "old" MAX reflective metal materials and apply them to this object. Then, you'll begin altering the materials to create a machined aluminum effect on the thruster.

2. Open the Material Editor. There are three different materials loaded: Chrome Blue Sky 2, Chrome Pearl 2, and Copper 2. Each has its own variations of Ambient and Diffuse Colors.

3. If you open the Maps section of each material, you'll also see different reflection bitmaps loaded, at different strengths, into each material. I've already applied fitted Cylindrical UVW mapping coordinates and the Chrome Blue Sky 2 material to the thruster model, so activate your Camera01 viewport and do a test rendering. It should resemble Figure 6.2.

Figure 6.2
The rocket thruster model with the Chrome Blue Sky 2 material applied.

As your rendering and Figure 6.2 indicate, the Chrome Blue Sky 2 material creates a very shiny object. For most purposes, MAX's Reflection mapping (including automatic reflections and cubic environment maps) can provide many of the same effects as true raytracing, but without the rendering slowdown inherent in raytracing. (In Chapter 11, you'll see how to use Release 3's Raytrace Map and material to create excellent reflective and refractive effects.) In this chapter, you'll concentrate on using Reflection maps only to create these reflective metal surfaces.

4. Select the thruster model, return to the Material Editor, apply the Chrome Pearl 2 material, and render another test shot.

5. When you're finished looking at the image, apply the Copper 2 material and then render a third test.

Other than changes in color, the model looks similar in each rendering. Although the rendering looks like metal, the thruster model seems too bright and shiny—the lack of further surface detail, as well as the soft wash of color across its surface, tends to flatten the 3D object.

Sharpening The Reflection

To add more definition to the surface, follow these steps to sharpen the Reflection map:

1. Return to the Material Editor, change the name of the Chrome Blue Sky 2 material to Chrome Blue Sky 3, and then apply it again to the thruster. Then, open this material's Reflection Map button, which contains the file SKY2.JPG. This is a modified version of the SKY.JPG bitmap that ships with MAX. Under General Parameters, you'll note that Blur is at 2.0 and Blur Offset is at 0.064.

2. Change Blur to 1.0 and Blur Offset to 0.01. Then activate your Camera01 viewport and render another test image.

As the image on your screen indicates, the whitish cloud shapes in the original SKY2.JPG image have placed additional reflective highlights on the object. The longitudinal detail of the map also helps better delineate the thruster's shape.

Scratching The Surface

Now, you'll add some surface relief to the thruster via a Bump map. Then, you'll begin tweaking the Reflection map settings. To start, follow these steps:

1. Click on the Bump Map button. In the Material/Map Browser, make New active, and select Bitmap.

2. From the \CHAP_06 directory of the companion CD-ROM, click on SCRATCH1.JPG and use File|View to examine it.

   As you see on your screen and in Figure 6.3, this 640-by-320 image consists of white and gray "scratches" and noise pixels on a black field.

3. Click on OK to load the image.

4. Now, you want to change the U and V Tiling. (Otherwise, when this image is used as a Bump map, the low resolution will make the

---

USE BLUR OFFSET

Always use at least a small amount of Blur Offset in your maps, particularly when using Bump and Reflection maps. This will help you avoid aliasing in your final renderings.

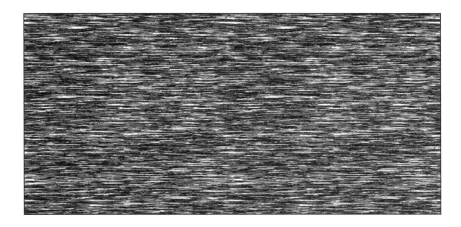

Figure 6.3
The SCRATCH1.JPG, used as a Bump map, helps break up the surface of the thruster object.

thruster look as if it were hammered out by a drunken blacksmith rather than machined by precision tooling.) Set U Tiling to 16.0, V Tiling to 32.0, and Blur Offset to 0.01 (to smooth out the bumps). Then, render another test image.

As the image on your screen indicates, the Bump map creates the appearance of slight scratches in the thruster surface and helps break up the overall specular highlight.

MAX Release 3's New Falloff Map

Although your Chrome Blue Sky 3 material is now more realistic than the original, you can still improve it. 3D Studio MAX's default Reflection mapping sometimes produces reflective objects that look self-illuminated (especially when the map level is set high and in 3D scenes with dim lighting conditions). Although we may tend to think of chrome objects as bright, they don't have a high ambient value as brightly colored or self-illuminated objects do.

One way to fix this is to knock down the levels of apparent illumination along the edges of a reflective object. By doing this, more of the reflection is visible in an object surface at an acute angle; at more oblique angles, the reflection appears to diminish in strength or brightness. (You might also want to reverse this concept to create a more edge-lit look.)

You can use MAX's improved Falloff map to achieve this effect. Falloff enables you to create interesting transparency effects—or blend between different materials—based on the face normals of your geometry. You can adjust the effect and the angle of attack based on world coordinates or based on the viewing direction relative to the object to which the map is assigned.

In addition, as shown in Figure 6.4, the new Falloff map type includes mixing curves for both Input and Output. The mixing curves for Input enable you to better control the blends between the colors or maps in the

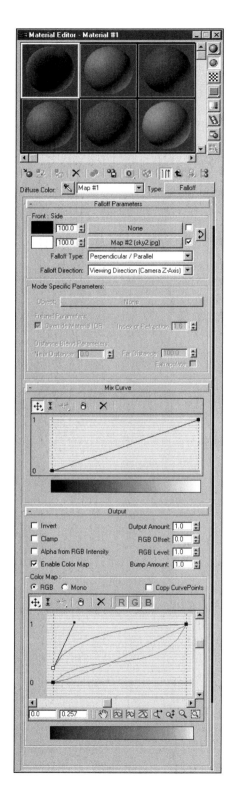

Figure 6.4
The Material Editor rollout for the enhanced Falloff Map type. (Note that this figure shows the entire rollout, with the Output Color map features activated.)

color swatch slots. The mixing curves for Output (shown activated in the figure) enable you to alter the individual RGB settings of the material and map within MAX. (This is similar to the RGB Tint map, which you used earlier in Chapter 5 to alter the colors of your Metal specular highlights.) This can help you alter the hue and saturation of your materials within MAX rather than having to load your original bitmap into a paint program and alter it there. (For more information on this map type, consult your 3D Studio MAX Release 3 manuals or the Release 3 Help file.)

Using The Falloff Map

Here, you'll modify your Reflection map by using the SKY2.JPG image as a subcomponent of the Falloff map, which will determine how the bitmap is masked on the thruster:

1. Return to the Material Editor and open the Reflection map for the Chrome Blue Sky 3 material. To load the Falloff map, click on the Type: Bitmap button. From the Material/Map Browser, click on Falloff, make sure Keep Old Map As Sub-Map is checked, and click on OK.

2. In the Material Editor, you should see that the SKY2.JPG bitmap is placed in the Falloff Color #1 swatch by default. For the proper rendering results, you need this map in the Color #2 (default white) slot. Click on the Swap Colors/Maps icon (the one with the arrows), then change the color swatches back to their original settings (Color #1 should be black; Color #2 should be white).

   You should see on your Material Editor sample sphere that the effect of the Reflection map seems to have disappeared. This is because the Environment mapping coordinates of the copied SKY2.JPG bitmap have changed to Texture: Explicit UVW mapping coordinates.

3. Click on the SKY2.JPG button to go to the Color #2 rollout, and change the mapping coordinates from Texture to Environ: Spherical Environment. Then, return to the Falloff map rollout.

4. You'll see that Falloff Type defaults to Perpendicular/Parallel in the new drop-down list. If you click on this list, you'll see several other choices: Towards/Away, Fresnel, Shadow/Light, and Distance Blend. For now, leave the settings at the default of Perpendicular/Parallel. Again, this setting makes the SKY2.JPG bitmap appear to reflect more toward your viewing angle and makes the bitmap's effects diminish as the faces of the thruster roll away from the Camera01 view.

5. Activate your Camera01 viewport and render a test image.

FALLOFF BASICS

As 3D Studio MAX's Online Help states, "The Falloff map generates a value from white to black, based on the angular falloff of the face normals on the surface of the geometry. The direction used to specify the angular falloff varies, depending on various methods you can choose. However, with the default settings, the map generates white on faces whose normals point outward from the current view and black on faces whose normals are parallel to the current view."

Notice in Figure 6.5 how the Falloff map has darkened the edges of the thruster reflection. You now get the benefits of the Reflection map without washing out the object, which might cause it to look flat or self-illuminated.

6. If you want, close your Camera01 VFB window and return to the Material Editor. Go to the Falloff map, select Towards/Away under Falloff Type, and re-render the scene. As the rendering appears, you'll see that this Falloff Type tends to clamp the colors of the Reflection map even more so than the Perpendicular/Parallel type.

7. Return to the Material Editor and select Fresnel under Falloff Type. As you do, you'll see the Fresnel parameters (under the Mode Specific Parameters section of the rollout) become active. Fresnel plots a geometric Falloff curve that somewhat simulates fisheye distortion that you see with an ultra-wide-angle lens or with certain raytracing effects. (You'll notice that there's an Index Of Refraction box, with a default setting of 1.6.) You'll also see the edges of the Reflection map become clamped more toward the outer edges of your sample object in Material Editor Slot #1.

8. Activate your Camera01 viewport and re-render the scene. Notice that the Reflection map tends to remain only on the outermost edges of the thruster model (relative to your Camera view). It looks as if

the model is lit with a rim light. (If you want, return to the Material Editor, change the Fresnel IOR settings, re-render and examine the results.)

9. Now, speaking of light, return once more to the Material Editor. Change Falloff Type to Shadow/Light, and then re-render your scene. You'll notice that the SKY2.JPG Reflection map appears only in the areas that are illuminated by the spotlights in the scene; it disappears in the shadowed areas.

New Falloff Features: The Output Curves

For the next Falloff/Reflection map trick, you'll take a quick look at Falloff's new Output features:

1. Return to the Material Editor, change Falloff Type back to Perpendicular/Parallel, then open the Output section of the rollout. Click on the Invert checkbox; the sample object in Material Editor Slot #1 turns a bright, washed-out hue. Well, it might look strange, but what the heck—render your Camera01 viewport. When the scene renders, you see a bright, ghostly image of the thruster as the luminance values are inverted.

   Okay, so that's kind of weird. (However, you need to find out what these features do, and they might be useful to you someday, so file this away for future use.)

2. Go back to the Material Editor and check Invert off again. Go down to Enable Color Map and check it; under Color Map, you'll see that Mono is the default. The Mono setting basically lets you increase the output of the map, but by adjusting the curves, you can also get some interesting edge effects.

3. You'll see that the Mixing window shows a straight line pointing diagonally up to the right. Click on the point on the upper-right end of the mixing curve to activate it; its value should be at 1.0. Now, you can drag this point upward and use the scrollbar to find it again, but because you're going to enter a large value, just go down to the spinner boxes below the Mix curve window. In the second spinner box, change the selected point's value from 1.0 to 5.0. Zoom—the point shoots up and out of sight. Click on the Zoom Horizontal Extents icon below the Mix curve window (use MAX's tooltips to find it, if necessary). This will recenter the entire curve in your Mixing window.

4. Now, right-click on the selected point, and you'll see a small Properties box appear. Change the point type from Corner to Bezier-Corner; a Bezier spline handle appears. Drag the handle down and to the left so that the end of the handle is almost parallel with the 0 value, and near-vertical, as well. (It should look something like Figure 6.6.)

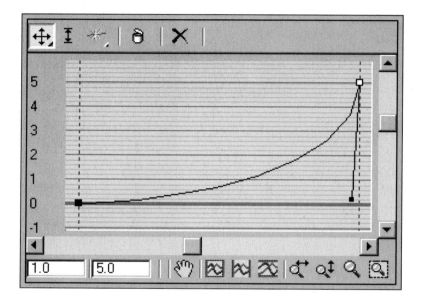

Figure 6.6

Changing the Mono Mix curve from a straight line to a Bezier curve (in Falloff Output).

5. Activate your Camera01 viewport and re-render the scene.

    As your scene renders, you'll see that the much higher Mono Output curve values have increased the reflection bitmap dramatically—but it's not a linear curve, so the bright reflections serve to highlight and silhouette the outlines of the thruster, as shown in Figure 6.7.

6. Return to the Material Editor and change the Color Map type from Mono to RGB. To the right of these checkboxes, you'll see three icons for the different Red, Green, and Blue mixing curves. Click on the Green and Blue icons to uncheck them, leaving the Red mixing curve. Select its endpoint, right-click to bring up the Properties menu, and change it to Bezier-Corner. Now, as you did before, go down to the second spinner box, and change its value from 1.0 to 2.0.

7. Return to the RGB icons, check Green to activate it, change its second point from Corner to Bezier-Corner, and change its value from 1.0 to 1.5.

Figure 6.7
The Mono Output Bezier curve
has increased the luminance
values of the SKY2.JPG
Reflection map.

8. Finally, activate the Blue icon, change its second point from Corner to Bezier-Corner, change its value from 1.0 to -1.0, and render your Camera01 viewport again.

   As your rendering shows, the Color Output curves have changed the SKY2.JPG RGB values, tinting the overall Reflection map from white and blue sky colors to hot oranges and yellows. This feature can be helpful when you need to change the color of a bitmap in the Falloff slots but you don't have the time or inclination to create an entirely new, color-adjusted map.

   Again, the Falloff map and its various features can be extremely useful for creating more realistic metals and other reflective materials for your scenes. With it, your reflective surfaces need no longer appear unnaturally flat and self-illuminated. (Personally, I almost never use a straight reflection bitmap anymore—I always mix it with Falloff instead.)

9. When you're finished viewing the rendering, close your Camera01 VFB and click on the Go To Parent icon several times to return to the main Chrome Blue Sky 3 rollout.

Note that variations of these scenes are saved in the \CHAP_06 directory of the companion CD-ROM as THRUST_2.MAX, THRUST_3.MAX, and THRUST_4.MAX.

Falloff Effects With Different Metals: A Robot Hand

For this tutorial, you're going to load a more complex object and examine its appearance under the effects of different metal materials. Each of the materials uses Falloff in the Reflection map slot, with Falloff toning down the effects of the reflection bitmap in either the Color #1 or #2 slots. To start out, follow these steps:

1. From the \CHAP_06 directory of the companion CD-ROM, load ROBOHAND.MAX. Your screen should look like Figure 6.8.

This model depicts a humanoid, robotic hand, and is reminiscent of the endoskeleton arm seen in the *Terminator* films. A primary white spotlight and a blue fill spotlight (hidden in the scene) illuminate the objects.

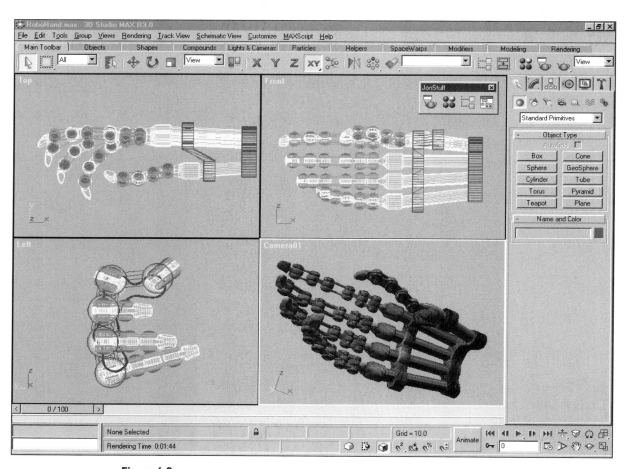

Figure 6.8
The geometry in the ROBOHAND.MAX scene helps demonstrate various metal textures that use the Falloff map as a Reflection map component.

Figure 6.9

The default metal material assignments on the robot hand.

2. Before you continue, do a quick test rendering of this scene. Your rendering should look like Figure 6.9.

    As your rendering indicates, the various model pieces have materials that are similar to the modified Blue Sky 3 material you created in the previous example.

3. If you open the Material Editor, you'll see three materials used in the scene: Chrome Burnish 1, Copper Burnish 2, and Chrome Pearl 2. The scratches in the surface of the various objects make the geometry resemble machined aluminum, copper, and pewter.

4. To better see how each material looks on the model, select all the geometry in the scene (press the H key to bring up the Select By Name menu, and Select All), apply one of the materials to the entire model, and then do a test rendering.

    The Chrome Burnish 1 material gives the entire model a very shiny, almost liquid metal-like appearance.

5. Now, assign and render the remaining two materials. The Copper Burnish 2 material is colorful and warm; the Chrome Pearl 2 material creates a satiny surface that resembles dark pewter.

6. When you're finished, close your Camera01 VFB.

Using Falloff For Iridescent Effects

Okay, that's enough scratchy metal textures for now. For the next tutorial, you're going to create some iridescent effects using the Falloff map to mix two widely varying material colors.

Webster's New Collegiate Dictionary (12th edition) defines iridescence as "a play of colors producing rainbow effects (as in a soap bubble)." From an optical—and computer graphics—standpoint, an object displaying iridescence refracts or reflects various spectra of light differently. This can depend on the viewing angle of its surface (a beetle's carapace, scratched aluminum, or stainless steel) or chemical reactions occurring on the surface (the aforementioned soap bubble, oil on the surface of water, and so on).

You can also see this effect in some translucent objects. For example, if you examine the inner surface of an abalone shell, you see a whitish mother-of-pearl look, with layers of bright color that appear inside the surface as you rotate the shell.

In the remaining tutorials in this chapter, you're going to create a simple iridescent material. You'll take a brief side trip into the land of retro-computer-graphics and X-ray effects and then take a simple material and enhance it with various maps to create the abalone-shell effect.

Now, because this tutorial and the one immediately following use similar materials, you're going to load a new model to use for both examples—and it's pretty creepy, as you'll soon see:

1. From the \CHAP_06 directory of this book's companion CD-ROM, load the file SKULL_1.MAX. The file loads, and your screen should look something like Figure 6.10.

   This model was constructed (and thoughtfully donated to this book) by James Bell (no relation to the author). James is a special effects artist working for Weta, Ltd., a special effects company based in New Zealand and founded by acclaimed film director Peter Jackson (*Dead Alive, Meet the Feebles, Heavenly Creatures, The Frighteners*, and the upcoming *Lord of the Rings* trilogy). James constructed the model originally in Alias Power Animator and took the textures from scanned photographs of a prop skull used in the horror-comedy *The Frighteners*. (And if you haven't seen this film, check it out—it's an over-the-top mixture of humor and horror, with dynamite special effects.)

2. Well, because you probably can't contain yourself, render the Camera01 view and check out the image, also shown in Figure 6.11.

3. Open the Material Editor, select an unused material slot, and change Material Type from Standard to Blend. (You can discard the existing material if you want.) Click on the Material 1 slot, change

SPECIAL EFFECTS DOWN UNDER

For more information on Weta, Ltd., visit its Web page at **www.wetafx.co.nz/**.

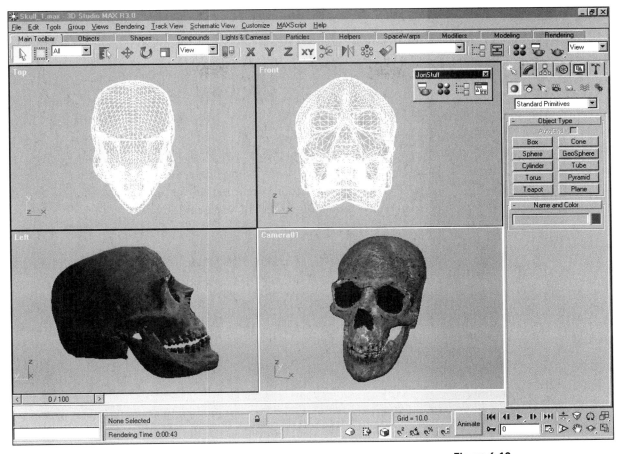

Figure 6.10

A high-resolution human skull model.

Figure 6.11

A moldy old human skull, cursing his digital existence.

its Ambient values to RGB 0, 0, 16, and change Diffuse to RGB 0, 0, 128, or dark blue. Change Specular Color to pure white (RGB 255, 255, 255) and Specular Level to 100. Change the material name to Blue, and then click on the Go To Parent icon.

4. Click on the Go To Parent icon again and open Material 2. Change the Ambient value to RGB 0, 16, 0, or dark green, and change the Diffuse value to RGB 0, 255, 0, or pure bright green. Change Specular Color to pure white (RGB 255, 255, 255) and Specular Level to 100, and then change this material name to Green. Click on the Go To Parent icon again and change this material name to Iridescent 1.

5. Click on the Mask button, and when the Material/Map Browser appears, make sure New is selected. Select Falloff, and when it appears in the Material Editor, you'll see the sample sphere (or box) in the Material Editor change to a dark blue with a bright green halo around its edges.

6. Next, select the skull geometry (either from your viewports or using the Select By Name menu) and assign the Iridescent 1 material to it.

7. When you're finished, activate your Camera01 viewport and render the scene.

Whoa! Pretty cosmic there, dude. (Looks like something you might've seen at an old Grateful Dead concert.) As you can see on your screen, the bright green material appears on the outer edges of the geometry, roughly parallel to your Camera01 viewpoint. (See Figure 6.12 for a black-and-white

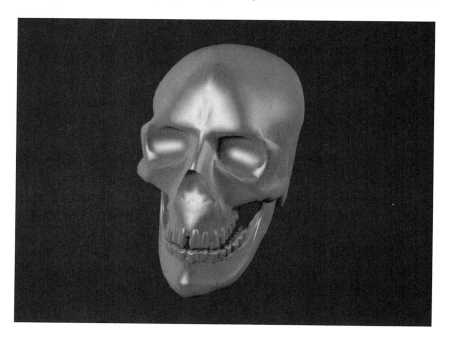

Figure 6.12
The Falloff map blends between two different material colors.

"REAL VIRTUALITY"

Although the graphics in 1981's *Escape From New York* appeared to be early computer graphics work, they were actually "simulated simulations." Instead of using early computer graphics, the film's effects technicians created the illusion of a wireframe cityscape by placing fluorescent pinstriping tape along the contours of matte-black miniature buildings. This miniature Manhattan was then bathed in heavy ultraviolet light and filmed with a snorkel camera rig.

Another interesting note: The effects supervisor in charge of this sequence was Jim Cameron, who has gone on to direct such groundbreaking films as *The Terminator* and *Terminator 2*, *Aliens*, *The Abyss*, *True Lies*, and *Titanic*.

---

version.) The green material then blends into the dark blue material, which appears predominantly on the surfaces that are more perpendicular to your viewpoint.

This iridescent effect can be quite striking when applied to complex geometry and enhanced with different Diffuse, Bump, or Reflection maps. (You'll play with these techniques at the end of this chapter.)

Again, as with the earlier examples when you played with the Falloff map, you can return to the Material Editor, change the Falloff type to Fresnel or other settings, and re-render to check the results.

Retro-CG And X-Ray Materials

Now, here's a simple way to modify the material you've just created to produce a retro-computer-graphics or X-ray effect:

1. Go to the Material Editor and drag-copy the Iridescent 1 material to another material slot. Change this new material's name to X-Ray Green, select the Skull model (if it's not already selected), and apply the X-Ray material to it.

2. Open the Green material component of the X-Ray Green material. Change Ambient Color to RGB 0, 0, 32; leave Diffuse Color as it is. Change Glossiness to 40 and Specular Level to 30. Uncheck the Color box under Self-Illumination, then change its value to 100.

3. Open the Extended Parameters section. Verify that Falloff is set to In, set the Amount to 100, and change Falloff Type to Additive.

4. Click on the Go To Parent icon, drag the Green Material #2 up to the Blue Material #1 slot, make it a Copy (not an Instance), and then open this new material. Change its name from Green to Inner, and then make Diffuse pure black, or RGB 0, 0, 0. Change Self-Illumination to 0.

5. Now, activate your Camera01 viewport, and render a test image, which should look like Figure 6.13.

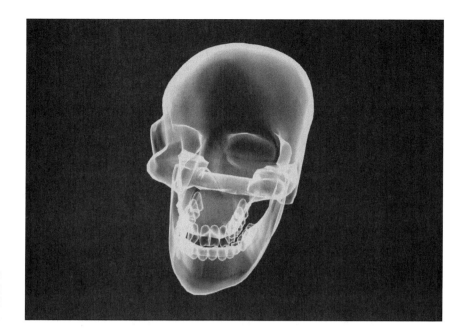

Figure 6.13
The new X-Ray Green material creates an old-fashioned computer-graphics look.

You've undoubtedly seen this computer-graphics look in some older movies and TV shows, where wireframe or edge-lit computer graphics illustrate technical data. (You'll see examples of this in the original *Star Wars* briefing scene, the *Nostromo* landing sequence in *Alien*, and Snake Plissken's flight by Manhattan skyscrapers in John Carpenter's film *Escape From New York*.)

I call this look "retro-CG." This type of 3D Studio MAX material could be very useful for showing off 3D imagery that's specifically intended to look synthetic or obviously computer-generated.

So, how else can we use this particular material? Well, as your previous rendering indicates, you could use it to simulate an X-ray look. It would be particularly effective used on a complex human skeleton mesh (especially if that mesh were itself inside another, properly proportioned human mesh object). By changing the green outer color to a bluish-white and adjusting the Glossiness and Specular Level values, you could simulate the spaceport X-ray scanner scene in the movie *Total Recall*, for example.

Varying The Materials

Here are some other things you could try:

- Change the Material Effects channel of Material 1 (the "outer" material) to 1 or above, and then apply a Lens Effects Glow to it. With a careful choice of material colors gradients (such as blue-white or purple, shading off to black) and Glow, you could simulate an eerie ultraviolet or black light look.

- Apply an automatic Reflection map to just one of the materials. (This would work best on an object surrounded by other geometry and an Environment map, of course.)

- Use a Raytrace map for one of the materials.

You should also experiment with the Falloff Type settings (as you did with the metal Reflection maps) to create iridescent material blending effects.

An Abalone Shell Effect

For the final tutorial, you'll create a new iridescent material that resembles the mother-of-pearl abalone effect I mentioned earlier. This material uses Falloff maps to mix Reflection maps and Bump maps.

1. For this example, you no longer need a moldering skull leering at you, so select File|Open, and from this book's companion CD-ROM, open the file VASE_1.MAX. The file loads, and your screen should look like Figure 6.14.

Figure 6.14

The test scene for the Iridescent Abalone texture.

This is a simple scene depicting a vase sitting on a small table in a room corner. If you were to render this scene as it stands, you would see that the walls have a beige, stucco surface, the table is light wood, but the vase is a flat blue. You'll change its material next.

2. Open the Material Editor and click on Material Slot #3, which has the simple, dark blue material already applied to the vase. Change Ambient to pure black, or RGB 0, 0, 0. Change Diffuse to RGB 16, 0, 32, or a dark purple. Don't worry about these colors being surprisingly dark for a pearl material; most of the bright colors for this material will come from the Reflection map mix. Change Specular to pure white, or RGB 255, 255, 255.

3. Change Glossiness to 50 and Specular Level to 100. Then, rename this material Iridescent Abalone.

   Okay, bear with me here for these next few steps. This Iridescent Abalone material is going to get complicated as you create layered maps for the Reflection and Bump map slots.

4. Go to the Maps rollout for this material, and open the Reflection map slot. When the Material/Map Browser appears, select Mix.

5. In the Mix Parameters rollout, click on the Maps slot next to Color #1, and select Mask. In the Mask rollout, click on the Map button and then select Bitmap. Now, click on the Bitmap Name button in the Bitmap Parameters rollout, and from the \CHAP_06 directory of the companion CD-ROM, click on the file COLRFOIL.JPG and view it.

   COLRFOIL.JPG is a 640-by-480 bitmap that I created in Autodesk Animator Pro. It began as a screen full of grayscale pixels to which I then applied various enlargement and pixelation effects. I then forced a rainbow-hued color palette into the grayscale bitmap to produce this op-art image. It serves as a colorful Reflection map for your Abalone texture.

6. Click on OK in the Select Bitmap Image File dialog box to load the image into the Material Editor. Under Coordinates, make sure Environment Mapping: Spherical Environment is selected. Verify that Blur is 1.0, set Blur Offset to 0.05, and then open the Output section. Change the Output Amount value to 1.5. (Again, as with the metal examples mentioned earlier in the book, you can experiment with the various Output Mixing Curve functions if you want.)

7. Click on the Go To Parent icon to return to the Mask Map rollout. Click on the Mask button, and then select Falloff from the Material/ Map Browser.

8. Now, click on the Go To Parent icon to return to the main Reflection map rollout, and then click on the Color #2 button. From the Material/Map Browser, select Bitmap; then, click on and view the ABALONE.JPG image from the \CHAP_06 directory of the companion CD-ROM.

    This 400-by-400-pixel image began as a scanned photograph of a colorful Victorian house in San Francisco. I loaded the image into Adobe Photoshop and used the Black Box 2.0 filters (renamed as Eye Candy) from Alien Skin Software to distort the original photo into the psychedelic mess you see here.

9. When you're finished viewing ABALONE.JPG, click on OK to load the image. Under Coordinates, make sure that Texture: Explicit UVW 1 is selected (this may seem like a strange setting for a reflection bitmap, but the final results look better). Verify that Blur is 1.0 and set Blur Offset to 0.05; then, click on the Mix button and select Falloff from the Material/Map Browser.

10. When the Falloff map loads, click on the Swap Colors/Maps icon, then click on the Go To Parent icon. Change this map name to Reflect Mask/Mix. Click on the Go To Parent icon again to return to the main Material Editor rollout.

11. Click on the Bump Map button and select Falloff from the Material/ Map Browser. Leave the settings as they are. Click on the Color #1 button and select Noise from the Material/Map Browser.

12. In the Noise rollout, change Noise Type to Fractal and Noise Size to 10.0. Then, click on the Go To Parent icon to return to the main Bump map rollout.

13. Now, if you were to click on the Get Material button and use the Active Slot option of the Material/Map Browser, you would see the entire Material tree of Iridescent Abalone in the Browser. By clicking on the various View icons (View List, View List + Icons, View Small Icons, View Large Icons), you can examine all the components that make up the Iridescent Abalone material. This tree diagram is shown in Figure 6.15.

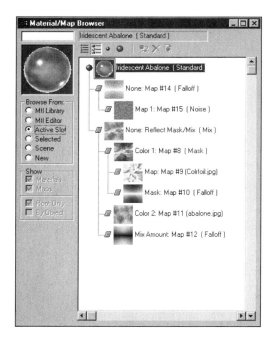

Figure 6.15
The Iridescent Abalone material shown in the Material/Map Browser (View List + Icons selected).

Figure 6.16
The Iridescent Abalone material creates a combination of bright edge colors (visible in your rendering) with a lighter pearly texture.

14. Close the Browser, activate your Camera01 viewport, and do a test rendering, as shown in Figure 6.16.

As your rendering indicates, this complex mix of maps combined with the Falloff masking places bright reflected colors along the edges of the geometry but leaves a bluish white pearly finish on the faces that are more perpendicular to the Camera01 view. The Bump map, using the Noise material and Falloff masking, creates slight variations in the surface and helps break up the specular highlights of the material.

Like the abalone shell inner surface, the material appears to have depth and complexity that belie its Standard material origins. This particular texture somewhat resembles a fine porcelain or translucent china and might be appropriate on a punch bowl, flower vase, or the like.

15. When you're finished looking at the rendering, close your Camera01 VFB.

Of course, you can experiment with other maps in the various Falloff slots to vary the final Abalone material. Try putting a Raytrace Reflection map or a Reflect/Refract cubic environment map in one of the Reflection slots and check out the final effect.

Note that all the materials you've created in this chapter are also saved in the MAXFX3.MAT Material Library, included on this book's companion CD-ROM. A version of this vase scene with materials is also saved as VASE_2.MAX in the \CHAP_06 directory.

Moving On

In this chapter and the preceding one, you've seen how you could create a wide variety of complex man-made and natural materials by using various custom bitmaps, procedural textures, and the Falloff map.

In the next two chapters, you'll see how to use MAX's new Oren-Nayer-Blinn, Multi-Layer, and Anisotropic shading types to create materials such as dry and wet rock faces and shiny car lacquer. Then, in Chapters 9 and 10, you'll see how to create animated materials, with an emphasis on such science-fiction-style effects as disintegrations and explosions.

MATERIALS III: OREN-NAYER-BLINN AND MULTI-LAYER

BY JON A. BELL

In the last chapter, you saw how using MAX's Falloff map helped you create better metal materials as well as unusual iridescent and X-ray effects. In this chapter, you'll expand on that work by exploring 3D Studio MAX Release 3's new Material Editor shading types, such as Oren-Nayer-Blinn and Multi-Layer.

Diffuse Shading: Blinn Vs. Oren-Nayer-Blinn

In this chapter, you're going to continue to explore different materials techniques on both a material and map level. You'll see how Release 3's new shading types enable you to create everything from realistic wet and dry rock surfaces to shiny car paint.

For the first material example, you'll take a look at a rock face texture and how MAX's new shading types alter the appearance of light across a 3D surface. You'll then modify the existing material and map settings to produce the illusion of wet, shiny rock and even simulate the appearance of water cascading down the rock face.

1. Load MAX, or else save your current work and reset the program.

2. From the \CHAP_07 directory of this book's companion CD-ROM, load the file ROCKDRY.MAX. The file loads, and your screen should resemble Figure 7.1.

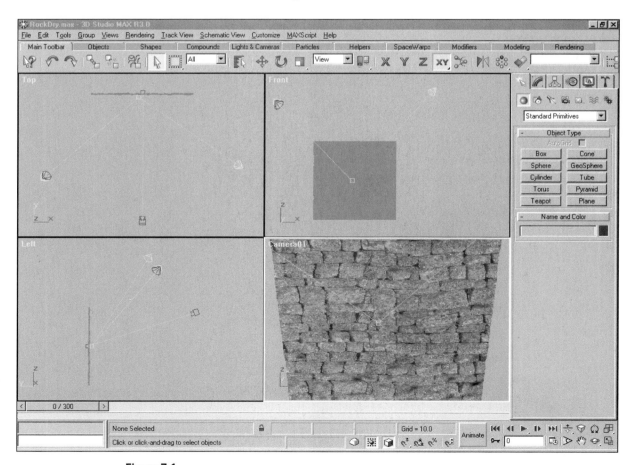

Figure 7.1

The ROCKDRY.MAX test scene.

The ROCKDRY test scene consists of a high-res QuadPatch object sitting in the middle of your MAX desktop, with several shadow-casting spotlights pointing at it. If you click on the QuadPatch object and go to the Modify panel, you'll see that the QuadPatch grid has a Displacement modifier applied to it, below the UVW Map. A bitmap called ROCKDRY.JPG is used to distort the patch geometry. (Note: The Displacement modifier is different from 3D Studio MAX Release 3's new Displace map, which can distort any polygonal geometry at render time. You'll explore the Displace map in the next chapter.)

3. Open the Material Editor and take a look at the material in Slot #1. This material, called Dry Rock, consists of a Blinn-shaded material with a single bitmap loaded in both the Diffuse and Bump map slots.

4. Open the Diffuse map slot and View the ROCKDRY.JPG image, which is shown in Figure 7.2.

Figure 7.2
A stone wall texture from the Great Zimbabwe Ruins, Zimbabwe, Africa.

I took this image in Africa, at the remains of an ancient city now designated the Great Zimbabwe Ruins. The ruins consist of giant stone walls and towers with light tan and brown rough-hewn rocks; the rocks are covered in various mosses and lichens, which give them a further mottled appearance. After taking the picture, I scanned it, loaded it into Adobe Photoshop, and made it seamlessly tilable using the Filter/Offset tool.

5. Close the Diffuse map, activate the Camera01 viewport, and render the scene. After a few moments, the scene renders and your screen should look like Figure 7.3.

Figure 7.3
The ROCKDRY.JPG texture
used on the Displaced
QuadPatch object.

As your rendering shows, the ROCKDRY.JPG bitmap, coupled with the bright multiple spotlights in the scene, produces a bright rock face.

6. Return to the Material Editor and change the shading type of the Dry Rock material from Blinn to Oren-Nayer-Blinn. As you do, you'll notice that the sample sphere in Material Slot #1 becomes darker.

7. Now, render the scene again and notice the differences between this rendering and the previous one with the Blinn shading type.

The Oren-Nayer-Blinn shading type produces what's known as non-Lambertian shading, which is well suited for rough, dry surfaces, such as rock, stucco, brick, and the like. The effect of this shader is to spread out or diffuse the light that plays across the surface of your object. Rough surfaces, such as this one, tend to absorb and scatter light with little falloff across their surface. For many rough, matte, or satin materials, this type of finish is more realistic than the standard light response you get with Phong- or Blinn-shaded materials, even if you've cranked down the specular highlights on the material. Although this is a subtle effect, altering the shading types of your materials to better match their real-world physical lighting responses can dramatically improve the overall realism of your renderings.

Diffuse Shading: A Wet Rock Surface

Okay, now that you've seen the differences between Blinn and Oren-Nayer-Blinn shading types for the dry rock, what about creating the illusion of wet rock? In the next example, you'll modify the textures used on this rock face to create the illusion of wet, shiny rock. You'll even see how using an animated Noise map in the Specular slot produces the effect of sheets of water cascading down the rock face. To create a wet rock surface, follow these steps:

1. Return to the Material Editor and activate Material Slot #2. Change the name of this material to Wet Rock 1, and then change the Ambient and Diffuse Colors as so: Make Ambient RGB 46, 17, 17 and Diffuse RGB 137, 50, 50. Make Specular pure white, or RGB 255, 255, 255.

2. Under Specular Highlights, change Specular Level to 100 and Glossiness to 50.

3. Go to the Maps section and open the Diffuse Color slot. When the Material/Map Browser appears, double-click on the RGB Multiply map to load it. In the RGB Multiply map, click on the name slot for Color #1 and select Bitmap from the Material/Map Browser. Next, from the Select Bitmap Image File menu, select the image ROCKDRY.JPG from the \CHAP_07 directory of this book's companion CD-ROM. When you return to the Material Editor, change UV Tiling to U 1.0, V 2.0. Then, click on the Go To Parent icon.

4. Drag-copy the ROCKDRY.JPG bitmap from the Color #1 slot down to Color #2, make it a Copy, not an Instance, then click on the Go To Parent icon again. Drag-copy the entire RGB Multiply map from the Diffuse map slot down to Bump map, but make this an Instance. (You want any changes you make to the Diffuse component to be updated for the Bump map.)

5. Click on the Glossiness slot, and from the Material/Map Browser, select Noise. Change the Noise type to Fractal, but keep the other settings as they are; then, click on the Go To Parent icon to return to the main Material Editor rollout.

6. When you're finished, select the Rock Face QuadPatch object in your scene, apply this new Wet Rock 1 material to it, then activate the Camera01 viewport and render the scene. After a few moments, the image appears, and it should look like Figure 7.4.

   Well, the rock face no longer looks completely dry, but the scene can still be improved to make the rock surface look wetter and more saturated.

7. Press the H key to bring up the Select By Name menu, and select the Spot03 spotlight. As your viewports indicate, the Spot03 spotlight is a duplicate of Spot01, which has been moved slightly along its local Z-axis. This produces a "doubled-up" light to greatly enhance the

Figure 7.4
The duplicated ROCKDRY.JPG image used in both slots of an RGB Multiply material darkens the overall image.

apparent illumination provided by the spotlight on the upper-left side of the rock face.

Now, you may be asking yourself, "Why duplicate the Spot01 light at all? Why not simply increase the existing Spot01's multiplier from 1.5 to an even higher setting?" The reason you're doing this is so you have greater control over the lighting on both the Diffuse and Specular components of the Rock Face object, as you'll see in a second.

8. With Spot03 selected, go to the Modify panel and check the Spot03 light to On. Then, under the Affect Surfaces area of the light rollout, uncheck Diffuse, but leave Specular checked. Now, the Spot03 light will affect only the specular highlights of the Rock Face object, but it won't add light to the Diffuse component of the material.

9. Next, return to the Material Editor and make the following changes to the Wet Rock 1 material. Go to the Diffuse map slot and open the RGB Multiply material. Click on the Color #2 slot, and from the \CHAP_07 directory of this book's companion CD-ROM, click on View, and then load the file ROCKWET.JPG.

As the image on your screen indicates, the ROCKWET.JPG image is a darker, more saturated version of the original ROCKDRY.JPG image, with more contrast. I created this image by loading the dry version into Adobe Photoshop and using the Multiply feature to layer it several times on top of itself. I then increased the brightness and contrast of the image to produce the final result.

10. When you've finished loading the ROCKWET.JPG image, click on the Go To Parent icon twice to return to the main Material Editor rollout, activate your Camera01 viewport, and render another test image. After a few moments, the image appears, and your screen should look like Figure 7.5.

Figure 7.5
The darker ROCKWET.JPG image, when used in the second RGB Multiply slot, creates an even more saturated rocky face.

Now, we're starting to get closer to our ideal wet rock surface. The combination of multiple spotlights—including Spot03, which is affecting only the Rock Face's specular component—and the dark, saturated, and very shiny material, create the illusion of a wet, mossy green surface.

Animating The Water Effect

This is a better effect—but if you wanted to use this in an animation, you would need to suggest that water is flowing down over the surface of the rock. You could do so in a couple of different ways.

First, of course, you could include a particle emitter (or several) to the rock face geometry. By adding a particle system with a high particle count, then applying deflectors, wind and/or gravity, you could suggest sparkling water droplets bouncing down the surface. However, if you want to produce a more subtle effect, you can still suggest flowing water without using a particle system. You can do this by simply animating the coordinates of the Noise map used in the Wet Rock 1 Glossiness slot.

1. Turn on the Animate button and go to the last frame (number 300) of the scene. Then, return to the Material Editor and open the

Note: The file you've just created is included in the \CHAP_07 directory as ROCKWET.MAX. The materials you've created are also included in the MAXFX3.MAT material library, which you can find in the \MATLIBS directory of this book's companion CD-ROM.

Glossiness: Noise slot of the Wet Rock 1 material. Under XYZ Coordinates, change the Y Offset value from 0.0 to 300, turn off the Animate button, and drag the Time Slider back to frame 0. As you do, you'll see the specular highlight on the sample sphere in Slot #2 change as the Noise coordinates animate.

At this point, you can save your current work to your local hard drive and then render a low-resolution test animation. However, I've already rendered a version of this sequence for you to examine.

2. Select File/View File, and from the \CHAP_07 directory of this book's companion CD-ROM, click on the file ROCKWET.AVI and play it. As the file plays, you'll see that the animated Noise texture, when used in the Glossiness slot, creates the impression that a thin sheet of water is flowing down the surface of the rock.

The Multi-Layer Material: Creating Lacquered Finishes

One of the new material shading types included with 3D Studio MAX Release 3 is the Multi-Layer material. This material is useful for creating shiny materials that have depth, such as lacquered paint surfaces. Although similar to a standard Phong or Blinn shading type, the Multi-Layer material gives you the ability to define multiple specular highlights. The blending between these multiple layers is additive, which produces an extremely glossy appearance.

Here's how to use it to create a shiny car lacquer surface:

1. Load MAX, or else save your current work and reset the program.

2. From the \CHAP_07 directory of this book's companion CD-ROM, load the file LACQUER.MAX. The file loads, and you'll see a simple sphere sitting in the middle of a room with several spotlights illuminating the scene, as shown in Figure 7.6. An Omni light provides additional illumination for the walls.

3. Open the Material Editor and select the first sample slot, or Material #1. You'll alter this material to create the red car paint. First, change the name to Red Lacquer Paint 1, then click on the Shading dropdown and change the default shading type from Blinn to Multi-Layer.

4. Next, go down to the Basic Parameters section and take a look at the settings. You'll see the standard color swatches for Ambient and Diffuse, but you'll also see a spinner box for Diffuse Level, and separate sections for two different Specular Layers. You'll also see

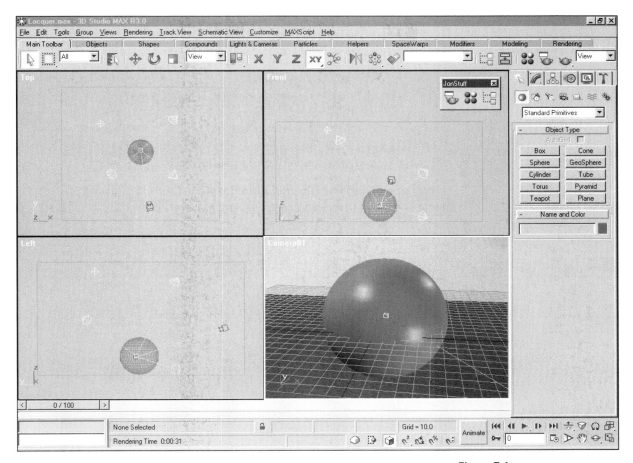

Figure 7.6
The simple test scene used to demonstrate the "car lacquer" example.

checkboxes for Anisotropy, which is another feature new to 3D Studio MAX Release 3. (You may remember the description of anisotropic shading from Chapter 5. I'll discuss this feature in the next chapter. For the moment, keep these settings as they are.)

5. If you open the Maps section of the rollout, you'll see several new map slots, including Diffuse Level and Diffuse Roughness, and separate Specular Color and Specular Level(s) 1 and 2 maps, Glossiness 1 and 2 maps, and Anisotropy (and Anisotropic Orientation) 1 and 2 maps. Each enables you to adjust the settings for the underlying base coat of the material and the overlaying lacquer or shellac coating.

6. Return to the Basic Parameters section and make the following changes. If the Ambient and Diffuse Color swatches are locked, unlock them, then change Ambient to RGB 0, 0, 0, or pure black. Change Diffuse to RGB 255, 0, 0, or pure red. Change Diffuse Level to 40—this will tend to mix the primary red Diffuse color with the black Ambient, making it darker and more rich.

7. Change the First Specular Layer color to pure white, or RGB 255, 255, 255. Then, change the Level value to 150 and the Glossiness value to 75. You'll see a bright, hot specular highlight appear on the sample sphere in Material Slot #1.

8. Next, go down to the Second Specular Layer section and change Color to RGB 255, 0, 0, or the same pure red you used in Step 6 for Diffuse. (You can also drag and drop this color swatch from Diffuse to Second Specular Layer, if you want.) Then, change the Level value to 75 and the Glossiness value to 35.

9. Select the Sphere01 object in your scene, apply the Red Lacquer Paint 1 material to it, activate your Camera01 viewport, and render a test image. After a few moments, the image appears on your screen, and it should resemble Figure 7.7.

Figure 7.7
The Red Lacquer Paint example.

The effect on your screen is somewhat subtle, but noticeable. What you should see is how the second Specular Layer spreads out underneath the overlaid hot-white specular highlight produced by the First Specular Layer settings. The image looks extremely glossy—almost wet—and simulates the effect of a shellac or lacquer car paint. These types of paint finishes invariably produce multiple specular highlights with underlying specular highlights that are softer and more diffused; the clear gloss coating on top of the surface then provides a sharper, additive highlight on the surface of the "paint."

Creating A Candy-Apple Finish

Okay, now let's dress up this effect a little further. What if you added a map to the second Glossiness slot? This will serve to spread out and diffuse the softer specular highlight even more than is happening currently. The effect you're striving for is similar to a candy-apple or metal flake car finish, where tiny bits of metal suspended in the car paint provide iridescent sparkles on the underlying layer(s). To create a candy-apple finish, follow these steps:

1. Return to the Material Editor and go down to the Maps rollout. Double-click on the Name button for Specular Level 2, and when the Material/Map Browser appears, click on Noise. Under Noise Parameters, change Noise Type from Regular to Fractal and then change Size from 25.0 to 0.25—you want the overall size to be fairly small. Change the name of this map to Noise Specular 2 (you're going to reuse this map in the next example).

2. Click the Go To Parent icon to return to the main Material Editor level, activate your Camera01 viewport again, and render another test image, as shown in Figures 7.8 and 7.9.

Figure 7.8
The addition of a Noise map in the Specular Level 2 slot serves to spread out the bottom specular highlight and also creates a speckled appearance in the highlight.

Adding Reflections

Let's keep going. If the sphere is extremely shiny, it would probably be reflecting the room, wouldn't it? So, let's add a Reflection map. However, instead of simply using a Reflection map alone, you'll combine it with Release 3's improved Falloff map to better control the final effect:

Figure 7.9
A close-up of the second
specular highlight on the sphere.

1. Go back to the Material Editor and click on the Reflection map slot. When the Material/Map Browser appears, click on Falloff from the Browser. This is an enhanced version of MAX's original Falloff map, and it provides additional control over how your maps appear in your final renderings. For our purposes, you'll want to leave the settings at their defaults; for example, Falloff Type set to Perpendicular/Parallel and Falloff Direction set to the Viewing Direction (Camera Z-Axis).

2. Click on the Name button next to the White (Color #2) swatch, and from the Material/Map Browser, select RGB Tint. When this map appears, click on the Green color swatch and set it to pure black, or RGB 0, 0, 0. Do the same for the Blue color swatch—you're going to want the final reflection map to be tinted pure red, or the same base color as the overall material.

3. Next, click on the Map Name button in the RGB Tint slot, and from the Material/Map Browser, select Reflect/Refract. When it loads, make the following changes. Under Source, select From File. Change Size to 256 and Blur Offset to 0.01.

4. Go down to the bottom of the rollout. Under the Render Cubic Map Files section, click on the To File button and save a file to your 3D Studio MAX \IMAGES subdirectory as RED_.JPG. Set Image Quality to the highest setting (100). When you do, you'll see the initial Cubic Reflection map created as RED_UP.JPG.

5. Now, click on the Pick Object And Render Maps button. Then, either click on the Sphere01 model, or use the Select By Name menu to select it from the list. When you do, you'll see a small Virtual Frame Buffer (VFB) window appear as MAX renders the 256-by-256-pixel Cubic maps, one right after the other. After a few moments, all of the maps will finish rendering, and you'll see the Red Lacquer Paint 1 sample sphere update with the new Reflect/Refract map tree.

6. Activate your Camera01 viewport and render another test image; after a few moments, it will appear, and your screen should resemble Figure 7.10.

   By using the Falloff map to mask the Cubic environment map, you're clamping the reflection more toward the outer edges of the sphere. In addition, the RGB Tint material changes the overall color of the Reflection maps to better match the existing red paint color.

Figure 7.10
The Red Lacquer Paint 1 material with a tinted Reflect/Refract cubic environment map.

7. To further see the effects of the Falloff material on this sphere, return to the Material Editor and click on the Go To Parent icon twice to return to the main Falloff2 level of this Reflection material. Under Falloff Type, change from Perpendicular/Parallel to Fresnel, then re-render the scene. As the rendered image indicates, the Fresnel falloff setting darkens the overall Reflection map, and restricts it further to the outer edges of the sphere, based on the viewing angle of the camera.

8. If you want, change the Falloff settings to Towards/Away or Shadow/ Light, re-render the scene, and compare the results.

Variations

Again, there are many ways to vary this Multi-Layer paint effect. You could try different combinations of colors in the Ambient, Diffuse, and Specular Layer sections (or even use complementary colors in these areas). Here are some other suggestions:

- Use different procedural or bitmap textures to modify the appearance of the Second Specular Layer. (For an interesting look, load the METAL7B.JPG image from this book's companion CD-ROM into the Specular Level 2 slot and re-render the scene.)

- If you don't mind the increased rendering times, use a Raytrace map instead of the Reflect/Refract map. (To speed things up, I suggest changing the Maximum Depth setting of the Ray Depth Control from 9 to 3, turning on Adaptive Antialiasing, and setting Maximum Number of Rays to 10. You can change these settings in the Global Parameters section of the Raytrace map.)

Note that the files you've just created are included in the \CHAP_07 directory of this book's companion CD-ROM as LACQUER2.MAX and LACQUER3.MAX.

Moving On

In this chapter, you've explored some of 3D Studio MAX Release 3's new Material types, and seen how you can create complex material effects through careful editing of your material parameters.

In the next chapter, you'll continue exploring Release 3's new materials, including the new Anisotropic shader, the RGB Multiply map, and Displacement.

MATERIALS IV:
ANISOTROPIC
TECHNIQUES
AND
DISPLACEMENT

In Chapter 7, you learned how to create realistic materials ranging from dry (and wet) rocky surfaces to shiny lacquered paint. In this chapter, you'll explore 3D Studio MAX Release 3's new Anisotropic shading type and see its specular effects on different types of geometry.

BY JON A. BELL

An Introduction To Anisotropic Shading

In this chapter, you'll see how you can use the Anisotropic settings for the Multi-Layer material as well as for the dedicated Anisotropic shader. You'll take a quick look at how you can use the RGB Multiply map to help you create richer materials. Finally, you'll examine Release 3's new Displacement options, which allow you to create complex surface distortions of any patch or polygonal mesh at render time.

In Chapters 5 and 6, I presented several tutorials on creating complex metal materials. The effects included blending Blinn-shaded (or Phong-shaded) materials with Metal-shaded materials using a complex combination of custom bitmap masks. The final result of these tutorials simulated an effect known as anisotropic specularity. Although this sounds like a *Star Trek* buzzword, it's the new rage for computer graphics imagery (CGI) users who want to create better-looking materials. Essentially, anisotropic specularity describes nonuniform specular highlights in shiny materials where the surface tends to break up the highlight or even produce multiple highlights.

There are many examples of this, both organic and man-made. The sheen of long human hair (just think of shampoo commercials or print ads) and glossy animal fur shows the effect of anisotropic specularity. Likewise, scratches in metallic surfaces (such as the faint lines you see in machined aluminum) display this effect. A good example of this is the METAL7.JPG texture map included with CD-ROM that ships with 3D Studio MAX. In addition, as you learned in the preceding chapter, a lacquered surface such as the surface on a well-waxed, newly washed car can also display multiple highlights. You'll often see a deep, soft highlight created by layers of paint—perhaps with metallic flakes—and then a hotter "kicker" highlight on the top surface of the clear lacquer.

Although earlier I described how to simulate this effect through some clever Material Editor workarounds, 3D Studio MAX Release 3's materials include the new Anisotropic shader, which lets you produce this effect automatically. For this tutorial, you'll quickly examine how to use it to produce interesting results.

Using Anisotropic Specularity With The Multi-Layer Shader

The first thing you'll do is load the Lacquer material you worked with in the preceding chapter and modify its anisotropic settings. You'll then work directly with the dedicated Anisotropic shader, new in 3D Studio MAX Release 3. To begin, follow these steps:

1. From the \CHAP_08 directory of the companion CD-ROM, load the file RACECAR1.MAX. The file loads, and your screen should look like Figure 8.1.

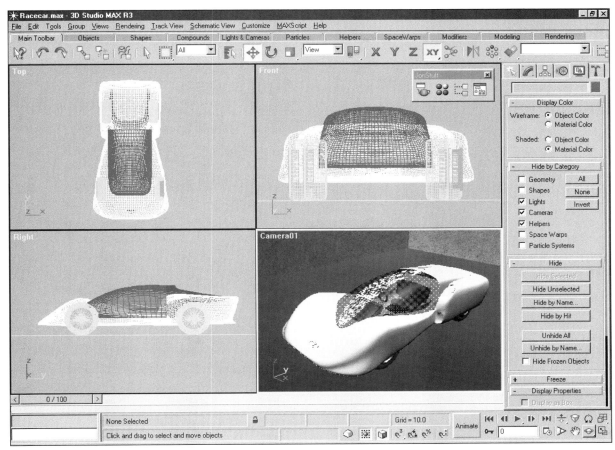

Figure 8.1

A sleek race car model sitting in a stark room.

This futuristic race car model has an interesting history. Jamie Clay, a former Autodesk employee and now the president of Digital Phenomena (San Rafael, California), constructed an early version of this model back in 1989 using a beta copy of 3D Studio Release 1 for DOS. When he first constructed it, he used 3D Studio/DOS's Deform/ Fit tools, then tessellated it to smooth out its surface. Over the years, Jamie has refined the design, and now, using MAX's MeshSmooth modifier, he has constructed the version you see here. Its sleek surfaces will show off the effects of anisotropic shading nicely.

2. Before you continue, activate your Camera01 viewport and render the scene at 640-by-480 resolution. Your screen should look like Figure 8.2.

Figure 8.2
A test rendering of the race car model.

As the rendering indicates, the car body is a very shiny yellow with hot specular highlights trailing off to softer highlights. A subtle Reflection map also enhances the glossy appearance of the car's finish.

3. Before you close your *Camera Virtual Frame Buffer* (VFB) window, click on the Save Bitmap icon (the Disk in the upper-left corner of the window) and save this image to your 3DSMAX3\IMAGES directory as ANI_TEST1.TIF. (You can use a different bitmap format if you want; if you choose JPG, make sure the Quality setting value is 100.) In a moment, you'll compare several test renderings by using MAX Release 3's RAM Player feature.

4. Open the Material Editor and take a look at some of the materials used in the scene. (If you don't have your Material Editor set up to display 24 materials simultaneously, right-click and change the Material Editor display to 6-by-4 Sample Windows, or use the Hand icon to scroll around and display the scene materials.) You'll notice various materials for the car's body, interior, and wheels, as well as the room's floor and walls.

5. In Material Slot #10, you'll see a material called Racecar Body. Make this material active, then take a look at the various settings. Under Shader Basic Parameters, you'll see that it's the Multi-Layer shader that you played with in Chapter 7 when you created various types of lacquer paint. Under Multi-Layer Basic Parameters, you'll see that the Ambient Color is set to solid black and the

Diffuse Color is set to RGB 255, 205, 7 to produce the strong yellow hue. The Diffuse Level value is set to 50, which blends some of the Diffuse Color with the Ambient and makes the surface appear richer and more contrasty.

6. As with the lacquer paint tutorials in the preceding chapter, you'll notice that there are multiple Specular Layer settings. The First Specular Layer color is pure white—or RGB 255, 255, 255—with a Level value of 200 and a Glossiness value of 90. This produces an intense hot specular highlight. However, you'll notice that the Anistropy setting and Orientation setting are both set to 0 (you'll change these in a moment).

7. Under Second Specular Layer, you'll see that the Color value is the same as the Diffuse shade above—yellow—and the Level and Glossiness values are set to 75 and 35, respectively. This produces a softer highlight surrounding the initial hard white specular "kicker."

8. Finally, if you open the Maps rollout and look under Reflection, you can see that there's the good old (new) Falloff map, with a Reflect/Refract map loaded into it. I created the bitmaps in the Reflect/Refract slot by selecting a Dummy object in the scene as the center point for creating the cubic environment maps of the room. (I did this with the entire car model hidden.) In addition, I placed self-illuminated white boxes on the ceiling (hidden in your scene) so that they would be included in the Reflection maps to suggest overhead lighting fixtures.

   Now, the rendering you saw a minute ago was interesting, but let's change some of the Racecar Body material settings—including the Anisotropic values—and examine the effects they have on the surface. First, change the overall color of the Car Body so you can see the highlights a little more clearly.

9. Return to the Material Editor, go to the Racecar Body material and click on the Diffuse color swatch. Change its RGB settings to 128, 0, 0, or dark red. Keep the Second Specular Layer color yellow; the contrast between the dark red Diffuse Color and the soft yellow highlights will enhance the final rendering.

10. Under First Specular Layer, change the Anisotropy value to 50; under Second Specular Layer, change the Anisotropy value to 25. Then, activate your Camera01 viewport and do another test rendering, but don't close your Camera01 VFB window when the rendering is finished. Your screen should look like Figure 8.3.

Figure 8.3
In the race car model, Anisotropy is set to 50 on the First Specular Layer, and 25 on the Second Specular Layer.

Comparing The Renderings With The RAM Player

As the new rendering appeared in your Camera01 VFB window, you could probably see the subtle changes made by the Anisotropic settings compared to the rendering you saw in Figure 8.2. However, you can compare the renderings more easily by using MAX Release 3's RAM Player feature:

1. Click on the Save Bitmap icon in your Camera VFB window and save this new image to your \IMAGES subdirectory as ANI_TEST2.TIF.

2. Minimize or close your Rendering menu and the Material Editor menu, then select Rendering|RAM Player. The RAM Player window appears.

   As you saw in Chapter 4, Release 3's new RAM Player lets you load image sequences and play them back—even high-resolution sequences—depending on how much RAM is in your computer (a fast video card helps as well). In addition, the new RAM Player lets you "scratch" back and forth between two different images to make quick comparisons between subtle rendering effects. It's a good way to check out the differences in the Anisotropic settings.

3. Click on the Open Channel A icon (the open folder icon), and from your 3DSMAX3\IMAGES directory, select the file ANI_TEST1.TIF. When the RAM Player Configuration menu appears, click on Okay

to accept the 640-by-480-resolution image. The first Anisotropic rendering loads into the RAM Player.

4. Next, click on the Open Channel B icon, and load the ANI_TEST2.TIF file from your \IMAGES directory. Click on Okay again to accept the image; when it finishes loading, you should see both images sitting in the RAM Player, with a scrollable dividing line running down the middle, as shown in Figure 8.4.

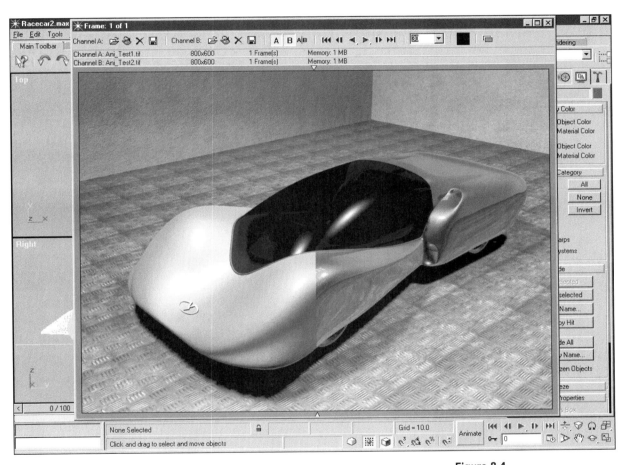

Figure 8.4

The ANI_TEST images loaded into the RAM Player. (These images rendered at 800 pixels by 600 pixels for clarity.)

5. At the top and bottom of your RAM Player screen, you should see small triangular markers, or arrows, pointing to the scrolling dividing line. Place your mouse cursor on this line, then left-click, hold, and drag the line back and forth across the two images. As you do, you'll see the RAM Player image change back and forth between your two ANI_TEST renderings. Of course, in this rendering, you'll mostly notice how the car colors change from bright yellow to a coppery orange, but pay attention also to the specular highlights.

The differing material specular colors add a depth and richness to the finish. (The darker surface color helps accentuate the reflected "ceiling lights" as well.)

6. Minimize your RAM Player, return to the Material Editor, and make the following changes to the Racecar Body material: Under First Specular Layer, change the Glossiness Value to 75 and the Anisotropy value to 75; under the Second Specular Layer, change the Anisotropy value to 50. Then, activate your Camera01 viewport and do another test rendering, but don't close your Camera01 VFB window when the rendering is finished. (Instead, save it to your 3DSMAX3\IMAGES directory as ANI_TEST3.TIF.) Your screen should look like Figure 8.5. The increased Anisotropic settings stretch out the highlights even more.

Figure 8.5
The increased Anisotropic values have lengthened the specular highlights along the car's contours.

7. Maximize the RAM Player again, but this time load the ANI_TEST3.TIF image you just rendered into the A Channel, then scroll the dividing line back and forth to note the Anisotropic setting changes.

8. Now you'll make one more change. Minimize your RAM Player, return to the Material Editor, and make the following changes to the Racecar Body material: Under both the First and Second Specular Layers, change Orientation to 90. Then, activate your Camera01 viewport and re-render the scene; your rendering should resemble Figure 8.6.

Figure 8.6
Changing the Anisotropic Orientation settings alters how the specular highlights lie on the car's surface.

9. Again, as you did before, save your Camera01 VFB to your \IMAGES directory as ANI_TEST4.TIF. Then, maximize your RAM Player again, and load the ANI_TEST4.TIF image you just rendered into the B Channel so you can compare it with the ANI_TEST3.TIF rendering. Scroll the dividing line back and forth to note the Anisotropic setting changes.

    Notice the differences? By changing the orientation of the Anisotropic value, you can alter how the specular highlights lie on the car's surface. The highlights now tend to follow the side contours of the car (this effect is especially noticeable along the left rear quarter panel and along the top of the left front wheel well).

10. At this point, you can continue playing with the various Multi-Layer Anisotropic settings, then save your current scene to your local \SCENES directory for further experimentation.

> **Note:** The scenes (and materials) you've just created are saved in this book's companion CD-ROM \CHAP_08 and \MATLIBS directories, respectively.

The Anisotropic Shader

Now that you've seen how to modify the Multi-Layer material to add anisotropic highlights, you'll take a quick look at MAX Release 3's new dedicated Anisotropic shading type.

The main difference between the dedicated Anisotropic shader and the Multi-Layer shader (with Anisotropy attributes active) is largely a matter of material complexity. If you don't need a Multi-Layer, lacquered finish but still desire anisotropic specular highlights, the dedicated shader should be fine for your needs.

Objects with anisotropic specular highlights often have a discernable grain or linear texture to them. Just as the 3D objects in your MAX scenes can have UVW coordinates for mapped materials, so can real-world objects have a latitudinal and/or longitudinal structure to them. A piece of lathed metal, for example, will have minute scratches that tend to gather and scatter the light across its surface both in the direction of the scratches and along the long axis of the object itself.

One way we can illustrate this effect is to take a look at a 3D model of a real-world object—an aluminum wheel (which might be appropriate for the race car example). You'll see what it looks like with a Standard Metal-shaded material, then you'll apply an Anisotropic shader to it and tweak the results. To begin, follow these steps:

Figure 8.7

The test aluminum wheel object used to demonstrate the dedicated Anisotropic shader.

1. If the RAM Player from the preceding tutorial is still sitting on your MAX desktop, close it. Then, from the \CHAP_08 directory of this book's companion CD-ROM, load WHEEL_1.MAX. The file loads, and your desktop should look like Figure 8.7.

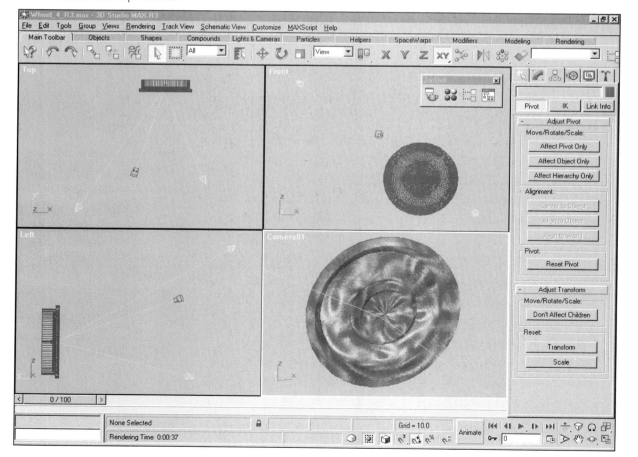

2. Open the Material Editor and take a look at the Chrome Wheel material in Slot #1. It's a Standard Metal shader material; the Reflection map consists of the metal image bitmap METAL_7B.JPG loaded as a sub-map in a Falloff map. Not surprisingly, this Metal shader material is currently applied to the Wheel and Rim models in the scene.

3. Activate your Camera01 viewport and render the scene; your rendering should look like Figure 8.8.

Figure 8.8
The aluminum wheel model with the Chrome Wheel material applied.

Okay, so this is a pretty straightforward metal material, similar to what you've seen in earlier chapters in this book. What we want to do is see the results we get when we change it to the Anisotropic shader and change the specular values. Then, we'll blend two different Anisotropic specular highlights together to create a striking effect.

4. Return to the Material Editor and make the following changes to the Chrome Wheel material: Under Shader Basic Parameters, change the shading type from Metal to Anisotropic. As you do, you'll see the sample sphere become washed out; the Diffuse Color has become white. Change Diffuse to pure black (RGB 0, 0, 0); this will darken the overall material.

5. Under Specular Highlight, make sure Specular Level is set to 150, with Glossiness at 75. Change Anisotropy to 65, then activate your

Figure 8.9
The Anisotropic shader and the Multi-Layer shader you worked with earlier produce similar results.

Camera01 viewport and render the scene again. Your rendering should resemble Figure 8.9.

As your rendering indicates, the bright Anisotropic specular highlights tend to follow the inner curvature of the wheel.

6. Return to the Material Editor, change the Anisotropic Orientation value from 0 to 90, then re-render the scene and note the differences between this rendering and the previous one. The specular highlights "gather" differently around the circumference of the wheel.

Blending Anisotropic Shaders With Shellac

Now, which rendering do you prefer? If it's sometimes difficult to decide how you want your anisotropic specular highlights to fall on your object surfaces, maybe you should simply combine the two different Anisotropic highlights, each with different Orientation settings. A nifty way to do this is to use MAX Release 3's new Shellac material.

The Shellac material was created by Blur Studios (**www.blur.com**), a special effects company located in Santa Monica, California. Blur Studios has used 3D Studio DOS and MAX on such TV and film projects as *The Visitor* and *Deep Rising*. During the last few years, their in-house development staff has created custom MAX plug-ins for Blur's various projects; a number of these plug-ins, including the Raytrace map and material, have been incorporated into the release copies of MAX.

The Shellac material is similar to the Multi-Layer material; it allows you to create layered Diffuse Color and specular material effects for your objects. However, unlike Multi-Layer, the Shellac material allows you to additively blend between two separate materials. This additive blending can afford you greater control over the final look of your materials, as you'll see here:

1. Return to the Material Editor, make the Chrome Wheel material slot active, and then click on the Material Type button (which should read Type: Standard). When the Material/Map Browser appears, change the material type to Shellac and click on Okay to make sure you keep the old material as a sub-material.

2. In the Shellac material rollout, you'll see the original Chrome Wheel material loaded into the first (Base Material) slot. Click on this slot to open it and change the material name to Chrome Base. Under Specular Highlight, make the following changes: Change Specular Level to 200, Glossiness to 50, and both Anisotropy and Orientation to 90. Then, click on the Go To Parent icon to return to the main Shellac rollout.

3. Drag-copy the Chrome Base material down to the Shellac Material slot and make sure it's a Copy, not an Instance duplicate. Then, click on this Shellac slot to open it. Change the copied material name to Chrome Top Layer, then make the following changes: Under Specular Highlight, change Specular Level to 150, Glossiness to 75, Anisotropy to 25, and change Orientation from 90 to 0.

4. When you're finished, click on the Go To Parent icon again to return to the main Shellac rollout and change the Shellac Color Blend value to 100. As you do, you should notice that the sample sphere in your Material Editor slot now has a cruciform-shaped specular highlight. Activate your Camera01 viewport again and render another scene. Your rendering should look like Figure 8.10.

   As your rendering indicates, the Shellac material has created an additive blend between the two different Anisotropic materials, producing multiple, accumulated highlights that run along both the U and V orientation of the wheel model.

5. If you think the Reflection map is too bright, remember that it's being blended (additively) in both materials just as the specular highlights are. If you want, open the Chrome Base material, uncheck its Reflection map, then re-render the scene. The Reflection map is added only to the Chrome Top Layer level of the Shellac material.

Note: Versions of this scene and associated materials are saved in the \CHAP_08 and \MATLIBS directories of this book's companion CD-ROM.

Figure 8.10
The Shellac material creates an additive blend between the two different Anisotropic materials.

Using RGB Multiply: Punching Up The Apple Scene

Well, that's it for the Anisotropic material techniques. Now, you're going to take a quick look at the RGB Multiply map and 3D Studio MAX Release 3's new mesh Displacement effects.

In Chapter 3, you took a brief look at how hand-painted texture maps created a convincing still life of an apple sitting on a tabletop. For this next material example, you'll see how you can punch up the saturation of the original Apple texture simply by reusing the Bump map as a component of an RGB Multiply material. Here's how to do it:

1. From the \CHAP_08 directory of this book's companion CD-ROM, load APPLE.MAX, then open the Material Editor. In Slot #1, you should have a material called Apple loaded (the actual material used on the apple in the scene is called Apple Raytrace; it uses a Raytrace map in the Reflection slot). For this example, you'll use the non-raytraced version of the Apple skin texture.

2. Press the H key to bring up the Select By Name menu, select the Apple mesh, then apply the Apple material to it (this will replace the Apple Raytrace material). Note that there's a slight Raytrace Reflection map on the table surface; to speed up rendering time, open this material and make sure the Reflection map option is turned off.

3. Go to the Maps slot of the Apple material and click on the APPLESKN.JPG map in the Diffuse Color slot. Next, click on the Type: Bitmap button, and when the Material/Map Browser appears, select RGB Multiply. Click on Okay to keep the old (existing) map as a sub-map. You'll now see the APPLESKN.JPG bitmap loaded into the Color #1 slot.

4. Click on the Color #2 slot, and when the Material/Map Browser appears, change Browse From to Scene instead of New. From the current Apple scene, click on the APPLEBMP.JPG image to copy it. However, make this a Copy, not an Instance—you're going to be altering this map from that of its existing Bump Map settings—then click on Okay.

5. Go to the Blur Offset checkbox of Slot #2 (where you just loaded the APPLEBMP.JPG image) and change the Blur Offset value to 0.1—this will blur out the existing grayscale map and "smear" the RGB values across the underlying bitmap in Slot #1.

6. When you're finished, click on the Go To Parent icon, close the Material Editor, and then render the scene. After a few minutes, the new Apple rendering appears on your screen. Compare this rendering with the apple rendering in Chapter 3. The two different renderings are shown in Figures 8.11 and 8.12, respectively.

Figure 8.11
The original Apple image from Chapter 3.

Figure 8.12
The modified Apple image, using the APPLEBMP.JPG image as the second component of an RGB Multiply material.

As you saw earlier, the APPLEBMP.JPG bitmap is a grayscale image used to produce subtle bumps and pits in the apple surface. However, when this bitmap is loaded into the second RGB Multiply slot, the grayscale values tend to punch up the underlying APPLESKN.JPG RGB values in Slot #1. Grayscale values below RGB 128, 128, 128, or neutral gray, tend to darken the underlying image; RGB values above neutral gray tend to lighten the Slot #1 image. The final effect is to increase the overall saturation of the current APPLESKN.JPG bitmap. As you load the APPLEBMP.JPG image, you'll see the Apple texture in the first material slot become darker; the apple turns from a Granny Smith to more of a Red Delicious, as it were.

Note: This scene is included in the \CHAP_08 directory of this book's companion CD-ROM as APPLE2.MAX.

7. When you're finished, save your existing work, if you want.

Using Displacement On Patch And Polygonal Objects

In the preceding chapter, you saw how you could create rocky surfaces, both dry and wet, using custom materials and a high-density QuadPatch. The stone wall had a Displacement modifier applied to it to distort its surface and enhance its rocky appearance.

Although this technique can work well for most scenes, there are times when you might want to add complex polygonal surface details only at render time—when you're working on your overall scene, you don't want to have huge numbers of polygonal faces bogging you down.

This is where MAX Release 3's new Displace material setting and polygonal object Properties attribute come in. Starting in Release 3, MAX's Displacement map can apply various levels of geometric distortion, or add surface details, to any object in your scene, whether it's a patch, polygon, or a non-uniform rational b-splines (NURBS) object. Unlike Bump mapping, which simply gives the appearance of surface depth based on face normals and lighting, Displacement details will actually distort the surface of your objects, including the edges visible to the camera.

You can use the new Displacement map to add scales, warts, or other features to the skin of your 3D creatures, create plating or piping details on industrial walls, or build architectural details such as ornate carvings on walls, ceilings, or trim. You'll experiment with these latter effects now:

1. Load 3D Studio MAX, or else save your current work and then reset the program.

2. From the \CHAP_08 directory of this book's companion CD-ROM, load DISPLACE1.MAX. The file loads, and you'll see a flat QuadPatch object sitting in the middle of your desktop with two targeted spotlights and a Targeted Camera facing it. The Camera01 viewport is displaying a Shaded view.

3. Select the QuadPatch, then open the Material Editor. Go to the first material slot, name it Sandstone Trim, and apply it to the QuadPatch object. Then open the Maps slot, double-click on the Diffuse Color slot, and click the Type: button to load the Material/ Map Browser. Under Browse From, make sure New is selected, and double-click on Bitmap. When the Bitmap browser appears, go to the \CHAP_08 directory of this book's companion CD-ROM and select the file SANDSTONE1.JPG. The file loads, and you'll see that it's a grainy, earth-tone image of a sandy surface. Click on the Show Map In Viewport icon to display the map in your Shaded Camera01 viewport.

4. Click on the Go To Parent icon, and then drag-copy the SANDSTONE1.JPG map from the Diffuse Color slot to the Bump map slot. (Make it an Instance, not a Copy.)

5. Click on the Displacement slot, select Bitmap from the Material/ Map Browser, and from the \CHAP_08 directory, highlight the DISPLACEDETAIL5B.JPG image and click on View. The image appears in Figure 8.13.

   This texture, as well as the other DisplaceDetail*.JPG images, is taken from *The Book of Victorian Alphabets and Designs*, by Graphics

Figure 8.13
A black-and-white scrollwork
image for Displacement mapping.

Arts Archives (New York: Sterling Publishing, 1990. ISBN: 0-8069-7340-4). This book contains black-and-white examples of various types of Victorian scrollwork; all the examples contained are in the public domain and, as the book asserts, are "free for all to use." Sounds good—this collection of ornate black-and-white textures can serve as excellent examples for showing off MAX Release 3's Displacement mapping.

6. If you want, click on the View button and take a look at some of the other textures; they range from Celtic scrollwork to more geometric Etruscan designs, as shown in Figure 8.14. When you're finished, load the DISPLACEDETAIL5B.JPG image back into the Displacement map slot. Click on the Go To Parent icon to return to the main Sandstone Trim material rollout and change the Displacement map value to 20. This will help you see the distortion quite clearly in your final rendering.

At this point, you're still not ready to render your scene. If you tried, you still wouldn't see any displacement of the QuadPatch surface; for the Displacement effect to work, you need to either collapse the

Figure 8.14
Some other examples of the DisplaceDetail textures.

object into an Editable Mesh (and adjust the Subdivision Displacement settings) or apply a Displace Approximation modifier. This will convert your parametric QuadPatch object into an Editable Mesh at render time yet give you the benefit of going back and changing the original QuadPatch's creation parameters. You'll see this now.

7. With the QuadPatch selected, go to the Modifier panel and click on More. Under the Object-Space Modifiers category, select the Displace Approximation modifier (not the Displace modifier). As you do, you'll see several settings under Displacement Approximation— Subdivision Displacement is checked, along with Split Mesh. (For the QuadPatch object, you don't have to worry about these settings.) Under Subdivision Method, you'll see that Spatial and Curvature is active; the default settings of Edge at 10.0, Distance at 10.0, and Angle at 4.0 correspond to the Medium button under Subdivision Presets, directly above.

8. Activate your Camera01 viewport and render the scene; your rendering should look like Figure 8.15.

Figure 8.15
The DISPLACEDETAIL5B.JPG image applied to the QuadPatch object as a Displacement map.

Well, you can definitely see a Displacement effect happening, but it's subtle; the rounded-off details make the sandstone wall look as if it's been eroded because of age and exposure to the elements. Of course, this might be the effect you might. However, let's say you want a more distinctive layering of detail.

9. Return to the Displace Approximation rollout and click on the High button under Subdivision presets. Activate your Camera01 viewport and re-render the scene. It should look like Figure 8.16.

Figure 8.16
A higher subdivision Displacement setting makes the details more distinct.

10. Okay, let's increase the tiling of the Displacement map so we can see more of the rosette details across the surface of the wall. Return to the Material Editor, open the Displacement map slot, and increase both the U and V tiling to 2.0.

    Now, we could render this image as is, but for the finer details to show up with clarity, we should increase the Displacement resolution even further. That's why it's useful to have the Displace Approximation modifier applied on top of a parametric object—you can still go back in the Modifier stack and increase the face count of the object. Let's do that now.

11. Return to the Modifier panel, click the Down arrow next to the Displace Approximation modifier in the Stack listing, and select QuadPatch. Change the QuadPatch Length and Width Segment values both to 5, click the Down arrow again, and return to the Displace Approximation level of the Stack.

12. Activate your Camera01 viewport and render the scene again; it should look like Figure 8.17.

Figure 8.17
The increased QuadPatch face count helps the fine Displacement details show more clearly.

Showing The Effect In Your Viewport

Okay, so now you know the basics of Displacement mapping. However, because true displacement occurs only at render time, it can be tough knowing exactly what effect your Displacement map is having on your geometry. If it's too much, your original shape is lost or perhaps not aligned properly with other geometry in the scene.

However, you can address this by using the World-Space Modifier (WSM) Displace Mesh. This will show you the effects of your Displacement map, right in your viewports:

1. Return to the Modifier panel and click on the Remove Modifier From Stack icon. The Displace Approximation modifier disappears. From the Modify panel, click on the More button, and under World-Space Modifiers, select Displace Mesh. Under Displace Approximation, check Custom Settings. You'll see that the QuadPatch becomes much more dense in the wireframe views and the Shaded Camera01 viewport actually shows off the effects of the displacement. (If you click on the Low, Medium, and High buttons, you can see the details become more clear in your Shaded viewport.)

2. Now, a final note: Return to the Modify panel and click the Remove Modifier From Stack icon to delete the Displace Mesh modifier. In any of your viewports, right-click to bring up the Properties menu for the selected QuadPatch and click on Convert To Editable Mesh. The QuadPatch then ceases to become a parametric Patch object and is instead a fixed-resolution polygonal mesh. (That is, unless you applied other modifiers, such as MeshSmooth or Tessellate.)

3. However, you can still apply true Displacement to this or any other polygonal mesh. Move your mouse cursor over to the Editable Mesh Modify panel, right-click, and select the Surface Properties rollout. As you do, you'll get bumped down to the bottom of the Editable Mesh rollout, and you can see the same Subdivision Displacement property options available. At this point, you can activate them and continue with your Displacement tests, by using the Presets buttons or by manually increasing the values for Edge, Distance, and Angle. (For more information on exactly what these options do, check your 3D Studio MAX Release 3 Help file.)

4. Now, here's a final Displacement experiment you can play with. If you go to the Display panel and click on Unhide By Name, you'll see several other basic MAX Primitive objects, such as a Box, Cylinder, and Sphere. Unhide any of them and try out different Displacement effects on them, using the techniques described in the previous steps. Try using your own custom bitmaps or procedural textures such as Noise, Smoke, Cellular, or Checker.

You can use Displacement mapping for a huge number of things beyond architectural details, of course. You could use a Noise map in the Displacement slot, applied to a horizontal QuadPatch, to create a landscape. You also could use a custom-painted grayscale bitmap to create mountains and other specific geography for your scene.

Now, here's another nifty trick: Instead of using a straight bitmap in your Diffuse Color slot, load a Mix map and put two different bitmaps in the Color #1 and #2 slots. Then, use your Displacement bitmap in the Mask slot of the Mix material. This will create the effect of the raised and sunken details being of different colors or textures than the generally flat areas.

Moving On

In the next chapter, you'll take a look at some pyrotechnic illusions: Specifically, you'll see how you can use combinations of animated Noise maps and masks to create disintegration effects. By combining these techniques with some of the metal material examples you saw in Chapters 5 and 6, you can create science-fiction-style effects worthy of *Star Wars* or *Star Trek*.

ANIMATED MATERIALS AND OPTICAL EFFECTS I

BY JON A. BELL

Now that you've explored complex, non-animated materials, it's time to make them move. In this chapter, you'll see how to create colorful animated material effects and combine the materials with the Lens Effects Glow filter to produce explosive results.

Making Glow Effects

First, you'll create glowing, animated optical effects using Blend materials and masks to restrict the glowing effect to specific areas of your objects. You'll then add animated Opacity maps (via Noise or animated bitmap sequences) to make objects disintegrate in a burst of glowing lightning a la *Star Trek*. Finally, you'll see how to create your own custom Opacity map bitmap sequences by animating some simple geometry and rendering the results.

In the many different incarnations of *Star Trek*—both the TV series and the films—you've probably seen a disintegration effect. In the original *Trek* series, for example, an alien beam weapon would often zap a red-shirted security guard. He would then disintegrate into a glowing mess and disappear with nary a residual smudge. Space cruisers, locked doors, and evil robots would also get blasted, with similar results.

It's easy to create this effect in MAX with Blend materials. To kick it off, you'll work on creating the glowing lightning effect. Then, you'll proceed to the actual disintegration. To create a glow effect, follow these steps:

1. Load the file DISINTEGRATE_1.MAX from the \CHAP_09 directory of the companion CD-ROM. You'll see that it's a simple sphere sitting on a flat Quad Patch, as shown in Figure 9.1. A couple of targeted spotlights and a camera complete the scene.

2. Open the Material Editor and take a look at the materials in the scene. The sphere and the ground plane are both mapped with the Metal 1 Single texture from Chapter 5. You're going to modify the Metal 1 Single texture for the sphere, so drag it over to the second material sample slot. Rename this material Metal 2, select the Quad Patch ground object, and apply this second material to it. (For this tutorial, you'll disintegrate only the sphere, not the ground upon which it sits.)

3. Select the original Metal 1 Single material to activate it and click on the Type: Standard button to bring up the Material/Map Browser. Select New and then choose Blend. When the alert box appears, make sure Keep Old Material As Sub-Material is checked. The Blend texture loads, and you'll see the Metal 1 material loaded into the Material 1 slot. Name this new Blend material Disintegrate 1.

4. Next, click on the Material 2 button. Change the name of this material to Glowing Lightning. This material will provide the basis for the crackling energy effect that crawls over the surface of the sphere.

5. Before you continue, click and hold on the Material Effects Channel icon and select Channel 1. The Lens Effects Glow filter will affect the second material only. (The Cellular map, which you'll load next, will

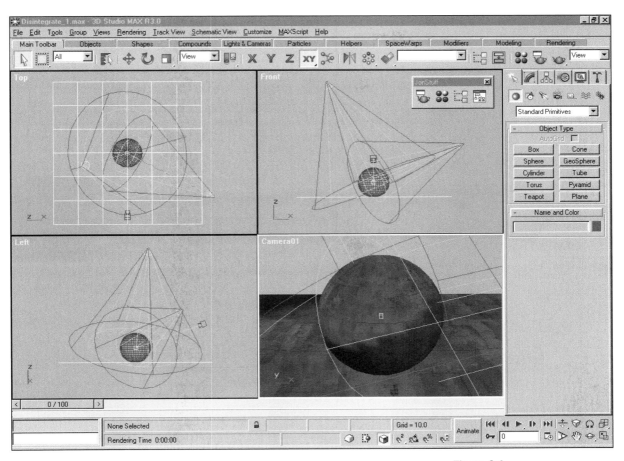

Figure 9.1
The test scene for the disintegration effect.

mask the Glowing Lightning material off to provide the actual spiky lightning.)

6. Change both the Glossiness and Specular Level values of the Glowing Lightning material to 0. Make sure the Self-Illumination Color checkbox is set to 100 and the Color box is unchecked.

7. Open the Maps rollout, click on the Diffuse Map button, and choose Noise from the Material/Map Browser. When the Noise Parameters rollout appears, change Noise Type to Fractal and Size to 10.0. Click on the black Color #1 swatch and change its RGB values to 128, 128, 255, or a bright blue. Leave Color #2 as white and double-click on the Go To Parent icon to return to the main Disintegrate 1 Blend material rollout.

Simplifying The Effect

You don't have to use a Noise Diffuse map for the Glowing Noise material. By making Material #2 self-illuminated and then changing the Ambient and Diffuse Colors to the desired shade, you can produce similar (although simpler) results. To do so, follow these steps:

1. Click on the Mask button under Basic Parameters and select Cellular from the Material/Map Browser.

   The Cellular map type is one of 3D Studio MAX's most powerful procedural textures. It's an extremely useful map that can produce "organic" imagery, including realistic ocean surfaces, cracked rocks or mud, and even scaly dragon skin. By tweaking some of its values, you can also produce convincing lightning effects, as you'll soon see.

   One caveat, though: The Cellular map type is probably the most processor-intensive map type you can use. Because it tends to increase your overall rendering times more than, say, using Noise, Checker, or another procedural, use it with caution.

2. When the Cellular map rollout appears, change the map name to "Cellular Mask". Then, make the following changes:

   • Under Coordinates, change Tiling to 0.5 on X, Y, and Z.

   • Under Cell Color, change the color swatch to pure black, or RGB 0, 0, 0.

   • Under Division Colors, make the first color pure white (or RGB 255, 255, 255) and the second color pure black (you can drag the Cell Color swatch down to this third swatch to copy it).

3. Under Cell Characteristics, select Circular, set Size to 25, and set Spread to 0.5. Check the Fractal box to activate it.

4. To produce the thin fractal lightning patterns, you need to change the thresholds. Set Low to 0.475, keep Mid at 0.5, and set High to 0.525. This will restrict the white Division color to thin fractal lines. Finally, to make the Glowing Noise material appear brighter, open the Output section and change Output Amount from 1.0 to 2.0. Click on the Go To Parent icon to return to the main Blend material level.

5. Because this is a "hot" material in your scene, activate your Camera01 viewport and do a test rendering to see the effects of this new material without the Glow effect.

As your rendering and Figure 9.2 show, the Cellular Mask map has restricted the blue-white Glowing Noise to thin fractal "worms" on the surface of the first Metal 1 material.

Figure 9.2
The Disintegrate 1 Blend material (without Glow) on the sample sphere.

Glow Worms?

Now, to keep the second material true to its name, you need to add a Glow effect to it. You can use 3D Studio MAX Release 3's new Rendering|Effects Glow filter, or you can create the Glow effect the old-fashioned way, via Video Post. For this example, you'll use Video Post, as described here:

1. Click on Rendering|Video Post to open the Video Post menu. Click on the Add Scene Event icon and select Camera01. Then, click on the Add Image Filter Event icon, and from your list of filters, select Lens Effects Glow.

2. Click on the Lens Effects Glow Setup button. The Lens Effects Glow setup menu appears, as shown in Figure 9.3. (Note that the Preview window has been activated for this figure.)

3. Click on the Preview button to display the Lens Effects Glow defaults, which are shown in the image window at the top of the menu. You'll be making some basic changes to the default settings, so make sure the Properties tab is active. Select Effects ID under Source and set it to 1 so it will affect only the Cellular "glowing worms" effect.

4. Click on the Preferences tab. Under Effect, change Size to 2.5, and under Color, change Intensity to 50.0. As you make these changes, you'll see the Glow effect in the Preview window change to match the new settings.

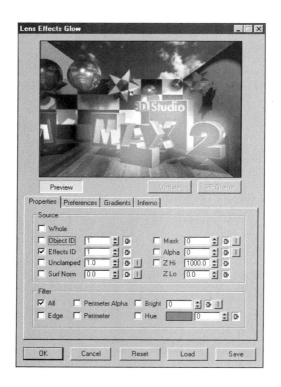

Figure 9.3

The Lens Effects Glow routine as it appears in Video Post.

5. Click on OK to return to the Video Post menu. Next, click on the Execute Sequence icon, select Single, and render a 640-by-480 image of the scene, which should resemble Figure 9.4.

Figure 9.4

The Disintegrate 1 material with the Lens Effects Glow applied.

As your rendering indicates, the Lens Effects Glow filter is operating only on the second material (the masked Glowing Noise texture). It has no effect on the first Metal 1 texture, which retains its metallic Diffuse characteristics.

There are many other uses for this technique. If you load a bitmap mask with rows of square or round pixels, for example, you can produce glowing windows on a distant building or on a vehicle, such as a large ocean liner or a spaceship. This type of Blend material can be more flexible and provide better results than a Standard material that uses separate Diffuse and Self-Illumination maps.

As mentioned earlier, you don't have to load a Noise map into the Diffuse slot of the Glowing Noise material. However, if an additional texture is revealed by the Noise mask, you can create—and animate—subtle or dramatic color variations in the glowing lightning itself.

Crawling Glow Worms?

I promised earlier that you would create animated glowing textures, so here's how:

1. Click on the Animate button, drag the Time Slider to 100, then return to the Material Editor. Click on the Cellular Mask button to open the Cellular Mask map. Under Coordinates, change the Z Offset value to 100.0. You'll see the lightning change position on the sample object in the Material #1 slot. Under Cell Characteristics, change the Roughness value to 0.1 and then turn off the Animate button.

2. If you have a minute or two, click on the Make Preview icon in the Material Editor to create an animated thumbnail of this lightning effect, sans Glow. If you would rather not wait, choose File|View File, and from the \CHAP_09 directory on the companion CD-ROM, click on the DISINTEGRATE_1.AVI to view the final effect, with the Lens Effects Glow added.

   The animated Cellular Mask creates a "crawling lightning" effect over the surface of the sphere, and the Glow accentuates the effect.

3. After you've viewed the animation, close the Preview window(s).

Making The Sphere Disintegrate

Now that you've seen the basic effect of the glowing lightning, you can combine it with animated Opacity maps to make it look as if the sphere is being eaten away while the lightning sparkles on the disappearing pieces.

The first step is to add an animated Opacity map to Material #1 and then use this same Opacity map as a submap in a masked Mask material.

Uh...what?!

Yes, I know this sounds confusing. However, I've already figured it out, which is the hard part; all you have to do is follow along, and you'll see how it works.

The first step is to create a new material. You'll use the Disintegrate 1 material to start:

1. In the Material Editor, drag the Disintegrate 1 material over to a free material slot to copy it. Name the duplicated material Disintegrate 2 and drag it to the sphere in the scene to apply it.

2. Open the Material 1: Metal 1 (Standard) material of Disintegrate 2. Change the Glossiness value to 75 and then go to the Maps section. Click on the Opacity Map button, select New, and select Noise from the Material/Map Browser. (You'll see the sample sphere in the Material Editor become ghosted as the soft Noise texture wipes out some of the Diffuse map.) Change the name of the Noise map to Noise Opacity—this is important because this specific name will help you select this material later from the Material/Map Browser.

3. Under Noise Parameters, change Type to Fractal, and under Noise Threshold, change High to 0.005. Keep Low at 0.0. By clamping the High Noise threshold so close to Color #2, or pure white, you'll create a solid Opacity map (you'll see the sample sphere turn solid again). Then, by animating the threshold, you can create the effect of the Opacity map eating away the Diffuse Metal material on the sphere.

4. Click on the Animate button, make sure you're on frame 100, and in the Material Editor, change the Noise Opacity Threshold settings so that High is 1.0 and Low is 0.995. In the Material Editor, the sample sphere disappears, leaving just the Cellular lightning and the Glossiness maps hanging around, like the smile of Alice's Cheshire Cat (you'll fix them in a moment).

5. Turn off the Animate button, but keep the Time Slider at frame 100—this will help you see the effects of the copied maps better. Click the Go To Parent icon to return to the Metal 1 material level of the Disintegrate 2 material.

Glossiness Maps And Masks

Next, you'll use the Opacity Noise map to mask the Glossiness and Specular Level maps of the Metal 1 material so an unwanted (and unrealistic) specular ghost of the original sphere isn't present:

1. First, check 2-Sided, then in the Maps rollout, open the Specular Color map, which now has RGB Tint loaded. Click on the Map

button (now loaded with the MTLSPEC.JPG bitmap) and then click on the Bitmap button next to Type. Select Mask from the Material/ Map Browser. When the Replace Map button appears, make sure Keep Old Map As Sub-Map is checked, and click on OK.

2. Under the Mask Parameters rollout, the MTLSPEC.JPG image is now loaded into the Map slot, and nothing (None) is loaded into the Mask slot. Click on the Mask button, and when the Material/Map Browser appears, click on Browse From: Mtl Editor. In the Browser window, double-click on the Noise Opacity map, load it as an Instance (not a Copy), and click on OK. This will mask the specular highlight as it also masks the Diffuse map.

3. Click on the Go To Parent icon until you're back at the Metal 1 material level, then click on the Glossiness Map button. Click on the Bitmap button next to Type, select New in the Material/Map Browser, and select Mask again. When the Replace Map button appears, click on Keep Old Map As Sub-Map and click on OK.

4. As you did with the Specular map, click on the Mask button and select the Noise Opacity map from the Material Editor to load it as the Glossiness Mask.

5. Click the Go To Parent icon and drag the Glossiness Mask map down to the Specular Level slot to copy it (you can make it an Instance, not a Copy).

Masking The Lightning

At this point, you should see only the Cellular lightning effect on frame 100 in the Material Editor sample slot. As you did in the preceding section, you can mask this lightning so that, as the sphere disintegrates, the electrical arcs only crawl over the (disappearing) surface—not across empty space. To do so, follow these steps:

1. Click on the Go To Parent icon to return to the Disintegrate 2 material level, and then click on the Mask: Cellular button. Click on the Type: Cellular button and select Mask from the Material/Map Browser (Browse From New). Keep the Cellular map as a submap, and click on the Mask button (below the Cellular map).

2. Under Browse From: Mtl Editor in the Material/Map Browser, select Noise Opacity, make it an Instance, and click the Go To Parent icon several times to return to the main Disintegrate 2 material level.

   In the same way you used the Specular, Shininess, and Glossiness maps in Material #1: Metal 1, you'll use the Opacity Noise map to mask the Cellular texture, which is itself masking the self-illuminated Material #2: Glowing Noise material. The end result is that, at frame 100, the sample sphere in the Material Editor should be completely invisible—or disintegrated.

3. Open the Glowing Lightning material, and make sure the Material Effects Channel is set to 1, not 0.

4. Before you render a test scene, select Spotlight01, open the Modify panel, and go down to Shadow Parameters. Under Cast Shadows, you'll see that Ray Traced Shadows is checked (Spotlight02, the blue fill light, uses shadow mapping instead of raytracing.) The raytraced Spotlight01 will cast shadows "through" the holes created by the sphere's Opacity maps; as the sphere disintegrates, its shadow disappears as well.

5. Click on Render|Video Post, click on the Execute Sequence button, and select Single under Time Output. Change the frame number to 50, set Output Size to 640 by 480, and click on Render.

As your rendering and Figure 9.5 show, the sphere on frame 50 is being eaten away by the animated Opacity Noise map while the glowing Cellular lightning crackles across its surface.

6. You can return to the Material Editor and render your own preview of the Disintegrate 2 material, but to speed up matters, choose File|View File, select DISINTGRATE_2.AVI from the \CHAP_09 directory on the companion CD-ROM, and view it.

Figure 9.5
The disintegrating sphere with glowing Cellular lightning applied.

You'll see how the sphere appears to be completely eaten away by the lightning (much like one of those hapless, red-shirted security guards from *Star Trek* I mentioned earlier).

A Better Disintegration Effect

The final disintegration effect you'll explore is an improved version of the one just shown. In the previous example, you saw glowing lightning crawling over the surface of the sphere, with animated "holes" appearing in the geometry.

However, a better version of this would be if the animated holes had glowing, sparkling edges around their perimeters to better suggest a burning away effect. You can create this effect by using a variation of your Noise mask, with modified thresholding, to produce the glowing edges around the animated holes. Here's how:

1. From your \CHAP_09 directory, load the file DISINTEGRATE_2.MAX. When the file loads, you'll see that it's largely a duplicate of the file you just created. If you open the Material Editor, you'll notice the Metal 1 Single and Disintegrate 2 materials in the sample slots.

   What you're going to do is modify the Disintegrate 2 material to create the enhanced disintegration effect.

2. Open the Disintegrate 2 material and then click on the Glowing Noise slot to open it. You need to change the Cellular lightning effect from blue lightning to orange glowing edges, so change the RGB settings of both the Ambient and Diffuse Colors to 255, 196, 0, or a bright orange. Also, make sure that the Material Effects ID value of this material is set to 1, not 0.

3. Click the Go To Parent icon, then click on the Metal 1 Single material slot to open it. You're going to start from scratch by replacing the Noise Opacity map, which will then be instanced in the Mask slot of the existing Mask material that blends between the Metal 1 Single and Glowing Noise materials. Click on the Opacity map slot to open it, then under Type, select Noise to bring up the Material/Map Browser. (You're going to replace the old Noise map with a fresh Noise map to clear out the existing animation keys on the Opacity map.) Select Noise from the Browser, make sure Discard the Old Map is checked, then click on OK.

4. Next, make the following changes to this new Noise map. Under Coordinates, change the Blur setting to 0.01. Under Noise Parameters, change the Size value to 50, then change Noise Type from

Fractal to Turbulence. (The Turbulence Noise type will produce more irregular edges than the other two Noise types.)

5. Click on the Swap button to reverse the order of the Color #1 and #2 swatches. (The white color swatch should now be Color #1.) Make sure High Threshold is set to 1.0, and then change Low Threshold to 0.994. Finally, rename this map Noise Opacity New (you're going to select it from your Material/Map Browser in a moment).

6. Click on the Go To Parent icon and take a look at the Specular Color, Specular Level, and Glossiness slots, which have Mask maps loaded. (Specular Color has a Mask map loaded into an RGB Tint map first.) You need to replace their old Noise Opacity masks with the new map you just loaded, so open the Specular Color slot, open the Mask map, and then open the old Noise Opacity mask slot. Under Type: Noise, click on the Noise button to open the Material/Map Browser. When it appears, click on Material Editor, find the Opacity: Noise Opacity New map, and double-click on it to select it. Make it an Instance, not a Copy, then click on the Go To Parent icon twice to return to the main Metal 1 Single rollout.

7. Open the Specular Level and Glossiness slots, and replace their old Noise Opacity masks with the Noise Opacity New map, as you did in Step 6 (make them Instances as well).

8. Click on the Go To Parent icon twice to return to the main Disintegrate 2 material level, then click on the Glow Mask button to open it. You'll see the Cellular texture used for the original lightning effect in the Map slot and the (old) Noise Opacity map used in the Mask slot.

9. Click on the Mask: Noise Opacity button, and under Type: Noise, click on the Noise button to open the Material/Map Browser. Again, you're going to clear out these old settings, so as you did earlier, click on Scene, find the Opacity: Noise Opacity New map, and double-click on it to select it. Make it an Instance, not a Copy, then click on the Go To Parent button again.

10. Next, drag-copy the Noise Opacity New map from the Mask slot up to the Map slot, *but make this a Copy, not an Instanced material.* (This is important.) As you do, you'll see the entire sample sphere in the Material Editor turn a bright orange. You're going to fix this by changing the new map's parameters.

11. Click on the Map slot to open it, and change this material's name to Noise Edge Glow. Then, under Noise Parameters, click on the Swap

button to reverse the order of the color swatches (Black should now be in the Color #1 slot.) When you do, you'll see the sample sphere return to the opaque Metal 1 Single texture. Change Low Threshold from 0.994 to 0.995.

12. Now, here comes the weird part. Turn on the Animate button, drag the Time Slider to 50, then return to the Material Editor. Change the Threshold High value of the Noise Edge Glow material to 0.5 and the Low value to 0.495.

13. Drag the Time Slider to frame 100, return to the Material Editor, and change the Noise Edge Glow Threshold High and Low values both to 0.0.

14. Drag the Time Slider back to frame 50, return to the Material Editor, click the Go To Parent icon, and open the Noise Opacity New slot of the Glow Mask material. Change the Threshold High value to 0.51 and the Low Value to 0.494.

15. Drag the Time Slider to frame 100, return to the Material Editor, and change the Threshold High value to 0. When you're finished, turn off the Animate button, drag the Time Slider back to frame 50, and render a 640-by-480 test frame. Your scene should look like Figure 9.6.

At this point, again, you could render a low-resolution test animation of the sequence, with a Glow effect (from either Video Post

Figure 9.6
The modified Noise Glow maps and mask result in highlighted edges around the growing "holes." (Note that there's no Lens Effects Glow added yet to this rendering.)

or the Render|Effects menu) to enhance the edges of the growing Opacity map. However, you can view a finished animation from this book's companion CD-ROM.

16. Select File|View File, and from the \CHAP_09 directory, view the file DISINTEGRATE_3.AVI.

As you can see in this rendering, the Glow filter adds some fiery pizzazz to this modified effect. In case it's still confusing, here's what's happening in the scene: The animated Mask material, of course, is masking off the Glowing Edge material from the Metal 1 Single Blend component. The glowing edges are created by having the virtually identical animated materials in both the Mask *Map* and *Mask* slots—but the Glow Edge map is made slightly larger than the Noise Opacity New Mask by offsetting the Threshold values a tiny amount from the Noise Opacity New map.

Again, if you want to save these scenes and materials to your MAX subdirectories and play with them later, feel free to do so. The scene files (DISINTGRATE_1.MAX, DISINTGRATE_2.MAX, and DISINTEGRATE_3.MAX) and materials are on this book's companion CD-ROM in the \CHAP_09 directory and MAXFX3.MAT Material Library, respectively.

Making Animated Opacity Sequences

In this chapter, you've seen how to create an animated Opacity map by using the procedural Noise texture. However, what if you want to create custom animated opacity bitmaps so you have greater control over the final disintegration effect?

There are a couple of ways you can do this. First, determine how long you want your finished disintegration effect to be. Then, paint an incremental series of bitmaps—using a program such as (the now discontinued) Autodesk Animator Pro/Studio, Adobe Photoshop, or the like—with the holes growing larger on each incremental frame. The advantage of this technique is that you can determine precisely where you want your openings, or translucent areas, to appear. The drawback, of course, is that this is extremely tedious, especially for a long sequence.

You can automate the process by building two simple objects in MAX, animating them, and using an orthographic rendering to produce the effect of holes appearing and growing in your image. This is a much faster process than, say, painting an incremental series of bitmaps entirely by hand. Once the bitmaps are rendered, you can then load them into a paint program and tweak them by hand, if necessary.

Here's an easy way to create such imagery:

1. In MAX, save your current work and reset the program. Press the S key to activate 3D Snap Toggle. Go to the Command panel and select Create|Patch Grids|Quad Patch. In the Top viewport, create a patch grid roughly 240 units long and 320 units wide.

2. In either the Left or Front viewport Shift-clone the QuadPatch01 object downward vertically 10 units to duplicate it. Make it a Copy, not an Instance, and then turn off 3D Snap.

3. Go to the Modify panel and change both the Length and Width Segments settings of QuadPatch02 to 20, which will produce a dense mesh object.

4. From the Modify panel, apply a Noise modifier to the QuadPatch02 object. Check the Fractal box, and under Strength, change Z to 25. The Quad Patch object distorts into a sort of terrain shape.

5. Open the Material Editor and change Material #1's Ambient and Diffuse Colors to pure black, or RGB 0, 0, 0. Change the Glossiness and Specular Level settings to 0, then apply this material to the selected QuadPatch02.

6. Change Material #2's Ambient and Diffuse Colors to RGB 255, 255, 255, or pure white. Change the Glossiness and Specular Level settings to 0, change Self-Illumination to 100, select QuadPatch01, and apply this material to it.

7. Next, click on the Animate button, go to frame 100, and in the Left or Front viewport, drag the top QuadPatch01 object down on the Y-axis until it's just below the solid black QuadPatch02 object. (Alternately, you can drag the bottom QuadPatch02 object up until it covers the entire top object.) Turn off the Animate button.

8. Activate the Top viewport and zoom into the Quad Patches until they fill the frame. (You may want to activate the Safe Frame option to help determine when the edges of the objects are just outside the field of view.) Then, go to frame 50 and render a test image at 640-by-480 resolution.

   As your rendering and Figures 9.7 and 9.8 indicate, the intersecting geometry creates the effect of holes appearing in the top, flat-white Quad Patch.

9. Now, choose File|View File, select OPACITY.AVI from the \CHAP_09 directory of the companion CD-ROM, and play it.

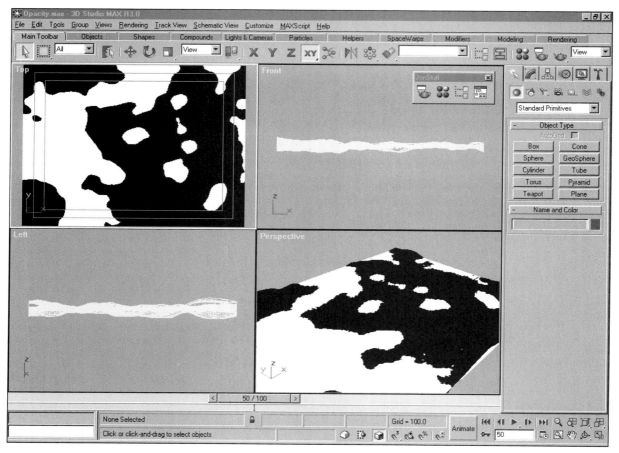

Figure 9.7

The intersecting geometry creates the effect of dark patches eating away the white field (when rendered from the Top viewport).

Figure 9.8

The Opacity bitmap rendering, Top viewport, frame 50.

As this animation shows, when the moving geometry is rendered from the Top viewport, it reveals the patches that appear to grow and devour the white field.

Variations Of Disintegrations

As with virtually all computer graphics techniques, there are many ways to vary this effect. Try these:

- Render this imagery at whatever resolution is necessary for your final animated Opacity map (either as a bitmap sequence or an animation, such as an AVI or FLC file). By changing the Quad Patch dimensions, your rendering resolution/aspect ratio, or both, you can create an animated sequence tailored to your particular needs.

- Change the overall frame rate to whatever length you need.

- Adjust the number of Quad Patch segments or Noise parameters to produce holes that are either relatively smooth or sharp and jagged.

- Apply a Bend or Taper modifier to either of the Quad Patches (producing a hill or valley) to restrict the growing black holes to specific areas, such as the center of the white field. This may be useful for creating a transparency effect that emerges from a specific spot, such as the middle of a door that's being disintegrated by a laser beam.

Note that the file you've just created is saved in the \CHAP_09 directory on the companion CD-ROM as OPACITY.MAX.

Modifying The Glow Effect

As with the previous tutorials, you should play around with the techniques presented in this chapter and vary them according to your needs. A particularly striking application might be to depict the outer hull of a damaged spacecraft being burned away to reveal the framework and superstructure underneath.

However, you don't have to use these techniques only for disintegration effects. As I mentioned earlier, by applying a Glow effect to only one material in a Blend, you can create glowing windows on office buildings, on the sides of ocean liners, in aerial shots of distant cityscapes, and so on. But if your heart is set on destroying things, here are some additional effects you can try:

- Change the Cellular lightning texture parameters (use Chips instead of Circular, for example) and animate the Roughness more for a jittery lightning effect.

- Animate the Glowing Noise parameters or change the map's color.

- Use different Noise types for the Opacity maps. You should also try using different procedural textures or even prerendered opacity bitmaps.

- Explore the various options available in Lens Effects (including Inferno) and animate the Glow effect.

Moving On

In this chapter, you saw how to use layers of materials, Opacity maps, raytraced spotlights, and Video Post filters to produce the illusion of a disintegrating object.

In the next chapter, you'll continue to explore animated materials and optical effects by deconstructing an explosion sequence. In Chapter 10, you'll see how you can use a combination of prerendered explosion bitmaps, conical geometry, Lens Effects Flare filter, and MAX's Particle Array system to blow up a deep-space asteroid.

ANIMATED MATERIALS AND OPTICAL EFFECTS II

In this chapter, you'll continue to work with animated materials and optical effects. You'll reverse-engineer an outer-space pyrotechnic scene—an exploding asteroid.

BY JON A. BELL

The Anatomy Of Explosions

One of the primary reasons many 3D graphics artists and animators got into the computer graphics imagery (CGI) field is because of their interest in TV and cinematic special effects. Basically, all CG shots are special effects: You're *simulating* events, both real and unreal, using 3D modeling, lighting, rendering, and compositing. This freedom to create, well, *anything*, makes CG especially suited to fantasy and science-fiction-oriented effects. With CGI, you can bring dinosaurs to roaring life or fly spaceships through the cosmos—and then blow them up spectacularly in the comfort of your own desktop computer.

In this chapter, we'll continue our look at science-fiction-style optical effects with a look at reverse-engineering some basic CG pyrotechnics. Here, you'll take a breather from creating specific MAX effects from scratch. Instead, you'll reverse-engineer an existing scene and its effects parameters and use them as starting points for your own pyro work. In a moment, you'll see how you can use digitized explosion imagery, courtesy of third-party vendors, combined with MAX geometry to create a realistic explosion effect.

How Do I Detonate Thee?

There are many different ways to blow up something in the 3D realm, and especially in MAX. You don't necessarily have to have the latest custom plug-ins to create convincing pyrotechnics (although they can definitely help). With MAX, you can use particle systems (both native and third-party), volumetric lights and/or atmospheric effects, post-processing optical effects (lens flares, highlights, and glows), prerendered image sequences, or a combination of all of these to produce the required effect.

Let's say you're rendering a typical 3D subject: an outer-space dogfight sequence, similar to shots in the various *Star Wars* or *Star Trek* films. For your shot, a spaceship flies through the scene, gets hit by an offscreen missile on frame 100, and gets blasted into atoms. You've got your spaceship model(s), your starfield backdrop, your scene lighting, and camera moves down pat. You have some or all of the previously mentioned tools available, but before you use them, you need to first figure out exactly how you want to choreograph your beautiful destruction. Here are some ideas:

- *Bait-and-switch*—On frame 100, when the ship gets hit, you decide to swap your "beauty" model for either a damaged version or big chunks of wreckage that follow some of the basic contours of your ship. You then hand-animate them flying willy-nilly through your scene. To do this, you might begin by linking the wreckage pieces to the beauty model. Then go in to MAX's Track View and set Visibility keys for both the beauty model and the wreckage. At frame 100, unhide the wreckage while simultaneously hiding the unblemished model. Then, "cover up" the transition with other elements in your scene, such as the ones that follow.

- *Particle systems*—You decide that at the moment the ship is hit, you want a burst of particles to erupt from the impact point. So, you link a particle system to your spaceship model and trigger a burst of particles right when the explosion is supposed to occur—say, at or before frame 100. The particles should be fairly numerous, erupt quickly, and dissipate chaotically. Because you're in space, there's no gravity; the particles should blast outward in a rough sphere shape or perhaps be blown directly at the camera. (You might want to have a stream of particles spewing out in a particular direction, though, to imply burning fuel being ejected from a fractured engine core.)

- *Volumetric Effects*—If you have volumetric or atmospheric effects options, then you might be able to create a plasma cloud or fireball, either singly or in conjunction with your particle systems. 3D Studio MAX's native Combustion atmospheric effect can create beautiful fire, smoke, and fiery explosion effects, as can Peter Watje's shareware Particle Combustion, Object Combustion, and Vertex Combustion plug-ins. Commercial MAX plug-ins such as Lumens's Afterburn and Digimation's Ultrashock can produce photorealistic effects, complete with billowing, pyroclastic clouds.

  An animated light with volumetric or optical effects may also fit your bill. 3D Studio MAX's Lens Effects feature enables you to create complex explosion effects by applying animated volumetric effects to lights in your scene. By keyframing the lights' density, brightness, colors, and fractal noise settings, you can produce explosions ranging from electrical to gaseous.

- *Animated Materials*—You've got the particle systems set up, but you also want to animate your material settings for the particle systems and perhaps the textures on the ship fragments. You decide that at the moment of explosion, you want the particles to be white-hot, so you keyframe their material settings to pure white. As the particles dissipate through your scene, you animate their colors from, say, white to yellow to orange to red, then finally to black.

  Finally, for the spaceship textures, you may want to show the hull of the ship (or the ejected wreckage) burning away; you could use the Disintegration effects you saw in the preceding chapter to create this effect.

- *Post-Processing Optical Effects*—To add additional visual "oomph" to your scene, you decide to incorporate some optical effects. For the initial blast, you might want to augment your particles with animated glows and/or sparkling highlights. Again, MAX's Lens Effects Video Post plug-in enables you to add these effects to elements in your scene, whether they're lights, particles, or mesh geometry.

Using Prerendered Sequences

Using procedural effects such as volumetric lights and/or complex particle systems in an elaborate 3D scene may increase your rendering times to an unacceptable level. However, there's another alternative: using prerendered imagery. Because many 3D artists enjoy creating pyrotechnic effects, a couple of companies have actually capitalized on this to provide cinematic spectacles for your 3D scenes.

Among these companies are Visual Concepts Engineering (VCE) of Sylmar, California, and Artbeats Software, of Myrtle Creek, Oregon. VCE, formed by special effects expert Peter Kuran (*Star Wars*, *Conan The Barbarian*, *Dragonslayer*) started the trend by digitizing 35mm film of real explosion elements used in his Hollywood effects work. VCE offers these sequences, along with digitized shots of fire, smoke, and electrical effects, on its Pyromania series of CD-ROMs for both the Macintosh and the PC. The animations consist of separate image sequences rendered as sequentially numbered, 24-bit TIF or TGA files, mostly at 640-by-480 resolution.

Artbeats Software offers various pyrotechnic wonders, including the ReelFire and ReelExplosion series of CD-ROMs. Both ReelFire and ReelExplosions are available (at the time of this writing) in four volumes. The sequences consist mostly of 720-by-486 resolution QuickTime MOV files, readable by both Macs and PCs. Some sequences include alpha mattes and high-resolution versions over 1024 pixels wide. Like the Pyromania CD-ROMs, the Artbeats offerings include numerous explosion sequences, including ground bursts, air bursts (affected by gravity), and zero-g (unaffected by gravity). A sample frame from one of the explosions is shown in Figure 10.1.

A Sample Artbeats Explosion

If you're trying to create an outer-space-style explosion effect, the zero-g sequences I mentioned are your best bet. To create zero-g explosions, a special effects company typically hangs an explosive charge from a crane at night or suspends the charge from a large black backdrop on the ceiling of a huge enclosure. Industrial Light + Magic filmed the final "Genesis" explosion (used in *Star Trek II: The Wrath of Khan*) in San Francisco's George Moscone Convention Center. Other companies have filmed similar effects in disused aircraft hangers.

Figure 10.1
A sample image from the Ares explosion sequence, Artbeats ReelExplosion, Volume 2.

Artbeats has provided a sample explosion sequence, which is included on this book's companion CD-ROM in the \CHAP_10 and \MAPS directories. This sequence, HOTF0000.JPG through HOTF0053.JPG, consists of 54 frames of lossless JPG images at 720-by-486 resolution. To see a low-resolution animation of this sequence, do the following:

1. Load 3D Studio MAX Release 3, or save your current work and reset the program.

2. Select File|View File, and from the \CHAP_10 directory of this book's companion CD-ROM, double-click on the file ARTBEATS.AVI to view it.

As the animation shows, the explosion starts off with a bright flash followed by sparks and then dissipates into a billowing blue cloud.

Deconstructing An Explosion

To see how this animation is incorporated into a final MAX effects scene, you'll load a file and examine how each element contributes to the final pyrotechnic effect. But first, let's take a look at the final effect, then we'll deconstruct it by examining the associated MAX scene file:

1. Select File|View File, and from the \CHAP_10 directory, select EXPLOSION.AVI and view it.

   As this 120-frame animation shows, the camera is rotating slowly around an asteroid when an energy bolt flies in from offscreen and blows the asteroid into glowing fragments. If you step through the sequence frame-by-frame, you'll see an initial bright flash as the weapon hits, then you'll see the asteroid break up. Simultaneously, you'll see the Artbeats explosion blast outward from the asteroid and the glowing rock pieces tumble past the camera.

2. Now, let's see how this effect was created. From the \CHAP_10 directory, load the file EXPLOSION.MAX. The file loads, and your screen should look like Figure 10.2.

Okay, let's take a quick look at the elements in this scene, one-by-one.

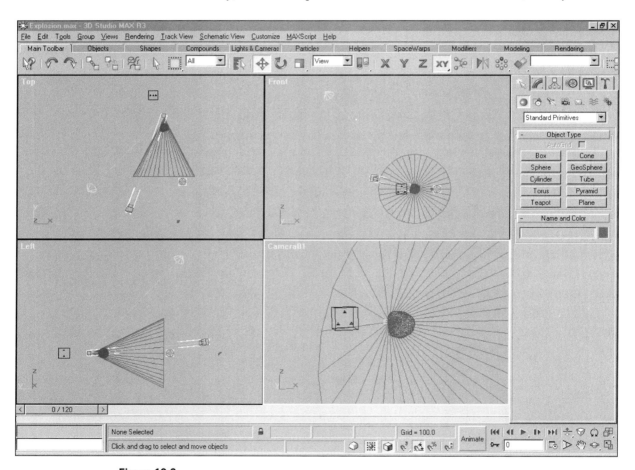

Figure 10.2
The EXPLOSION.MAX test scene.

The Asteroid Model

First, you'll notice the asteroid model in the middle of the scene. I built this by creating a low-resolution Gsphere, and then I distorted its surface with a Noise modifier. I then applied MeshSmooth to round off its sharp corners and collapsed it into an Editable Mesh object. A targeted Spotlight illuminates the asteroid.

The Explosion Cone

Surrounding the asteroid model is an open-ended Cone primitive, with its bottom faces deleted and its remaining face normals inverted so as to be visible to the camera. This cone provides the geometry for the "flat" Artbeats explosion bitmap sequence.

Now, why use a cone? For some scenes, you might be able to use a planar object, such as a QuadPatch, on which to map your explosion imagery. This is especially true if your original explosion sequence's imagery doesn't go beyond the edges of its frames. For best results, the QuadPatch should be of the same proportions as the bitmap image sequence you're going to use. You would then apply Planar mapping coordinates to it and place this geometry in your scene where you want the explosion to occur. The QuadPatch should face perpendicular to your camera; to keep it perpendicular even when your camera is moving, you might consider applying a Look-At controller to the explosion object. (You could do this to the cone as well.)

The size of the plane or cone determines how large your explosion will be, of course. You can place the planar geometry in front of, behind, or smack in the middle of your subject if you want. To make it look as if the explosion is instantly engulfing your spaceship or asteroid, you may want to first place the explosion geometry slightly behind the object (relative to the Camera view). At the time of detonation, you then keyframe the explosion geometry so that it makes a quick move—perhaps occurring on only five or six frames—toward the camera, sliding "through" the object. This will help offset the "2D" nature of the explosion effect, especially if you're mapping it to a QuadPatch.

A problem you might encounter with this flat planar technique is that some of your favorite explosion bitmap sequences have imagery that flies off the edges of their frames. Both VCE and Artbeats offer explosion sequences that stay "in frame" throughout the sequence. However, some of their best sequences have fire, smoke, or sparks that fly "offscreen." If you use these sequences on your planar geometry, the explosion will appear to be cut off as it hits the edges of an invisible rectangle.

One way to fix this is to simply scale up the plane so that your 3D camera doesn't see the boundaries of the object. However, this may make the initial explosion effect too large or the bitmap sequence too "grainy" or fuzzy to be appropriate in the scene. If this solution is unacceptable, then mapping the explosion imagery onto a cone (with an open mouth that extends beyond the camera) may do the trick.

The advantage of the cone technique is that, with planar mapping applied to the mouth of the cone, the explosion imagery will appear to stretch along the Z-axis toward the camera, heightening the 3D effect dramatically. Sparks or fire elements that go beyond the edges of the frame in the original texture sequence will appear to fly behind the camera and not off the edges of a rectangular QuadPatch.

If you select the Cone, you'll see that it has Planar mapping coordinates applied to it so that the explosion appears to emanate from the apex of the cone and then fly outward to the edges. (As long as the camera remains inside the mouth of the cone during the animation, it doesn't matter if the original explosion sequence goes beyond the boundaries of its frames.) Finally, the Explosion Cone's Properties have been modified so that it neither casts nor receives shadows on the asteroid object.

The Energy Bolt

Drag the Time Slider to the right and take a look at the Camera01 viewport. You'll see an Omni light fly into the scene, from right to left, and strike the asteroid. The Omni light serves as the node for a Video Post Lens Effects Flare (you'll examine its settings in a moment). This helps create an "energy bolt" effect (similar to a "photon torpedo" from *Star Trek*).

The Particle Array

Behind the Explosion Cone object is a Particle Array helper object. Click on it to select it. In the Modify panel, under Basic Parameters, you'll see that it's using the asteroid model itself as a particle emitter.

In the Particle Array Modify panel, go down to the Particle Type panel and open it. You'll see that Particle Type is set to Object Fragments. This produces the effect that the object itself is exploding into actual chunks and not just face normals (as would be produced with the Bomb spacewarp, for example). Under Object Fragment Controls, you'll see that Thickness is set to 5.0; this ensures that the asteroid pieces look like boulders instead of eggshell fragments. The minimum number of chunks is set to 25, which produces sufficient debris for the shot.

Go down to the Particle Spawn rollout and open it. You'll see that Spawn Trails is active. This creates additional particles that fly outward from the initial asteroid chunks. The Affects percentage is set to 25, with a multiplier value of 1. (Higher multiplier values may add a huge number of particles to this scene and slow down rendering substantially. Use caution when adjusting this setting.) Direction Chaos is set to 5 percent; this makes the spawned particles deviate only slightly from their parent particles' paths. In addition, Speed Chaos is set to 25 percent, with Slow and Fast (Both) active, to create more variation in the spawned particle speed. (Note that the spawned particles are also picking up speed from their parents because Inherit Parent Velocity is checked.) The Scale Chaos Factor is set to 100 percent, with Down checked; this makes sure the spawned particles tend to be smaller (of course) than the initial fragments.

Particle Fragments

Finally, behind the camera (as seen from the Top viewport), you may notice a tiny piece of geometry out of camera range. Activate the Top viewport and select it. This small piece of geometry, called Asteroid Fragment, is loaded into the Object Mutation Queue of the Particle Array rollout. The Asteroid Fragment serves as the basis for the Spawned Particles.

Hiding The Asteroid Geometry In Track View

If you open Track View and select the Asteroid model, you'll notice that it has Visibility keys set on frames 30 and 31. From frames 0 to 30, the Asteroid is visible; starting on frame 31, it becomes hidden, and the particles it emits make it look as if the asteroid itself has exploded.

Materials And Scene Timing

Now that you've examined the basic geometry in the scene, let's take a look at the materials the sequence comprises:

1. Open the Material Editor and take a look at Slot #1. This contains a material called, simply enough, Explosion. Under Basic Parameters, you'll notice that Self Illumination is set to 100. If you open the Extended Parameters rollout, you'll see that Advanced Transparency Type is set to Additive (you want the explosion to be as bright as possible in the scene).

2. Open the Maps rollout. You'll see the HOT50000.IFL entry in both the Diffuse Color slot and the Opacity map slot (the latter entry is an Instanced copy of the Diffuse Color slot). Open the Diffuse Color rollout and then open the Time rollout. You'll see that Start Frame is set to 25. This is also the frame at which the Omni light "torpedo" hits the asteroid and the asteroid starts to break up (that is, emit particles). You'll also see that Hold is checked under End Condition; the image sequence ends on a black frame, which remains for the rest of the animation. (You don't want to see the 54-frame explosion bitmap "start up again" during the course of the animation.)

3. Click on Slot #2 to activate it. This contains a Blend material called Asteroid Blend; it consists of a rocky material (called Asteroid Rock) in Material Slot #1, a second material called Molten Rock (pretty self-explanatory), and a Noise material loaded into the Mask slot.

4. Open the Asteroid Rock material, then open the Maps rollout and the Diffuse Color slot. This slot is loaded with a bitmap called CRACKED_MUD_2.JPG. Under the Bitmap Parameters rollout, click on View Image to view it. This image is also shown in Figure 10.3.

STARTING YOUR EXPLOSION OFF RIGHT

The Start Frame feature in MAX's Material Editor will "freeze" the bitmap sequence in your scene until the specified frame. This is fine if the first frame of your explosion sequence is completely black. However, if it's not, you might have to resort to a little trickery to keep a still image of the first explosion frame from appearing "frozen" in your scene. To fix this problem, you could set Visibility keys for the Explosion geometry timed to the appropriate keyframes. You could also keyframe the Diffuse and Opacity components of the material so that they're at a 0 percentage until the "detonation frame"; then, they instantly pop up to 100 percent at the appropriate time. If you've set up this effect correctly, the explosion should appear to blow apart the subject with fire and fury.

Figure 10.3
The CRACKED_MUD_2.JPG texture.

As I've mentioned earlier in the book, this is yet another texture that I obtained on a trip to Africa in October 1998. I shot this image among the sand dunes of Namibia, in a region called Sossusvlei, on the west coast of Africa. After scanning this image of cracked mud, I loaded it into Adobe Photoshop. I then made it seamlessly tilable by using the Offset filter (with Wraparound turned on) and cut and pasted pieces of the image over the visible edges until the final 1522-by-969-pixel image was seamless. This earth-tone image serves as an acceptable asteroid texture.

5. Click on the Go To Parent icon twice to return to the main Asteroid Blend material rollout and then open the Molten Rock rollout. It's simply a bright orange, self-illuminated material, with no other maps used. However, you'll see that the Material Effects Channel has been set to 1. This creates a lava effect when rendered with the appropriate Lens Effects Glow filter (which you'll see in a bit).

6. Click on the Go To Parent icon and then open the Noise Mask slot. Under Noise Parameters, you'll see that Noise Type is set to Turbulence, with a size of 10. In addition, you'll see red brackets around the High Threshold slider. (This indicates that keyframes have been set for this particular slider.) The High value is set to 0.001 and Low is set to 0.0; the High color is white, or Color #1; the Low color is black.

7. If you drag the Time Slider to frame 25 and beyond, you'll see that the High Threshold value begins to animate from 0.0 to 0.2 between frames 25 and 30. (You'll also see the Phase value animating throughout the course of the animation; it changes from 0.0 on frame 0 to 5.0 on frame 120, thus animating the Noise mask.) And you'll notice that the sample sphere in Slot #2 begins to show animated orange "lightning" appearing quickly on the rocky surface.

As you saw in Chapter 9, by animating a Noise Mask's Threshold value, you can create the appearance of flickering lightning appearing on the surfaces of your objects. I created this material to suggest that the exploding asteroid pieces have become superheated due to the impact of the energy bolt. This asteroid texture is quite similar to the Disintegration textures you saw in Chapter 9 when you made the metal sphere disappear in a burst of energy. However, unlike those examples, here I'm not making the overall asteroid textures disappear; I'm simply adding another layer of glowing texture to the rocky surface.

Polishing Off The Effect: Video Post

Okay, now it's time to take a final look at this sequence by examining the Video Post settings:

1. Close your Material Editor and then select Rendering|Video Post to open the Video Post menu, which should resemble Figure 10.4.

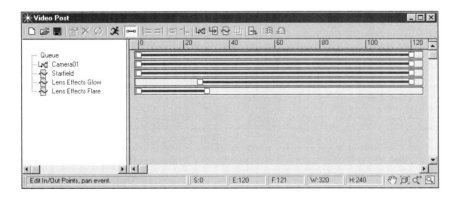

Figure 10.4
The Video Post menu for the explosion scene.

2. As the menu and figure indicate, the Camera01 entry dominates the queue, of course, with the MAX-standard Starfield filter immediately following. You then see the Lens Effects Glow filter. This keys off of Material Effects Channel 1, which makes the Molten Rock material appear to glow, although it's masked off by the animated Noise Mask. You'll also notice that the Glow effect track doesn't begin until frame 27. This gives the HOT5 explosion sequence time to begin

expanding "through" the asteroid geometry before the asteroid starts to glow.

3. The last entry is the Lens Effects Flare. You'll notice that the end of its track is frame 30; this "turns off" the energy bolt light effect after the Omni light flies into the center of the asteroid mesh, and the explosion takes over. If you click on the Edit Current Event icon and then click on Setup, the Lens Flare menu appears. Click on Preview; after a moment, you see a flattened oval ring of bluish light appear in the Preview window. In addition, you'll see red brackets around the Lens Flare Properties: Size spinner. The overall Lens Flare size starts out at 10.0, shrinking in size (down to 2.5) by frame 30. This makes it appear as if the energy bolt is traveling far into the distance as it flies past the camera and strikes the asteroid. However, for a few brief frames—25, 26, and 27—I animated the Size settings going back to 10, then to 25, then 50, to suggest a bright impact flash. It then diminishes back to 2.5 by frame 30 as the actual explosion effect takes over.

4. When you're finished looking at the Lens Effects Flare menu, close it and the Video Post menu as well.

Figure 10.5

The asteroid sits in space, with the energy bolt approaching (frame 15).

5. Finally, if you examine Figures 10.5 to 10.8, you'll see the progression of pyrotechnic events in the sequence. (Note that these figures are also in the \CHAP_10\FIGURES directory of this book's companion CD-ROM; you can use MAX's File|View File feature to view them.)

Figure 10.6
The energy bolt strikes the asteroid, creating a bright flash on frame 26.

Figure 10.7
The asteroid begins to break up (frame 31). The Molten Rock component of the Asteroid Blend material becomes visible, and the explosion bitmap begins to become more noticeable.

Figure 10.8
The asteroid is blown into fragments (frame 55).

Variations

To make this effect even more spectacular, there are some other techniques you could try.

You could create multiple cones of the same length, but of varying end sizes, all with their apexes in the same spot. (Ideally, the camera should still be able to move inside the mouth of the smallest cone, or else you should animate the cones so that they always face the camera.) The thinner the cone, the more the explosion bitmap will appear to "stretch" toward the camera. If there are sparks in the original bitmap imagery, they will appear to elongate into fast-moving streaks of light that whip by the camera, producing a spectacular three-dimensional effect.

By using multiple cones of varying widths, you could produce complex multiplanar effects, with explosion sparks and fire appearing to move at different rates of expansion—even if you're using the same bitmap sequence on all the cones! (To help conceal the map's similarities, you could rotate the texture coordinates or the cones themselves and also offset the starting frame times of each explosion.)

PLASMA.MAX And RING OF FIRE.MAX

If you want to take a look at some other interesting explosion effects, there are two other scenes included in the \CHAP_10 directory. (Both of these scenes, along with complete tutorial descriptions, appeared in my previous book, *3D Studio MAX R2.5 f/x and Design*.)

The first scene, PLASMA.MAX, consists of a rapidly expanding Sphere that has distortion applied to it via a Noise modifier. By animating the Noise modifier and the material applied to the sphere, I've produced a simple geometry-based effect that resembles a volumetric cloud. (View the file PLASMA.AVI in the \CHAP_10 directory to see the final results.)

The second scene, RING OF FIRE.MAX, consists of a rapidly expanding toroidal ring with a multicolored fiery texture map applied to it. (To produce the textures, I processed a fire sequence from the VCE Pyromania Volume 1 CD in Adobe Photoshop. By applying several sets of filters using Photoshop's Batch processing feature, I created a psychedelic fire effect. These modified textures are included in the \MAPS directory of this book's companion CD-ROM, and are used by permission of Peter Kuran, VCE.) If you view the RINGFIRE.AVI file, you'll see that it's an expanding "shockwave" ring, similar to those optical effects you might've seen in some of the Star Trek films, and in the Special Editions of *Star Wars* and *Return of the Jedi*.

I've included both of these scenes for your perusal. To best understand their techniques, examine each scene's Material Editor, Track View, and Video Post settings carefully.

Moving On

With a little bit of experimentation, the techniques in this chapter can help you achieve the pyrotechnic effects you want. Whether you're collapsing a building for an industrial video or creating your own version of *Star Wars*, the wide variety of features available in MAX gives you "Vishnu-like" power. With them, you can be both the creator—and destroyer—of worlds.

Okay, that's enough destruction for now. In the next chapter, you'll see how you can use MAX's Raytrace Material and Map types to create striking material effects—from glass and shiny metals to fluorescence and even rubber.

MAX STUDIO

On the following pages, you'll see color examples of the effects tutorials presented in this book. In addition, you'll see the work of several noted 3D Studio MAX artists for film, TV, multimedia, games, and print.

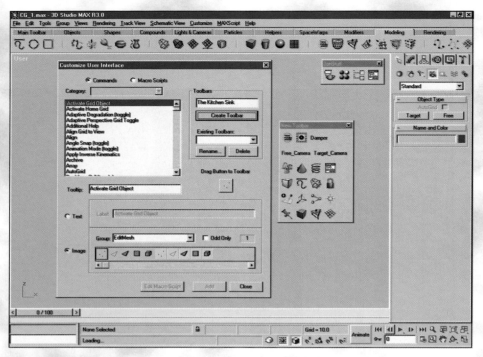

From Chapter 1, among the new features of 3D Studio MAX Release 3 is that it allows you to create customized interfaces, as shown here.

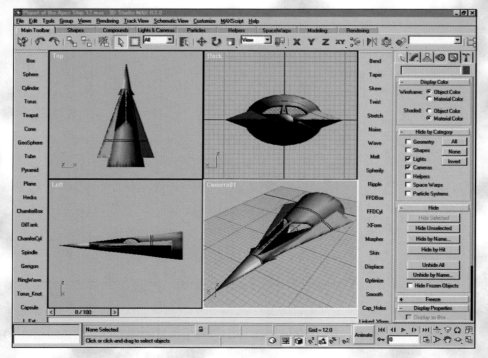

This is another example of a custom 3D Studio MAX Release 3 interface. In this one, the majority of the icons have been replaced with text-only buttons.

From Chapter 2, this example of a standard studio lighting setup helps illustrate good lighting techniques for 3D scenes, too.

A finished rendering of the studio lighting setup shows front, fill, and rim lighting on the objects.

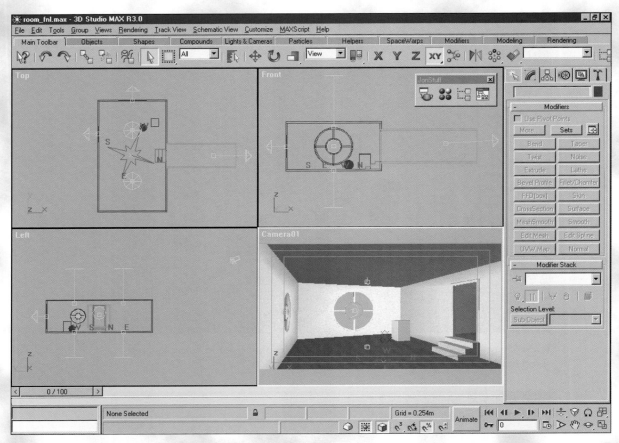

A demonstration file (ROOM_FNL.MAX) from the \CHAP_02 directory of this book's companion CD-ROM shows advanced lighting techniques for room interiors.

This example of a realistically illuminated room is from Chapter 2. With careful placement of lights, you can create interiors that display a richness in color values and tonality that rival images produced with a radiosity renderer.

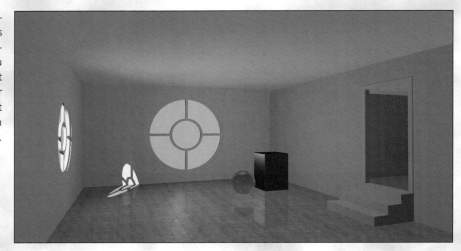

Real-world textures—such as digitized images of rocks, bricks, metals, tree bark, and animal skins—can improve the quality of your final 3D renderings. Jon A. Bell used Adobe Photoshop to make this digitized photo of muddy earth seamlessly tilable on the top and bottom edges and on both sides. (This map is included in the \CHAP_03 and \MAPS directories of this book's companion CD-ROM.)

By loading textures, such as this digitized photo of an old clunker car's door, into an image-editing or painting program, you can cut and paste interesting sections of the image together to form new maps. (This map is included in the \CHAP_03 and \MAPS directories of this book's companion CD-ROM.)

This digitized photo shows the side of an old metal door exposed to the weather. The effects of weathering, paint leaching, stains, and other textural effects are discussed in Chapter 3.

Although it's a simple technique, the use of beveled and chamfered edges on 3D geometry can enhance the appearance of your renderings. In this simple example, note how the bevels on the foreground box catch specular highlights, resulting in a less-flat appearance.

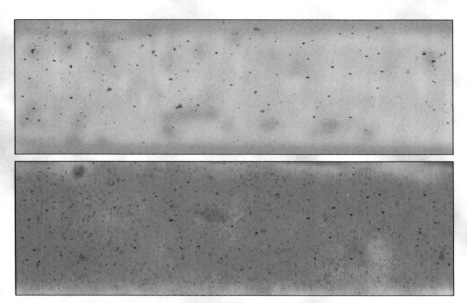

If you're a skillful 2D artist with a good eye, you may be able to paint Diffuse and Bump maps to make your 3D objects look indistinguishable from their real-world versions. The grayscale Bump map (top) and the colorful Diffuse map (bottom) serve as the outer skin texture for an apple. (These maps are included in the \CHAP_03 and \MAPS directories of this book's companion CD-ROM.)

The finished apple rendering. (This file, APPLE.MAX, is in the \CHAP_03 directory.)

A digitized sheep's eye texture (seen horizontally in this rendering) combined with a raytraced corneal lens provides a startling 3D effect. (This file, EYE.MAX, is in the \CHAP_03 directory; various eye texture maps are included in the \MAPS directory.)

An example of a Top/Bottom material that uses a Noise procedural to blend between the darker, more saturated lower part of the sphere and the dustier top surface. (This file, DUSTY.MAX, is in the \CHAP_03 directory.)

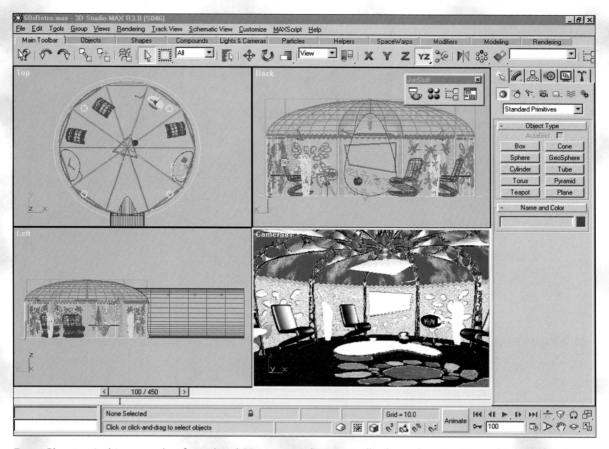

From Chapter 4, this example of a stylized 3D scene with organically shaped geometry, multiple Reflection maps, and unusual textures serves as an interesting test subject for 3D Studio MAX Release 3's new antialiasing filters and Material Editor supersampling features. (This file, 60SRETRO.MAX, is in the \CHAP_04 directory.)

This rendering of the final 1960s retro set uses MAX Release 3's Mitchell-Netravali filter to sharpen the details.

A close-up shows the martini glass in the 1960s retro set. The foreground elements were rendered with the sharp Catmull-Rom filter. The soft-focus background was rendered separately using the Gaussian filter, which simulates a depth-of-field effect in this shot.

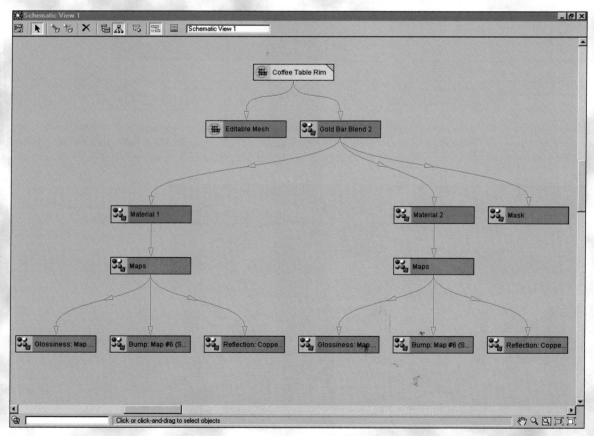

3D Studio MAX Release 3's new Schematic View window (shown full screen here) enables users to link and unlink various elements in their 3D scenes and to examine the structure of complex object and material trees. This tree shows the Coffee Table Rim component of the 60SRETRO.MAX scene.

This rendering of an underwater scene demonstrates MAX Release 3's Gaussian Soften rendering filter. (This file, UNDERWATER.MAX, is in the \FX3 Extras directory of this book's CD-ROM.)

A close-up shows the tabletop in the 1960s retro set. The heavy Bump map on the stucco walls and the Bump map on the sculpture have been softened with MAX Release 3's new Supersampling filters.

A combination of the Diffuse Color, Specular Level, Glossiness, Specular Color, and Bump maps, combined with Phong- and Metal-shaded materials in a Blend material, creates the appearance of a scratched, scuffed metal surface. (The files METAL_1.MAX and METAL_2.MAX are in the \CHAP_05 directory; example maps are included in the \MAPS directory of this book's companion CD-ROM.)

The Diffuse Color map.

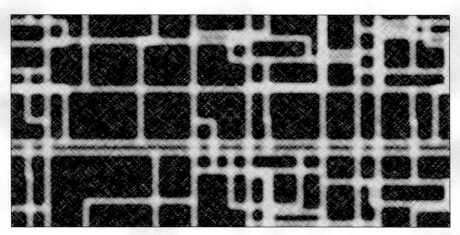

The Specular Level map.

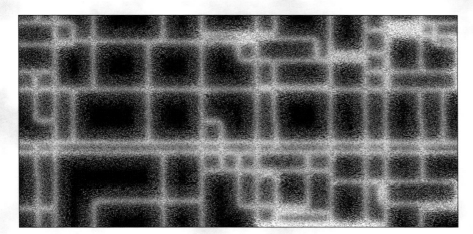

The Glossiness map.

The Specular Color map.

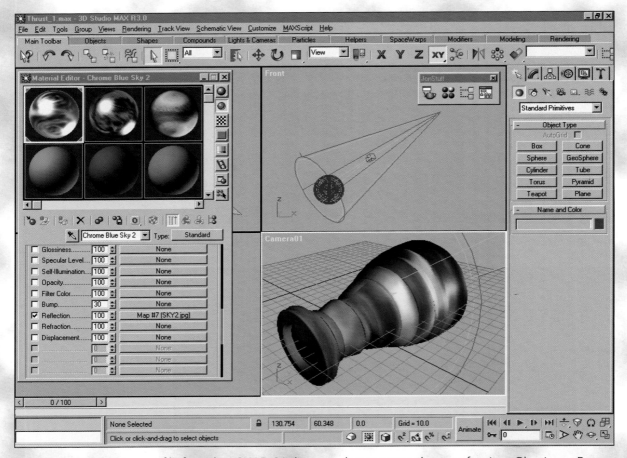

The THRUST_1.MAX scene file from the \CHAP_06 directory demonstrates the use of various Glossiness, Bump, Reflection, and Falloff maps to create convincing metallic textures.

The final rendering of the THRUST_1.MAX scene file shows the Blue Sky 2 material, which uses 3D Studio MAX Release 3's enhanced Falloff map type to reduce the amount of reflection on the edges of 3D objects.

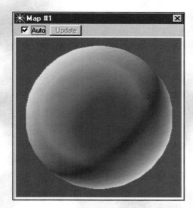

Perpendicular/Parallel

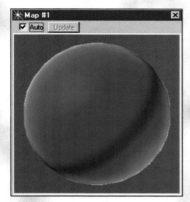

Fresnel

Shadow/Light

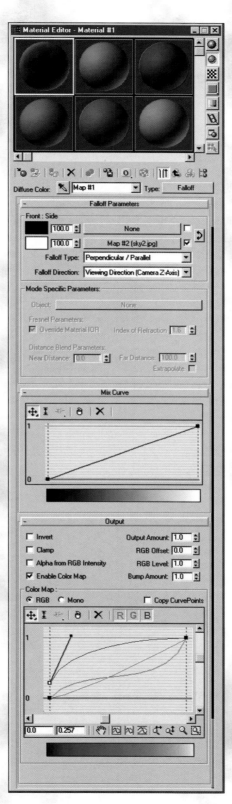

3D Studio MAX Release 3's improved Falloff map type includes controls that allow you to select different types of falloff attributes, such as Towards/Away, Fresnel, Shadow/Light, Distance Blend, and Perpendicular/Parallel. The Falloff map also includes Mix curves for greater Falloff control.

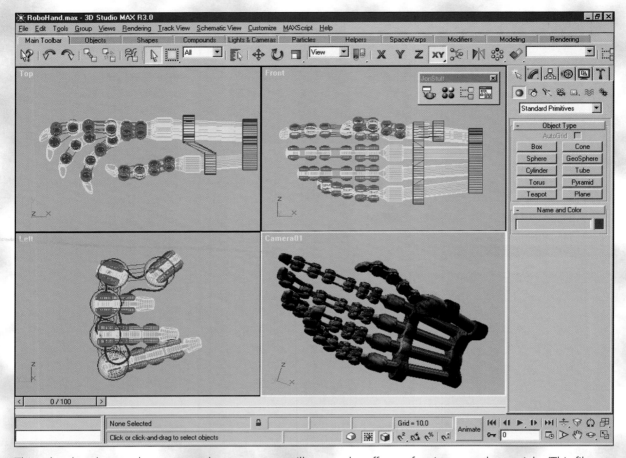

This robot hand example uses complex geometry to illustrate the effects of various metal materials. (This file, ROBOHAND.MAX, is in the \CHAP_06 directory.)

In this rendering, different metal textures (included in this book's MAXFX3.MAT Material Library) are applied to the various finger "bones" and joints.

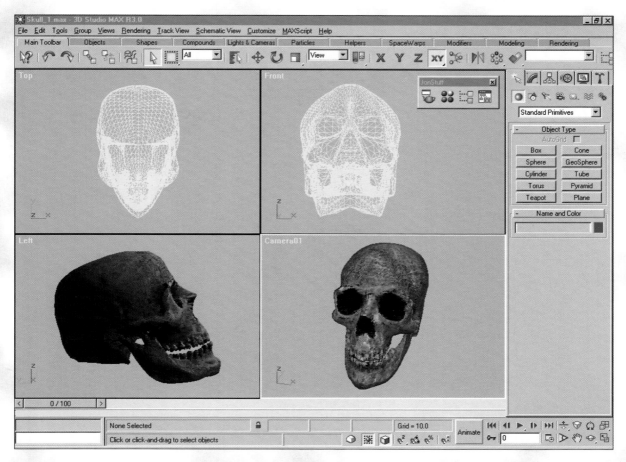

A human skull model (courtesy of 3D artist James Bell, Weta Ltd., New Zealand). This model is useful for demonstrating the use of MAX's Falloff map to create iridescent and X-ray effects. (The model, SKULL_1.MAX, is included in the \CHAP_06 directory of this book's companion CD-ROM.)

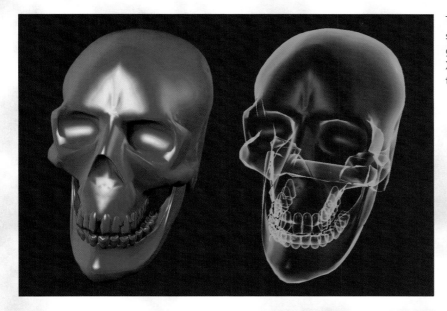

The same human skull model is shown with an iridescent blue/green texture and a translucent X-ray texture, both created with the Falloff map.

By using the Falloff map to blend between two Reflection maps, you can create an abalone-shell, mother-of-pearl texture.

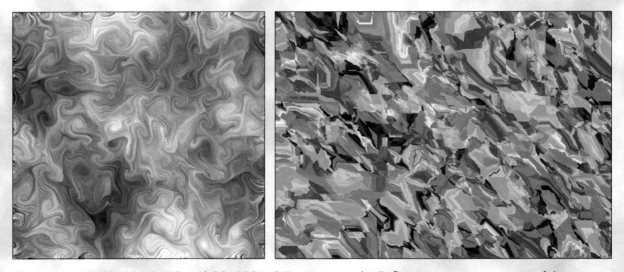

These images—ABALONE.JPG and COLRFOIL.GIF—comprise the Reflection map components of the vase texture.

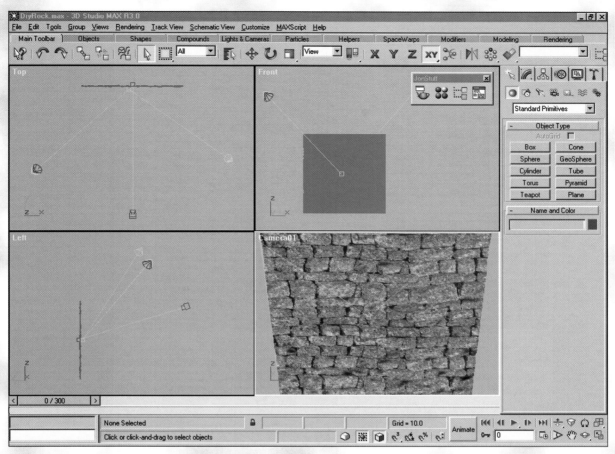

In this test scene, DRYROCK.MAX, from Chapter 7, you can see how digitized bitmaps of real rock faces are combined with MAX Release 3's new shading types to create both dry and wet stone surfaces.

In these variations of the same rock texture, the one on the left looks dry; the one on the right has had its saturation and contrast increased so that it appears wet. In materials with a high Specular Strength value, RGB Multiply maps help create the effect of realistically wet surfaces.

This final rendering shows a wet rock face. By animating the Specular highlight (using a Noise map), you can produce the illusion of water cascading down the rock face. (The file, WETROCK.MAX, is in the \CHAP_07 directory.)

The LACQUER.MAX test scene is from Chapter 7. This example shows how 3D Studio MAX Release 3's new Multi-Layer material—when combined with custom Glossiness and Reflection maps—can create the effect of shiny car lacquer. The hot-white specular highlight, along with the softer, more diffused highlight underneath, creates a convincing car paint surface.

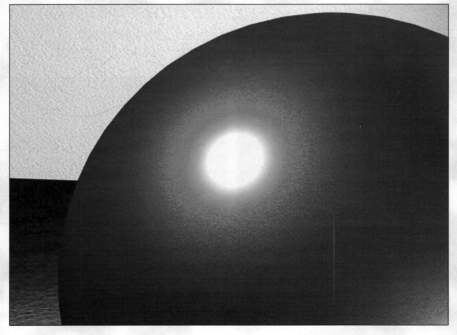

A close-up of the metal flake car paint example shows how the Noise procedural map creates a speckled secondary specular effect.

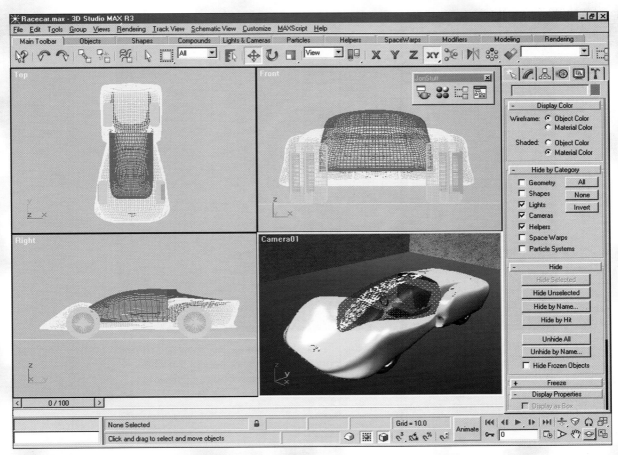

A futuristic race car model provides an interesting test subject for demonstrating the new anisotropic specularity features in MAX Release 3's Material Editor.

A rendering of the race car model shows off the Anisotropic settings of MAX's Multi-Layer shading type. (This file, RACECAR1.MAX, is in the \CHAP_08 directory.)

An aluminum sports car wheel shows the effects of MAX Release 3's new Anisotropic shader. Note the stretched specular highlights around the periphery of the wheel. (This file, WHEEL_1.MAX, is in the \CHAP_08 directory of this book's CD-ROM.)

Here is an example of true polygonal Displacement mapping, which occurs at render time in MAX Release 3. (Grayscale Displacement maps are included in the \CHAP_08 and \MAPS directories of this book's CD-ROM.)

A combination of the Cellular texture and MAX's Lens Effects Glow filter creates the illusion of lightning arcing across this spherical surface. (This file, DISINTEGRATE_1.MAX, is in the \CHAP_09 directory.)

Animated Noise maps and masks, combined with the Glow filter, create the effect of a disintegrating sphere with glowing edges around its expanding fissures. The lattice underneath makes the disintegrating skin effect more obvious.

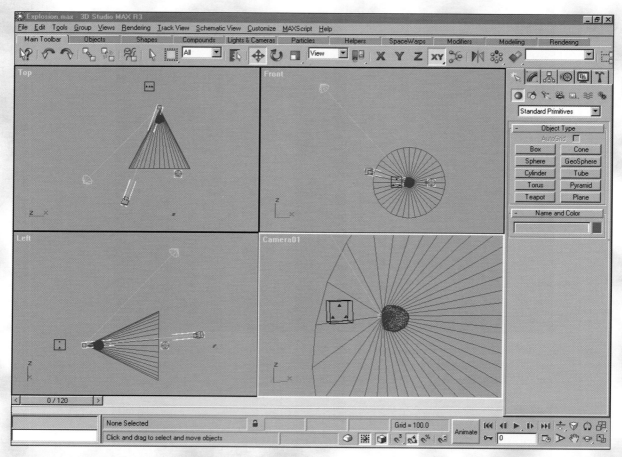

In Chapter 10, conical geometry, a Particle Array system, a distorted GeoSphere, prerendered explosion imagery, and a Lens Effects Flare produce an outer-space asteroid explosion.

This is an image from a 54-frame explosion sequence provided courtesy of Artbeats Software. (The files, HOTF000-HOTF0053.JPG, are in the \CHAP_10 directory of this book's CD-ROM.)

A finished frame shows the final asteroid explosion sequence. (This file, EXPLOSION.MAX, is in the \CHAP_10 directory of this book's CD-ROM.)

In a later frame in the ateroid explosion sequence, the Particle Array system, explosion texture map, and Lens Effects Glow filter create fiery asteroid debris.

From Chapter 11, this example of three metal spheres illustrates how you can use the Blur settings in MAX's Raytrace material to create different metal types—polished steel, plain steel, and sandblasted steel.

A tabletop setting illustrates MAX's Raytrace material and map types. Note how the teapot lid reflects its own handle and the purple tinted shadow cast by the purple glass sphere. (This file, TABLETOP.MAX, is in the \CHAP_11 directory.)

A golden watch demonstrates both the refractive qualities of MAX's Raytrace material (on the crystal) and the Fluorescence feature on the glowing green hands. (This file, WATCH.MAX, is in the \CHAP_11 directory.)

MAX's Raytrace material enables you to set the index of refraction (IOR) for your specific material needs. This image from Chapter 11 shows five spheres, each with a different IOR that corresponds to real-world refraction properties. From left to right, top: underwater (IOR 0.7) and hot air (IOR 0.98); bottom: water (IOR 1.22), glass (IOR 1.5), and diamond (IOR 2.42.)

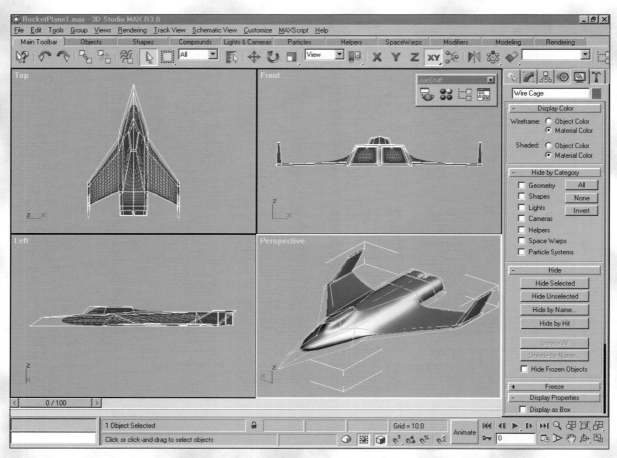

From Chapter 12, a low-resolution proxy object, combined with a MeshSmoothed Reference copy, creates this futuristic rocket plane. (This file, ROCKETPLANE.MAX, is in the \CHAP_12 directory of this book's CD-ROM.)

The low-resolution proxy sculpting cage is visible in this rendering of the rocket plane model.

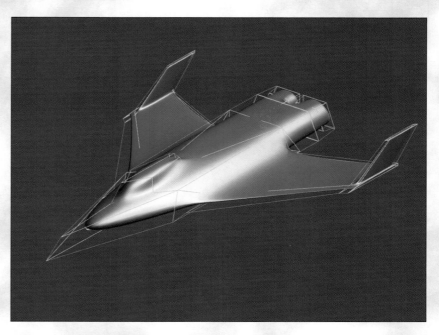

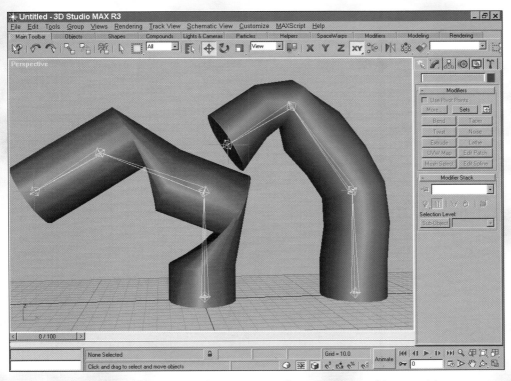

From Chapter 13, 3D Studio MAX Release 3's new Skin and Flex modifiers enable you to use MAX's Bones to deform polygonal geometry and add secondary movement.

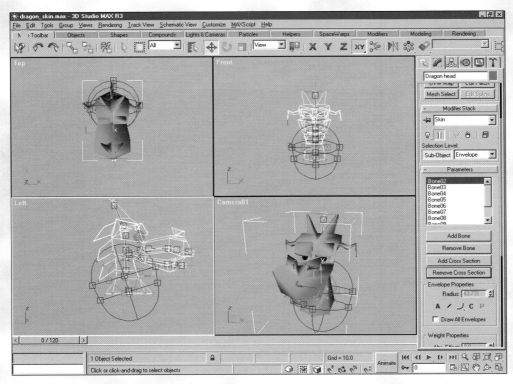

Bones and the Skin modifier have been applied to this low-resolution cartoon dragon model.

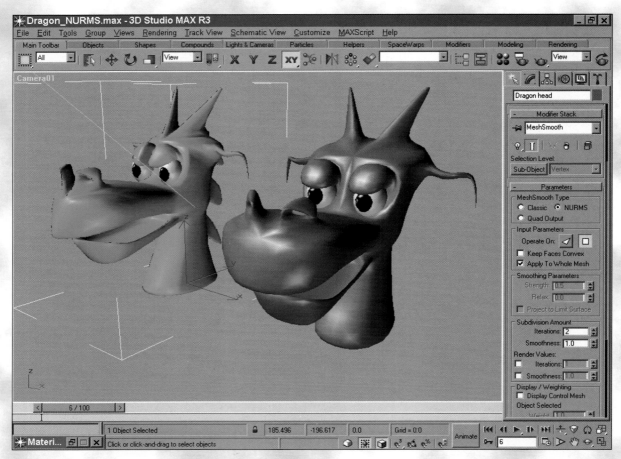

Two versions of the cartoon dragon are shown after the MeshSmooth modifier has been applied. The eyelid geometry on the left dragon has been modified in preparation for animation.

The rendering of the final MeshSmoothed dragon uses Cellular Diffuse and Bump maps for the skin texture.

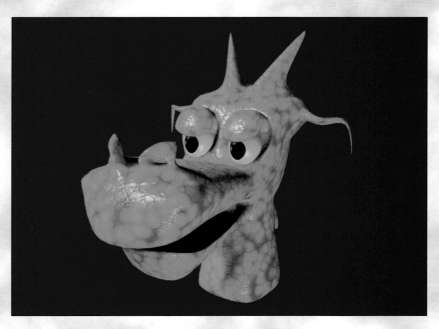

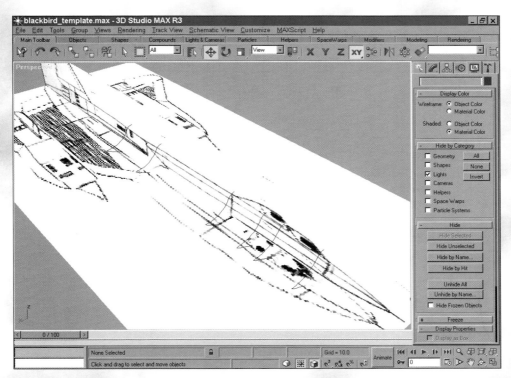

From Chapter 15, this SR-71 spy plane model was constructed using the new Surface Tools plug-in, which is included in 3D Studio MAX Release 3.

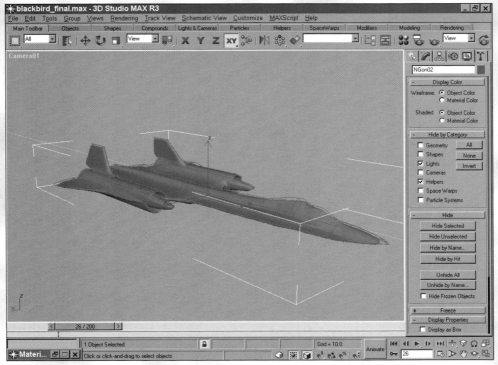

The finished SR-71 model was built using Surface Tools. (This file, BLACKBIRD_FINAL.MAX, is in the \CHAP_15 directory of this book's CD-ROM.)

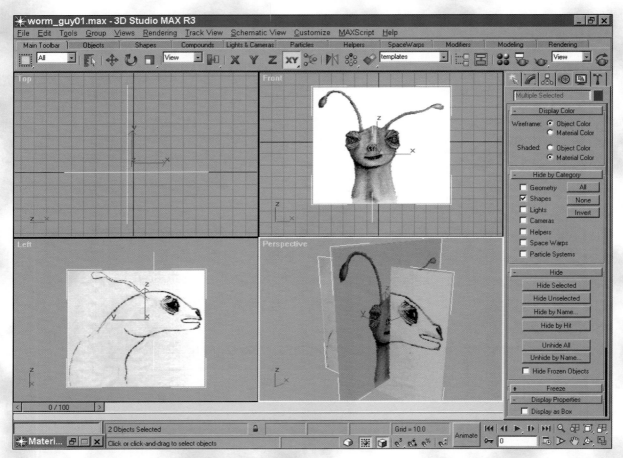

Chapter 15 features another Surface Tools project—an insect-like alien called Worm Guy (included in the \CHAP_15 directory of this book's CD-ROM). This image shows the sketch templates for the Surface Tools splines in preparation for construction.

The preliminary Worm Guy pencil and charcoal sketch was created by Ken Allen Robertson.

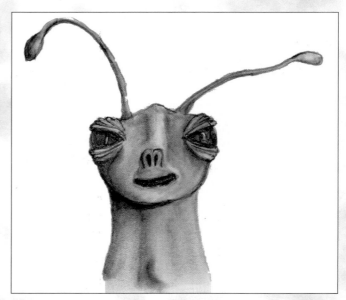

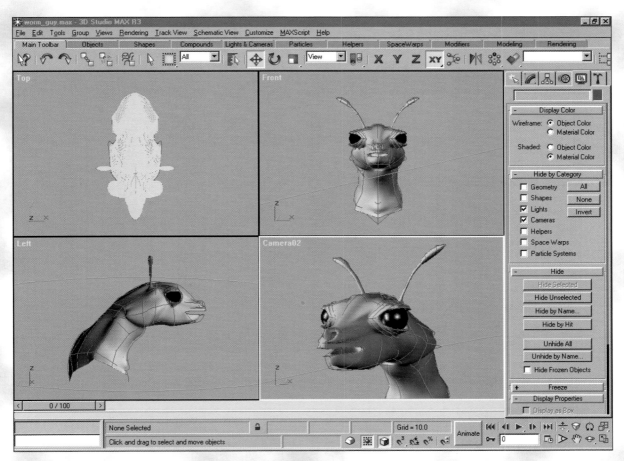

This is the final Worm Guy Surface Tools model.

In this rendering of Worm Guy, a subtle Cellular texture has been applied to his skin. (This file, WORM_GUY.MAX, is in the \CHAP_15 directory of this book's CD-ROM.)

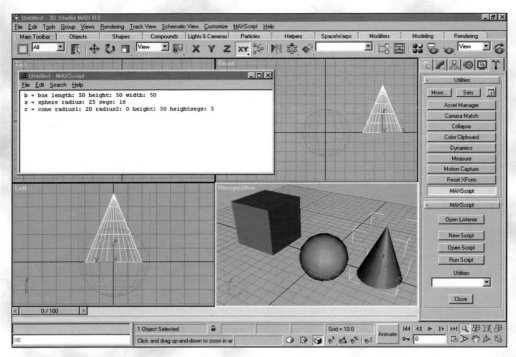

In Chapter 16, Scot Tumlin shows you various MAXScript techniques, including how to create standard MAX Primitives with only a few lines of code.

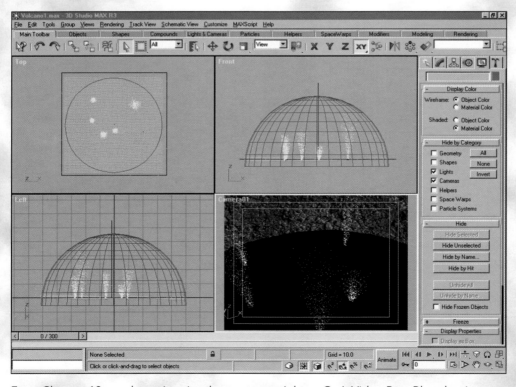

From Chapter 18, a volcano interior demonstrates Johnny Ow's Video Post Blur plug-in, which was applied to the particle systems to create heat distortion in this scene. (The file, VOLCANO1.MAX, is in the \CHAP_18 directory of this book's CD-ROM.)

A finished rendering shows the volcano interior from the previous page.

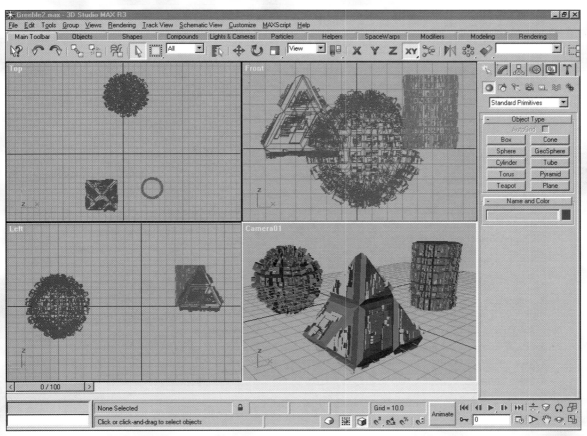

Tom Hudson's Greeble plug-in has returned, and it's been recompiled for MAX Release 3! These Standard Primitives show the effects of the Greeble modifier, which creates procedural details on selected faces or objects.

Here is a rendering of the Primitive objects, with the Greeble modifier and custom metal textures applied.

Another example shows the Greeble modifier applied to selected faces of a QuadPatch object.

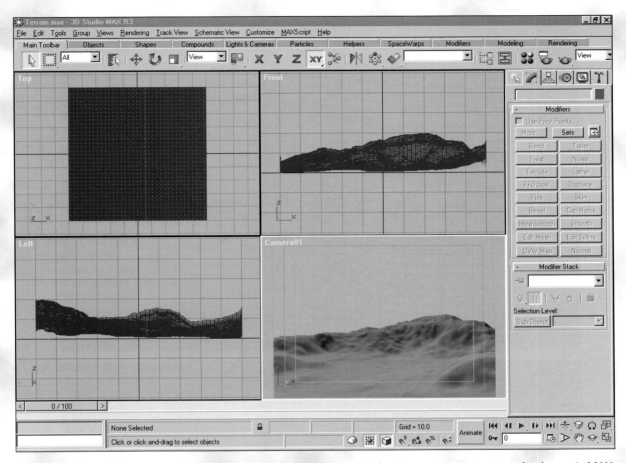

High-resolution geometry, coupled with Johnny Ow's Terrain material plug-in, create an interesting landscape in MAX.

A final rendering of the landscape has the Terrain material applied. (This file, TERRAIN.MAX, is in the \CHAP_18 directory of this book's CD-ROM.)

Matte World Digital

These before and after images for Martin Scorcese's film *Casino* (Universal, 1995) demonstrate the addition of 3D Studio architectural elements to live-action plate photography. The live-action street scene was photographed at the old Howard Hughes' Landmark hotel off of the Las Vegas Strip. The final composite establishes a scene on the Strip that re-creates the 1960s period marquees and hotels, which have long since been torn down. Special lighting effects for the 3D Studio models were rendered with Discreet's Lightscape radiosity software.

These before and after images for Peter Weir's film *The Truman Show* (Paramount Pictures, 1998) demonstrate the effects work of Matte World Digital (**www.matteworld.com**). Only the first stories of the buildings were constructed on set. Matte World Digital created models in 3D Studio MAX Release 2.5 to provide lineup reference for matching the camera moves. The last frame of this 13-second pan shows the completed buildings, with photorealistic textures and lighting created in MAX.

Aiken

by John W. Stetzer

A reptilian alien (armed
with a Louisville Slugger!)
contemplates his existence.
(The artist can be reached at
jwsttzr3@iw.net.)

Mechanical Dragon
by John W. Stetzer

A mechanical dragon trundles across a (Greeble-filled) industrial landscape. Depth of field blurring and soft glows on the specular highlights enhance this image.

Hatred3
by Neil Blevins

This is a dark and scary image from the master of the MAX macabre. (For more information, go to **www.soulburn3d.com**.)

Light Me Up
by A.Wiro

This image started as a material exercise and ended in an attempt to create a photoreal scene, as well as a small parody on the old glass ball-on-checkerboard theme. No particles were used; the smoke is actual geometry. (For more information, go to www.datacomm.ch/ phlug.)

SheBot
by A.Wiro

In this composition, the artist focused on the environment and overall scene composition. Only simple textures were used; most of the appearance is derived from colored lights. The robot was modeled in Rhino, and the cables and environment in MAX R2.5.

Still Life With Rose
by Jerry McManus

The artist's intent in this image was to create a "painterly" effect to give the feeling of soft brush strokes and diffused lighting instead of the hard, harshly lit effect so common in computer generated graphics. Models and textures were built in MAX 2.5; the image was slightly retouched in Photoshop. (The artist can be reached at **jerrymcm@uswest.net**.)

Intruder
by Jerry Potts

This image shows an encounter between a mounted guard and a traveling trader. All of the models were created using "box modeling" with MeshSmooth, and the maps were either composites of real photos or, as in the case of the lizard skin, hand-painted. All maps were made with Photoshop. (For more information, go to **www.geocities.com/SoHo/Studios/1038**.)

Gothic
by Gary "Smeggy" Butcher

This interior was inspired by a set in the film *Bram Stoker's Dracula*. (For more information, go to **www.3dluvr.com/smeggy** and **www.cyan.com**.)

Racecar
by Ken Ray

This model for the B&H Jordan F1 Team was built with a mix of standard Lofting and NURBS. The driver started life as Demi from Character Studio (with a little tweaking!). Although it looks simple, the biggest challenge was the texturing—the model ended up with 32 sub-maps in the main body texture. (The artist can be reached at **kenbo@ rayk.freeserve.co.uk**.)

Balcony
by Scott Malerbi

A photoreal, Tuscan-styled balcony features excellent textures and lighting. (The artist can be reached at **scott@drealm.net**.)

Oasis
by Erick Gravel

Backlighting, a reflective water surface, and area fog provide a moody feel to this image. (The artist can be reached at **erickg@home.com**.)

Nina
by Christian Zürcher

A female warrior, with disturbing mime face paint, strikes a pose. (The artist can be reached at **grimrepoman@ mindspring.com**.)

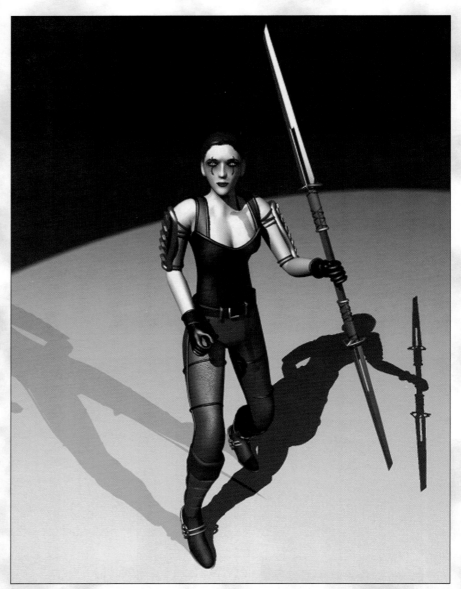

Fallen Angel
by Neil Blevins

Another dark, complex work featuring Neil's typical attention to object details is enhanced by volumetric lighting.

Snake
by Gary "Smeggy" Butcher

A small snake explores a garden. Complex skin textures and depth of field add greatly to the realism of this shot.

Mountain Cabin
by John Manning

The artist built this model in 3D Studio MAX R2.5 and R3. The smoke effect was created with the free Pyro plug-in from Cebas. Many of the textures are from Marlin Studios Rustic Exterior Surfaces collection and the pickup truck is from Espona 3D Encyclopedia. (The artist can be reached at **jm3d@home.com**.)

Bugship
by Jon A. Bell and Michael Spaw

An organic-looking, bug-shaped vessel plies the starways. (This model is included in the \FX3 Extras directory on this book's CD-ROM.)

BENDING LIGHT: EFFECTIVE RAYTRACING TECHNIQUES

11

Although raytracing can produce excellent results, there are various issues you should consider when you use it in your MAX work. In this chapter, you'll find some hints on how to use MAX Release 3's improved raytracing features in your 3D scenes. You'll also learn about some specific settings to create particular effects.

BY
MICHAEL SPAW
AND
JON A. BELL

Raytracing: A Little History

Raytracing has long been considered the pinnacle of 3D rendering technology. Even though scanline renderers, such as Pixar's Photorealistic Renderman, are capable of completely believable results, true raytracing can produce extraordinary renderings and create "hyper-realistic" reflections and refractions on shiny, translucent, or transparent surfaces.

Although 3D Studio/DOS (versions 1 through 4) and 3D Studio MAX R1 relied on native scanline rendering, since 3D Studio MAX Release 2, MAX has included selective raytraced rendering. Developed by special-effects house Blur Studios, of Venice, California, MAX's raytracer works on either a material or map basis. This selective raytracing enables you to apply raytracing rendering to objects that specifically need it and use more conventional scanline rendering for the rest of your 3D scene. And, like many of 3D Studio MAX Release 3's features, the underlying raytracer code has been optimized to produce better results more quickly.

As a rendering method, raytracing originated in the 3D graphic research labs in the early 1980s and has worked its way into commercial 3D software—first on high-end workstation platforms, then on less-expensive desktop computers.

Raytracing works by calculating, or "tracing," the path that your light would take through your 3D scene. In the real world, a light source—either natural, such as the sun, or artificial—emits light, which then propagates throughout an environment, either outdoors or indoors. The light strikes surfaces, where it's reflected or absorbed until it finally reaches your eye.

Raytracing generally works in the opposite direction—that is, a 3D program traces light by starting out at a particular pixel and working its way through the scene until it reaches the light source. Raytracing works in this apparently backward manner because it would take an unbelievably large number of rays cast from the light to eventually strike the image plane that makes up the final image. By working from the image plane to the light, the program can guarantee that each ray that is calculated will count toward the final image. As the rays travel through the scene, they gather information about the color, reflectivity, refractivity, and intensity of the surfaces they strike. The program then combines this information to form an image of where the light has been. It can take quite a while to calculate this path, especially if the scene is complex. For this reason, raytraced renderings are almost always slower than standard scanline renderings of the same scene. However, the resultant raytraced image can contain accurate reflections and refractions that you can't easily achieve any other way.

In The Beginning...

At first, 3D computer graphics artists thought raytracing was the perfect solution for creating realistic imagery. This was mainly because of its ability to reproduce accurate reflections and refractions in materials such as glass and metals. However, the computational cost limited the use of raytracing in most production animation environments, thus it was reserved for stills and short animation experiments. Oddly enough, another problem with raytracing is often the ultrarealistic look it provides. Although it can produce physically correct reflections and refractions for ideal surfaces, the result is sometimes "too perfect," leading to a cold, sterile look. What's often missing are the imperfect reflections and blurring caused by irregularities in the surfaces of most objects. Very few real-world surfaces are perfectly reflective like a mirror. You should take these considerations into account when you do your 3D renderings.

In this chapter, you'll learn how to use MAX's raytracing for both "perfect" reflective surfaces, such as chrome and glass, and nonshiny surfaces, such as rubber.

A Look At MAX Raytracing

With raytracing, you can reproduce two things—reflections and refractions—with excellent results. When you're re-creating the look of polished chrome or a wineglass from a standard material, almost no amount of tweaking will beat the look of raytracing.

The reflections generated by MAX's Raytrace map and Raytrace material are more accurate than those created by using the Reflect/Refract map. Raytracing also allows you to generate reflections in surfaces where neither Flat Mirror nor Reflect/Refract maps will work. It is also possible to use raytracing to create multiple reflections within an object's surface (something you can't do using Reflect/Refract maps). All of these abilities come at a price. It is typically much slower to render objects with raytracing than it is when you use other techniques. Even so, depending on the complexity of the scene and the relative size of the objects in the view, raytracing in MAX can be less of a speed hit than you would think.

> **Note:** Because raytracing is computationally intensive, the renderings in this chapter's tutorials may require that you exercise a little patience for the final results—especially if you have a slower computer. Example renderings are included in the \CHAP_11\ FIGURES directory of this book's companion CD-ROM.

Reflections

When you use raytracing to capture the reflective qualities of a surface, it's often more important to consider what the surface reflects than the surface itself. This is especially true when you are creating polished metal materials. Chrome is a perfect example of a surface defined by what it reflects.

To take a look at a raytraced chrome material, select File|View File in MAX and click on TEAPOT1.TIF in the \CHAP_11 directory of this book's companion CD-ROM. This image is also shown in Figure 11.1.

The material on this teapot is called RT Polished Chrome; it's included in the MAXFX3.MAT Material Library. In a moment, you'll load this teapot scene and create your own raytraced chrome material.

Figure 11.1
The look of this metal teapot is determined almost completely by its surroundings.

Refractions

The second real strength of raytracing is its ability to replicate the look of transparent materials. When light passes through a transparent surface, the light is typically bent or distorted. This distortion is known as refraction, and the amount of refraction is known as the index of refraction (IOR). The IOR results from the relative speed of light as it passes through a transparent material relative to the medium the viewer is in. Often, the more dense the object, the higher the IOR will be.

At 1.0, the approximate IOR of air, the object behind the transparent object does not distort. At 1.5, the object behind distorts greatly, like a glass marble. At an IOR slightly less than 1.0, the object reflects along its edges, like an air bubble seen from underwater.

Table 11.1 includes indexes of refraction for several common transparent materials. You can use these settings to simulate a particular material correctly, or you can use them as a starting point for materials of your own.

Table 11.1 Index of refraction.

Material	IOR
Air	1.0003
Water	1.33
Ethyl alcohol	1.36
Glass	1.50
Lucite or Plexiglas	1.51
Crown glass	1.52
Sodium chloride (salt)	1.53
Quartz	1.544
Flint glass	1.58
Diamond	2.42

An example of how various refraction indexes change the look of transparent materials is shown in the following scene:

1. In 3D Studio MAX Release 3, reset MAX and load IOR.MAX from the \CHAP_11 directory of the companion CD-ROM. You'll see a simple scene consisting of five spheres sitting on a striped floor.

2. Activate the Camera01 viewport and render the scene; your rendering should look like Figure 11.2.

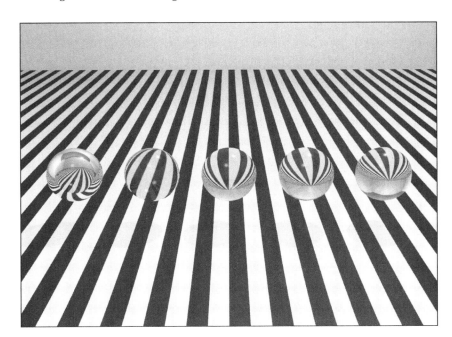

Figure 11.2
Here are several spheres, all with differing indexes of refraction. From left to right, the materials are underwater (IOR: 0.7), hot air (IOR: 0.98), water (IOR: 1.33), glass (IOR: 1.5), and diamond (IOR: 2.42).

3. To see the materials for the five spheres and how they differ, open the Material Editor and examine the IOR settings for each of the raytraced materials. (Note that these materials are all saved in the MAXFX3.MAT Material Library on this book's companion CD-ROM.)

4. Hide all but one of the spheres, change the refractive index on one of the materials, and apply it to the sphere. Then, create your own test renderings and check the results.

The Raytrace Map And Raytrace Material

As mentioned at the beginning of this chapter, MAX's raytracing is selective—rather than raytrace the entire scene, you only need to apply a raytraced map or material to the objects in your scene that require physically correct reflections and refractions.

MAX's raytracing features also enable you to select the objects in the scene that will and will not be "seen" (either locally or globally) by the raytracer. This selectivity is a substantial time-saver when you're rendering complex scenes. Finally, both the Raytrace map and Raytrace material give you a great deal of control over the depth to which the surface will be traced (that is, the number of reflections) and the amount of antialiasing that will be used.

You may be wondering: Why does MAX have both a Raytrace map and a Raytrace material type? Simple—if you have both, you'll have a great deal of flexibility when you're tweaking your final renderings.

The Raytrace map provides an easy way to integrate either raytraced reflections or refractions into a material you've already created or a preexisting one you're modifying. This is the easiest way to get raytraced effects on your objects—you simply load the Raytrace map as you would any other map type.

If you have a metal or glass material in your Material Library that you would like to use in your scene, just add the Raytrace map to the Reflections and/or Refractions map slot in the material. (For special effects, you can place the Raytrace map in material slots other than Reflection or Refraction, which I'll discuss later in this chapter.) The biggest plus to using the Raytrace map is that it usually renders more quickly than the Raytrace material.

The Raytrace material is a new material type, and it enables you to create accurate reflections and refractions for objects in your scenes. Unlike the Raytrace map, the Raytrace material gives you the ability to create translucency, fluorescence, and other special effects in your scene.

The Tabletop Scene

Now that you've learned the basics of MAX's Raytrace material and map types, you'll load a simple scene and experiment with the material settings. After you work through this tutorial, you may want to play with the materials in the scene to become more familiar with the new raytracer's possibilities.

Note: The Raytrace map and Raytrace material share the same raytracer rendering code and Global Parameters settings. It's important to keep this in mind when you're modifying any of the global parameters because all of the materials in the scene will be affected. If you need to change the parameters for raytraced antialiasing, raytrace depth, and blurring, you'll most likely want to change them at the Local Parameters level.

You'll start out by using both the Raytrace map and material in a simple MAX scene:

1. Select File|Load File (or press Ctrl+O), and load TABLETOP.MAX from the \CHAP_11 directory of this book's companion CD-ROM. You'll see a small tabletop set up inside a room.

    For those of you who started out with 3D Studio/DOS, this scene should look vaguely familiar. It's an homage to Jack Powell's original 3D Studio/DOS modeling tutorial, in which you created a tabletop, wine goblet, and covered serving tray. Here, I've replaced the serving tray with the ubiquitous rendering teapot. This scene provides a good environment in which to try out various settings with both the Raytrace map and Raytrace material.

2. Activate the Camera01 viewport and render the scene; your rendering should look like Figure 11.3.

Figure 11.3
Here you will see the tabletop with all standard materials in place. Note that, at this point, raytracing hasn't been applied to any of the materials.

Now, you'll make some improvements to the materials in the scene. To start out, you'll create a chrome material for the teapot. Previously, if you wanted to create materials that re-created the look of chrome, you would use either Automatic Reflection mapping or a standard Reflection map. Although this type of "cheat" is fine for many scenes and objects, the resultant reflections are not physically correct and, in some cases, simply look wrong. For example, automatic Reflection maps can work well for curved surfaces but often fall apart when there's a combination of curves and flat areas. Moreover, both of these mapping types fail to capture reflections within reflections. The Raytrace map can solve these limitations.

3. Open the Material Editor and click on the Polished Chrome material in Material Slot #1. Open the Maps rollout and scroll down to the Reflection map slot. Currently, there is a Reflect/Refract map in place. To make this material more realistic, change it to a Raytrace map.

4. Click on the Reflection Map button, select New, and choose Raytrace from the Material/Map Browser. When the Replace Map dialog box appears, discard the old map. Click on the Go To Parent icon to return to the main Polished Chrome Standard material rollout.

5. Next, activate the Camera01 viewport and re-render the scene to see the change in the teapot's reflection. Your rendering should look like Figure 11.4.

Figure 11.4
With the use of the Raytrace map, the teapot correctly reflects its surroundings.

One of the first things you'll notice is that the reflection is more realistic—you can see the reflection of the knob on the teapot lid in the rest of the lid, for example. The base of the teapot also reflects the table correctly, unlike the earlier example with the Reflect/Refract map. Now that the teapot is done, it's time to move on to the goblet.

6. In the Material Editor, click on the Polished Gold material in the second material slot. Open the Maps rollout and go to the Reflection map slot. Like the material for the teapot, there's a Reflect/Refract map in the Reflection map slot. To make this material more realistic, you'll change it to use a Raytrace map.

7. Click on the Reflection Map button and choose Raytrace from the Material/Map Browser. When the Replace Map dialog box appears, click on Discard Old Map As Sub-Map, then click on Okay.

8. Look a little closer at the settings for the Raytrace map. The Trace Mode options are located in the Raytracer Parameters section in the Material Editor rollup. These radio buttons tell the raytracer whether the rays should reflect or refract the scene. As long as you use the Raytrace map in either the Reflection or Refraction map slots, the Raytrace map should know how it is being applied. (There is one exception—when you use a strong Bump map, you should not use the Auto Detect option but instead select either Reflection or Refraction.)

9. Click on the Global Parameters button to display the Global Raytracer Settings dialog box.

    The Global Raytracer Settings dialog box gives you a great deal of control over how the raytracer will render the raytraced objects in the scene. It controls the reflection recursion level, Global antialiasing, and renderer acceleration. By familiarizing yourself with the various controls, you can sometimes decrease the amount of time the render will take to raytrace materials within the scene. For example, you can do a few things now to speed up your final renderings.

10. Under Ray Depth Control, you'll see that Maximum Depth is set to 9. The Recursion depth tells the render how many levels deep the reflections should extend. If two or more reflective surfaces reflect one another, the reflections will continue to bounce back and forth in the surfaces. This is the "hall of mirrors" effect. By default, Maximum Depth is set to 9, but you often don't need this high of a recursion level. To speed up the rendering, set this value to 3.

11. Next, take a look at the Adaptive Antialiasing section. This controls how the raytracer applies antialiasing to the materials. Click on the checkbox next to Adaptive and change Max.Rays to 10. This will

allow at most only 10 rays per pixel to be calculated for antialiasing. Then, click on the Close button and click on the Go To Parent icon to return to the main Polished Gold Standard material rollout.

12. Activate the Camera01 viewport and re-render the scene to see the change in the goblet's reflection and the teapot; your rendering should look like Figure 11.5.

Figure 11.5
The goblet now reflects its surroundings correctly, as well as the reflections in the teapot.

Like the teapot, the goblet is now reflecting its environment accurately. Some of the visible changes include the reflections captured inside the goblet and the reflection of the goblet itself in its base.

The glass ball sitting on the tabletop could also benefit from some raytracing. You could use the Raytrace map again for both the reflection and refraction, but here, you'll use the Raytrace material instead. To use the Raytrace material for the glass ball, you'll need to create a new material in the Material Editor.

13. The fourth material slot in the Material Editor currently contains the Glass Ball material as it is applied in the scene. To create the new Glass Ball material, click in Material Slot #5. Next, click on the Type: button to bring up the Material/Map Browser. Choose Raytrace from the Material/Map Browser, then click on OK. Finally, in the Name field, change the name of this material to RT New Glass.

14. At this point, the new Raytrace material looks much like the Standard material. Look at the Basic Parameters rollup. The first thing you'll do is change the material's Specular attributes. In the Specular Highlight section, change Glossiness to 80 and Specular Level to 175. (Previously, only the Raytrace material allowed you to put this value above 100; now, all of MAX Release 3's materials allow you to do this.) You'll see the material changes occur on the sample sphere in the RT New Glass slot.

15. Click on the color swatch box next to Transparency: Value to bring up the Color Selector. Set Value to 255, or pure white. Notice how the material sample sphere is now transparent. The Raytrace material uses the value to control the material's opacity. Black makes the material opaque; white is fully transparent.

16. Next, you'll set the Diffuse Color. Click on the color swatch next to Diffuse: Value and change the colors to RGB settings 0, 0, 255, or pure blue. You'll see that the sample sphere is still transparent. Reflection and transparency effects are layered on top of the Diffuse result. When Reflect or Transparency are pure white, the Diffuse Color isn't visible.

17. To create the effect of colored glass, you'll need to do one more thing. Click on the Diffuse color slot and drag the saturated blue color to the Transparency slot. When the Copy Or Swap Colors dialog box appears, select Copy. Now, in the material sample slot, you will see that the sample sphere looks like tinted glass.

18. The ball should also reflect its environment, so click on the color swatch next to Reflect: Value. Set the value to 30, then close the Color Selector.

19. Finally, you'll need to set the IOR for the material so that it will refract the scene as real glass does. Set the Index Of Refraction value to 1.5.

20. Select the glass ball in the scene and click on the Assign To Material Selection button (or drag this material to the glass ball).

21. Activate the Camera01 viewport and re-render the scene; your rendering should look like Figure 11.6.

As a final touch, you could change the Table material to use the Raytrace map to add subtle reflections (keep the level of reflection low).

Figure 11.6
The glass ball now correctly refracts and reflects its surroundings. (In your rendering, you'll also notice that it casts a colored shadow.)

Creating Raytraced Metals

One of the primary reasons you may want to use raytracing in MAX is to produce accurate reflections in metal and other reflective materials. However, as I mentioned earlier, raytraced reflections are often "perfect," and very few real-world surfaces, with the exception of mirrors and polished metal, are perfectly flat and reflective.

Most reflective materials have some degree of roughness to them. Small surface imperfections or grime on the surface of an object will blur out the reflection. Oily fingerprints on glass or the brushed aluminum of an auto wheel are good examples of this effect. By blurring the reflection slightly in a raytraced material, you can add a great deal of realism to the surface.

In the following example file, I've created three raytraced materials, each with different amounts of blur to its reflections. These differences in blurring create vastly different-looking surfaces. Now, you'll take a look at the materials for the three spheres and see how their settings differ:

1. In MAX Release 3, load SPHERES.MAX from the \CHAP_11 directory of the companion CD-ROM. You'll see three spheres inside a box environment.

2. Activate the Camera01 viewport and render the scene; your rendering should look like Figure 11.7.

3. Open the Material Editor and click on the RT Polished Steel material in Slot #1. Notice that the material is not 100 percent reflective. You can see this by clicking on the Reflect color slot. It currently contains

Figure 11.7
Here are three metal spheres with differing amounts of blur in their reflectivity. The left sphere could represent polished steel. The middle sphere is less polished, and the right sphere looks as if it's been sandblasted.

a Value setting of 180. Unless they're mirror-smooth, most metals will retain some of their diffuse color.

4. Notice that Specular Level is set to 130, which creates strong specular highlights. Finally, look at the Soften parameter. This lets you soften and spread out the specular highlight, creating the look of a more matte surface.

5. Click on the second material slot, look at the RT Steel material, and compare its settings with that of Material #1. Finally, click on Slot #3 and compare the RT Sandblast Steel material to the previous two. The main changes between the three materials are in the appearance of their specular highlights. As the surface becomes more matte and less reflective, the highlights become broader and softer.

6. Next, take a look at what really makes the reflections appear differently between the three materials. Click once again on the RT Polished Steel material and open the Raytracer Controls rollup. In the middle of the rollup is a checkbox that enables you to override the global antialiasing settings; this allows you to modify each Raytrace material or map to meet specific antialiasing or Blur/Defocus needs. The Blur/Defocus parameters enable you to change the reflection blurring of the three materials. For the RT Polished Steel material, I've used the default settings.

7. Click on the RT Steel material and examine the Blur/Defocus settings. You'll see that Blur Offset is increased to 5.0. This new setting softens the reflection and gives the appearance of a less-polished surface.

8. Click on the RT Sandblast Steel material. Blur/Defocus is set to 10.0, which softens the reflections further. Note that you can also use the Blur/Defocus parameter to eliminate aliasing in reflections or refractions. If you see aliasing in these areas in your renderings, increase the Blur/Defocus value in small increments until you get the effect you want.

9. Note that the Blur Aspect parameter has also been changed for the RT Sandblast Steel material. When the reflection is blurred by a large amount, you may need to change the Blur Aspect parameter to change the shape of the blurring. As MAX's online documentation notes, "If you see aliasing that occurs mostly along horizontal lines, try increasing Blur Aspect to 1.5. This changes the shape of the blurred effect. The reverse is also true. If aliasing occurs mostly along vertical lines, try decreasing Blur Aspect to 0.5."

10. Finally, look at the parameters in the Adaptive Control area of the rollup (I've changed them for the last two materials). When Adaptive has been checked, it allows you to set the initial and maximum number of rays that will be sampled for each pixel. The greater the number of rays cast, the better each pixel will be antialiased against its neighbors. Generally, the default settings are adequate, but in the case of very blurry reflections, the number of rays may need to be increased.

11. Look at the Initial Rays and Max Rays settings for all three materials and compare the settings. (Although blurring the reflection can add realism to some materials, it's important to note that it can also add considerably to your rendering time.)

The Lantern Scene: Translucency

One material effect that's been difficult to render properly in MAX (until now) is true translucency. Translucent materials permit light to pass through but diffuse it so that an object on the other side is not clearly visible. Frosted glass, rice paper, and candle wax all show this effect. Another result of this effect is that shadows cast on a translucent surface from the back will be visible from the front.

To see an example of translucency in action, you'll take a look at frosted glass in a lamp:

1. Load LAMP.MAX from the \CHAP_11 directory of the companion CD-ROM. You'll see a cylindrical lamp sitting on a flat surface.

2. Activate the Camera01 viewport and render the scene. Your rendering should look like Figure 11.8. (Note that I've turned off
   antialiasing in this file to speed up the render time.)

Figure 11.8

This image shows how a semitransparent raytraced material
with a light inside the object
looks when rendered without the
use of translucency. Notice that
the glass does not appear to be
lit from within.

3. Now, take a look at how the material for the lamp is set up. Open
   the Material Editor and click on the RT Frosted Glass material in Slot
   #1. In the Basic Parameters rollup, you'll see that the material is set
   up to replicate a semitransparent, matte-finished surface. The Diffuse Color is off-white to help convey the warmth of the light from
   the lamp. The Transparency value is set to 210 so that the glass is
   only partially transparent. I've set the IOR value to less than that of
   glass (perhaps it's some type of plastic). Finally, the Glossiness and
   Specular Level values provide a soft specular highlight.

4. Open the Extended Parameters rollup. At the top of the rollup is the
   section for Special Effects. In the center of the effects section are the
   Translucency controls. The controls consist of a color swatch box and
   a map slot button.

5. Click on the Color box next to Translucency. When the Color Selector
   appears, change the RGB values to 243, 243, 219. As you modify the
   color, you'll notice that the material sample window displays the
   changes.

6. Activate the Camera01 viewport and re-render the scene. Your rendering should look like Figure 11.9.

Figure 11.9
Now, the frosted glass looks as if it's diffusing the light from within the lamp.

As your rendering shows, the translucency effect can add a great deal of realism to semitransparent materials.

When you re-create these types of (Standard) materials with the new Raytrace material, make sure you set up the rest of the parameters for the material to reproduce the desired look before you play with the translucency. This is important because adding translucency may have the tendency to hide some of the subtlety of the material's Specular component.

To further explore the effects of translucency, set up a translucent glass block lit from behind. Place a second object between the light and the block to cast a shadow onto the block to see the effect's shadow-catching ability. You can also play with the color of the translucency or map the effect to replicate the look of sandblasted or acid-etched art glass.

Other Cool Effects

By now you've seen the advantages of using raytracing for creating reflections and refraction. As if basic raytracing wasn't enough, there are other options in the Raytrace material that can help you create specific effects. In many cases, these techniques don't require the use of either the reflection or refraction capabilities of the material, which decreases the time it takes to render them.

Rubber

You can create a subtle but cool surface effect with the Raytrace material's Soften parameter, which lets you soften the specular highlights that are visible on the material.

In Standard materials, the Soften feature helps soften specular highlights when they're seen at glancing angles on the surface of your objects. However, unlike the Standard Soften feature, which has values that range from 0.00 to 1.00, you can set Soften in the Raytrace material to values larger than 1.00. If you create a Raytrace material with a large soft highlight, it can give the material a semimatte appearance, much like that of a rubber ball. To see an example of this effect, follow these steps:

1. Load RUBBER.MAX from the \CHAP_11 directory of the companion CD-ROM. When the scene appears, activate the Camera01 viewport and render it. The resulting image should look like Figure 11.10.

Figure 11.10
The ball has a raytraced Soften material; with the Soften setting set above 1, the ball takes on a rubbery appearance.

2. Take a look at the Material settings for the ball's material. Open the Material Editor and click on the Rubber Ball material in the first material slot. Unlike the previous examples of the Raytrace material, the Rubber Ball material uses neither the Reflection nor the Refraction properties typically associated with raytraced renderings.

3. Next, look at the Soften parameter in the Specular Highlight section of the Basic Parameters rollup. Currently, Soften is set to 2.5, which gives the ball its soft, matte appearance.

4. To see how Soften can change the appearance of the Specular highlight, change the setting to 2.0, 1.5, and then 1.0, and render each setting.

SOFTER SPECULAR HIGHLIGHTS WITH OREN-NAYER-BLINN

If you want to create softer, more diffused specular highlights without using the Raytrace material, consider using a Standard material with the Oren-Nayer-Blinn shader. See Chapter 7 for more information on this shader type.

Fluorescence

Fluorescence is an effect often associated with 1960s and 1970s psychedelic posters and roller-skating rinks. Technically, fluorescence is the emission of radiation, especially visible light, from a material when it is exposed to external radiation. More importantly for us, this new MAX Raytrace material effect can simulate the look of commercial fluorescent paints and black light. It can be used to imitate phosphorescent pigments of certain animals, such as deep-sea fish.

To accomplish this effect, the Raytrace material uses the lights within your MAX scene, regardless of their color, to illuminate the material as if it were lit by purely white light. This gives the effect of the material glowing by itself. The effect is especially apparent when the lights in the environment are colored very differently than the color of the fluorescent material. The effect also uses a Bias to increase or decrease the influence of the lights.

As the MAX Online Help feature notes, "At 0.5, the Bias makes Fluorescence behave just like diffuse coloring. Bias values higher than 0.5 increase the fluorescent effect, making the object brighter than other objects in the scene. Bias values lower than 0.5 make the object dimmer than other objects in the scene." To see an example of Fluorescence in action, follow these steps:

1. Load FLUORESC.MAX from the \CHAP_11 directory of the companion CD-ROM. The scene contains a watch body within a gray room environment. Activate the Camera01 viewport and render the scene. The resulting image should look like Figure 11.11.

2. Next, take a look at the Material settings for the watch hands. Open the Material Editor and click on the Fluorescent Green material in Slot #1. Open the Basic Parameters rollup and take a look at the settings. Currently, the material has a soft specular highlight and no added Luminosity value.

3. To make the material appear to fluoresce, you'll need to modify the Fluorescence value. Open the Extended Parameters rollout. The Fluorescence color swatch box is under Special Effects. By simply setting the Fluorescence value to the same value as the Diffuse Color, you can give the watch hands an appropriately colored glow.

4. Click on the Diffuse color swatch and drag it to the Fluorescence color swatch; you'll see the sample material slot change to reflect the new effect.

5. To make the effect brighter than the environment, set the Fluorescence Bias value to 1.0. If you want, close the Material Editor.

Figure 11.11
The watch hands on this model could benefit from the Fluorescence effect in the Raytrace material. (I've hidden the watch's crystal, which has a raytraced glass material, to speed up rendering times.)

6. Finally, drag the Time Slider to frame 100; you'll notice that the lighting dims. (I animated the light value settings in this file.) As with most Fluorescent materials, you can see the effect better when the surrounding environment is darkened.

7. Activate the Camera01 viewport and re-render the scene; your rendering should look like Figure 11.12.

Figure 11.12
The watch hands appear to glow (bright green, in your rendering) regardless of the blue color present in the room light.

Fog

You can also use the Raytrace material to simulate the look of fog within an object. This effect is much like having a volume light inside the surface; as the MAX Online Help states, Fog "is a thickness-based effect. It fills the object with a fog that is both opaque and self illuminated." To see an example of this effect, follow these steps:

1. Load FOG.MAX from the \CHAP_11 directory of the companion CD-ROM. When the scene appears, render the Camera01 view. The resulting image should look like Figure 11.13.

Figure 11.13

Each of the three spheres is filled with differing densities of self-illuminated fog.

2. Now, you'll take a look at how the materials for the three spheres differ. Open the Material Editor and click on the Full Fog material in the first material slot. Open the Extended Parameters rollup; in the Advanced Transparency section you'll see that the Fog box is checked. This enables the fog to be rendered in transparent materials.

   The Start and End controls modify how the fog appears within a material based on the object's overall size. Start sets the position within the object where the fog begins to appear. End sets the location within the object where the fog reaches its full Amount value. The Amount value sets the fog's overall density. In addition to controlling the color of the fog, you can use a map to modify its appearance.

3. Take a look at the next two materials and compare their Fog settings. The Medium Fog material has a higher End value, giving the fog a less-dense appearance. The Light Fog material has an even higher End value, further decreasing its density at the sphere's edge. It also has the Fog Amount value decreased to 0.8, lessening the overall density possible.

RAYTRACING TIPS AND TRICKS

Here are some suggestions for getting more out of MAX's raytracer:

- Turn off antialiasing in the Global Options dialog box when you're first designing raytraced materials. This will save you a great deal of time when you're waiting for the final result and you're still tweaking the materials' appearance.

- As you look around your real-world environment a little closer, you'll notice that many surfaces are slightly reflective. You can increase the realism of a surface by adding a small bit of reflectivity to it. However, make sure the reflectivity is generally less than 5 percent for most nonmetals. Higher values look interesting, but they aren't realistic.

- To help speed up rendering times with the raytracer, make sure you've welded the cores of Lathed objects. You should also check to make sure your objects' faces have unified normals and that the objects aren't degenerate, that is, have missing faces, overlapping vertices, and so on.

- If you don't need to keep the modifier stack for your raytraced objects, collapse them into Editable Meshes before rendering your scene.

In addition to these suggestions, here are some additional tips from MAX animator Greg Tsadilas:

- If Object #1 is inside transparent Object #2 (which uses the Raytrace material), Object #1 will have its Material ID passed through to Video Post filters. Consequently, you can have an object glow inside another object.

- As mentioned earlier, for creating good metallic materials, crank up the Specular Level of the Raytrace material to above 100 to create very "hot" specular highlights.

- Under Globals, you'll find that the default setting for Maximum Depth is 9. That's overkill for most basic scenes. Unless you want a "hall of mirrors" effect in reflective objects that are also reflecting each other, a setting of 2 or 3 is usually sufficient, and much faster.

- Many people seldom use the Manual Acceleration settings under Globals. Depending on your scene, you can decrease your render time by using Single or Dual pipeline. I usually start by using Single in complex scenes; if necessary, I'll try switching to Dual. One of them usually decreases render time significantly.

- Here's a fun trick to try. Let's say you want your Raytrace Material object to reflect the background (or more correctly, a plane with an image that's acting as your background mapped to it), but you don't want the plane with the image to appear in the render. For the solution, follow these steps:

  1. Create a duplicate plane that's in front of the one with the image mapped to it. (Actually, it just needs to be between the camera and the image-mapped plane.)

  2. Assign this plane a Shadow/Matte material.

  3. Exclude this Shadow/Matte plane from the Global Exclude list in the Raytrace material.

The final effect is that your objects will reflect the image that's mapped onto the plane, but the plane itself will not be rendered because it's hidden by the Shadow/Matte plane. Naturally, this works if you want to reflect any object but still exclude it from the final rendered image.

—*Information courtesy of Michael Spaw and Phillip Miller of Discreet*

Moving On

Now that you've learned some of the basics of raytracing, I hope you'll be able to use this new and exciting MAX feature in interesting ways. (Just don't go overboard with chrome spheres sitting on checkerboard floors—and for heaven's sake, keep those scenes off your MAX demo reel!)

This chapter concludes the look at MAX Release 3's materials, maps, and shaders. In the next section, you'll see tips on polygonal and patch modeling and have fun with some cool new modifiers, including MAX Release 3's improved MeshSmooth.

PART III

MODELING
AND
MODIFIERS

MeshSmooth I: Polygonal Modeling Techniques

12

By Jon A. Bell

In the preceding section of the book, we focused on materials editing and optical effects. In this section, "Modeling And Modifiers," we begin to focus on different ways to use MAX Release 3's new tools to create the geometry for your 3D scenes.

Sculpting With MeshSmooth

In this chapter and the next, you'll see how to use one of MAX's most powerful tools, the MeshSmooth modifier, to turn a simple box into a streamlined rocket plane or organic objects, such as a cartoon dragon.

In addition, in Chapter 13, you'll see how to use MAX Release 3's new Non-Uniform Rational MeshSmooth (NURMS) setting to fine-tune the details and curvature of your models to produce exactly the contours you want. You'll then see how you can animate your creations using the new Skin and Flex modifiers.

"How To Do It!"

There's an old, very funny *Monty Python's Flying Circus* skit that portrays a phony TV show called "How To Do It!" In this skit, the members of the Monty Python troupe describe how to do a wide range of amazingly complex tasks, all in laughably quick, simplistic fashion. The tasks included how to play the flute, how to split the atom, how to build box-girder bridges, and how to irrigate the Sahara and make vast new areas cultivatable. And perhaps most apropos to this chapter was a brief moment in which the late Graham Chapman held up a beautiful model of a race car and extorted to kids, "How to build this swell race car?! First, you get a block of wood, and then you carve the car!" That was the sum total of instruction!

Well, in this chapter, you're actually going to do something like that: You're going to take a "block" (actually, a basic Box primitive) and sculpt it into a cool futuristic rocket plane, courtesy of the MeshSmooth modifier. However, unlike the one-sentence throwaway instructions of Monty Python, I'm going to use this entire chapter and step-by-step, augmented with copious illustrations, show you exactly how to do it.

(By the way, in case you were wondering how to play the flute: "You blow in one end and move your fingers up and down the outside." And you thought this was just a computer graphics book!)

Flash Forward...

Before you begin creating your spacecraft, you'll first take a look at a finished MeshSmoothed model. Then, you'll begin to approximate it by sculpting a Box primitive, using extruded faces and moving and welding vertices.

To start, do the following:

1. Load MAX, or save your current work and reset the program. (Note that for this tutorial, I am assuming that your MAX session is set at the original program defaults, especially for the Units, Grid, and

---

MESHSMOOTH TECHNIQUES FOR MAX R2.5 AND R3

With the exception of the NURMS feature, the MeshSmooth techniques covered in this chapter can also be accomplished in 3D Studio MAX R2 and R2.5.

Snap settings. If not, please change them to the default settings; consult your MAX Release 3 manuals and/or the Help file to set them properly.)

2. From the \CHAP_12 directory of this book's companion CD-ROM, load the file ROCKETPLANE.MAX. The file loads, and your screen should look like Figure 12.1.

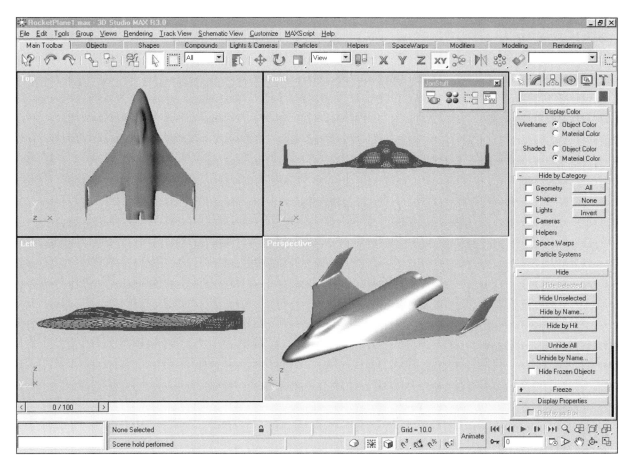

Although it's an original design, I was inspired in its creation by several published examples of 21st-century NASA "rocket plane" concepts for suborbital transports.

3. Take a moment and, using the Arc Rotate feature, rotate around the model in the Perspective viewport. You'll notice that, although the overall craft is smooth and rounded off, the aft end of the ship has two rocket exhaust ports; their edges are fairly sharp and defined. In addition, the vertical stabilizers that project up from the outboard wings have strongly delineated transitions into the tops

Figure 12.1

A futuristic rocket plane model, inspired by several NASA designs. (The Grid background is hidden in this figure.)

of the wing surfaces themselves; the tops of the stabilizers and the wingtips are also squared off more than the rest of the ship, as shown in Figure 12.2.

Now, you'll see how the basic geometry was built.

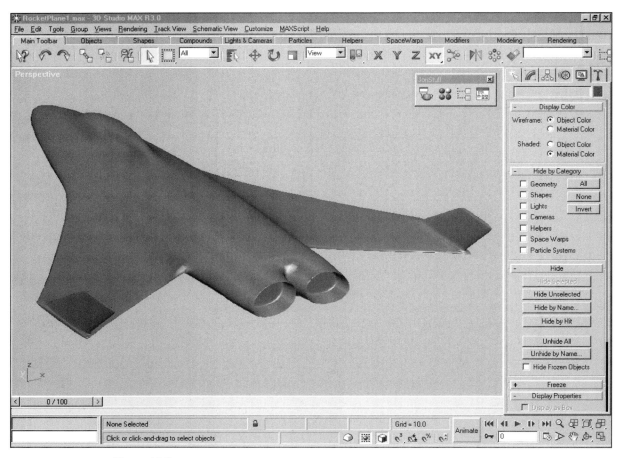

Figure 12.2

Certain details, such as the backs of the exhaust ports, the vertical stabilizers, and the wing tips, are far less rounded off than the overall rocket fuselage.

4. Go to the Display panel and select Unhide All. When you do, you'll see a low-resolution wireframe cage appear around the higher-res rocket plane model. This cage is a low-resolution proxy model that I used to actually sculpt the final, high-resolution version of the plane, as shown in Figure 12.3. (The proxy model has a wireframe texture applied to it so that it still appears as a wireframe model in Shaded viewports.)

5. Next, select the high-res model of the plane and go to the Modify panel. You'll see that there's a MeshSmooth modifier applied to the Rocket Plane object. If you examine the modifier's settings, you'll note the following: Under Parameters, Quad Output is checked. This

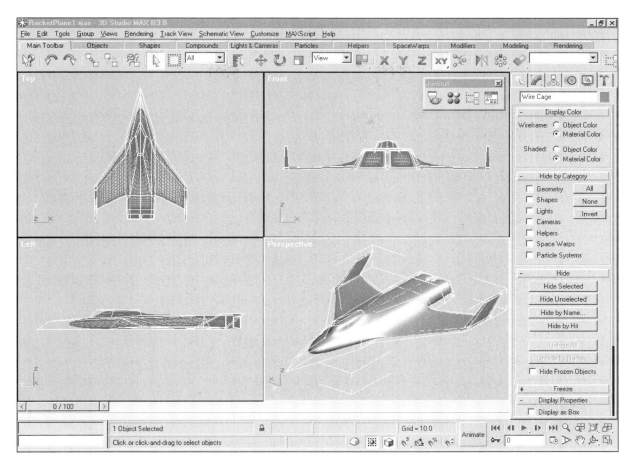

Figure 12.3

A low-resolution proxy model of the rocket plane surrounds the MeshSmoothed model.

indicates that the modifier will produce only four-sided polygons (minus hidden edges, of course; the quads are actually composed of two triangles apiece).

6. If you were to select Classic, the MeshSmooth modifier would tessellate and relax the original object by using a combination of quads and individual triangular polygons. Try this out: Activate the Top viewport, press the W key to enlarge it to full screen, then click on the Classic button in the Modify panel. You'll notice a subtle change in the smoothed tessellation of the model; the Classic setting doesn't seem to round off the model as much as the Quad setting.

7. Next, click on NURMS. NURMS stands for Non-Uniform Rational MeshSmooth, which is a new MeshSmooth feature added to 3D Studio MAX Release 3. With it, you can adjust the overall curvature of your model by adjusting the "weight" of selected vertices. (You'll play with this feature in the next chapter; the controls are under the Display/Weighting section of the MeshSmooth rollout.) For now, select Quad again to return the model to its original form.

8. Finally, if you look at the Smoothing parameters, you'll see that Strength is set to 0.5 (its default) and Subdivision Amount/Iterations is set to 3. Note that, unlike 3D Studio MAX 2.x, MAX Release 3 enables you to apply a higher number of MeshSmooth iterations onto your model. (You should use this with caution, however, as you can quickly create models with *enormous* face counts.) However, you'll also see the new Render Values feature. With it, you can adjust your MAX desktop to display a lower-resolution version of a parametric MeshSmoothed model (to speed up screen redraws) and a high-resolution version that appears only at rendering time.

9. You can test this out now. Under Subdivision Amount, change Iterations to 0; you'll see the rocket plane revert to a blocky version of itself that's identical to the original low-res proxy. Then, under Render Values, check the box next to Iterations and change this to 3.

10. Next, click on the Min/Max Toggle button (or press the W key) to return to your four viewports, activate the Perspective viewport, and render it. Your screen should look like Figure 12.4.

Okay, that's enough messing around with this model right now. Let's see how we can build something like this from scratch.

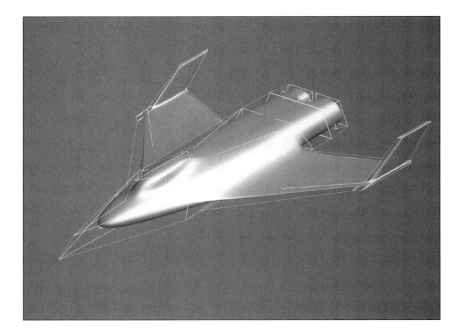

Figure 12.4
The new MeshSmooth Subdivision settings enable you to specify separate Iterations for desktop display versus final rendering.

You Start With A Box...

For the next few pages, you're going to build a model similar to the rocket plane you've just been examining. Although I'll give specific instructions for most steps involving face and vertex manipulation, as you get more comfortable with "sculpting" details, you can begin modifying the original low-res proxy object as you wish. But first, you start with a box:

1. Reset MAX, and make sure your Grid and Snap settings are set to their original defaults. Make sure that the Grid background is showing in all your viewports.

2. Press the S key to activate 3D Snap, then activate your Top viewport and enlarge it to full screen (press the W key or the Min/Max Toggle button).

3. Go to the Create panel, select Geometry|Standard Primitives|Box. Place your mouse cursor at XYZ coordinates X –80, Y 190, and Z 0, and draw out a box (diagonally, down to the right) with a length of 400, a width of 160, and a height of 60. (The Parameters fields of the Create panel will help you with the exact settings, as will the 3D Snap option.) Don't worry about turning on Mapping Coordinates; you won't need them. Leave the Length, Width, and Height Segments options all set to 1.

4. Now that you've got your box, you'll want to collapse it into an Editable Mesh. You can do this from the Modify panel, but you don't need to; simply right-click to bring up the Properties menu on the still-selected Box, and choose Convert to Editable Mesh. When you do, you'll see the Modify panel appear, with the Box01 object appearing as an Editable Mesh. Go to the Modify panel and change Box01's name to Wire Cage.

5. Click on the wire cage model to select it, right-click to bring up the Properties menu again, and select Move.

6. Without actually moving the model, hold down the Shift key and click on the wire cage model again until it's selected. The Clone Options menu appears.

7. This step is important: Under Object, click on Reference. Do *not* select Copy or Instance. Rename the object from Wire Cage 02 to Rocket Plane, then click on Okay.

Now, why did you make this duplicated model a Reference rather than a Copy or Instanced object? Because you're going to be applying a MeshSmooth modifier only to the Reference Rocket Plane object. Consequently, changes made to the parent wire cage model are passed down to the Reference Rocket Plane model, but not back the other direction. A Copy would have MeshSmooth changes made only to it; an Instance would've passed the MeshSmooth modifier changes in either direction, ruining the final effect.

The MeshSmooth Setup

At this point, you're almost ready to start sculpting the plane. However, you still need to do a little bit of setup work before you continue (and you need to apply the MeshSmooth modifier, of course). Now, you'll finish setting up the objects for sculpting:

1. With the rocket plane still selected, go to the Modify panel and apply a MeshSmooth modifier—again, only to the rocket plane and not to the wire cage model.

2. With the MeshSmooth modifier applied, make the following changes: Under MeshSmooth Type Parameters, check Quad Output. Under Input Parameters, check both Keep Faces Convex and Apply To Whole Mesh.

   Note that this latter command is *extremely* important. As you work on a sub-object level on the Wire Cage proxy object, you don't want the MeshSmoothed rocket plane model to respond only to the selected sub-objects. Instead, you want the overall MeshSmooth effect to be visible over the entire object all the time.

3. Under Smoothing Parameters, keep Strength set to 0.5 and Relax at 0.0. Under Subdivision, set Iterations to 3. If you have a slower computer, you might set this to 2, but don't set it higher than 3, even if you have a scorchingly fast PC. For the purposes of this tutorial, interactive modeling speed is paramount; you can always increase the overall Subdivision (Tessellation) Amount value after you've got the model looking the way you want.

4. Skip Display/Weighting, and under Surface Parameters, make sure Smooth Result is checked. You're going to do much of your sculpting with a Shaded viewport active, so you want to be able to see a smoothly shaded version of your rocket plane rather than a faceted one.

5. Press the W key or click on the Min/Max Toggle button to return to your four viewports.

Setting Up The Display Materials

In your viewports, you should be seeing a single Box primitive; the MeshSmoothed Box is basically hidden inside. For best results, you're going to apply two different materials to these objects. These will help you differentiate the models as you're sculpting:

1. Open the Material Editor and click on the first sample slot. Rename this material Wire Cage and then make the following changes: Change the Diffuse Color to RGB 255, 255, 0, or a bright yellow. Under Shader Basic Parameters, check both Wire and 2-Sided, turn off the Self-Illumination Color checkbox, and change the Color slider from 0 to 100. You should have a pure yellow, self-illuminated wireframe material showing in the sample sphere #1 slot.

2. Go to the second sample slot, change this material name to Rocket Plane, and make the following changes: Change the Diffuse Color to RGB 0, 124, 255, or a bright blue-green. Under Specular Highlights, change Specular Level to 100 and Glossiness to 50. This smooth "plastic" material will help outline the overall smooth curves on your high-res rocket plane model.

3. Next, apply the Wire Cage material to the wire cage model and the Rocket Plane material to its namesake. (You can press the H key to bring up the Select By Name menu and apply the textures, or you can drag and drop them from the Material Editor to the two different models.) When you're finished, close the Material Editor.

4. As a final step, it's useful to be able to see both a Wireframe and a Shaded view of your Perspective window, so I suggest setting up your desktop as shown in Figure 12.5. The Perspective viewport in the upper right has Shaded mode active; the Perspective view below has Wireframe mode active.

Now, you're ready to begin creating your rocket plane. (As you progress through these tutorials, it's wise to periodically save your work, or choose Edit|Hold, to hold your scene before you perform a major step.) Also, please note that the JonStuff floater menu appears in only some figures in this chapter; in others, I've removed it for clarity. In addition, in some of the figures, I've turned off the Grid background so that you see some of the polygonal details in the scene more easily.

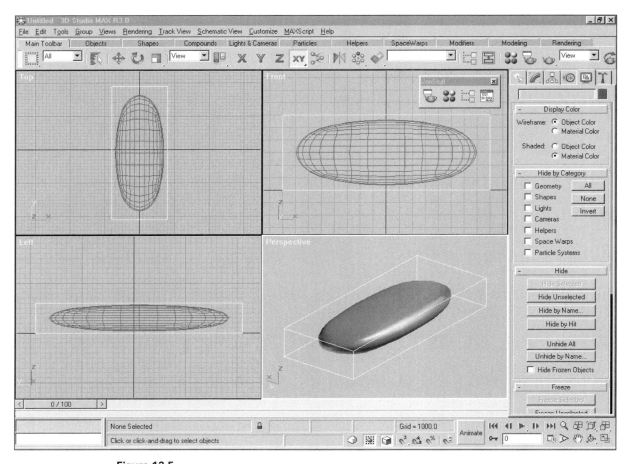

Figure 12.5

The low-res Wire Cage proxy and the Reference MeshSmoothed object.

Taking Shape: Extruding Faces

Now, you're ready for the fun part: the actual sculpting. (Actually, at this point, I was sorely tempted to say, "Okay, now you simply modify the box until it looks like the cool rocket plane you saw earlier, and you're done! Moving right along, in the next chapter...") But, because we're still working in MAX and not watching *Monty Python*, here's what to do:

1. Using the Arc Rotate button, rotate your Perspective viewports so that you're looking at the two objects in a roughly three-quarter view, as shown in Figure 12.5.

2. Select the Wire Cage object and go to the Modify panel. Go to SubObject: Polygon mode and make sure Ignore Backfacing is unchecked. Then, click on the end face (pointing down, to the left) of the wire cage model in the lower Perspective window to select it.

3. Under Edit Geometry in the Modify panel, click on Extrude, then begin dragging the slider up to extrude the selected end faces.

4. Whoa! That's interesting—as you extrude the Wire Cage faces, you'll see that the MeshSmoothed Rocket Plane object begins to extrude additional faces, and those faces stretch out and curve inward toward the end faces of the low-res Wire Cage proxy. The more you increase the slider value, the more the underlying faces stretch and smooth out.

5. Go to the toolbar at the top of your screen and undo your slider values; the objects should snap back to normal. With the end faces still selected, go back to the Extrude button, type "50" into the number field, and press Enter. You'll see the rocket plane faces appear and stretch out to follow the contours of this modified low-res wire cage, as shown in Figure 12.6. (Note that this figure has been retouched for clarity.)

> ### CAN'T FIGURE OUT WHICH FACES TO SELECT?
>
> If you have trouble determining which faces or vertices to select, based on my descriptions or the book's illustrations, note that you can use MAX's File|View File feature to view JPG versions of each figure from this book's companion CD-ROM. They're located in the \CHAP_12\FIGURES directory.

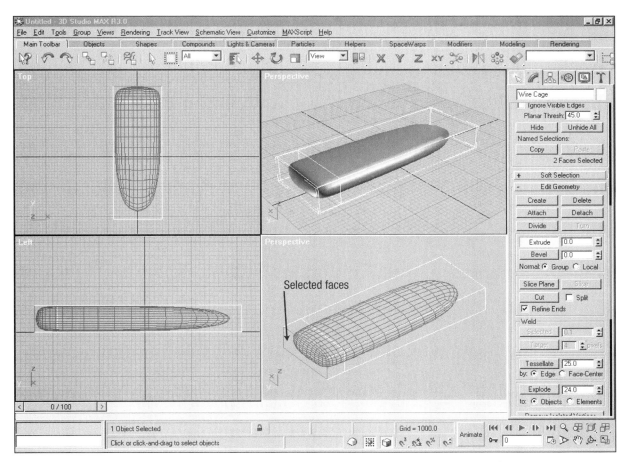

Figure 12.6

The underlying rocket plane faces stretch out to follow the contours of the extruded Wire Cage end faces.

6. Now, repeat this process on the other (long) end of the wire cage. In the Top viewport, select the end faces (at the "bottom" of the viewport, opposite the faces you just extruded). From the Modify panel, set the Extrude value to 50 again and press Enter. The faces opposite the "nose" end extrude as before. Your screen should look like Figure 12.7. (Again, this figure has been retouched for clarity.)

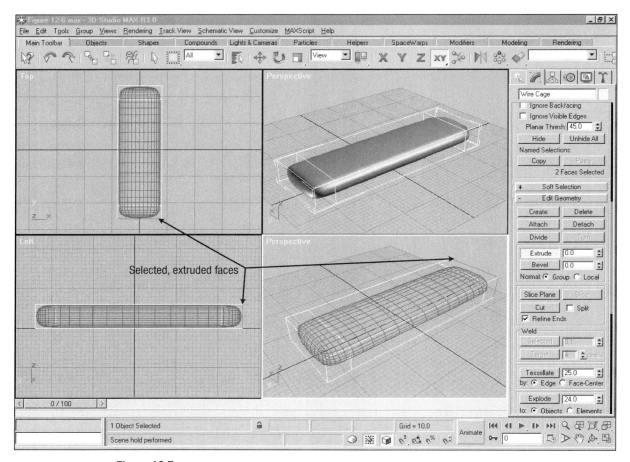

Figure 12.7

The second round of extruded faces.

Face And Vertex Editing

Now, it starts getting interesting. You've made your original box a little more complex by adding extruded faces to it. It's time to start combining vertex and face manipulation with face extrusion and scaling to start turning this rounded-off plank into an aerodynamic form. You'll start by sculpting the nose:

1. Go back to the Modify panel, switch to Sub-Object: Vertex mode, and make sure Ignore Backfacing is unchecked. You're going to start moving vertices to form the vessel's pointed nose.

2. From this point forward, it's going to be useful to have the Transform Type-In window up so that you can move faces and vertices an exact distance along any given axis and so you can type in exact scaling values. Choose Tools|Transform Type-In, and place this floating menu off to one side (say, in the lower-right corner of your screen). You can always move it out of the way as you switch to different viewports and begin selecting different faces and vertices.

3. Activate the Top viewport and enlarge it to full screen. Next, select the vertices in the upper-right corner of the Wire Cage box, as shown in Figure 12.8.

Note: As you progress through this chapter, you'll notice that you're only working on one side of the model. As you'll see a little later on, when you've gotten the model's details finessed, you'll detach, mirror, and weld the selected faces to create the final rocket plane.

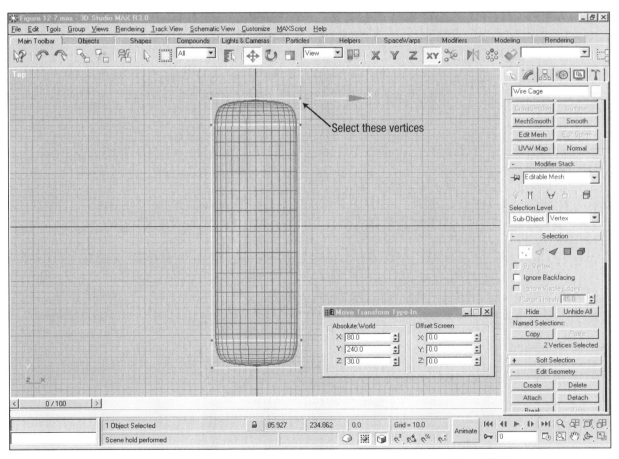

Figure 12.8

Select the vertices indicated here.

4. Right-click to bring up the Properties menu and select Move. In the Transform Type-In floater, enter a value of "400" in the Offset: Screen Y field and press Enter. As you do, you'll see the vertex move up, off screen. Click the Zoom Extents All icon to recenter the objects in your Top viewport, as shown in Figure 12.9.

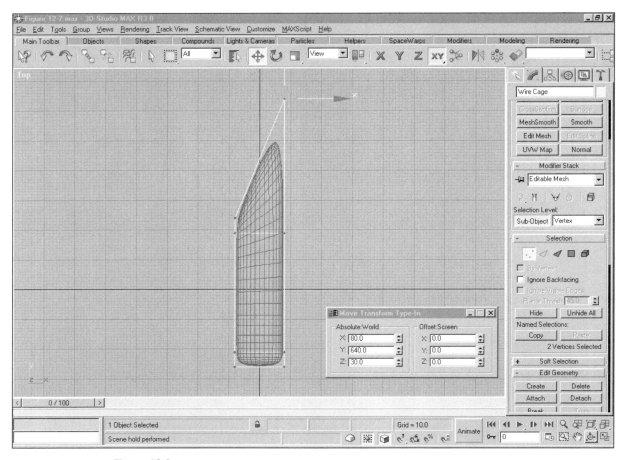

Figure 12.9

The vertices moved up on the Y-axis 400 units.

5. For this next bit, you may want to zoom back into the geometry in your scene somewhat. You're going to extrude some faces and start building the left (port) wing of the plane. From the Modify panel, select Sub-Object: Polygon again and then select the middle row of faces on the left side of the wire cage model, as shown in Figure 12.10.

6. Return to the Modify panel, go down to Extrude, enter a value of "5.0", and press Enter. As you do, you'll see a slight bulge extend out the middle-left side of the craft, as viewed from the Top viewport. This first extrusion serves as the wing "root" where it joins the fuselage.

7. Now, to edit the wing properly (and see what you're doing), you need to return to your four viewports. Press the W key (or click the Min/Max icon) to return to your four viewports. Activate your Left viewport, then from the toolbar, select Non-Uniform Scale from the Scale flyout (or pop-down) menu.

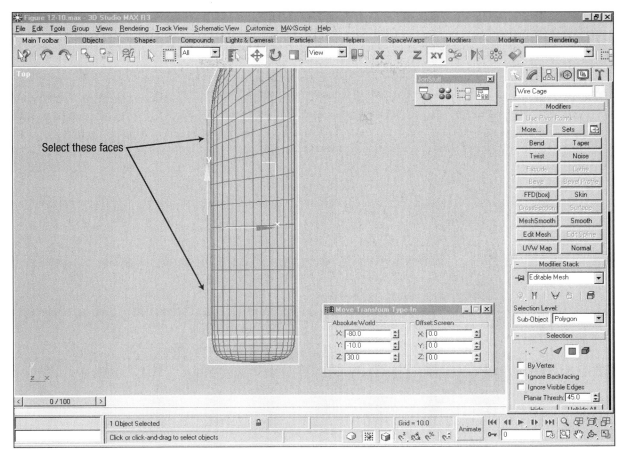

Select these faces

Figure 12.10
Select the middle row of faces.

8. With the Left viewport active, go to the Transform Type-In floater and enter a value of "25.0" in the Y field. This will squash the selected face down to one-quarter of its original height.

9. Return to the Modify panel, make sure the Extrude button is still selected, type in a value of "200", and press Enter. As you do, you'll see a flattened, rounded-off wing extend out of the left side of the ship, as shown in Figure 12.11.

Sharp Corners: Fixing The Wingtip

Okay, so the preceding example doesn't look too much like a wing, yet; it looks like a tongue. At this point, you may be thinking, "Yeah, MeshSmooth is cool; it makes nice, smooth organic shapes. But what if I want to make certain parts of my model have sharper corners? I don't want my rocket plane to have these big Dumbo ears sticking out the side of it!"

There are two ways to sharpen the edges of your geometry using MeshSmooth. First, you can extrude specific faces again, but only a short distance, so that

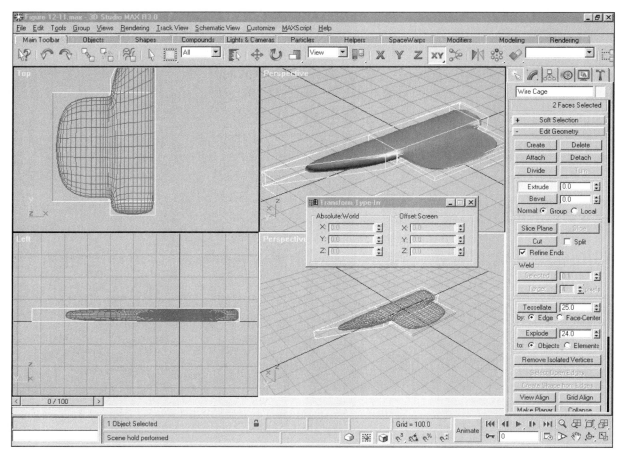

Figure 12.11

Another face extrusion begins to form the wing.

the resultant smooth faces have far less space in which to curve. The second option is to use MeshSmooth's NURMS feature and change the weighting on specific vertices.

At the moment, you'll work just with face extrusion to create sharper angles. (Again, in the next chapter, you'll see how to tweak your models with NURMS.) To begin, follow these steps:

1. Activate the Top viewport and click on the Non-Uniform Scale icon again. From the Transform Type-In menu, type "50.0" in the Offset: World Y field and press Enter. You'll see the wing become more pointed. Click on the Move icon, and in the Transform Type-In menu, enter a value of "–200" in the Y field. This moves the end of the wing down, as shown in Figure 12.12.

2. Okay, now you want the end of the wing to be squared off, so return to the Modify menu, select Extrude, and enter a value of "10". Press

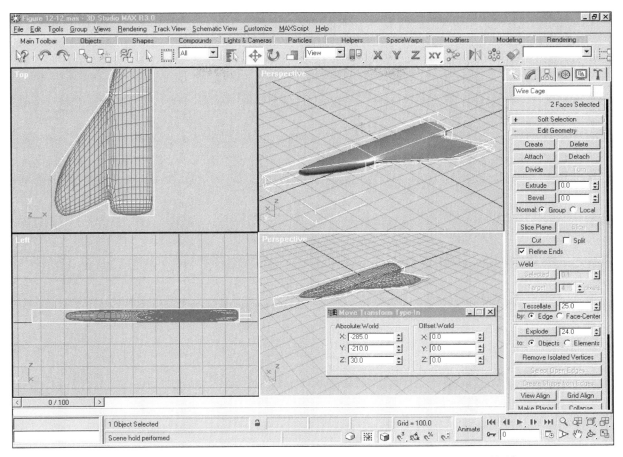

Figure 12.12

Use the Transform Type-In menu to move selected vertices and faces precisely.

Enter. As you do, you'll see the wingtip flatten out, as shown in Figure 12.13. (Note that, for clarity, the figure shows a close-up of the wing as seen in the Top viewport.)

3. Before you create the vertical stabilizer, you need to move this selected face down a bit along the Top Y-axis. Activate your Top viewport and enlarge it to full screen, then zoom in somewhat to see a close-up portion of the wing (similar to Figure 12.13). Right-click to bring up the Properties menu, select Move (if it's not already selected), then go to the Transform Type-In menu. Enter a value of "–25" in the Y field and press Enter. You'll see the selected wingtip faces move down somewhat.

4. Return to the Modify panel, make sure Extrude is selected, and enter a value of "5.0". You should see the wingtip extrude out slightly again and flatten out a little more. Click on and hold on the Scale

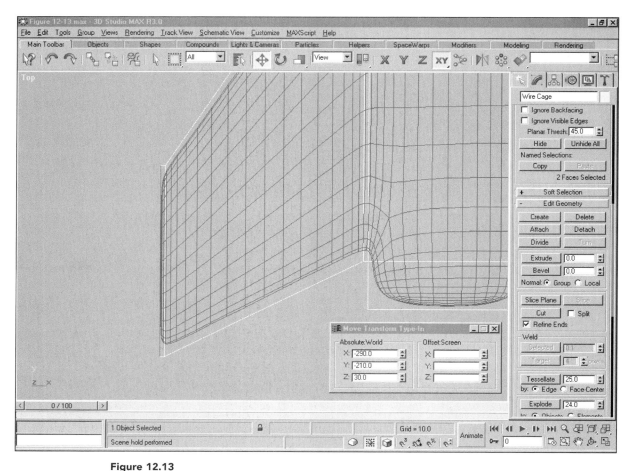

Figure 12.13

Extruding the selected face only a small amount flattens out the wingtip.

flyout from the toolbar, change it to Uniform Scale, and enter a value of 75 percent in the Transform Type-In menu. This will create a nice, tapered end for the wingtip.

5. Now, before you continue, select Edit|Hold to hold your scene in its present form (you'll see why in a moment).

Your next step is to build the vertical stabilizers.

Building The Vertical Stabilizers

Now that the wingtip looks the way you want it to, you need to extrude faces from the top, outer edge of the wing to create the vertical control surfaces. Here's how:

1. In the Top viewport, make sure you're zoomed in on the wingtip, then click on the top, middle polygon at the wingtip, as shown in Figure 12.14. Do *not* draw a bounding box around these middle faces. Simply select the top, middle face alone.

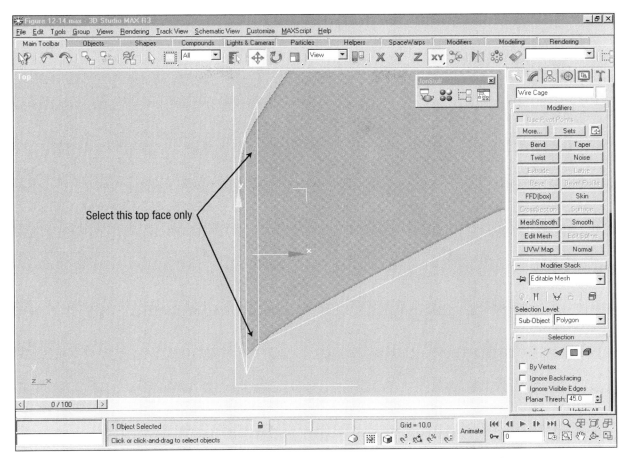

Select this top face only

Figure 12.14

The proper selected face to extrude for the vertical stabilizer. (For clarity in this figure, the high-res rocket plane model is displayed in Shaded mode with a translucent material applied.)

2. Return to the Modify panel, make sure the Extrude button is selected, type in a value of "100", and press Enter. As you do, you'll see (in the Top viewport) that new faces have been generated at the wingtip.

3. Press the W key (or the Min/Max Toggle icon) to return to your four viewports, then change the Left viewport to a Front view (press the F key) and zoom into the wingtip area to take a look at the vertical stabilizer. It should resemble Figure 12.15.

As you've probably guessed, this is wrong. You don't want the vertical stabilizer to have such a thick base. What you need to do is create a much sharper fillet where the vertical fin begins to extrude out from the top end of the wing.

As with the wingtip example you did earlier, you need to extrude this top face only a short distance to create a small fillet and then extrude again to create the main vertical fin. Step 4 starts the extrude process.

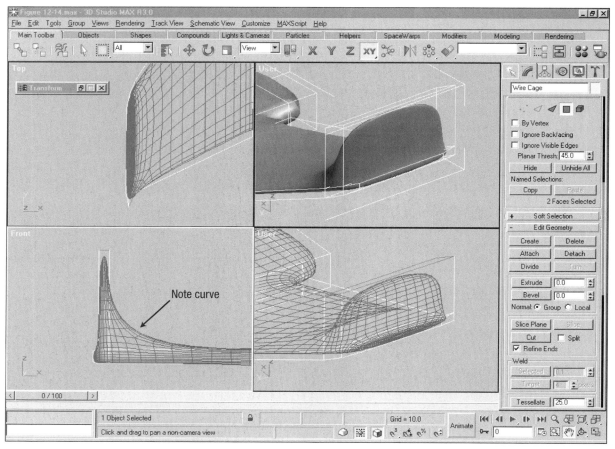

Figure 12.15

The extruded vertical stabilizer. Note that the extreme curve in the top surface of the wing stretches up to the top of the fin.

4. First, select Edit|Fetch, and fetch your scene from the point before you extruded the vertical fin. (If you can undo this extrusion successfully, do that instead.)

5. Before you extrude the fin again, press the W key to return to your four viewports. Change your Left viewport to a Front view and zoom in on the wingtip, similar to what's shown in Figure 12.15.

6. Return to the Modify panel. With the Extrude button selected, type in a value of "1.0" and press Enter. You should see a slight nub extend out from the top of the wingtip. Type in "100" and press Enter again. You should now see a new vertical fin appear, but with a much tighter fillet between the base of the fin and the wingtip, as shown in Figure 12.16.

7. Now, you're ready to finish the fin. Activate your Front viewport, and press the L key to change it to a Left viewport (you may have to click

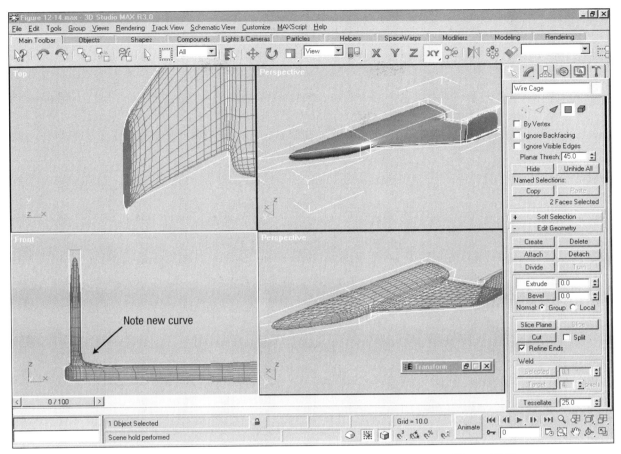

Figure 12.16

Creating a short, initial extrusion produces a tighter fillet at the base of the vertical fin.

the Zoom Extents icon to center the geometry in your Left viewport). Select the Move icon (or right-click and choose it from the Properties menu) and then, in the Transform Type-In menu, type "100" into the X field and press Enter. The fin slants back, away from the leading edge of the wing, or off to the right as viewed from the Left viewport.

8. From the toolbar, select the Scale flyout, select Non-uniform Scale. In the Transform Type-In menu, type "50" in the X field and press Enter. This tapers the vertical stabilizer at the top.

9. Return to the Modify panel, enter a value of "5.0" in the Extrude field, and press Enter. This will flatten out the top of the vertical fin and turn it into a more conventional aircraft shape, as shown in Figure 12.17.

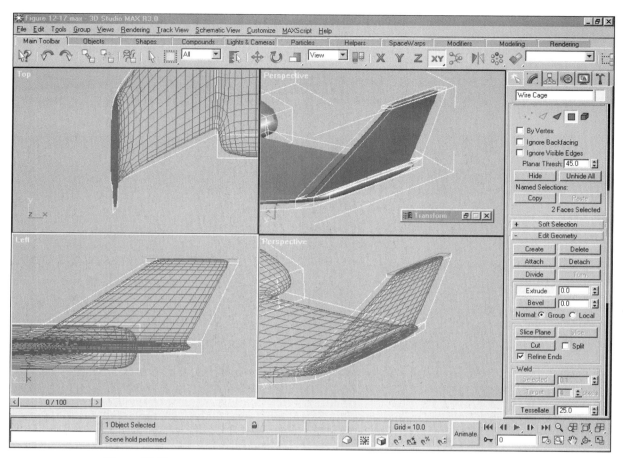

Figure 12.17

The final design for the vertical stabilizer.

Making It Symmetrical

You've now got the basic shape of the rocket plane model, but you're getting a little tired of looking at only one side of the thing. To better gauge the final look of the model, you need to mirror the smoothed details from the left side to the right side and then stitch the model back together. Here's how:

1. For safety, select Edit|Hold, and hold your present scene. (You want to be able to undo this work if you don't get this right the first time.)

2. Enlarge your Top viewport to full screen and press the Zoom Extents All icon to center the plane geometry in your scene. You should still be in Sub-Object: Polygon mode, so draw a bounding box rectangle around the faces running down the far right of the low-res wire cage model. When you have them selected, press Delete; you'll see the MeshSmoothed faces of the Rocket Plane geometry suddenly stretch

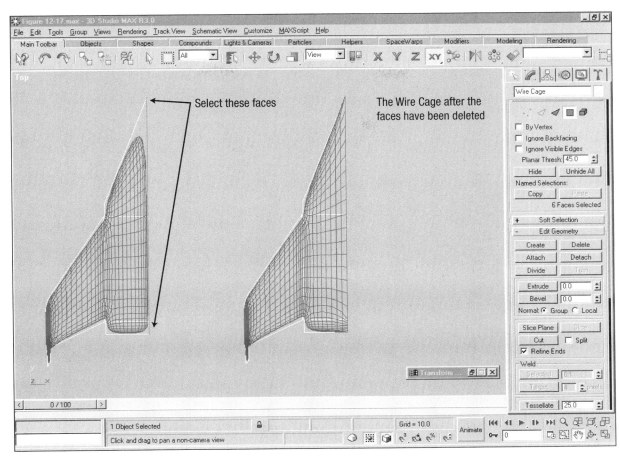

Figure 12.18

On the left, the selected faces of the Wire Cage object, and on the right, the results after you delete those faces. (Figure modified for clarity.)

out to the open "hole" of the Wire Cage mesh. Both the before and after images are shown in Figure 12.18.

3. Now comes the tricky part. You need to mirror both pieces of geometry to create the final smoothed fuselage. Press the H key to bring up the Select By Name menu, select All to choose both the wire cage and rocket plane models, and click on Select. Both pieces of geometry should be selected.

4. Click on the Mirror Selected Object icon on your toolbar. When the Mirror: Screen Coordinates menu appears, make sure Mirror Axis: X is selected, and under Clone Selection, choose Copy. Then, click on Okay. You should have a mirrored duplicate of the Wire Cage and Rocket Plane geometry, as shown in Figure 12.19.

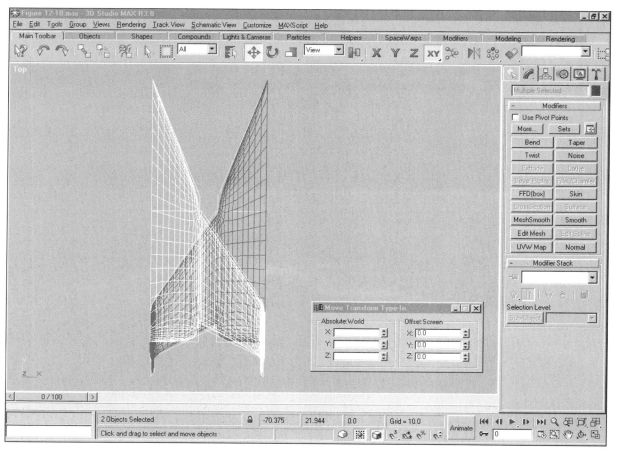

Figure 12.19

The mirrored, duplicated Wire Cage and Rocket Plane geometry, ready for attachment.

5. Now, you need to align the selected right (or starboard) side objects with the left side objects. Make sure your Transform gizmo is displayed, press the spacebar to lock your selection, and drag the selected objects on the X-axis to the right until the selected objects'

A DARK MATERIALS SECRET REVEALED

Here's a bit of news that typically surprises many MAX newbies: 99 percent of the time, I *never* use Multi/Sub-Object Mapping for my models. I find it to be incredibly cumbersome for most tasks, and when I see newcomers to MAX struggling with Material ID numbers and assignments, I ask them why they're making their life harder than it needs to be. Yes, there are instances (especially in creating graphics for low-polygon computer games) where you need to use Multi/Sub-Object Mapping, but when you're doing work for stills, game cinematics, or video, treat your 3D models as if they were plastic model kits. Cut them into separate, logical pieces and apply custom UVW mapping coordinates and individual materials to each piece. Then, link them to a dummy object, Group them, or reattach them, but without welding the vertices of the final model. (To eliminate the appearance of a seam between the pieces, apply a Smoothing modifier to the entire selected model.) You can always detach the pieces again later using the Sub-Object: Element feature.

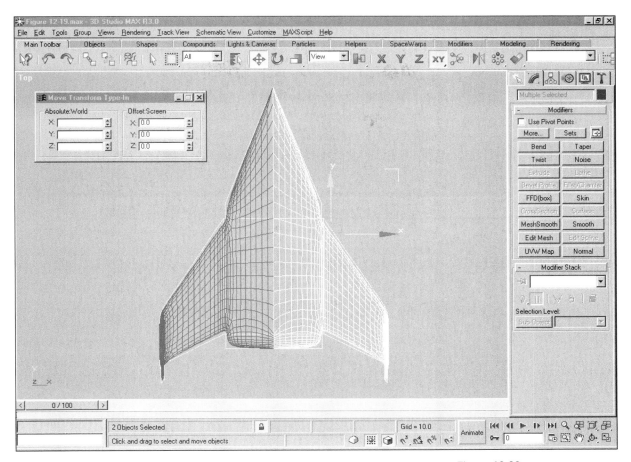

Figure 12.20

Aligning the mirrored objects.

left vertical edge is lined up with the right vertical edge of the original objects, as shown in Figure 12.20.

6. With the Top viewport still active, select the Region Zoom icon and draw a bounding box around the tip of the rocket plane to zoom in closely to the split model pieces. The two halves are probably not completely aligned, so click on the Restrict To X icon on your toolbar and move the selected geometry over slightly to the right until it's lined up more precisely with the unselected geometry, as shown in Figure 12.21.

7. Once you have the selected objects lined up more precisely, click the Zoom Extents icon to center the scene geometry in your Top viewport and then press the spacebar again to unlock the selected geometry. Press the H key to bring up the Select By Name menu, click on Wire Cage01, and click on Select.

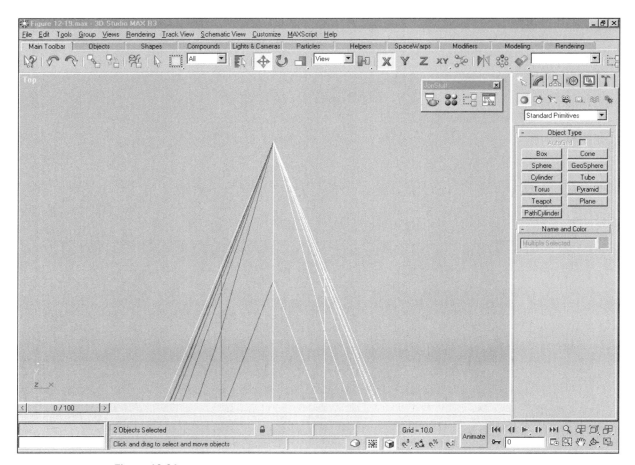

Figure 12.21

Aligning the selected objects with greater precision.

TROUBLE WELDING VERTICES?

If you have trouble welding your centerline vertices using this MeshSmooth proxy technique, your Weld tolerance may be too low. You can increase the Weld tolerance amount in the Modify panel, or you can set Non-Uniform Scale to scale the selected vertices toward each other on one axis (to pinch them together) and then weld them.

8. Go to the Modify menu, and under Edit Geometry, click on Attach. Then, either click on the original wire cage model (make sure you don't accidentally click on either of the rocket plane pieces) or use the Select By Name menu to select the correct object. The Wire Cage01 model is now attached to the original wire cage.

Fusing The Parts

At this point, you're ready to "fuse" the two parts. To do so, follow these steps:

1. Return to the Modify menu and select Sub-Object: Vertex. In the Top viewport, draw a bounding box vertically down the centerline vertices of the Wire Cage geometry, as shown in Figure 12.22 (make sure you don't select any other vertices).

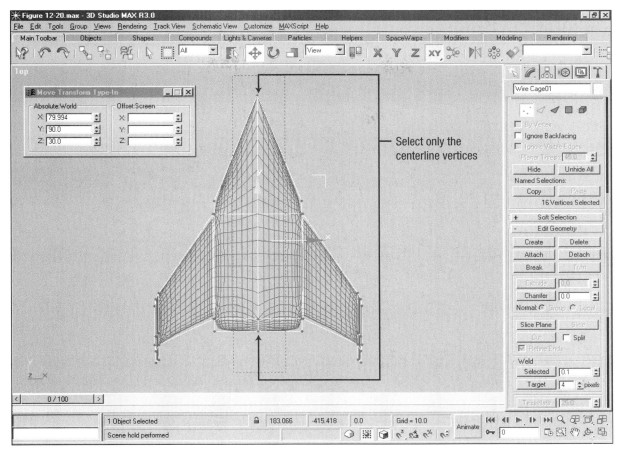

Figure 12.22
Selecting only the centerline
vertices.

2. Return to the Modify panel, and under Weld, click on the Selected
   button.

   When you do, you should see something interesting: A new,
   smoothed, bilaterally symmetrical rocket plane model is created. In
   addition, you have a "leftover" original half of the rocket plane
   model, with one sharp, open side remaining.

3. Because you don't need this spurious half-plane, you can discard it.
   Click on the Sub-Object: Vertex button again to turn it off, then click
   on the half-Rocket Plane geometry (or select it from the Select By
   Name menu) and press Delete to get rid of it. (You'll see the correct
   geometry to select in Figure 12.23.)

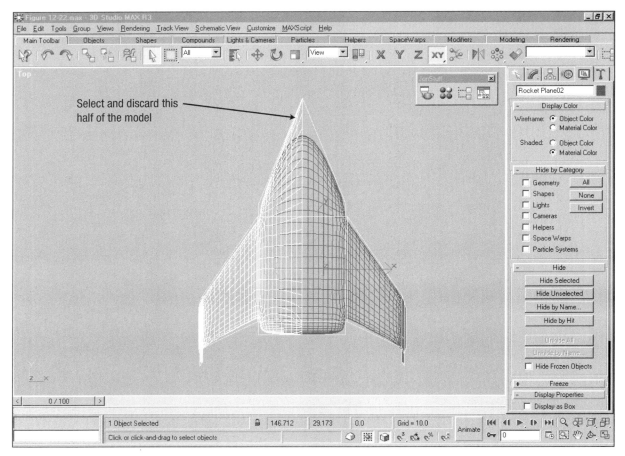

Figure 12.23

Select and discard the half-Rocket Plane geometry.

4. Although you might like the overall look of the rocket plane, the fuselage seems a little wide. You can thin it down on the X-axis (in the Top viewport) by selecting all the vertices left of the centerline and using the Transform Type-In menu to move them on the X-axis to the right, say, 50 units. Then, deselect the vertices, select all the vertices to the right of the centerline, and with the Transform Type-In menu, move them to the left X: -50 units. The rocket plane (before and after) should now look like Figure 12.24.

Creating The Cockpit

Now, you're ready to create the cockpit, as shown here:

1. Select the Wire Cage01 geometry and go to the Modify panel. Select Sub-Object: Polygon, and in the Top viewport, single-click on the top

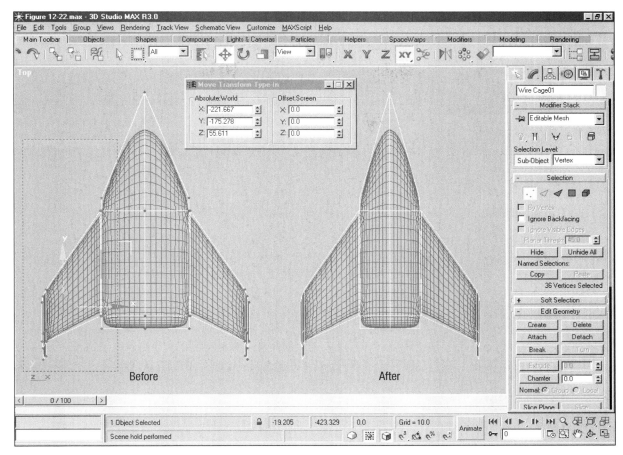

Figure 12.24

Thinning down the
fuselage geometry.

four polygons of the model, starting at the nose of the plane and
working down. Don't select the bottom two polygons, near where the
engines will be, and don't draw a bounding box around the fuselage
of the Wire Cage01 object—that would select the sides as well. The
correct faces are shown in Figure 12.25.

2. Go to the Modify panel, click the Extrude button, type in a value
   of "25", and press Enter. Select the Non-Uniform Scale icon from
   your toolbar, and from the Transform Type-In menu, enter "25" in
   the Offset: Screen X field and "50" in the Y field. As you do, you'll
   see the top faces of the plane stretched toward the center of the
   aircraft.

3. Go to the Modify panel, type a value of "25" in Extrude, and press
   Enter. When you're finished, click the W key again (or the Min/Max

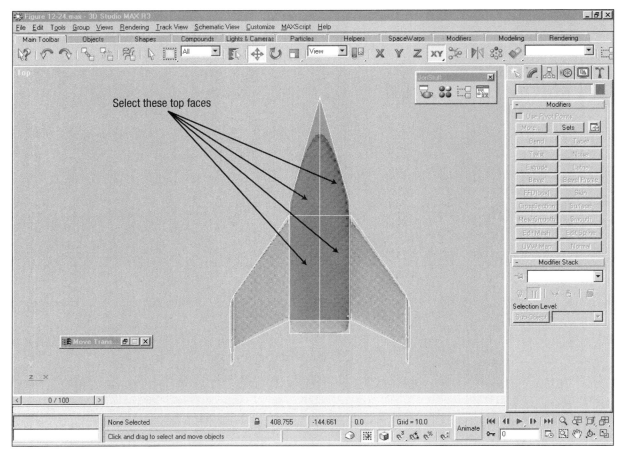

Figure 12.25

Select these top faces to begin creating the cockpit. (The rocket plane model is shown in translucent shaded mode for clarity.)

Toggle icon) to return to your four viewports. Your desktop should resemble Figure 12.26.

4. Now, the top of the cockpit is still somewhat flat, and the leading edge of it could probably be more rounded off instead of pointy. Because this is a matter of personal taste, you might perform an Edit|Hold on your current scene and then push and pull specific vertices around the cockpit area until you get the effect you want. When you're finished, you can save your current work to your local \3DSMAX3\SCENES directory (call it ROCKETPLANE2, say) and then continue.

Building The Engines

Now, as you'll remember from the beginning of this chapter, you loaded a completed rocket plane model from this book's companion CD-ROM and examined it. I built that model the same way you've just created your current

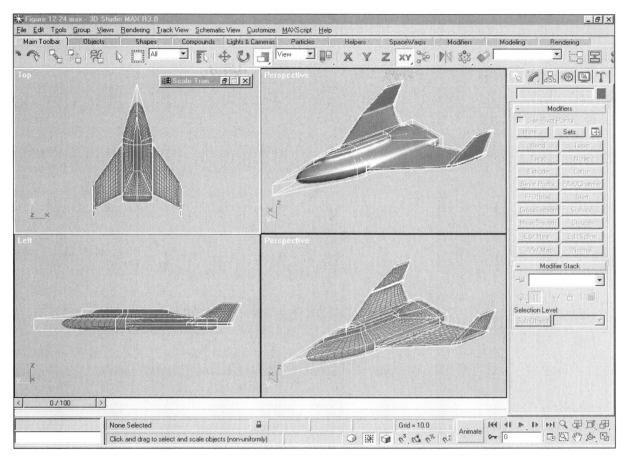

Figure 12.26

The rocket plane with the extruded cockpit.

Rocket Plane geometry, although there are some cosmetic differences based on how specific faces and vertices have been extruded, moved, or welded.

Because you should already have a good grasp of how this MeshSmooth sculpting process works, I'll simply give you some basic instructions on creating the engine exhausts. The back end of the Wire Cage01 model (between the wings) is divided into two rectangular faces. You'll perform the same operation on each one to create the thrusters:

1. Select your Wireframe Perspective viewport and enlarge it to full screen. Using the Arc Rotate icon, rotate around the geometry so you can see the back of the craft, looking down on it in a three-quarter view.

2. From the Modify panel, make sure Sub-Object: Polygon is selected, then select the left-side end polygon of the fuselage, as shown in Figure 12.27.

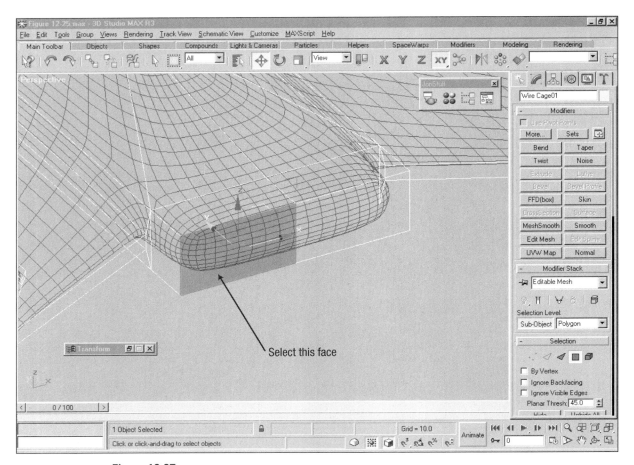

Figure 12.27

The correct face for the left engine thruster.

3. Okay, here are the quick procedures to create the left thruster:

• Extrude the selected face 75 units.

• Use Uniform-Scale to scale the selected face 90 percent (use the Transform Type-In menu).

• Extrude the face again 1.0 units.

• Use Uniform-Scale to scale the selected face 80 percent.

• Extrude the face again –75 units (this will push it inward).

• Extrude the face again –1.0 units, then use Uniform-Scale to scale it 95 percent. This will flatten out the inner surfaces of the thruster.

When you're done with the left polygon, select the end polygon on the right and repeat the preceding steps. Your finished engine thrusters should look like Figure 12.28.

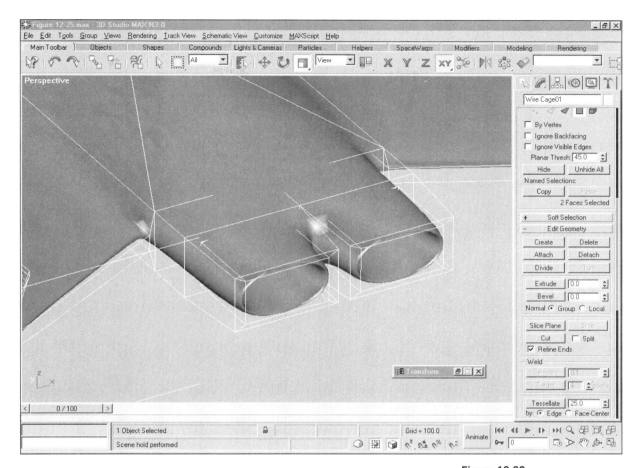

Figure 12.28
The finished engine thrusters.

At this point, you can continue to modify the model or collapse it into an Editable Mesh object and begin applying materials to it. For smooth-skinned models such as this, I typically use Sub-Object: Face mode and the Lasso selection tool, select specific components of the model, detach their faces, name them appropriately (Cockpit, Left Vertical Fin), and map each piece separately.

4. If you want, save this model to your local \3DSMAX3\SCENES directory again as ROCKETPLANE2.MAX.

Moving On

Now that you've seen how to use MeshSmooth to sculpt inorganic models, you'll see how you can use it for organic ones as well. In the next chapter, you'll examine MeshSmooth's new NURMS feature and see how you can use its vertex weighting capabilities to create sharper angles on your smoothed models.

You'll then see how MAX Release 3's new Skin and Flex modifiers can help you animate your MeshSmoothed creations.

MeshSmooth II: NURMS, Skin, and Flex

By Ken Allen Robertson

In the next few chapters, we'll examine some powerful tools for complex character modeling (such as Surface Tools in Chapter 15) and facial animation (with the new Morpher modifier in Chapter 14). But in this chapter, we're going to explore the major modifiers that allow you to breathe new life into characters at a level never before possible within MAX: Skin and Flex.

An Introduction To NURMS

In the preceding chapter, we took an in-depth look at the wonders of subdivision surface modeling, better known in MAX as MeshSmooth. But, along with most other features in MAX, MeshSmooth has been turbo-charged with a new feature that allows modelers unprecedented control over the look of smoothed models. That new feature is better known as NURMS.

For MAX Release 3, Discreet has added several modifications to the original MeshSmooth modifier. First, they've increased the number of smoothing iterations (the old maximum value was 4). In addition, they've added the ability to have different iteration levels in the interactive workspace and the renderer (allowing you to work faster at a lower level of smoothing, yet render at a very high level). But the most curious addition is the new radio button right at the top of the panel marked NURMS.

The most astute MAX users will undoubtedly notice the similarity between this strange acronym and NURBS. And rightfully so; the two do share a core modeling methodology.

NURBS stands for non-uniform rational b-spline, a long complex name with a rather simple meaning. "Non-uniform" means that curvature can be at varying levels in various places of the model. "Rational" means that this curvature can be defined through mathematical formula (fortunately, this doesn't have to be manually defined by the modeler or we'd all have to be rocket scientists). "B-spline" means simply a spline that has multiple curves, like the letter *B*. NURBS models are created by skinning multiple curves, and curvature can be defined by adjusting the weight of control vertices (CVs) along the defining splines. The higher a CV's weight in relation to its neighbors, the more it tends to draw (or pull) the curve to itself, resulting in a sharper level of curvature at that particular CV. Neighboring CVs that have the same weight value will attract the curvature equally.

NURMS stands for Non-Uniform Rational MeshSmooth. If we borrow from the NURBS definition, we already have an idea of what "non-uniform" and "rational" stand for. With the inclusion of the word MeshSmooth, we know that this modifier affects polygonal objects rather than surfaced b-splines.

But, just like its namesake, NURMS uses weighted control vertices to define curvature. The higher a control vertice's weight (again in relation to its neighbors), the more it wants to "pull" the mesh toward it, resulting in sharper curvature. Although it doesn't sound terribly impressive in this simple definition, the results can be amazing.

One of the greatest challenges with MeshSmooth modeling has been the fact that the MeshSmooth modifier smoothes equally across all of the visible edges of an object. If you had two edges far away from each other, the result was a subtle gentle curve. If you had two edges fairly close together, the curve amount was simply squashed into the smaller area. To create harsher edges or sharper curves, one had to add more geometry and position it in such a way that curvature was defined in a smaller area.

However, with NURMS and weighted vertices, you can now create varying levels of curvature within the smoothed surface with less geometry. It's more for less, and you've got to love that!

Okay, enough talking about the theoretics. Let's put all this theory into practice.

Working With NURMS: The Dragon Head

You'll start working with a character that will become a fast friend over the next few chapters: a cartoon dragon. You'll be working with slight variations of this character all through the exercises in this chapter. To start, do the following:

1. From the \CHAP_13 directory of this book's companion CD-ROM, open the file called DRAGON_NURMS.MAX. When you open the file, you'll find the cartoon dragon head, shown in Figure 13.1. This

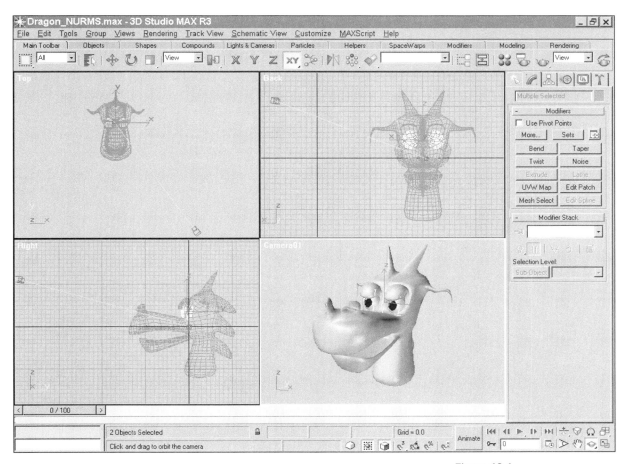

Figure 13.1
The contents of the Dragon NURMS file.

model was designed and constructed by Scot Tumlin and Jon A. Bell using the MeshSmooth techniques described in Chapter 12. It started out as a simple box and, with careful face extrusion and vertex welding, has become the fire-breathing cutie that you see now. The model already has the MeshSmooth modifier applied to it, using the Quad output option introduced in MAX 2. (Feel free to see how the low-res mesh looks by dropping down the Modifier stack.) Also present are a targeted camera and the dragon's eyes.

2. Click on the Dragon Smooth model to select it, then go to the Modify panel and click on the NURMS radio button at the top of the MeshSmooth Modifier panel (in the MeshSmooth Options area). You'll see some slight changes to the model, but some big changes will take place in the MeshSmooth panel itself. The entire Smoothing Options panel (with the Strength and Relax spinners) becomes grayed out.

3. Now, let's start making some adjustments to our friendly dragon. First, go to the Right viewport and locate the three bony plates, or scales, protruding from the back of the neck. Notice that they are rather rounded off. You'll want to make these a bit sharper, giving the dragon more chiseled scales. Slide the Modifier panel up until you locate the area labeled Display/Weighting (or right-click to bring up the Modifier menu and go to the Display/Weighting level of the rollout). Place a checkmark in the box marked Display Control Mesh. An orange-colored representation of the low-res mesh (before Smoothing) appears.

4. Turn on the Sub-Object button and select Vertex from the drop-down list. The vertices of the control mesh now appear as blue dots. Notice also that all of the Transforms on the Top toolbar (Move, Rotate, and Scale) become grayed out, indicating that you can't reposition anything you select.

5. Scroll back down the Modifier panel to the Display/Weighting menu again. In the Top viewport, use the Fence Zoom feature to zoom in on the vertices that run down the middle of the neck scales. Select the vertices down the middle of the scales, go to the Display/Weighting area of the Modifier panel, and in the Weight box, type a weight value of 5.0. In the Right viewport, notice how the scales have gotten sharper, with more defined points at the ends and the mesh moving closer to the vertices whose weights you modified.

6. Now, you'll adjust the bottom of the neck to make it a cleaner line. Select all of the vertices on the bottom of the neck, go to the Modifier

panel, and change their weight to 10.0. Notice how the neck flattens out at the bottom.

7. Now it's your turn. Select a few vertices, change their weights, and notice the changes. In particular, pay attention to vertices that lie at the extents of various features (the lips, jaw, nostrils, and so on). Adjust the vertices on the eyelids, alternating between the vertices on the outside of the eyelids and those closest to the nose. Try setting some vertex weights below 1.0 as well, creating the opposite effect of a higher weight. Indulge yourself!

If you ever find yourself unhappy with the results, just change the weights back to their original settings or clear the slate by clicking on the Reset All Weights button. A sample of what NURMS can do in a very short amount of time is shown in Figures 13.2 and 13.3. The original dragon head is on the right side in the darker material. Notice the difference in the personality of the two models.

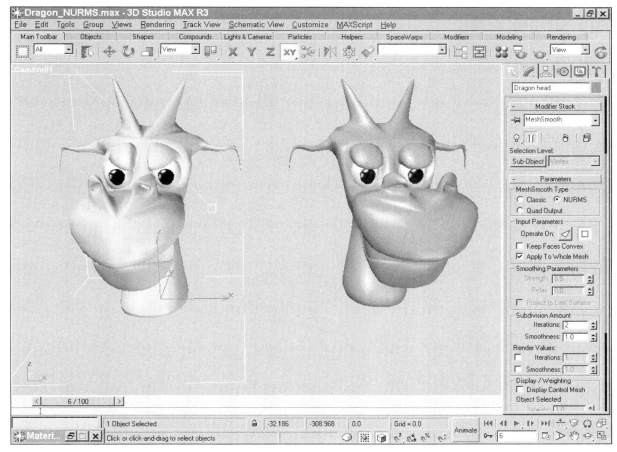

Figure 13.2

The NURMS-adjusted dragon and the original model, version 1.

Figure 13.3

The NURMS-adjusted dragon and the original model, version 2.

The Skin Modifier

Since the first release of MAX, a single question has plagued MAX users, neophytes and hardened professionals alike. The question has been about the Bones system built into MAX. Until MAX Release 3, the built-in Bones system served mainly to help animate jointed models and to support third-party polygonal deformation systems, such as Digimation's Bones Pro. For advanced character animation and skeletal deformation, Kinetix (now Discreet) relied on MAX users buying the Character Studio plug-in.

However, with 3D Studio MAX Release 3, Discreet has included several skeletal deformation systems that enable users to produce basic character animations and polygonal deformations. These are in the form of the Skin and Flex modifiers. The Skin modifier allows MAX's built-in bones to distort polygonal geometry; the Flex modifier provides secondary animation characteristics, such as wiggling flesh, bobbing antennas, and so on.

In a moment, you'll take a look at these modifiers. But first, you'll take a brief detour to look at the general principles of skeletal deformation in MAX.

Skeletal Deformation: The Basics

For those unfamiliar with the idea behind skeletal deformation, here's a brief primer.

Almost every creature on the face of the Earth (with the exception of insects, arthropods, and invertebrates) would be a simple gooey bag of liquid without the aid of a hardened interior skeleton (or endoskeleton). The skeleton defines bodily structure from the inside out, providing support to the bags of fluids and tissue we call bodies. The hardened bones are linked together with ligaments and tendons (so they don't float away from each other), and are moved by a complex muscle structure running between the points along the length of the bones.

When a muscle contracts, it draws the midpoint of one bone toward another, but because the ligaments and tendons bind the ends of bones together, the effect is a rotation of one bone around another at their respective end points. The muscle itself maintains a constant volume, getting thicker and shorter when contracted, longer and thinner when relaxed. The massive number of muscles beneath the skin keep us from looking like a balloon animal wrapped around a flagpole. Now, granted, physiology is a bit more complicated than this (okay, it's a *lot* more complicated), but these are the basics of how we move around the world.

In the world of 3D animation, the concept of using a few hundred constant volume muscles to deform a single skin is impractical at best, due to CPU calculation requirements and memory constraints. But the idea of several solid objects rotating around each other's end points (like bones in a skeleton) is a piece of cake...in fact, it's one of the most basic elements that makes 3D animation possible.

Therefore, just as skin deforms based on which bone is being moved by which muscle, a 3D mesh object can be deformed by having vertices move in relation to a bone object placed beneath the object's solid surface. Simple, huh?

Well, not quite as simple as that. Remember that our skins are deformed not *just* by the bones, but by the muscles that connect across the joints between the bones. For example, take a look at your hand. Hold it up and look at the area near the base of your fingers. Now move just one finger while holding the others still (or at least give it the old college try if your digits aren't that flexible). Notice how the skin at the top of the hand (but still below the finger joint) moves with the finger. Also, notice how the skin on the fingers on either side of the one you moved deforms as well. Skin is pretty rubbery stuff, and muscles overlap all of those joint areas, providing some pretty complex deformations. Therefore, you need something a bit more complex than just assigning vertices to bones. You need a solution that takes into account the movements of other bones in proximity to the one moving.

This solution is to add a weighted value to the vertices. More specifically, you need to add multiple weighted values for each vertex in relation to each bone. Look at your hand again. Notice that the skin on the hand at the base of the fingers doesn't move *as much* as the skin surrounding the finger itself. In fact, the farther the distance down the hand from the finger, the less the movement. But if you fold your fingers over in a waving "bye-bye" sort of movement, that skin inherits the movement completely. You could speculate that, to create this effect on a 3D object, that area of skin would have a lower weight in relation to the lower bone of the finger and a higher weighted value in relationship to the bones of the hand. Your speculation would be correct.

Simply assigning vertices to multiple bone objects is known as *absolute vertex assignment*. The process of assigning weights to vertices in relation to multiple bone objects is known as *weighted vertex assignment*. The different results provided by the two options are shown in Figure 13.4.

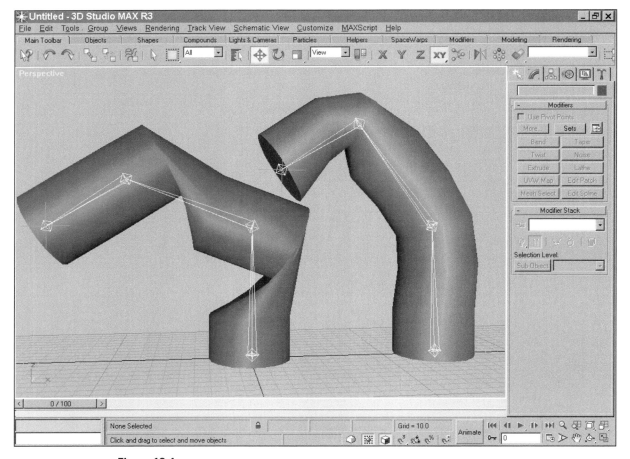

Figure 13.4

The results of an absolute vertex assignment (left) versus a weighted vertex assignment (right).

Skeletal Deformation Plug-Ins

Ever since the first release of MAX, there have been commercial options that use different methodologies to accomplish weighted skeletal deformation. The most used are Physique (part of Discreet's Character Studio) and Digimation's Bones Pro.

The deformation plug-in that gives Character Studio its deformation abilities, Physique, uses the idea of envelopes to define vertex weights. Physique uses elliptical volumes to define what vertices fall within a bone's influence. The envelopes have an inner and outer range to determine the weight value, and envelopes overlap each other at bone joints to give the illusion of muscle contraction. Users can add and manipulate various cross sections to better define a bone's area of influence.

Bones Pro uses a simple range value to determine vertex weights, but it also allows you to select any vertex (or group of vertices) and assign a weight value to them or force them to ignore/include certain bones in the weight-value calculation. This allows for very precise control over deformation in tricky areas, such as fingers and toes, where multiple vertices are in close proximity to each other but require very specific assignments to particular bones (you don't want part of one finger to wander off with another).

Both of these plug-ins have other features that still make them attractive options (such as the Jiggler modifier in Bones Pro 2 or the interactive muscle bulge capabilities in Physique). However, with the advent of MAX Release 3's Skin modifier, you no longer have to rely solely on these external plug-ins for advanced skeletal deformation power.

How Skin Works Its Magic

MAX Release 3's new Skin modifier, having two very powerful commercial applications to build upon, has learned from its predecessors. Like Physique, it uses elliptical envelopes to generate the basic vertex weight values. But it also gives you the ability to assign a specific weight to a selected vertex (or vertices) in relation to a particular bone object, similar to Bones Pro. But Skin doesn't stop there. It also allows you to "paint" vertex weight values with a 3D brush. This brush even has the ability to paint falloff values, meaning a weight is higher in the center of the brush and lower at the outer perimeter. With all these tools in place, Skin is a powerful tool for making correct vertex assignments and weight values in a very short amount of time. So let's put Skin to the test by adding a skeleton to our dragon's head and watching him "bust a move."

USING THE STACK EFFECTIVELY WITH SKELETAL DEFORMATION

The biggest challenge one faces when working with skeletal deformation in a complex model is proper vertex assignment. Improper vertex assignment can easily result in harsh creases when a Skinned object is animated. An easy method for minimizing the risk of this happening is to create the model low-res, exactly as you would for MeshSmooth modeling. But before you apply the MeshSmooth modifier, add the Skin modifier and make the vertex assignments. This will make assigning the vertices a much easier and cleaner process because there will be fewer of them to deal with. Animate your model, then add the MeshSmooth modifier on top of the stack. This will have the same effect as adding it lower in the stack, but the smoothing process will be applied as your model is deformed, drastically reducing the risk of those unexpected and unwelcome Skin creases. In addition, you will be able to animate the low-res model faster (toggle off the MeshSmooth modifier or make it active only in the renderer) and see the deformations in realtime.

Working With Skin: Adding Bones To The Dragon

Now that you know the basics of skeletal deformation, it's time to add some bones to the meat of the dragon:

1. Open the file in the \CHAP_13 called DRAGON_SKIN.MAX. You'll find your old friend the dragon without the MeshSmooth modifier applied but with an IK skeleton set up, complete with an animation cycle.

2. Select the dragon head object, go to the Modifier panel, and add the Skin modifier. In the Skin Modifier panel, click on the Add Bones button, and from the pop-up list, select either Bones 2–11 or the selection set Bones in the Selection Set drop-down list (both options will assign the proper Bones to the object). Then, press the Play button to watch the animation.

The head is indeed deforming with the bones, but there are a number of problems. The ear pieces are staying rooted in space, and parts of the mouth are distorting in painful ways, as shown in Figure 13.5. The eyes aren't moving with the head, but you'll fix that with another method later on.

3. Turn on the Sub-Object button to access the Bone Envelope settings. The first envelope you'll see is the last bone assigned; in this case, it's Bone11, which is at the end of the lower jaw. You'll adjust this bone later, but for now, you'll work your way up the chain.

4. In the Bone list, select Bone02. This is the first bone in the chain, the one at the base of the neck. You should see the envelope for Bone02 appear. As you can see, it doesn't completely include all of the vertices of the neck base.

VERTEX ASSIGNMENTS AND ANIMATION

Most of the time, vertex assignments are done before a skeleton is animated. However, adding just a single frame of animation can make assignments easier because it will expose where vertices are improperly assigned. Of course, you can assign vertex weights at any point in the process and the result will be applied to the whole animation, but it can bring your animation process to a halt when you find those vertices flying off in strange directions.

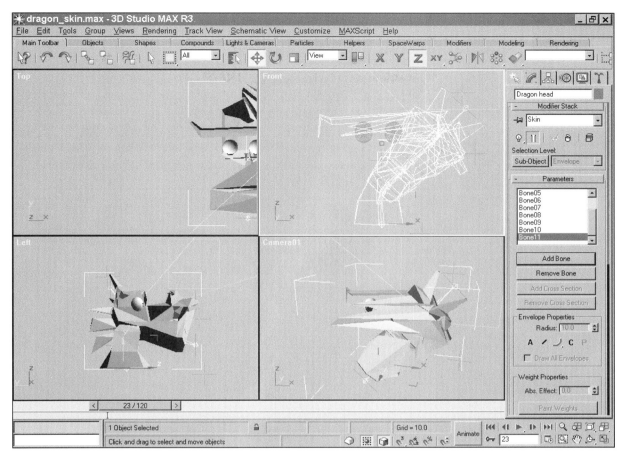

Figure 13.5
The Skin modifier applied to the head without correct vertex assignments.

5. Go into the Left viewport and zoom in on this envelope.

   There are actually two envelopes present for each bone: a red one and a brownish one. The red envelope is the area of complete influence (where vertex weights are set to a value of 1.0). The brownish envelope represents falloff, where vertex weights are interpolated from absolute (1.0) to no influence (0.0) based on their relative proximity to the inner envelope. Also notice that the vertices within the influence of an envelope take on different colors. These colors represent the weight value of the vertex. A red vertex has a value of 1.0, and a blue vertex has a value of 0.0. A yellow vertex has a value of more than 0.5 and green vertices have weights of less than 0.5—the darker the green, the lower the value.

   Each envelope also has two lines across it, with several squares on each line. These lines are called Cross-Sections (not to be confused with the Cross-Section modifier used in Surface Tools modeling, shown in Chapter 15). When you click on one of those squares, it

Note: The total weight value on a vertex always adds up to a value of 1.0, no matter how many bones are exerting influence over it. So if a value of either 1.0 or 0.0 is assigned to a vertex in relation to a particular bone, the other bones influencing it will compensate. If only two bones exert influence on a vertex, a value of 1.0 or 0.0 will cause the vertex to be affected by only one bone.

DEM BONES

Even though skeletal deformation objects (the objects inside the mesh "skin" that determine the deformation) are almost always called bones, in MAX 3, they need not actually be bone objects. In fact, any object will do. Using simple boxes as bone objects allows you to animate with forward kinematics, unlike the Bones system, which limits you to inverse kinematics. Just make sure that whatever you use for bone objects has a proper hierarchy in place and uses very simple geometry. No matter how complex your bone object may be, Skin only cares about its volume when it generates the envelopes.

will turn bright pink, indicating that you are now editing that particular Cross-Section. By moving your cursor in the active viewport, you cause the Cross-Section to expand or contract, increasing or decreasing the influence radius of that particular bone.

In addition, you can select a Cross-Section point and adjust its radius by using the Radius spinner at the top of the Envelope Parameters menu in the Skin Modifier panel. By selecting the squares on the bone just above the bottom cross section or below the top cross section, you can rotate the angle of the entire envelope. You can also create new Cross-Sections points between the two that are initially created within the envelope. With these options, you have a great deal of control over exactly how a bone's influence is defined.

Now, with all that in mind, let's get back to the business of getting the head to behave properly with the underlying Bone structure.

6. In the Bone list, select Bone02 again. The envelope for this bone should appear.

7. In any viewport, select one of the squares on the bottom Cross-Section and move it until it expands over the vertices on the lower neck scale, or bone plate. Do the same with the upper Cross-Section on Bone02 until the envelope resembles Figure 13.6. You may also wish to rotate this envelope (at the top) so that it tilts toward the back of the head, reducing the influence on the vertices of the lower jaw. It isn't necessary for proper performance, but it can yield some nice results.

8. Continue this process with Bones 3 through 5 (all of the neck and head bones, none of the mouth bones), extending the envelopes as necessary to cover all of the vertices of the head (including the ear pieces). Do not expand the envelopes of Bones 3 through 5 over the mouth vertices any more than is necessary to cover the main part of the head.

9. Now, play the animation to check and see that the ear pieces and the neck scales are behaving with the underlying bone structure the way they should.

10. At this point, let's start getting the dragon's mouth fixed. Select the Bone at the tip of the upper jaw (Bone08). Move the Cross-Section points until the outer envelope covers the vertices of the nostrils and (in the Top viewport) covers the vertices on the outside of the upper jaw.

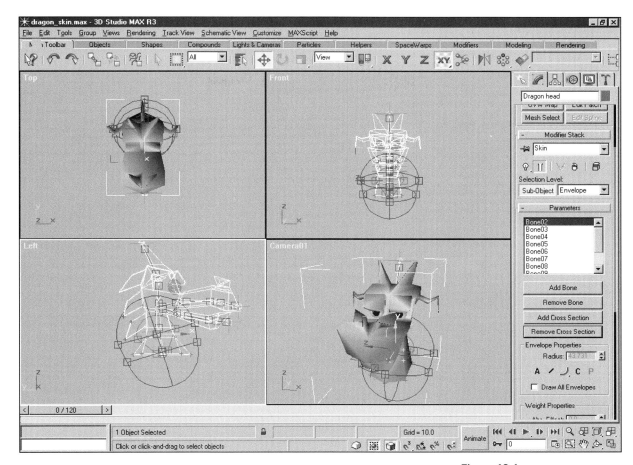

Figure 13.6
The envelope for the first bone.

11. Play the animation to see the results.

    You've solved most of the problems by now. All of the vertices are
    moving with the bones, and none are left hanging in space the way
    many vertices were when you first assigned the bones. However, you
    have a new problem. When the envelopes engulf every vertex they
    should, they also grab vertices they shouldn't. For example, the
    bones of the upper jaw are influencing the vertices of the lower jaw
    and vice-versa. To correct this problem, simply adjusting the enve-
    lopes will be time consuming at best and impossible at worst. For
    this you need to directly access the vertices themselves and directly
    control their bone assignments.

12. Scroll the Skin Modifier panel down until you see the Filters menu.
    By default, Envelopes and Cross-Sections are checked, but Vertices is
    left off. Place a checkmark in the Vertices box and go into the Left
    viewport. With Bone08 still selected, carefully select all of the
    colored vertices that appear on the lower jaw. A small white box will

surround each of the selected vertices. These are the vertices that are receiving at least some influence for the movement of Bone08.

13. Find the Weight Properties menu in the Skin modifier menu. In the blank box next to Abs Effect (Absolute Vertex Effect), enter a value of 0.0. Notice that the selected vertices not only lose their color, but no longer appear as vertex ticks at all, indicating that they are no longer influenced by the selected bone (shown in Figure 13.7).

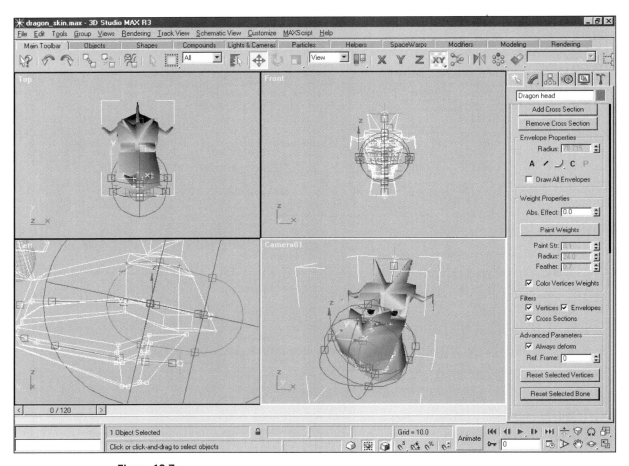

Figure 13.7

The jaw vertex assignments are assigned correctly here.

14. Play the animation again to see the result.

You can now very easily see the mouth opening and closing in the animation. However, there still appear to be some vertices on the lower jaw being affected by the upper jawbones, so you still have a bit of work to do. (Note that, when selecting vertices for absolute weight assignment, it can be helpful to turn off the filter buttons for Cross-Sections and Envelopes.)

ROAMING EYES

External eyes are often used on a cartoon character like the dragon. But how do you get them to work with skeletal movements? Simple! You use an Attachment controller! After the MeshSmooth modifier is applied, simply select the eyes (one at a time), go to the motion panel, expand the Assign Controller rollout, and select the Position controller. Click on the Assign Controller button (the green triangle with the arrow next to it) and select Attachment from the controller list. In the Attachment Parameters rollout, click on the Pick Object button and select the object you want the eyes to move with (in this case, the head). A little further down the Attachment rollout, find the Position menu. Click on the Set Position button, then left-click and hold while dragging over the dragon head mesh. The eye will travel with your mouse, aligning the eye's pivot point to the face normal of whatever polygon you position your mouse over. When you find the desired position for the eye, just release the mouse button. The eye will now stick to that face as the skeletal structure deforms the mesh. Rotate the eyes around their local axes to get the orientation just right.

The Attachment controller is just begging to be used in conjunction with boned objects like this. The results can be seen in the file DRAGON_SKINNED03.AVI in the \CHAP_13 directory on this book's companion CD-ROM.

15. Repeat the preceding step with all of the jawbones, making sure that the top bones do not influence the bottom jaw vertices and vice versa. Leave the vertices at the corner of the mouth assigned and weighted just as they are so that these vertices are equally affected by both the upper and lower jaws as well as the bones of the head.

16. Finally, turn off the Sub-Object button and apply a MeshSmooth modifier to the dragon's head. Feel free to make NURMS vertex and edge weight adjustments to the model as you did in the preceding project. Then, set Sub-Division Iterations (in the Subdivision Amount menu) to a value of 2. Render or make a preview of the animation to see the results.

The Flex Modifier

Okay, so you have complex character modeling tools and the ability to animate them with a skeleton. Now, it's time for the icing on the cake.

Reactionary motion has long been one of the primary principles of character animation. Getting reactions out of the floppier parts of a 3D character, though, is much simpler said than done...until now.

In 3D software, reactionary or secondary motion (bobbing bellies, and so on) is called *soft body dynamics*. The Dynamics system introduced in MAX 2 is called *rigid body dynamics*. To illustrate the difference between the two, imagine the differences in reactions between a bowling ball dropped on a wooden plank and a water balloon dropped on a trampoline. The former is rigid body, and the latter is soft body.

SOFT BODY PLUG-INS

MAX users wanting additional soft body dynamics control in MAX should go to the Digimation Web site (**www.digimation.com**) and look at the features for its programs, Hypermatter and Bones Pro.

With MAX 3's focus on character tools, a limited soft body system would be a natural progression from the tools you've already explored. That natural progression is incorporated in the form of MAX's Flex modifier. Flex is a limited soft body system in that it does not take into account collisions (something certainly desired in future MAX upgrades). However, it does take into account many dynamic forces not available in other 3D commercial systems, such as MAX's Wind, Gravity, and Particle Bomb features.

Flex uses the space warps available under MAX's Particles and Dynamics category to determine its effects. However, it can be very useful even without using space warps. Simply applying the modifier allows MAX to calculate flexible reactionary motion based on the simple transforms (or skeletal motions) applied to an object.

Just as in the Skin modifier, effective use of the modifier stack can make the use of Flex simple, fast, and controllable, or slow and painful. The best method is to create a low-res "proxy" version of your model (as seen in this chapter and the previous one), as you would in preparation for using MeshSmooth. Apply the Skin modifier (if necessary), *then* apply the Flex modifier. Finally, put the MeshSmooth modifier on the top of the stack, allowing it to smooth across the Flex deformations, greatly reducing the possibility of nasty folds or creases in the animation. Flex animations can also be used quite effectively on Surface Tools models by applying the modifier to the splines before surfacing.

So with that in mind, let's get to the final project of this chapter, using Flex.

Working With Flex: Blowing In The Wind

To see the effects of the Flex modifier, do the following:

1. Open the file in the \CHAP_13 directory called DRAGON_FLEX.MAX. In this file, you'll find our old friend the dragon, complete with Skin modifier and properly adjusted bone assignments. Also present is a Wind Space Warp, preset and ready for incorporation into the Flex modifier.

2. Select the dragon head object. Go to the Modify panel and apply a Flex modifier to the dragon head.

3. Play the animation. You'll notice that parts of the dragon's head now seem to flop around quite a bit more as the animation plays (to clarify the difference, you may wish to toggle the Flex modifier off using the Active/Inactive modifier toggle button).

   When you apply a Flex modifier, by default all of the vertices of the mesh are subject to reactionary motion calculations. This would be fine if you wanted the entire character to be very "gooey." However, you only want parts of the character to bounce in reaction to the skeleton. That's why Flex, similar to Skin, has weights assigned to the vertices, with adjustable values of negative 100 to positive 100. However, weight assignments are a bit counter-intuitive. A weight of positive 100 means that a vertex *is not* subject to soft body calculations, whereas a value of negative 100 means that a vertex is *completely* influenced by all possible soft body forces.

Vertices are assigned a weight by default based on their distance from a controllable Center Sub-Object (the default center is placed at the object's pivot point). The farther a vertex is from the Center Sub-Object, the lower its weight and, therefore, the higher the amount of reactionary motion it inherits. The closer the vertex, the higher the weight is set, resulting in less motion. Vertex colors are indicated in the same way they are in the Skin modifier: Lighter colors equal higher weight; darker colors equal lower weight. (A yellow vertex represents a value of 100, however, unlike the red vertices used in Skin.)

You can also "paint on" weights, the same way you can in the Skin modifier. But the most control resides in assigning absolute weights to the vertices (accessible by choosing the Weights sub-object from the Sub-Object drop-down list).

With all of these parameters in mind, let's set about making only the flexible parts of the dragon's head subject to reactionary motion.

4. Turn on the Sub-Object button and select Weights from the drop-down list. (You may have to turn on Absolute Weights to keep the value that you enter.) In the Front viewport, select all of the vertices on the main part of the head, leaving the vertices on the ear pieces unselected. In the Vertex Weights menu, enter a value of 100 in the box.

5. Now, select just the vertices on the tips of the ear pieces. Set these to a value of 0.0.

6. Select the vertices in the middle of the ear pieces and set them to a value of 50.

    You've defined the floppiest parts of the dragon's anatomy and set up a decreasing value as they move closer to the head. Now, you can define some areas that may be floppy, but not as floppy as the vertices of the ear pieces.

7. Switch to a Left viewport and select the vertices on the top of the nostrils. Set these to a weight of 80.0.

Your vertex colors should now be yellow throughout the main part of the head, darkening on the ear pieces and a little darker on the tops of the nostrils, as seen in Figure 13.8. (To see this figure in color, select File|View File and select the image 13_08.JPG from the CHAP_13\FIGURES directory of this book's companion CD-ROM.)

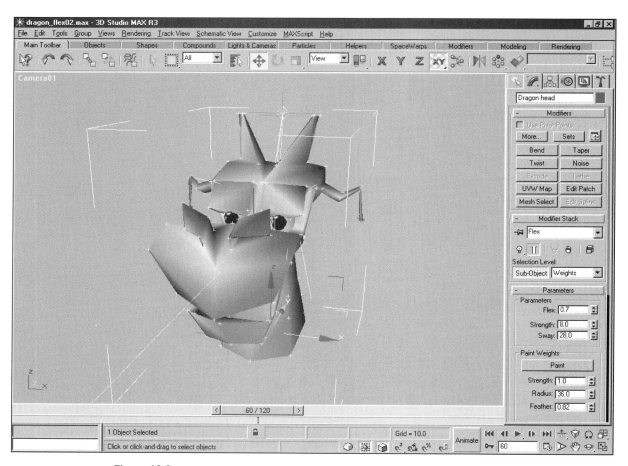

Figure 13.8

The Flex vertex weight values.

8. Scroll forward through the animation. You should be able to see the ear pieces bouncing around quite a bit and the nostrils bouncing a little.

9. For more control, go to the Parameters menu (at the top of the Flex Modifier panel) and use the following values:

   • Set Flex to 0.7. The Flex amount determines the maximum number of frames a vertex will lag behind the main motion (actually, it's the Flex amount times the vertex weight as a percentage).

- Set Strength to 8.0. Strength controls the springiness of the reactionary motion.

- Set Sway to 28.0. Sway controls how long a vertex will stay in motion before final resting (again, imagine the jiggling of a sturdy water balloon that's been dropped on a hard surface).

Now you could use just one more thing. The ear pieces appear to be swaying *through* the head as it bounces back and forth. So, in keeping with the jolly feeling of our happy dragon, let's set up a little breeze to blow through his ears.

10. Scroll down the Modifier panel and find the Advanced Parameters menu. Click on the Add Force button and click on the Wind space warp in one of your viewports. Scroll the animation forward to frame 60 and click on the Set Reference button to make the Wind force active. You should immediately see the ear pieces move back a bit, as in Figure 13.9.

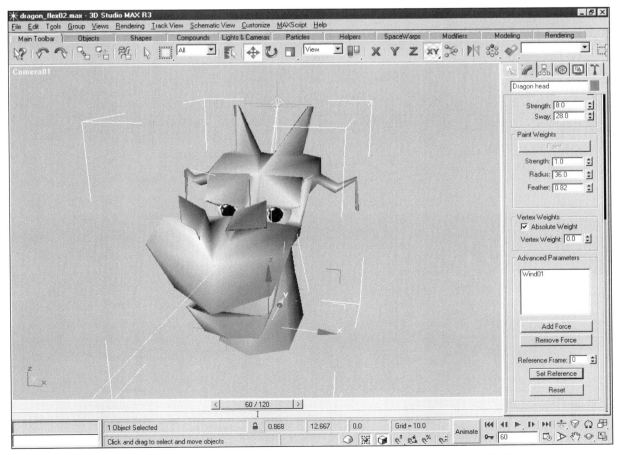

Figure 13.9
The Wind force added to the Flex parameters.

11. Play the animation and take note of the effects.

12. Finally, let's apply the MeshSmooth modifier again. This will smooth out the dragon and make him into a more pleasing, higher-resolution version.

13. Feel free to make any NURM weight adjustments that you wish, or you can render or preview the animation. If you want to see the final effect, select File|View File and choose the DRAGON_FLEX.AVI animation from the \CHAP_13 of this book's companion CD-ROM.

Moving On

Now that you have a strong arsenal of character modeling and animation tools, let's give some real personality and life to our dragon. In the next chapter, Scot Tumlin takes us through the ins and outs of making a characters face come alive, using MAX 3's powerful—and very useful—Morpher modifier.

THE MORPHER MODIFIER

14

BY SCOT TUMLIN

This chapter looks at 3D Studio MAX Release 3's new Morpher modifier. You'll use it to animate the head of the cartoon dragon you first saw in Chapter 12.

Morphing: A Primer

Changing an object's topology from one shape to another is called three-dimensional object morphing. For example, you could morph a sphere into a sharp-edged cube over a period of time, or you could take two similar organic models and morph between them to create fluid effects. Both 2D (image) morphing and 3D object morphing were popularized by Industrial Light + Magic's effects in the 1991 film *Terminator 2: Judgment Day*. It took the best resources of ILM's talented computer graphics imagery (CGI) artists running proprietary software on a network of powerful workstations to create these effects. Today, you can produce this now-common effect using desktop PCs and off-the-shelf software.

When you morph between two objects, your 3D software keeps track of the vertex positions of both objects. Each vertex in the first object is matched up with a vertex in the second object. As the frames advance, each vertex in the first object is moved until it reaches the position of its matching vertex in the second object. This is called *linear morphing*; you're simply morphing from one discrete shape into another. It gets the job done, but sometimes you want more control over the final effect—including the ability to derive entirely new shapes by morphing among multiple 3D objects.

Today, 3D Studio MAX Release 3 and most other professional 3D programs have enhanced morphing technology with a capability called *weighted interpolation*. With weighted interpolation, you can mix among a series of similar objects, each with a different amount or percentage of influence, and apply the results to the final object. The similar objects are called *targets*. The final object is called the *base*.

To produce this particular morphing effect in 3D Studio MAX Release 3, you're going to use the new Morpher modifier, written by Harry Denholm, now a full-time MAX developer working in Discreet's London office. (You may remember Harry's shareware Ishani plug-ins, which were included on the CD-ROM of *3D Studio MAX R2.5 f/x and design*.) With the Morpher modifier, you can create weighted morphs for complex, yet subtle, organic animation.

In this chapter, you'll experiment with morphing between some cartoon dragon heads that Jon A. Bell and I designed and constructed as low-polygon objects. The techniques we used to construct them were identical to those detailed in Chapter 12. We began with a Box primitive; then, through a combination of face extrusion and vertex moving and welding, we roughed out the basic dragon head as a low-resolution wireframe proxy object. We used a Reference copy of this object with a MeshSmooth modifier applied to help us sculpt and check (in real time) the higher-resolution results. When we were finished sculpting, we discarded the low-resolution "cage" and

BEYOND YOUR MORPH LIMITS

When you create your target shapes, make sure all targets have the same vertex count. Also, pose your characters in extreme poses, well beyond the limits you plan to use. This way, you won't always have to crank a target shape up to 100 percent.

collapsed the object stacks of the higher-resolution dragon heads. We attached the eyes to the head geometry and then used MAX's Free-Form Deformation (FFD) modifiers to adjust the heads so they could bend or tilt; the heads became the target objects.

The Dragon Blinks

For the first tutorial, you'll animate a character's eyelids. You'll start by using one target object to create this animation:

1. Start 3D Studio MAX Release 3, or save your current work and reset the program.

2. From the \CHAP_14 directory of this book's companion CD-ROM, load the file BLINK.MAX. The file loads and the dragon heads appear, as shown in Figure 14.1.

> ### THE BLINK2.MAX FILE
>
> If you get into trouble or want to save time, you can load the completed tutorial file from the \CHAP_14 directory of this book's companion CD-ROM. The file is called BLINK2.MAX.

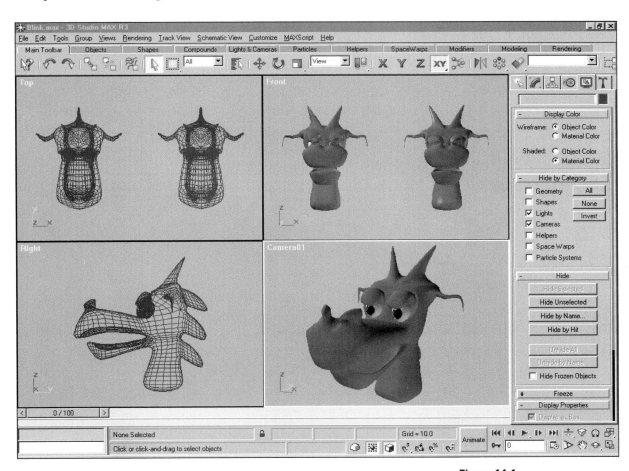

Figure 14.1

The dragon heads used for the Morpher example.

Weighted Morphing For Computer Games

When Jon A. Bell and I were working together at a computer games company, we used a weighted morphing technique (in another 3D program) to animate a series of low-polygon cartoon faces for a Nintendo 64 game. Two of the company's other animators, Ken Cope and Clifford Lau, created a methodology to blend 26 different target faces onto one base character face. By moving null objects linked to expressions that controlled each weighted morph face object, we could apply a specific percentage (or weight) of each target face to the base. The higher the percentage, the more influence the target face had on the base face. This technique let us isolate different parts of the face and mix them at will to create characters who could talk, blink, and look around. (We could even "dial in" and keyframe specific null object values to produce phonemes for dialogue.) These animation tests provided the inspiration for this chapter. If you're comfortable with MAX's expressions and the Morpher controller, you can easily duplicate these same techniques.

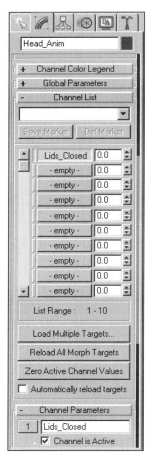

Figure 14.2
The Morpher Modifier panel. The Lids_Closed object is in the Target 1 slot.

This scene contains two dragon heads. The first head, to the left, is named Head_Anim. This head is the base object. The second head is named Lids_Closed; this is the target object. The second head started out as a copy of the first; I then used Release 3's polygon editing tools to move the vertices that make up the eyelids.

With the heads ready, let's apply the Morpher modifier to the base object.

3. Select the Head_Anim object and then select the Morpher modifier from the Modifiers panel. (You may want to add the Morpher modifier to your Modifier tab. Click on the Configure Button Sets icon to create a new set of modifiers and add the Morpher to your list.)

4. Click on the Morpher button; the Morpher Modifier rollout appears. Scroll down, click on the Pick Object From Scene button, then click on the Lids_Closed object. (You can also right-click on the empty slot to activate the Pick Object From Scene feature.)

5. Scroll up to the Target list; the first item should contain the Lids_Closed object, as shown in Figure 14.2.

At this point, the base face has one target: Lids_Closed. Changing the spinner value will change the base face. Let's give it a try.

6. Select the spinner next to the Lids_Closed object and increase the spinner value. As you do, note how the eyelids of the Head_Anim object close, as shown in Figure 14.3.

Now, you can set keyframes for the Lids_Closed spinner.

7. Your Time range should be set to the default of 0 to 100. Make sure the Time Slider is at frame 0, turn on the Animate button, and go to frame 2.

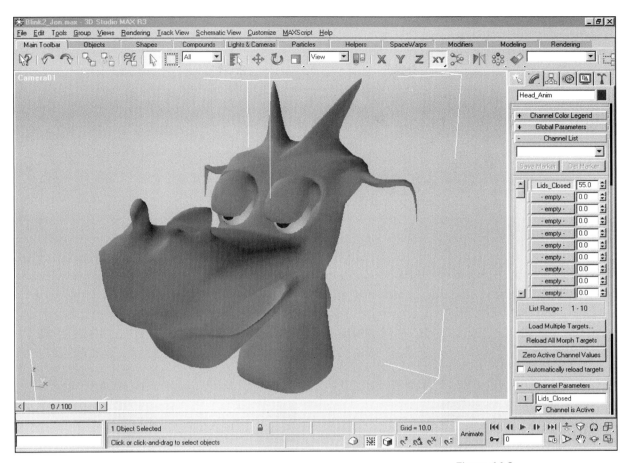

Figure 14.3

Increasing the spinner value for the Lids_Closed target causes the eyelid vertices of the base object to move.

8. Set the spinner next to Lids_Closed to 30 percent. The eyelids close partway. (A red bracket appears on the spinner indicating that MAX has recorded a keyframe for this value.)

9. Next, go to frame 4 and set the spinner to 100 percent. The eyelids close completely.

SAVING ON MEMORY

For this chapter, I used the final, higher-resolution, MeshSmoothed dragon heads for both the base object and the targets. However, if you have a large number of morph targets, you *don't* have to make duplicates of your first, high-res base object. Instead, you can duplicate the low-resolution proxy "cage" (as you saw in Chapters 12 and 13) surrounding the (MeshSmoothed) Reference base object and use those duplicates as your morph targets. By manipulating the vertices of the low-res proxy targets, but applying the MeshSmooth modifier *only* to the first base object, you can save on memory and processing power. The MeshSmooth modifier acts to smooth the animated, low-res morph targets. (It's also easier to move the vertices around on the lower-resolution proxy objects to produce your morph targets.) One point to remember, however, is don't extrude any new faces or weld vertices on any of the duplicates; this will result in a different number of vertices for the morph objects, and the morph effect won't work.

10. Go to frame 6 and set the spinner to 60 percent. The eyelids are closed almost completely.

11. Finally, go to frame 8 and set the spinner to 0 percent; the eyelids are completely open again. Turn off the Animate button.

12. Press the Play button and view the results. (You may want to turn off Smooth Shading in your Perspective viewport to speed up playback.) The eyelids of the base object close and open between frames 0 and 8, creating a realistic blink.

As an experiment, try moving the keyframes to adjust the timing of the blink sequence. Longer delays make the dragon look tired. Shorter delays make the dragon more alert or anxious.

This example used just one morph target to create the blinking animation. In the next example, you'll use three morph targets to add a breathing motion.

Multiple Morph Targets: Breathing And Blinking

Now, let's get the dragon breathing. You want the dragon's head to move slightly, indicating deep breaths. You also want the nostrils to flare during the inhalation. You could use one morph target for both, but using two separate targets gives you more flexibility. To get the dragon breathing, follow these steps:

1. Start 3D Studio MAX Release 3, or save your current work and reset the program.

2. From the \CHAP_14 directory of this book's companion CD-ROM, load the file BREATHE.MAX. The file loads and another series of dragon faces appear, as shown in Figure 14.4.

   The scene contains four dragon heads. As in the preceding example, the first head is named Head_Anim. This head is the base object. The second head is named Head_Up; this is the first target object. This head started out as a copy of the Head_Anim object. I used an FFD modifier to bend the neck, thus raising the head slightly. The third head is named Head_Inhale. This head is also a copy of the Head_Anim object; I scaled up the vertices that make up the nostrils, making them flare. You've already seen the fourth head, which is Lids_Closed.

   With the heads ready, let's apply the Morpher modifier to the base object.

Figure 14.4
The faces used to create the blinking and breathing animation.

3. Activate your Perspective viewport and press the C key to change it to the Camera01 viewport (this will help you see the Base head more easily). Select the Head_Anim object and then go to the Modifier panel. Click on the Morpher button; the Morpher Modifier rollout appears.

4. Scroll down to the Channel Parameters area. The number "1" should appear and the word "empty" should appear in the field next to it.

5. Click on the Pick Object From Scene button, then click on the Head_Up object. The "empty" changes to "Head_Up", and the Head_Up object is added to the first channel.

6. Click on the second Target slot, directly below the Head_Up target. The "1" in the Channel Parameters area changes to a "2."

7. Click on the Pick Object From Scene button again, then click on the Head_Inhale object. Again, the "empty" in Slot 2 is replaced with "Head_Inhale."

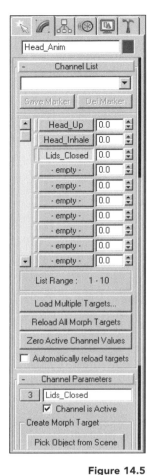

Figure 14.5
The Channel Parameters area of the Morpher modifier. The Lids_Closed object is placed in the third Target slot.

8. Click on the third Target slot, directly below the Head_Inhale target. The number "2" in the Channel Parameters area changes to a "3."

9. Click on the Pick Object From Scene button again and then click on the Lids_Closed object. Again, the "empty" in Slot 3 is replaced with "Lids_Closed." Your final Morpher rollout should look like Figure 14.5.

   Now, the base face, Face_Anim, has three target faces assigned: Head_Up, Head_Inhale, and Lids_Closed. Changing the spinner value of each target will change the Head_Anim object. In the preceding example, you had one target object, but with multiple targets, you can begin to really see the power of doing weighted, mixed interpolation via the Morpher modifier. Let's give it a try.

10. Select the spinner next to the Head_Up object and increase the spinner value to 100 percent. The Head_Anim object tilts up.

11. Select the spinner next to the Head_Inhale object. Increase the spinner value to 100 percent. As you do, you'll see the Head_Anim object's nostrils flare, but more importantly, the Head_Anim object remains tilted up. You can combine or blend multiple targets to create new expressions.

   Using all three targets, let's create a quick animation of the head blinking and breathing.

12. Right-click on the Play Animation button to bring up the Time Configuration menu. Set the End Time value to 120.

13. Turn on the Animate button and move to frame 60.

14. Set the Head_Up spinner to 30 percent. The Head_Anim object rises.

15. Go to frame 120 and set the Head_Up spinner to 0 percent. The Head_Anim object falls back to its original position. Turn off the Animate button.

16. Play the animation. The Head_Anim object rises and falls.

Flaring Nostrils

Now, let's add the flaring nostrils to enhance the breathing effect:

1. Go to frame 0 and turn on the Animate button.

2. Go to frame 50 and set the Head_Inhale spinner to 90 percent. The Head_Anim object's nostrils expand.

3. Go to frame 110 and set the Head_Inhale spinner to 0 percent. The Head_Anim object's nostrils contract.

4. I want the nostrils' expansion to start on frame 10, not frame 0. So go to frame 10 and set the Head_Inhale spinner to 0 percent. (Alternatively, you could go into Track View, isolate this specific Morpher track, and drag the key set at frame 0 to frame 10.)

5. Turn off the Animate button.

6. Play the animation. Now, the Head_Anim object's nostrils flare as the head rises and falls.

Eye Blinks

Now, let's complete the animation with eye blinks:

1. Go to frame 0 and turn on the Animate button.

2. Go to frame 2 and set the Lids_Closed spinner to 30 percent. The Head_Anim object's eyelids close slightly.

3. Go to frame 4 and set the Lids_Closed spinner to 100 percent. The Head_Anim object's eyelids close completely.

4. Go to frame 6 and set the Lids_Closed spinner to 60 percent. The Head_Anim object's eyelids open slightly.

5. Go to frame 8 and set the Lids_Closed spinner to 0 percent. The Head_Anim object's eyelids open completely.

6. Turn off the Animate button and play the animation. The Head_Anim object blinks, flares his nostrils, and tilts his head.

This simple example demonstrates the power of Release 3's new Morpher modifier. Blending different targets provides a great deal of flexibility. For example, you can use the flaring nostrils for deep breathing, sneezing, or preparing to blow dragon fire. You can use the tilted head for breathing as well as for laughing or looking at an object overhead. You could have even gone one step further and separated the Lids_Closed object into Left_Lid_Closed and Right_Lid_Closed (you would have to modify the vertices for each object separately, of course). This would add winking to the dragon's library of movement.

Before you continue, here are some suggestions to enhance this animation:

• Play with the timing of the keys. Try making two breaths for a more agitated or exhausted effect.

• Move the blink sequence away from frame 0 so it doesn't appear so robotic. (You could add additional blinks or slide the keys over in Track View to change their timing.)

• Finally, in Track View, change to Function Curve mode (instead of Key mode) and play with the tangency of the Morpher function curves.

THE SLEEP2.MAX FILE

If you get into trouble or want to save time, you can load the completed tutorial file SLEEP2.MAX from the \CHAP_14 directory of this book's companion CD-ROM.

The Dragon Falls Asleep

Now, let's animate the dragon falling asleep. The animation sequence starts with the eyes closing and the head tilting down. Next, a sudden noise wakes the dragon. Finally, the dragon falls into a deep sleep. You'll use some head targets from the previous examples combined with a new target called Ears_Down.

1. Load 3D Studio MAX Release 3, or save your current work and reset the program.

2. From the \CHAP_14 directory of this book's companion CD-ROM, load the file SLEEP.MAX. The file loads and another series of dragon faces appear, as shown in Figure 14.6.

As with the previous scenes, this example scene contains four heads. The first head is named Head_Anim and again serves as the base

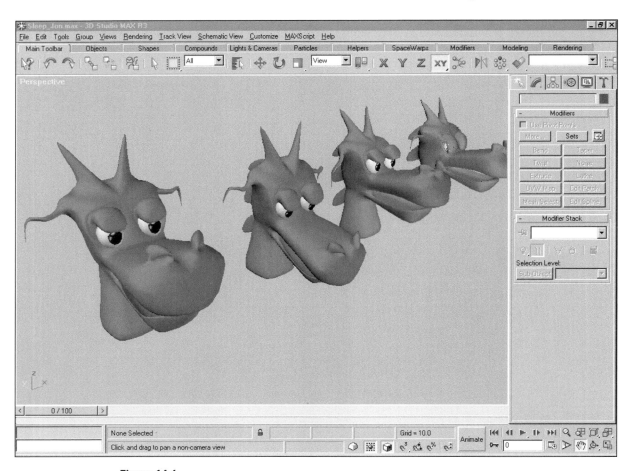

Figure 14.6
The faces used to create the sleeping animation.

object. The second head is named Head_Down; this is the first target object. This head started out as a copy of the Head_Anim object. As with the Head_Up object in the preceding example, I used an FFD modifier to bend the neck and make the head look down. The third head is named Ears_Down. This is also a copy of the Head_Anim object, with separate FFD modifiers applied to the selected ear faces to make them droopy. Finally, the fourth head is Lids_Closed.

With the heads ready, let's apply the Morpher modifier to the base object.

3. Select the Head_Anim object, and from the Modify panel, apply the Morpher modifier to the selected object.

4. From the Modify panel, scroll down to the Channel Parameters area. The number "1" should appear and the word "empty" should appear in the first field.

5. Click on the Pick Object From Scene button and click on the Head_Down object. The "empty" changes to "Head_Down", and the Head_Down object is added to the first channel.

6. Click on the second Target slot, directly below the Head_Down target. The "1" in the Channel Parameters area changes to a "2."

7. Click on the Pick Object From Scene button and click on the Ears_Down object. Again, the "empty" in Slot 2 is replaced with "Ears_Down."

8. Click on the third Target slot, directly below the Ears_Down target. The number "2" in the Channel Parameters area changes to a "3."

9. Click on the Pick Object From Scene button and click on the Lids_Closed object. Again, the "empty" in Slot 3 is replaced with "Lids_Closed." Your Morpher Modifier panel should look like Figure 14.7.

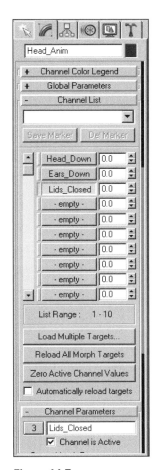

Figure 14.7

The Channel Parameters area of the Morpher modifier. The Lids_Closed object is placed in the third Target slot.

Pose-To-Pose Animation

At this point, the base face, Head_Anim, has three target faces assigned: Head_Down, Ears_Down, and Lids_Closed. Changing the spinner value of each target will change the Head_Anim object:

1. Select the spinner next to the Ears_Down object, then increase the spinner value to 100 percent. As you do, you'll see the Head_Anim object's ears droop.

Now, using all three targets, let's create an animation of the dragon falling asleep. The previous examples used straightforward animation; you started at the beginning and continued until the last frame was keyed. Another animation method, called pose to pose, begins with the creation of each important pose. Once the poses are completed, you move them along a timeline to create the animation sequence.

You'll use pose to pose for this example.

2. Using the Time Configuration menu, set your frame range from 0 to 10 and turn on the Animate button.

The first pose is the dragon wide awake. The Head_Anim object starts in this pose, so you don't have to create it. The second important pose is the dragon tilted slightly forward, eyes slightly closed and ears slightly down. Let's create this pose at frame 1.

3. Go to frame 1, then set the Head_Down spinner to 30. The Head_Anim object tilts forward slightly.

4. Set the Ears_Down spinner to 55; the ears on the Head_Anim object droop slightly.

5. Set the Lids_Closed spinner to 25; the eyelids on the Head_Anim object close halfway.

The second important pose is completed. The third important pose is the dragon with a startled expression. You could use the first pose, but the eyes aren't wide enough. Let's add another target face to the Head_Anim object.

6. Turn Off the Animate button, drag the Time Slider to frame 0, then select File|Merge. From the \CHAP_14 directory of this book's companion CD-ROM, click on the file LIDS_WIDE.MAX to merge it. When the Merge File dialog box appears, click on All, then Okay (if prompted for a material source, select Use Scene Material). The new target object Lids_Wide appears in the scene, as shown in Figure 14.8.

Now, you have to add the Lids_Wide target to the Head_Anim object.

7. Select the Head_Anim object, go to the Modify panel, and click on the empty Slot 4 button directly under the third target Lids_Closed.

8. Click on the Pick Object From Scene button, then click on the Lids_Wide object. Slot 4 is now filled with the Lids_Wide object.

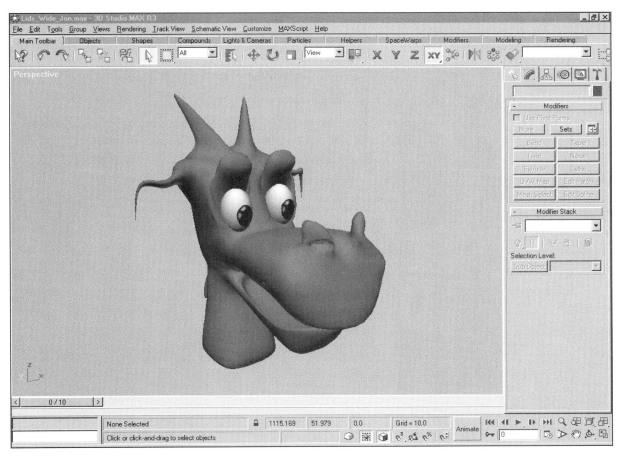

Figure 14.8

The Lids_Wide object (shown in close-up view, by itself) merged with the SLEEP.MAX scene file.

9. Change the Lids_Wide spinner to 100 percent. The eyes on the Head_Anim object widen, and the dragon's "eyebrows" also rise. Drag the slider back to 0 (you can right-click on it to zero it out).

10. Now, did you lose your keyframes? To check, move the Time Slider from 0 to 1. The keyframes were not deleted. So if necessary, you can add additional morph targets and not lose your original keyframes.

Startled Dragon

Now, let's create the third important pose—the dragon, startled.

1. Turn on the Animate button again, then go to frame 2. Set the Head_Down spinner to 0; the Head_Anim object rises.

2. Set the Ears_Down spinner to 0; the ears on the Head_Anim object rise.

3. Set the Lids_Closed spinner to 0; the eyelids on the Head_Anim object open.

THE FACE_LINEAR.MAX FILE

If you want to save time, you can load FACE_LINEAR.MAX from the \CHAP_14 directory of this book's companion CD-ROM. This file has all the Morpher animation keys set to Linear.

4. Set the Lids_Wide spinner to 90; the eyelids open wide and the eyebrows rise.

   The third important pose is completed. The last two poses are the dragon sleeping. Both of these latter poses feature closed eyes and lowered ears; the only difference is the position of the head. The fifth pose will tilt lower than the fourth. Moving between the two will produce the same breathing sequence from the example in "Multiple Morph Targets: Breathing And Blinking" earlier in the chapter.

   Let's create the forth pose.

5. Go to frame 3. Set the Lids_Wide spinner to 0; the eyelids and eyebrows return to normal.

6. Set the Head_Down spinner to 50; the Head_Anim object tilts forward.

7. Set the Ears_Down spinner to 90; the ears on the Head_Anim object drop.

8. Set the Lids_Closed spinner to 100; the eyelids on the Head_Anim object close completely.

   The fourth important pose is completed. The fifth important pose uses a higher Head_Down percentage.

9. Go to frame 4. Set the Lids_Wide spinner to 1, then back to 0. This forces the creation of a keyframe.

10. Set the Head_Down spinner to 60; the Head_Anim object tilts forward.

11. Set the Ears_Down spinner to 91, then back down to 90. (Again, this forces a new keyframe on frame 4.)

12. Set the Lids_Closed spinner to 99, then back up to 100.

You "forced" these keyframes because you're going to copy and move them across a longer timeline. Your spinner values should match Table 14.1.

Off On A Tangent

With the important or "key" frames done, you can animate the face. First, though, you need to change the tangents of the keyframes.

Table 14.1 The spinner values for keyframes 0 to 4.

Keyframe	0	1	2	3	4
Head_Down	0	30	0	50	60
Ears_Down	0	55	0	90	90
Lids_Closed	0	50	0	100	100
Lids_Wide	0	0	90	0	0

1. Select the Head_Anim object, then click on the Track View icon to open the Track View menu.

2. To make it easier to see the correct keys and items, you can pare down the available items in Track View. Click on the Filters button. Under Show, uncheck the following items: Note Tracks, Visibility Tracks, Sound, Materials/Maps, Material/Parameters, and Static Values. In the Show Only section, check Selected Object. Leave the remaining items in this list unchecked and click on Okay.

3. Under Objects, right-click and select Expand All. This will open all the remaining, unfiltered tracks associated with the selected Head_Anim object.

4. In the Head_Anim object tree, you should see the following hierarchy under Modified Object|Morpher:

   • [1] Head_Down (Target Available)

   • [2] Ears_Down (Target Available)

   • [3] Lids_Closed (Target Available)

   • [4] Lids_Wide (Target Available)

   Click on the Head_Down item under Morpher, then click on the Function Curves icon to show the curves for the Head_Down target object. Click on each of the remaining objects; as you click on each object, note its function curves. (If you hold down your Ctrl key and click on each object, you can then see all their function curves in Track View, as shown in Figure 14.9.)

5. Click on the Zoom Horizontal Extends icon to see frames 0 through 4. Currently, the tangents for the function curves are set to Smooth. A Smooth curve produces an arc between each keyframe.

   Imagine how a Smooth curve affects the spinner values in the Morpher modifier. Let's say you set the Head_Down spinner to 10 at frame 0. On frame 50, you set the Head_Down spinner to 30. You want the spinner value to change from 10 to 30 between frames 0 and 50. A smooth arc would produce numbers higher than 30 or lower than 10 because it arcs above or below the two keyframes. What you really want is a Linear (or straight) curve to get the initial animation. Later, you can use other types of curves for final tweaking.

   So, let's change the keyframes of the four target shapes to Linear curves.

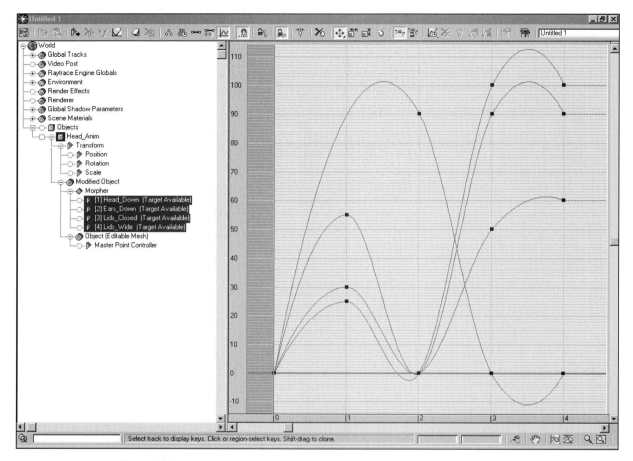

Figure 14.9

The function curves for all the Morpher targets (shown with Track View enlarged to full screen and zoomed in to show only frames 0 through 4).

6. Select the Head_Down target in Track View, then right-click on the keyframe at frame 0. A new window appears displaying the In and Out curves for this keyframe, as shown in Figure 14.10. Change both to Linear, as shown in Figure 14.11.

7. Repeat these steps for the Head_Down object's remaining keyframes and all the other target objects. (Select each object to display its function curves, then draw a bounding box around all the frames to select them. You can then change them en masse to Linear tangents by right-clicking to bring up the Key Properties box.)

Now, you can move and copy the keyframes to create the sleeping animation.

8. Click on the Time Configuration button and set the End Time value to 100.

Five gray-filled circles appear directly under the Time Slider. These are the five keyframes you created earlier. The initial pose is the dragon at rest; the first keyframe at frame 0 generates this pose. Next, you want the dragon to get sleepy and lower his head.

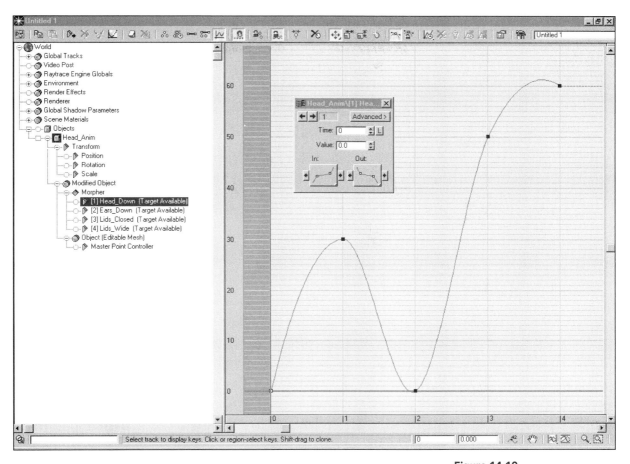

Figure 14.10
The In and Out curves for frame 0.

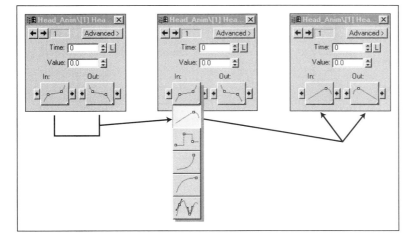

Figure 14.11
Changing the key tangents (both In and Out) for frame 0 to Linear.

9. Click on the second keyframe, at frame 1; this key tilts the head forward slightly. The frame changes from gray to white. Move the keyframe to frame 45.

Now, you want the dragon to get startled and momentarily wake up. The key at frame 2 produces this pose.

10. Select the key at frame 2 and move it to frame 50.

    At this point, the dragon tilts his head forward and quickly lifts it. You want the dragon to hold this startled pose for a moment.

11. Select the key at frame 50, then press the Shift key and drag a copy of this selected key to frame 85. Now, the dragon holds the surprised pose for a moment.

    Next, you want the dragon to fall into a deep sleep. The keys at frames 3 and 4 will produce this result.

12. Use the Time Configuration menu to increase the End Time value to 225. Select the key at frame 4 and move it to frame 165.

13. Select the key at frame 3 and move it to frame 220.

    Now, let's see what you have.

14. Move the Time Slider to frame 0 and play the animation. The dragon tilts his head forward and quickly lifts his head. He pauses for a moment and then lowers his head slowly. Finally, his head rises slightly to show subtle breathing.

15. Let's add a few more breaths. Again, use the Time Configuration menu to extend the end frame to 350.

16. Select the key at frame 165 and Shift-drag to place a copy at frame 265.

17. Select the key at frame 220 and Shift-drag to place a copy at frame 305.

18. Finally, select the key at frame 265 and Shift-drag to place a copy at frame 345.

19. Move the Time Slider to frame 0 and play the animation. You'll see that a few deep breaths are added to the end of the animation.

As you can see, the pose-to-pose technique differs from the straightforward keyframing technique used in the earlier examples. In this example, you created the poses that you needed first. Then, you moved them into position to get the overall timing.

So, what's left to do? Here are some suggestions:

• First, you should change the tangency of the function curves. The current Linear tangency is good for controlling the Morpher spinner values, but the resulting animation looks too robotic. Instead, try using the Custom (Bezier Curve) tangent. The Custom tangent displays two Bezier Curve handles for both In and Out. Moving the handles adjusts the shape of the curves, changing the overall ease in/ease out movements of the Head_Anim object.

- Try moving the keys around and see what effect this has on the overall timing.

- Use MAX Release 3's new Bones and Skin features (described in Chapter 13) to create your facial morph targets.

- Finally, use the Lids_Closed target object to add slow blinking.

Moving On

In this chapter, you used Release 3's Morpher modifier to animate a dragon's face. The first two examples used the straightforward technique, and the last one used the pose-to-pose technique. With MAX's new Morpher modifier, you can blend and combine numerous target shapes. You can also add and remove targets as needed without losing your existing set of keyframes. A thorough discussion of character animation techniques is beyond the scope of this chapter (and would take up an entire book in itself). However, a number of good animation books are listed in Appendix C of this book; you should consult those references for further study.

In the next chapter, guest contributor and *3D Studio MAX R2.5 f/x and design* alumni member Ken Robertson will show you how to do organic modeling using 3D Studio MAX Release 3's new Surface Tools. Originally a $99 plug-in from Digimation, Surface Tools, written by Peter Watje, allows you to create smooth, organic models with the strength of spline and patch-based modeling but without the difficulties of NURBS trims and blends. Stay tuned!

15

PATCHWORKS: AN INTRODUCTION TO SURFACE TOOLS

BY KEN ALLEN
ROBERTSON

In this chapter, you'll see how to use Peter Watje's Surface Tools, an excellent spline modeling plug-in that's included in the core 3D Studio MAX Release 3 program.

Welcome To Surface Tools

With the release of 3D Studio MAX 2, Kinetix (now Discreet) implemented a development strategy that pleased many MAX artists, a strategy almost obscured by the 1,000 or so new features added to the package. That strategy was to purchase popular third-party plug-in software and include it into the base MAX package, without charging more for it. The inclusion of such plug-ins as Digimation's Lens Effects filters made for a lot of very happy 3D graphics artists.

In 3D Studio MAX Release 3, Discreet has added another former Digimation tool to the MAX arsenal: Peter Watje's "must-have" spline/patch modeling plug-in, Surface Tools. Surface Tools's capabilities give MAX world-class organic and character modeling tools. It's long been the favorite tool of MAX artists heavily involved in facial modeling and animation.

In this chapter, I'll show you some of the techniques that make Surface Tools so powerful and popular. In the first part of this chapter, you'll see how to model a sleek SR-71 spy plane using Surface Tools. In the latter part of the chapter, you'll see how to use the plug-in to create a whimsical insectile alien head.

An Introduction To Patches

Although patches have been a part of the MAX tool set since Release 1, many MAX artists tend to misunderstand their efficacy, and patches therefore tend to be underutilized. So, before I get into the patch modeling aspects of Surface Tools, it might help to clarify exactly what a patch is and what the benefits of using them are.

First, one of the most difficult 3D modeling jobs is the creation of compound-curved surfaces. A compound curve is any surface that curves on more than one axis, which is almost any organic surface. To create such shapes, 3D artists usually have to resort to one or more of several different 3D modeling techniques.

If you want to create a smoothly curved surface from polygons (which inherently have straight edges), you often have to use a large number of small polygons that vary in small-degree increments from their neighbors. The greater the number of polygons, the greater the computer resources required to manipulate the dense mesh object.

On the other hand, you could opt to use non-uniform rational b-splines (NURBS) to define a surface. NURBS curves are always rounded, and straight edges are difficult to create with NURBS. The parametric (the curves defining the parameters) surface is derived from "skinning" a multitude of curved lines scattered about in 3D space. The problem is that the 3D program might build the solid surface in unpredictable ways. The 3D modeler, who might have a great deal of control over the curves that *define* the surface, often has only limited direct control over the surface itself.

Sitting in the middle of these two options is the humble patch surface. A patch is parametric, like NURBS, but is defined by Bezier handles at each corner rather than curves across the entire surface. The patch itself comprises a regular grid of polygons. Because it's a regular grid, the number of polygons can be redefined. Once the Bezier handles have been adjusted to define curvature, adding polygons to the grid makes the curvature smoother and more refined, as determined by the angles in place at each of the Bezier handles.

Patch Modeling: A Brief Fable

Now, once upon a time, when MAX 1 first shipped, many MAX users noticed these nifty-looking buttons called Patches under the Create|Geometry tab. They came in only two varieties—quad and tri—but whichever one you picked, you ended up with a flat grid and four Bezier handles, with which you could organically sculpt the grid with great speed and ease.

More adventurous MAX modelers discovered that you could adjust these handles, and then add an Edit Patch modifier to the object. At that point, you could "grow" other patch surfaces by selecting the Edge sub-object of the patch and clicking on the Add Quad or Add Tri buttons. The new patch would grow seamlessly out of the selected edge, maintaining whatever curvature the modeler added when he or she adjusted the Bezier handles. Better yet, the MAX modeler could weld the vertices of two different patches together; when the weld happened, the patch surface maintained smoothness across the welded vertices.

This in itself is a powerful capability, but this method of modeling, say, a complex, one-piece organic figure by "growing" it from a single patch proved to be too difficult for many MAX artists. Most MAX modelers used patches for modeling small organic pieces, but not complex models. A few modelers tried using the Edit Patch modifier on varieties of polygonal objects. However, this too proved daunting because the new patch surface had Bezier handles so densely arrayed across the surface that it was difficult to efficiently modify them to get a recognizable model.

So, things looked dire for the humble MAX patch, until a kindly programmer named Peter Watje noticed that patches and splines had something in common—Bezier-handled vertices. Peter set about creating a system whereby MAX users could sculpt splines into something that looked like a polygonal object, but with much less face density. Users could adjust the splines with the Bezier handles, and when they had the desired result, they could cover the spline network with a patch surface. Even better, you could adjust the new surface with the original spline handles, allowing the patch surface to exist at a density higher than the spline vertices would seem to indicate.

Thus, Surface Tools was born, to the delight of MAX modelers everywhere.

OTHER MAX RELEASE 3 PATCH ENHANCEMENTS

Although Surface Tools may be the most noticeable addition to MAX's patch modeling arsenal, Discreet has made other refinements to make patches a viable and desirable tool for everyday modeling. In particular, the ability to extrude and bevel patches in the Edit Patch modifier (or at the Editable Patch base level) enables modelers to sculpt patch objects by starting from a primitive, just as one would sculpt a mesh object for MeshSmooth modeling (as seen in Chapter 12). The addition of the Editable Patch object means that a patch model can be much more memory efficient because a patch object no longer has to be created as an Editable Mesh object with an Edit Patch modifier sitting on top of its stack. Combining these abilities with the power of Surface Tools allows for even more detailed modeling and quicker results.

Surface Tools: Cross-Section And Surface

Myth and magic aside, Surface Tools and several supporting utilities Peter created for it (some of which are now included in MAX Release 3) are readily accepted by many MAX users as the best way to model complex compound-curved objects. In fact, Surface Tools has basically become synonymous with MAX patch modeling.

Okay, that's enough background. Now, let's take a look at what makes up this miracle tool.

Surface Tools actually consists of two MAX modifiers—Cross-Section and Surface. The Cross-Section modifier creates connecting splines through existing Spline sub-object "cross sections" (as shown in Figures 15.1 and 15.2). This modifier is used primarily to "block out" your model and to add extension pieces to a model (such as fins, nostrils, antennae, and so on). Cross-Section

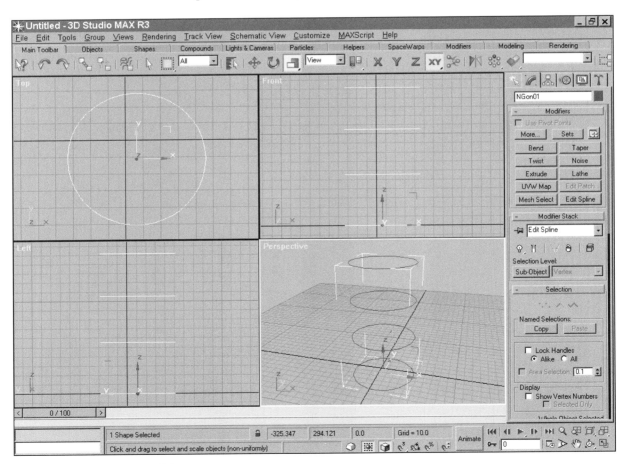

Figure 15.1

A spline object before adding the Cross-Section modifier.

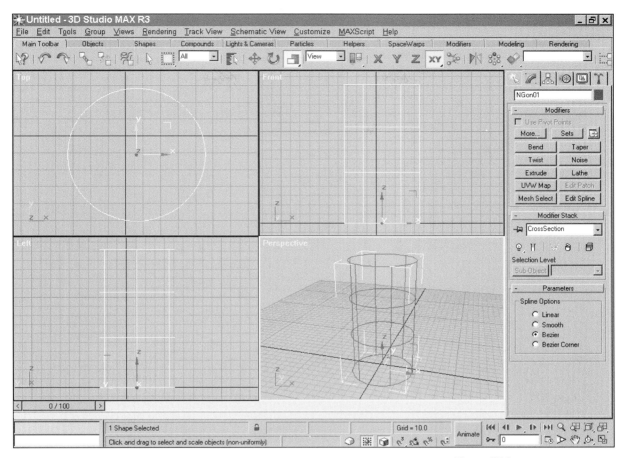

Figure 15.2
The spline object with the
Cross-Section modifier applied.

looks at the order in which you created the initial Spline sub-objects and
creates connecting splines in the same order (from the first spline created to
the second, the second to the third, and so on). In some cases you may find
that you've created an entire Surface Tools model without ever using the
Cross-Section modifier.

The Surface modifier is the meat and potatoes of Surface Tools modeling.
When Surface is applied to a spline model, patches are arranged so that the
patch vertices are placed precisely over spline vertices, thus inheriting the
curvature properties of the spline. But, because patches only have three or
four vertices (tri or quad patches), spline segments must enclose an area
with only three or four vertices. An area with more than four vertices will
not receive a patch covering, as seen in Figure 15.3.

Surface Tools Modeling Tips

In the years since the introduction of Surface Tools, several techniques have
been created (and occasionally abandoned) to make the power of Surface
Tools easier and more controllable. Although many techniques have been

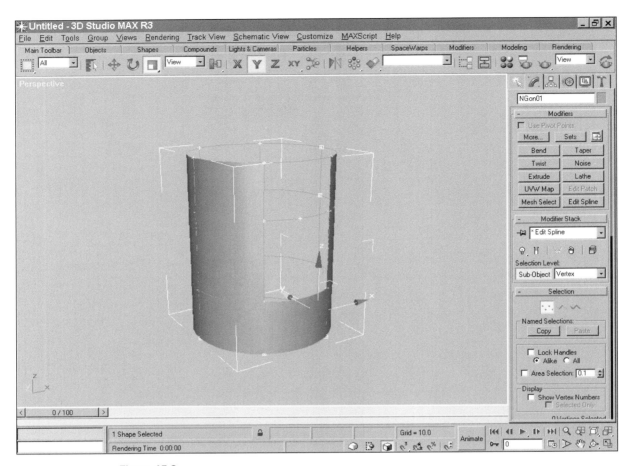

Figure 15.3

A surfaced spline object with an open area due to too many vertices.

developed for specific types of modeling challenges (facial models, for example), many more techniques have universal value when used with Surface Tools. The remainder of this section includes a discussion of those universal principles.

Always work from a scanned template.

This principle alone can save you many hours of torturous tweaking. Whether you use a photo of an object or orthographic drawings, make sure you have scanned materials that you can apply as either a MAX Viewport background or, preferably, as a material on a planar object like a QuadPatch. This will allow you to "trace" the templates, creating higher accuracy and less tweaking.

Work in halves.

Even though you may be working on a character that needs asymmetrical features, you will save an enormous amount of time and effort by creating half the model (split down the middle), then creating a mirrored copy and attaching it to the original. You can then add the asymmetry by making simple adjustments to the mirrored copy rather than treating it as a separate modeling task. Ideally, the mirroring and attaching should take place at the spline level, before you apply the Surface modifier.

Set up your 3D Snaps and use them in a User or Perspective viewport whenever you create connecting splines.

The Cross-Section modifier won't be able to provide all the splines you need when you're modeling a spline object for surfacing. You'll need to create new splines to generate those three- or four-sided areas for patches to be placed into. And, when you create those splines, you'll want to build them from existing vertices.

In MAX's Grid And Snap Settings menu, set the Snap priorities to Vertex only (Figure 15.4), turn off Use Axis Constraints (Figure 15.5), and make sure the Snap Toggle button (at the bottom of the MAX interface, just below the Time Slider) is set to 3D. Then, when you need to create new splines, turn on the 3D Snap Toggle (press the S key) and Arc-rotate a User or Perspective viewport so that you can clearly see the two vertices you need to connect with the new spline.

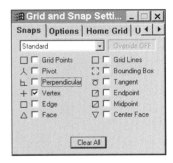

Figure 15.4
The Snap priority settings.

Snaps work well most of the time, but if you can rotate your view so that the two vertices you want to use are cleanly isolated with little or few other vertices behind them, the less likely you are to have a vertex created in a place you didn't expect. Always check the new spline in the other viewports right after they are created rather than risk getting a nasty surprise when your model is completed.

As soon as you have even part of the object "surface-able," make a Reference clone of the spline object and add the Surface modifier to the reference.

As you saw in Chapter 12, when you make a Reference copy of an object, the reference inherits all of the modifier data from the original object, and it can have other modifiers applied above the original object's modifier list without affecting the original object. And, if the Reference copy's properties are set to See-Through (a new feature in MAX Release 3, shown in Figure 15.6), you will be able to affect the splines and see simultaneous adjustments to the solid model.

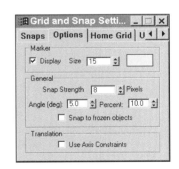

Figure 15.5
Turn off Use Axis Constraints.

This gives you unprecedented control of the surfaced object in a couple of ways. First, when you create the initial splines, new patches will appear automatically when you create a new three- or four-sided section. This means you will have fewer "snap accidents" because you'll have immediate visual feedback. Second, when making subtle adjustments to the model, having the shaded geometry underneath the splines allows you to use Bezier handles with maximum precision and immediate feedback. This can slow down the viewport redraw speed (especially in a complex model), but the results are usually worth it.

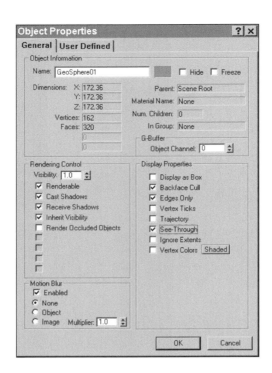

Figure 15.6

Making an object see-through in
the Properties menu.

You should also place a Relax modifier on the top of the Reference object's
Modifier stack. This will create a smoother model that requires less vertex
tweaking to get that organically curved smooth surface, which makes patch
modeling so desirable in the first place.

Use Fence selections for moving vertices.

Despite appearances, MAX does not support branching splines. What this
means is that every vertex in a spline object can have only one segment
going into it and only one segment exiting. When you see an enclosed
section, those vertices that appear to have more than a single spline going
through them are actually two vertices lying in exactly the same coordinate position in 3D space. If you simply click on a vertex to move it, you
will find that these splines are pulled apart and that area is no longer viable for surfacing. By Fence-selecting (drawing an area around) the desired
vertex, you'll be able to move both vertices as one and keep the enclosed
section intact. Figure 15.7 shows the results of proper and improper vertex
selection methods.

Also, when you start moving vertices, very often you will see a pop-up dialog box asking if you want to Weld Coincident End Points. Although many
MAX users will tell you to always click on No, this can be useful at times,
making splines smoother and easier to adjust across evenly curved areas.
The best advice is to click on Yes and immediately undo the operation if the
patch geometry disappears on your reference model. On the opposite extreme, you can set the Weld threshold to 0.0 in the Edit Spline/Editable

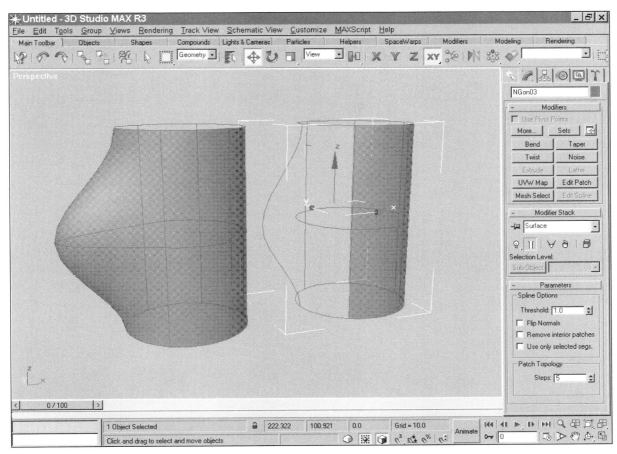

Figure 15.7

The results of moving a Fence-selected vertex (left) and a clicked vertex.

Spline dialog box for the original object. This latter option ensures that the Weld dialog box will never pop up at all.

Don't try to build the object in one piece—build it in sub-assemblies and "stitch" them together.

Imagine that you are trying to model a human hand, using splines. You have five fingers that need a minimum of four splines to define their appropriate roundness. You have to put them in the right place on the hand object so that the fingers show up where they should instead of ending up as a surprise mutation. Now, wouldn't it just be easier to make five cylindrical objects for fingers and a rounded rectangular sort of object for the hand and stick them together? Sure it would!

Fortunately, the easier way is the preferable way when working with Surface Tools. Building objects such as fingers, noses, antennae, and so on, separately and then "stitching" them together with new splines is the best way to get control and detail. In a larger sense, facial modeling is all about building features (eyes, lips, nose) and stitching them to the head outline. With the Relax modifier sitting on top of the model's Modifier stack, the hard-edged splines you created for stitching will smooth out into nice organic detail. A few Bezier adjustments later and you'll have a much more controllable result in less time than it would take to model the object in one solid piece, as shown in Figure 15.8.

So with all these principles in mind, let's use them to build something, shall we?

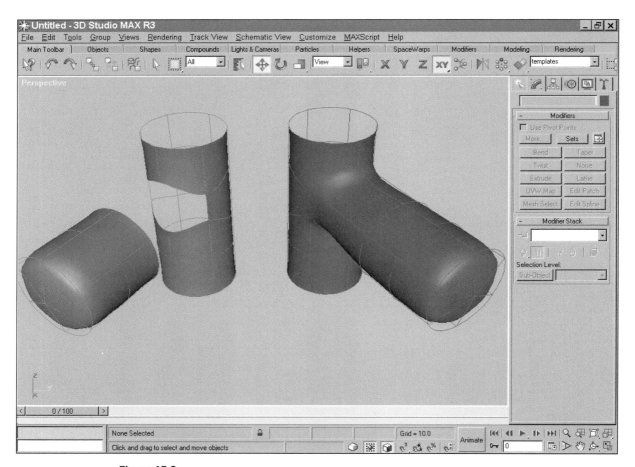

Figure 15.8

A spline object before and after adding "stitched" sub-assembly.

Building A Spy Plane

Let's start off by creating an inorganic object that has a lot of complex curved surfaces and, of course, just plain looks cool. To fulfill these requirements, you're going to create one of the most interesting and distinctive aircraft ever built: the Lockheed SR-71 spy plane, code-named Blackbird. You're actually going to create a little-known variation of the Blackbird, the SR-71B, which had a secondary cockpit bubble behind the front cockpit so the aircraft could be used as a trainer vehicle.

Now, remember the first principle, "Always work from a template"? Fortunately, that part is already done for you:

1. Load 3D Studio MAX, or save your current work and reset the program.

2. From the \CHAP_15 directory of this book's companion CD-ROM, open the file BLACKBIRD_TEMPLATES.MAX. When the file loads, you should see three Planar objects with line drawings of the top, side, and front views of the Blackbird, as seen in Figure 15.9. In this scene, I've also created a Named Selection Set called Templates. You'll be using this quite a bit, hiding and unhiding the templates, while you work on the spline model.

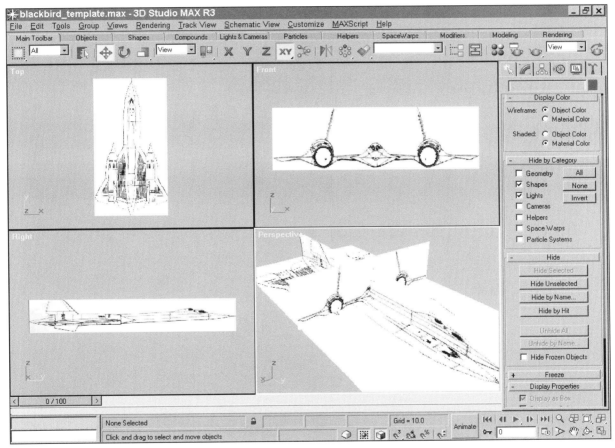

Figure 15.9
The Blackbird templates.

You'll build this model in sub-assemblies. The assemblies you'll work on will be the front fuselage, the engine, the wing, and the tail fins, in that order. The only stitching you'll need to do is when you connect the fuselage to the engine. The other pieces (tail fins and outer wings) you will create by extracting parts from the original model, building the new spline objects, and reattaching them back in place.

Creating The Front Fuselage

To build the front fuselage, follow these steps:

1. Begin by going to the Create panel and clicking on the Shapes button. In the Front viewport, create a 12-sided NGon (with Circular checked), centered roughly on the fuselage of the Blackbird. Go to the Modify panel and add an Edit Spline modifier to this shape. Select the Segment Sub-Object mode, and delete all of the segments on the right half of the shape in the Front viewport. You should now be left with a semicircle consisting of seven vertices, as shown in Figure 15.10.

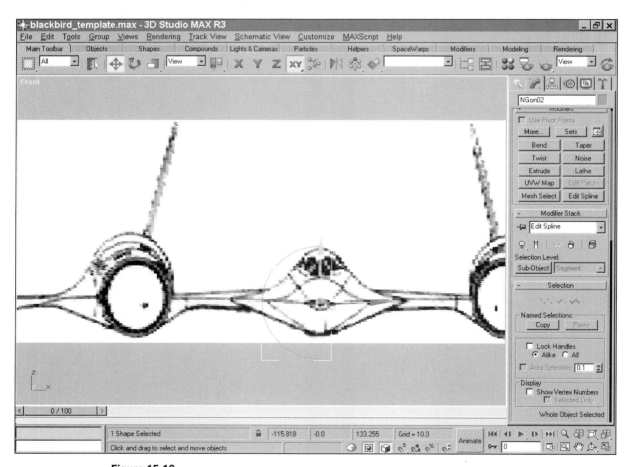

Figure 15.10

The first spline of the Blackbird.

2. Select the Vertex Sub-Object mode, and in the Front viewport, move the vertices to trace the outline of the fuselage, creating the rounded "V" shape shown in Figure 15.11. Don't move the vertices on the open ends of the spline left or right, only up and down.

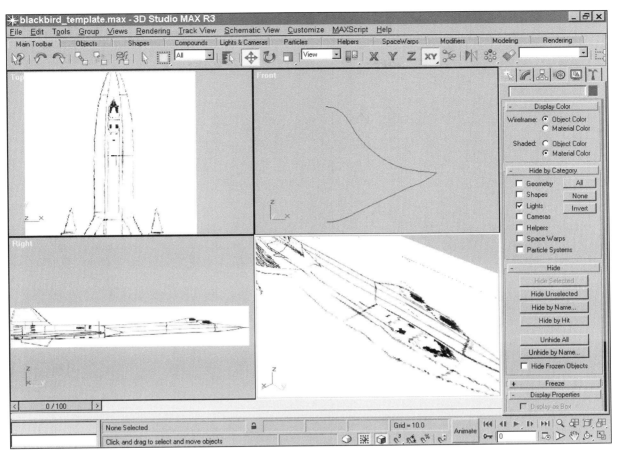

Figure 15.11
The spline vertices traced around the fuselage line.

3. Select the Spline Sub-Object mode and select the spline. In the Right
    viewport, move this spline along the X-axis to the point where the
    front cockpit meets the fuselage. With the spline still selected, hold
    down the Shift key and make a clone of the spline, moving it back to
    the point where the upper cockpit meets the front cockpit. Create two
    more clones by moving the splines (in order) to the highest point of
    the upper cockpit and to the back of the upper cockpit.

4. In the Top viewport, select the last spline you created and create two
    more clones (again, in order), placing the first one where the wing
    begins to diverge from the fuselage and the second where the inner
    wing terminates into the engine. You should now have six identical
    splines arranged down the fuselage, as shown in Figure 15.12.

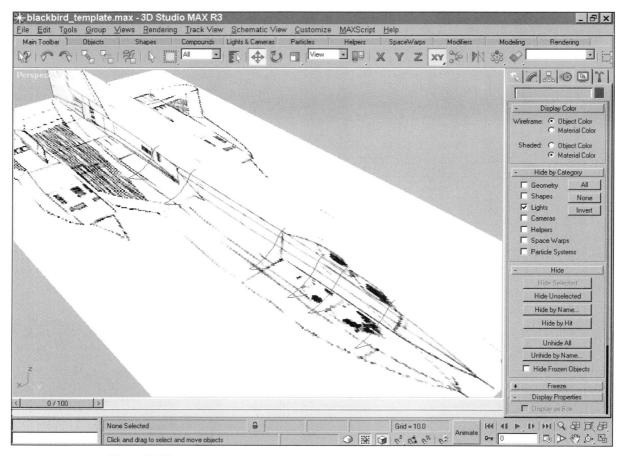

Figure 15.12

The splines of the front fuselage.

5. Adjust the vertices of these splines to match them up with the Top and Side images on the template. Then, go to the Modify panel and apply a Surface Tools Cross-Section modifier (with the Bezier radio button checked in the Spline Options panel) to the spline object. If you created splines in the proper order (in Step 4), your spline model should now have clean connecting splines between those created in the last step, as shown in Figure 15.13.

6. At this point, make a clone of the model by clicking on the Move button on your toolbar, selecting the spline model, and holding down the Shift key. Do not move the cloned model at all—leave it so it rests in the same identical place as the original. In the Clone Options pop-up menu, select the Reference button under the Object panel. (Note that you may want to rename this Reference object so you can more easily pick it later.)

7. When you're finished, go to the Modify panel and apply a Surface modifier to the cloned object. Leave all of the options in the Surface

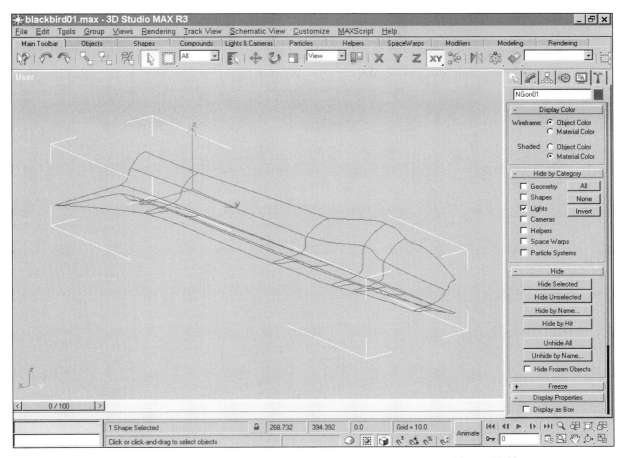

Figure 15.13
The splines of the front fuselage adjusted with a Cross-Section modifier added.

Modifier panel at their default settings (unchecked) except for Remove Interior Patches—place a checkmark in this box *only!*

8. Now, from the Modify panel, apply a Relax modifier on top of the Surface modifier. Make sure the Relax value is set to 1.0 and Iterations set to 4. The result is that you now have a solid copy of your object beneath the spline model, which will react to every change you make, no matter how subtle, except that it will have a superior amount of smoothness from the addition of the Relax modifier. The results are shown in Figure 15.14.

Now that you have a major and recognizable piece of the aircraft built, let's complete the front of the plane by building the nose cone.

Creating The Nose Cone

To create the nose cone, follow these steps:

1. Select the original spline object, and activate the Vertex Sub-Object mode. Turn on the Snap Toggle. (You did remember to set up your

SOLID REFERENCES

Having a solid object beneath the spline model allows you to see subtle adjustments to your model. But for easier modification, make the solid object see-through. Select the Reference clone, right-click on it, and select Properties from the pop-up menu. In the Display Properties menu, check See-Through. The solid model is now transparent in the viewport but renders as solid.

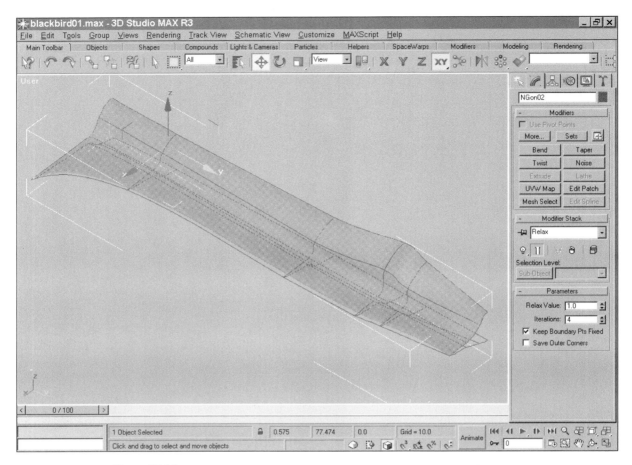

Figure 15.14
A solid reference object beneath the spline model.

Note: When creating new lines in a Surface Tools model, you don't have to have a Sub-Object mode turned on. However, if you do, it will show you the vertices on the existing splines, allowing you to create new lines precisely between existing vertices without guess work. Any sub-Object mode will do this, but the Vertex Sub-Object mode will let you create new lines, then turn off the Create Lines button, and immediately adjust your model.

Snap priorities earlier, right? If not, go to the top toolbar, select Customize, and select Grid And Snap Settings from the drop-down list. In the Grid And Snap Settings panel, place a checkmark in the Vertex box *only!* Now, you're ready to continue.)

2. Turn on the Create Line button in the Edit Spline modifier panel. In a User or Perspective view, use the Arc-rotate feature to orbit around the model until you can easily see every vertex of the frontmost spline of the fuselage (the first spline that you created). Create a line connecting the two vertices at the open ends of this spline, as shown in Figure 15.15.

3. Switch to the Segment Sub-Object mode and select the line you just created. In the Segment panel, click on the Divide button, with the Division number set to the default of 1, to create a new vertex exactly in the center of the new line. With Snap Toggle still on, begin creating new lines from each of the other vertices on the frontmost fuselage spline (the V-shaped spline created first) to the new vertex

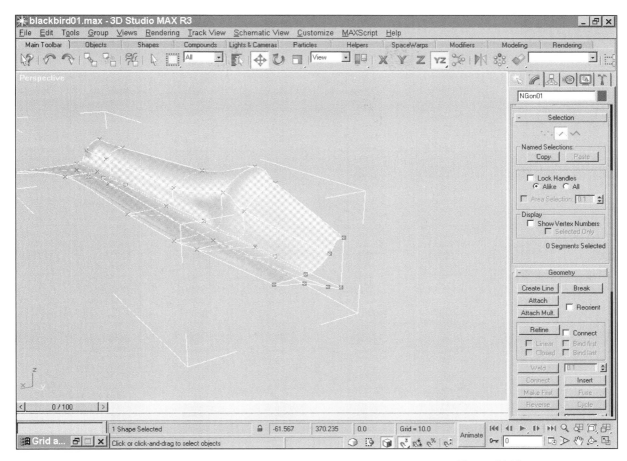

Figure 15.15
The new line created at the front
of the fuselage for the nose cone.

in the center of the new line. You should have a collection of new
lines that resemble pie slices.

4. Switch back to Vertex Sub-Object mode and Fence-select the center
   vertex that you just connected all those new lines to. In your Top
   viewport, move this vertex along the Viewport Y-axis until it's in the
   same place as the tip of the nose cone in the template drawings. The
   result should look like Figure 15.16. You may wish to adjust the
   Bezier handles of the splines connecting back to the original fuselage
   spline at this time to create more of that recognizable Blackbird
   curvature. But don't feel obligated; there'll be ample time for subtle
   adjustments later.

Now it's time to move on to building the back half of the aircraft. You'll
start with the most noticeable feature, the massive engines, and then use
the engine splines and the splines you've already created for the fuselage to
build the rest of the plane.

WHERE'S MY MODEL?

When creating stitch lines for a
Surface Tools model, the face
normals of the shaded reference
copy may become reversed.
Normals for Surface Tools
models are determined by the
direction in which the splines are
aligned. Fix this problem by
selecting the Reference model
(the solid-surfaced one) and
going back to the Surface level
in its modifier stack. Check the
Flip Normals box.

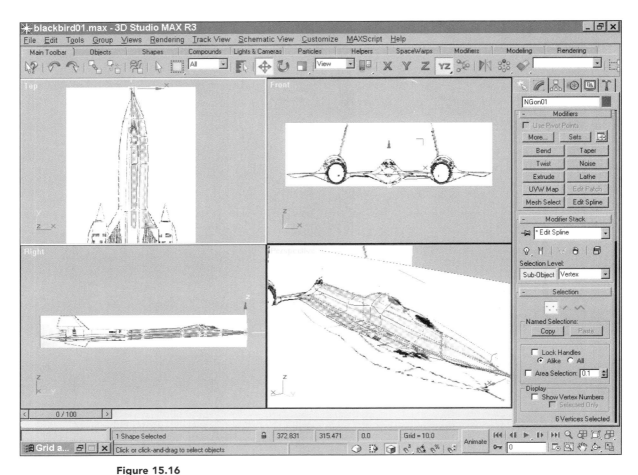

Figure 15.16
The completed nose cone.

Creating The Engine

The engine is a simple shape: It's a cylinder with open ends, and you could build it simply by creating a few circular shapes and using the Cross-Section modifier on them. But for the Cross-Section modifier to do its job predictably, you must make sure that the circular shapes you build are created in the order in which you want the Cross-Section splines to connect them. Otherwise, you'll end up with splines that loop back and forth chaotically from each sequential circular shape. So, while the following procedure may seem a bit strange, it will ensure that you get the results you desire from Cross-Section:

1. Start the engine construction by going to the Create tab and clicking on the Shapes button. Select NGon and create an eight-sided circular shape that lines up with the inner circumference of the engine in the template. Create the shape on the same side of the template where you created the front fuselage and, in the Top viewport, move the spline to the front of the engine.

2. Go to the Modify panel and apply an Edit Spline modifier to the NGon. Activate Spline Sub-Object mode, click on the Uniform Scale button, and then uniformly scale this spline down to about 80 percent of its original size. Move this spline down toward the back of the plane, about one-fifth of the way down the length of the engine (this doesn't need to be precise; it will be hidden by the engine cone later on).

3. Next, create a scaled-up clone of this spline (while still in the Spline Sub-Object mode) by holding down the Shift key and using Uniform Scale to scale the shape up again until it fits the inside circumference of the engine (as it did originally). Move this spline forward to an area just behind the front of the engine.

4. While still in Spline Sub-Object mode, create another scaled-up spline clone using the last spline (holding down the Shift key) and uniformly scaling it to now fit the outer circumference of the engine. In the Top viewport, move this spline between the previous two, a bit closer to the previous spline (the one closest to the front of the engine). The result should look like Figure 15.17.

Figure 15.17
The first splines of the engine.

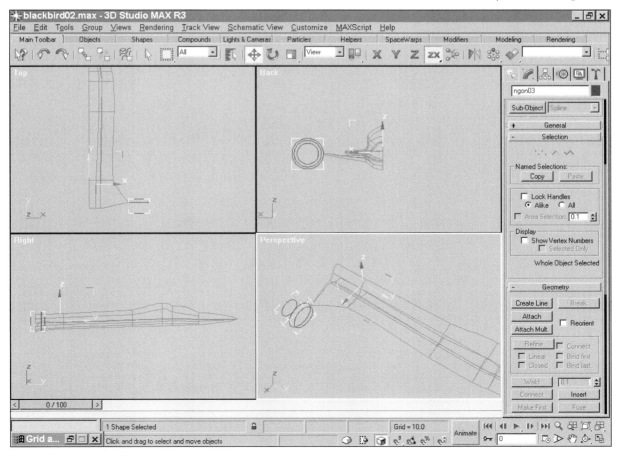

WELL-ORDERED SPLINES

There are other ways to make sure your splines are ordered correctly for the Cross-Section modifier. The most notable is to create the splines within the object in any order, then use the Explode command at the bottom of the Edit Spline modifier panel with the Objects button checked. This makes every spline its own new object. From there, simply select the spline that you want to be at either end of the Cross-Section shape, click on the Attach button, and begin attaching the splines in the order that you want Cross-Section to follow.

5. In the Top viewport, you'll create two clones of the last spline. So, click on the Move button and create the first clone by holding down the Shift key and moving it down the Viewport Y-axis to near the middle of the engine on the template. Create the second clone by holding down the Shift key and moving it down the Viewport Y-axis to near the rear of the engine on the template (about one-fifth of the way up the engine).

6. Now, click on the Uniform Scale button again and create a clone of the last spline you created, uniformly scaled down to match the inside of the engine. Then, move this spline almost to the very bottom of the engine. Finally, create the last circular shape for the engine by selecting the last spline you created, holding down the Shift key, and scaling it down to about 80 percent of its original size. Move this spline along the Viewport Y-axis to just above the first spline created in this step.

You should now have three splines at the back of the engine that almost mirror the scale and arrangement of the splines at the front of the engine and one circular shape right in the middle of the engine's length, as seen in Figure 15.18.

7. Apply the Cross-Section modifier to this spline object (with the Spline options set to Bezier) and check to make sure that the new splines follow uniformly down the length of the engine. The Bezier interpolation of the Cross-Section modifier (when it connects the outside splines of the engine to the inner shapes) will create a smooth rounded line that will serve as the front and back edges of our engines.

Attaching The Engine And The Fuselage Seamlessly

Now, you need to put these two parts together:

1. In a User or Perspective viewport, rotate the view until you can clearly see the inside of the engine (the side closest to the fuselage). Go to the Modify panel and apply an Edit Spline modifier to the engine spline object, then go into Segment Sub-Object mode. On the center circular spline, select the two segments on either side of the centermost vertex facing the fuselage (the segments just above and below). Hold down the Control key and select the two segments of the Cross-Section spline that lie on either side of this

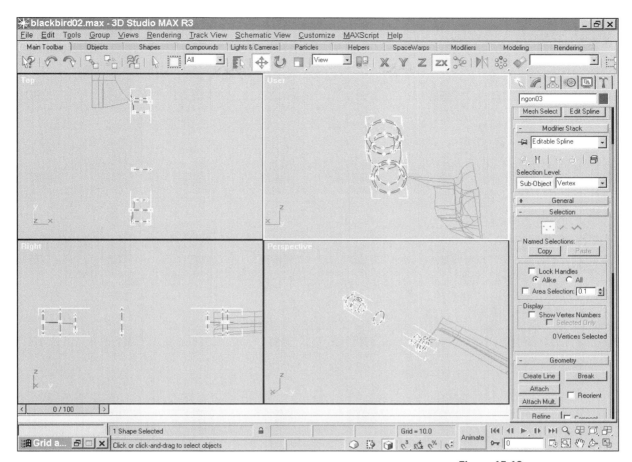

Figure 15.18

The completed engine splines before adding the Cross-Section modifier.

vertex to add them to the selection. You should now have the four segments that are shown in Figure 15.19 selected. Delete these segments, as this will create the area you will use to connect the fuselage and the engine to create the wing.

2. Select the Fuselage spline model and, in the Edit Spline modifier panel, click on the Attach button. Then, select the Engine splines to attach them. If you've done everything correctly, you'll now see the Reference model (the shaded copy of the spline model) add solid (or see-through) geometry where the engine splines are.

3. Now, you need to "stitch" the engine to the fuselage geometry. Toggle the 3D Snaps button back on, and in a User or Perspective viewport, rotate the view so you can easily see the backmost spline of the fuselage and the inside of the engine. Go into the Vertex

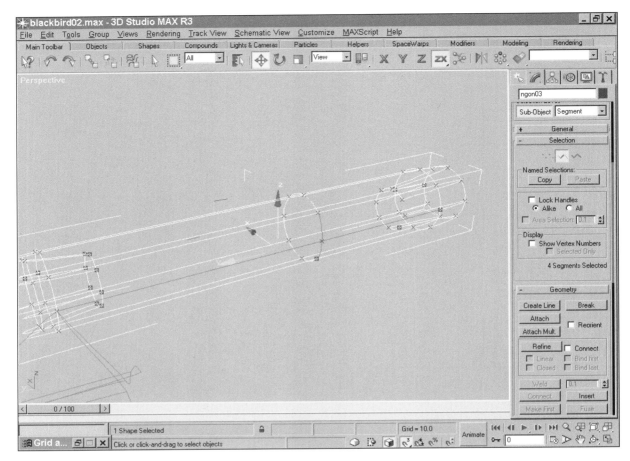

Figure 15.19
The segments to be deleted.

Sub-Object mode of the Edit Spline modifier and Fence-select the vertex on the wing of the fuselage. Move this vertex so that it snaps to the center vertex of the spline on the front, outer circumference of the engine, as shown in Figure 15.20. If done correctly, geometry will appear automatically around the engine.

4. Switch to the Segment Sub-Object mode and select the segment of the backmost fuselage spline (the segment that leads from the vertex you just moved to the rounded part of the fuselage), as shown in Figure 15.21. Delete this segment and the corresponding segment on the bottom of the model. Solid geometry in the reference model will disappear, but don't worry, you'll rebuild it so that it will be better suited to the model.

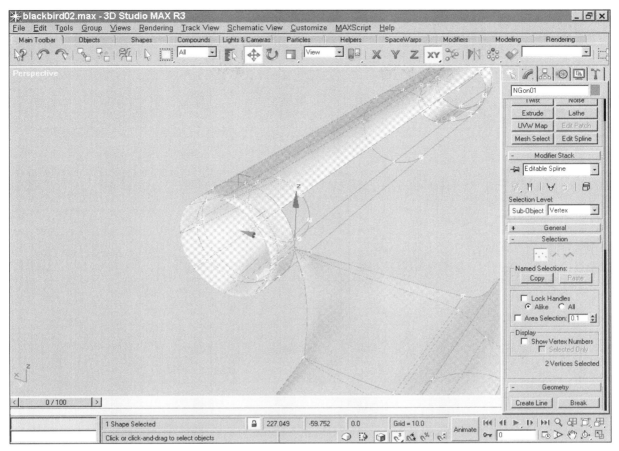

Figure 15.20
The fuselage wing snapped to the engine.

As I mentioned earlier, in the next few steps, you'll be creating new lines, and more likely than not the Weld End Vertices message will pop up. Remember, you have a few choices when this happens. You can automatically click on the No button, or you can click on Yes and see if the results work or not. If not, then immediately undo the weld operation. Or, you can just set the Weld Threshold setting to 0.0 in the Edit Spline modifier dialog box and ensure that you'll never have to deal with that obnoxious little pop-up at all.

5. Turn on the Create Line button in the Edit Spline modifier. With the Snap Toggle still activated, create a new line from the bottom vertex of the rounded backmost fuselage spline to the vertex on the spline

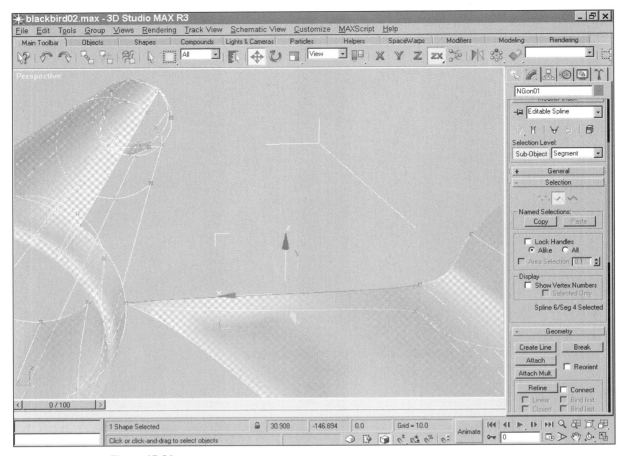

Figure 15.21

The segments of the fuselage spline to be deleted.

on the front, outer circumference of the engine (the vertex just above the engine vertex you snapped to in Step 3). The new line should look like that shown in Figure 15.22. Create the corresponding line on the bottom of the aircraft.

No new geometry appears, so you must have more than four vertices defining this area. To remedy this, you need to add one more segment.

6. With the Create Line button still on, create another new line from the wing vertex on the fuselage spline, just in front of the backmost fuselage spline. Connect it to the vertex at the bottom

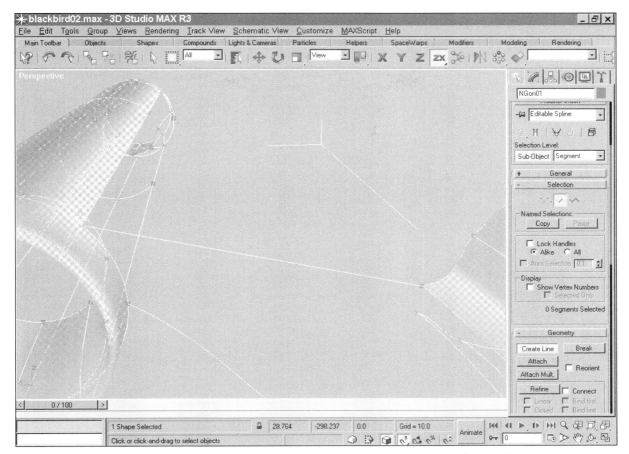

Figure 15.22
The new line from the fuselage to the engine.

of the rounded area on the backmost fuselage spline, shown in Figure 15.23. If done correctly, new geometry will automatically appear. Create another line between the corresponding vertices on the underside of the aircraft.

At this time, you may want to adjust the vertices of the new lines to create a more rounded and smooth look for the front of the wing. But if you just can't wait, that's okay—you can always adjust these later as well.

Now, you'll extend the fuselage geometry and create the back half of the aircraft.

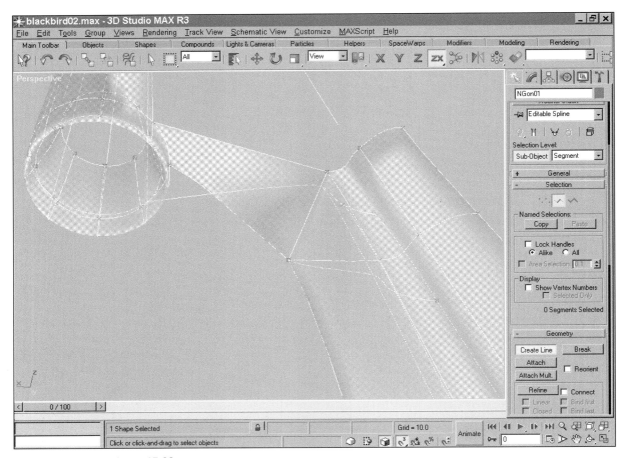

Figure 15.23

The new line creating the four-sided areas to "skin" the area between the fuselage and the engine.

Creating The Rear Fuselage And Wing

To create the back half of the aircraft, follow these steps:

1. Go to the Top viewport and switch to Segment Sub-Object mode. Find the backmost spline of the fuselage and select the segments of the fuselage and the wing. (Don't select any of the segments on the engine itself.) In the Edit Spline modifier panel, find the Detach command. Place a checkmark in the box labeled Copy, then click on the Detach button. A copy of the segments will be created as a new spline object. The default name of this object is Shape01, but feel free to name it anything you wish. It won't remain an independent entity for very long, though.

2. Turn off Segment Sub-Object mode and select the new shape, then turn on the Vertex Sub-Object mode for this shape. Select all of the vertices and click on the Weld button. This will ensure that you are dealing with a single spline over the next few steps, which will be important for the final result.

3. Switch to Spline Sub-Object mode and select the new spline. Holding down the Shift key, create a clone of this spline by moving it down the Viewport Y-axis in the Top view. Move the cloned spline down so it aligns with the middle circumference spline of the engine. You may wish to have your 3D Snap Toggle on and move the spline by positioning the cursor over the vertex on the engine side of the spline and snapping it to the inner vertex of the spline on the circumference of the middle of the engine. Make another clone of this new spline, positioning the last clone so that it aligns with the spline on the circumference of the rear of the engine. The final splines should look like Figure 15.24.

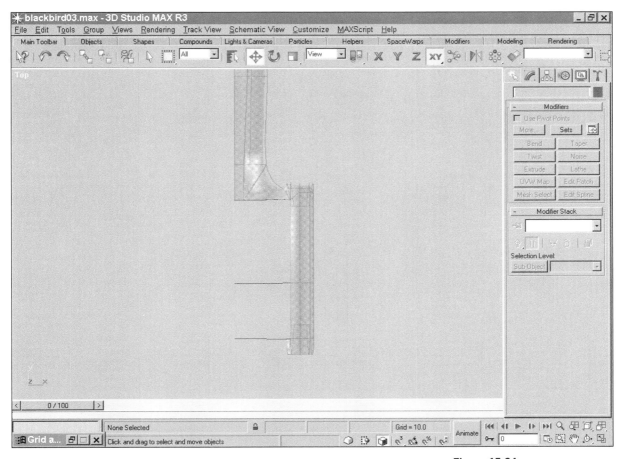

Figure 15.24
The splines for the rear fuselage/wing area.

4. Go to the Modify panel and apply a Cross-Section modifier to this new shape. Then, select the original spline model and attach the rear-fuselage wing spline object. New geometry should immediately appear when this object is attached. If not, you may need to adjust the vertices on the engine side of the new splines so that they are snapped close enough to be surfaced.

Repeat the four steps in this section with the corresponding spline on the bottom of the aircraft, creating the wing and rear fuselage geometry for the underside.

Creating The Tail Cone And Rear Flaps

Now, you can move on to creating the tail cone and rear flaps for the aircraft:

1. In a User or Perspective viewport, rotate the view so that you can clearly see the open end at the back of the plane. Turn on Vertex Sub-Object mode and check the Create Line button. Create a new line between the two open vertices on the top and bottom of the rounded fuselage body, closing off the open area. Create another line between the next set of top-bottom fuselage vertices on the fuselage side of the wing. This should produce a solid area right at the end of the fuselage, as seen in Figure 15.25.

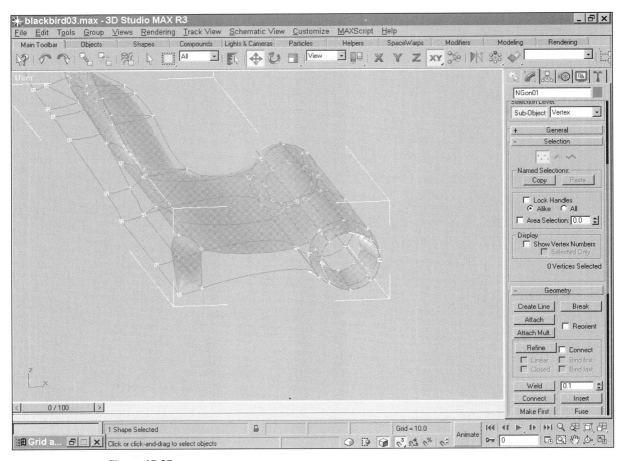

Figure 15.25

The splines for starting the tail cone.

2. Switch to Segment Sub-Object mode and select the two new lines created in the preceding step. Go down the Edit Spline panel until you find the Divide button and click on it, dividing the selected lines with a new vertex in the middle of both.

3. Go back to the Create Line button and turn it on once again; also make sure that your 3D Snap Toggle is on. Create a new line from the vertex in the center of the spline at the inside of the plane fuselage, through the vertex in the middle of the spline next to it, and ending at the vertex in the center of the spline on the outer circumference of the rear engine. The new line is shown in Figure 15.26. If new geometry doesn't appear in the Reference model, check your vertices to make sure they are snapped up tightly to those of the engine.

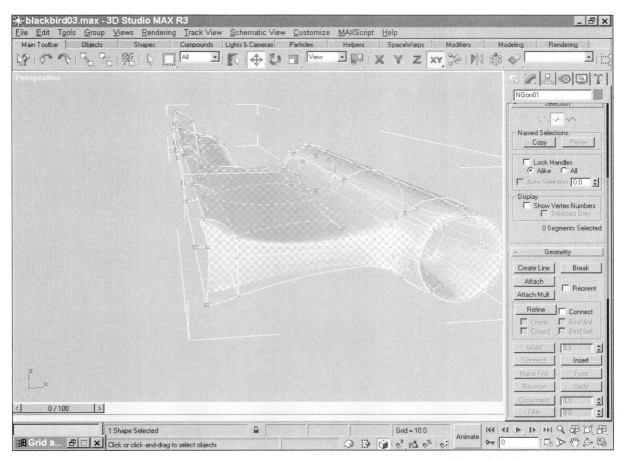

Figure 15.26

The splines for the rear flap.

4. With Create Line still on, go back to the rounded center of the fuse-lage. Create new lines from each of the vertices to the vertex in the center of the line at the middle end cap of the fuselage, resulting in pie-shaped sections similar to those of the nose cone. If your template objects are hidden, you may wish to unhide them so you can move the center vertex of the tail cone to match the position on the template, as seen in Figure 15.27. Feel free to make Bezier adjust-ments to create the appropriate curvature in the solid reference model geometry.

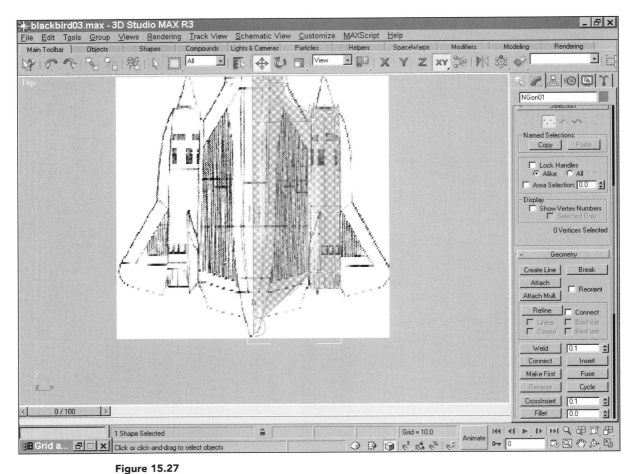

Figure 15.27

The splines adjusted for the tail cone.

5. Now, you need to finish up the rear flap. Find the line you created in Step 3 and locate the segment between the fuselage and the engine. Go into Vertex Sub-Object mode and click on the Refine button. Click on the segment to add a vertex to it. Geometry will disappear in the solid shaded model, but don't worry about that, you'll correct it in the next step. Move this new vertex to correspond with the position of the corner of the rear flap in the template drawings, as shown in Figure 15.28.

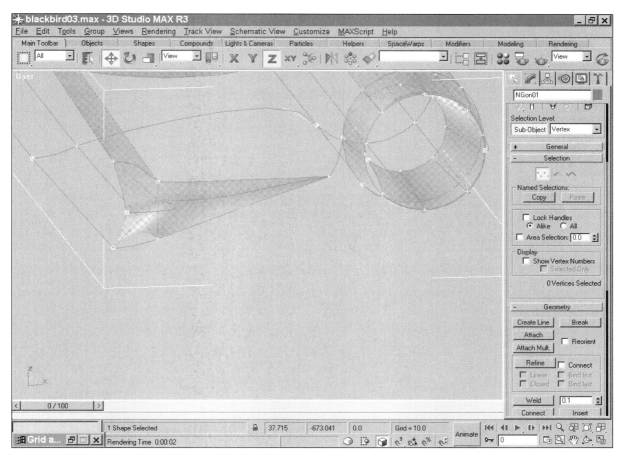

Figure 15.28
The corner vertex of the rear flap.

6. Now, you need to re-create the surfaces so that the model is solid
    again. Turn on the Create Line button again and check your 3D Snap
    Toggle (if you have turned it off). On the top of the aircraft, create a
    line from the lower rounded fuselage corner to the vertex on the
    spline on the rear, outer circumference of the engine; solid geometry
    should appear in the solid reference model, as shown in Figure 15.29.
    Create the corresponding spline on the underside of the aircraft.

Now that you have a complete aircraft body, all that's left to create are the
tail fins, the engine cone, and the smaller wings on the outside of the engines. These pieces are quite a bit simpler than anything you've done so far
and yet still use many of the principles you've employed.

Creating The Tail Fin

To create the tail fin, follow these steps:

1. In the Top viewport, find the engine splines toward the rear. Switch
    to Segment Sub-Object mode and select the segments that form a

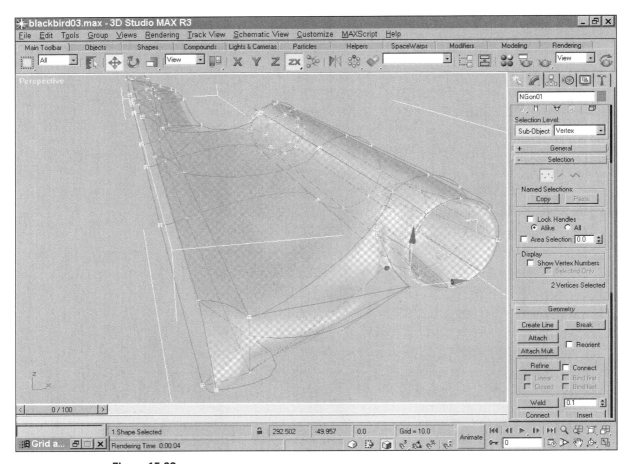

Figure 15.29

The completed rear flap.

square on the inside of the engine on the area just below the mid-engine circumference spline, as shown in Figure 15.30. Go down to the Detach button, place a checkmark in the box marked Copy, and detach a copy of these segments.

2. Turn off Segment Sub-Object mode and select the newly detached shape. Turn on Vertex Sub-Object mode and select all of the vertices. Click on the Weld button to make these segments one continuous spline.

3. Switch to Spline Sub-Object mode and select the spline. In the Front viewport, make a clone of this spline by holding down the Shift key and moving the spline up along the Viewport Y-axis, just slightly above the original (about 1 unit).

4. Go to the Right viewport and make another clone of this shape the same way (holding down the Shift key and moving the shape

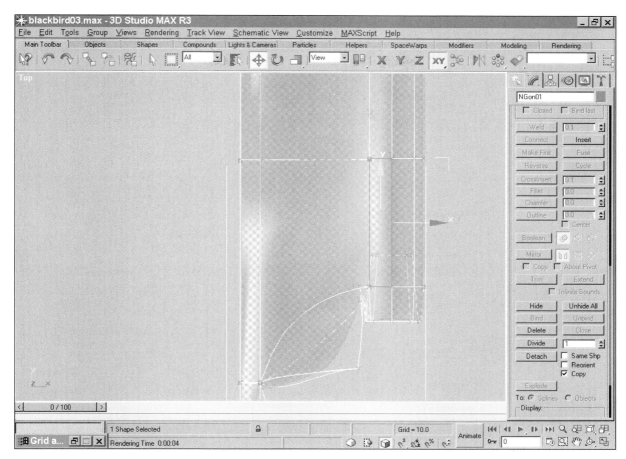

Figure 15.30

The segments to be selected to start the tail fin.

upward). This time, move the clone up to the first level of change on the template tail fin drawing (the sharp angle change at the back of the fin). Switch back to Vertex Sub-Object mode and select all of the vertices of this spline. Right-click over any one of the selected vertices, and in the pop-up dialog box, change them all to smooth vertices. Note that you may now need to rescale the spline again to fit the template. You should also adjust the vertices at the back of the fin shape so that they are thinner, giving a more aerodynamic look to the tail fin.

5. Create one more clone by switching back to Spline Sub-Object mode and selecting the spline you just created. Clone this spline by moving it up (in a Front or Right viewport) to the top of the tail fin in the template drawing. The completed splines are shown in Figure 15.31.

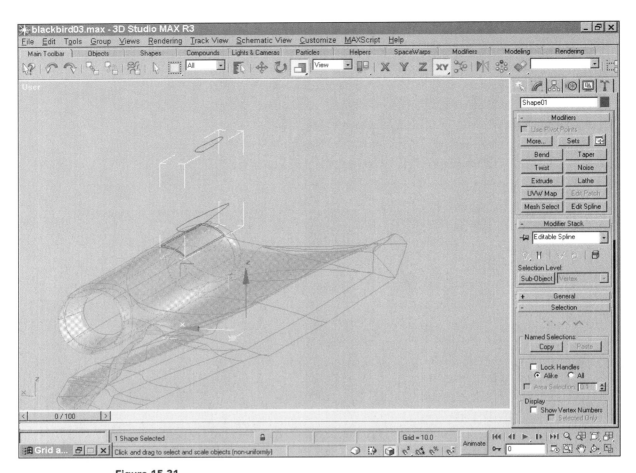

Figure 15.31
The splines for the tail fin.

6. Go to the Modify panel and apply a Cross-Section modifier to this object (with Spline Options set to Linear this time), then apply an Edit Spline modifier. Go into the Spline Sub-Object mode, select the bottommost spline in the object, and delete it. Turn off the Sub-Object button and select the main spline model of the aircraft. Click on the Attach button and select the Tail Fin spline object. The splines should readily attach to the aircraft model and new solid geometry should appear in the Reference model.

Creating The Wingtips

To create the wingtips, follow these steps:

1. Start by turning on the Create Line button and, in a Top viewport, creating a line from the outside of the engine tracing the outer wingtip. Be miserly with vertices, placing them only where the line meets the engine and where there is a sharp direction change in the wingtip. A total of five vertices should be sufficient for this line.

Note: If artifacts or holes appear in the solid geometry, select the reference model and go down in its Modifier stack to the Surface modifier. Check to see if the box marked Remove Interior Patches is checked. If not, place a checkmark in this box. Checking this box should be almost automatic whenever you apply a Surface modifier.

2. Go to Vertex Sub-Object mode. Turn on the 3D Snap Toggle and snap the vertices at each end of the wingtip spline to the corresponding center vertices of the outer-engine splines. Then, switch to Segment Sub-Object mode and select the segments in the center of the engine on the outer side (the mirror of the segments that you selected for the engine/fuselage attachment). Delete these segments. The geometry on the reference model should disappear, leaving a clean square hole along the outside of the engine, as seen in Figure 15.32.

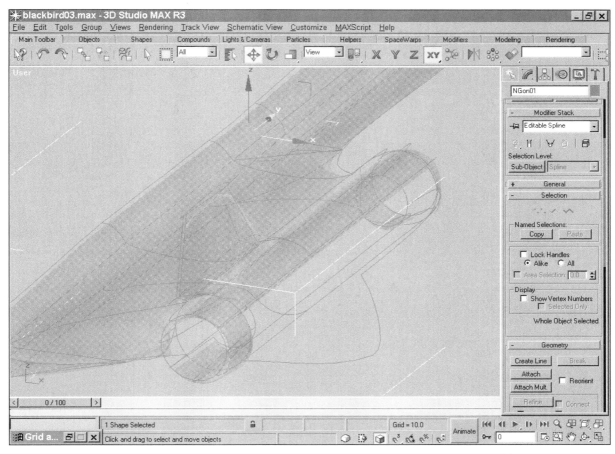

Figure 15.32

The wingtip spline and the open area on the outer engine.

3. With the 3D Snap Toggle still on, turn on the Create Line button and create a new line from the top vertex of the wingtip spline to the next-to-last vertex on this same spline (the one at the last sharp direction change on the trailing edge of the wing). This line is shown in Figure 15.33.

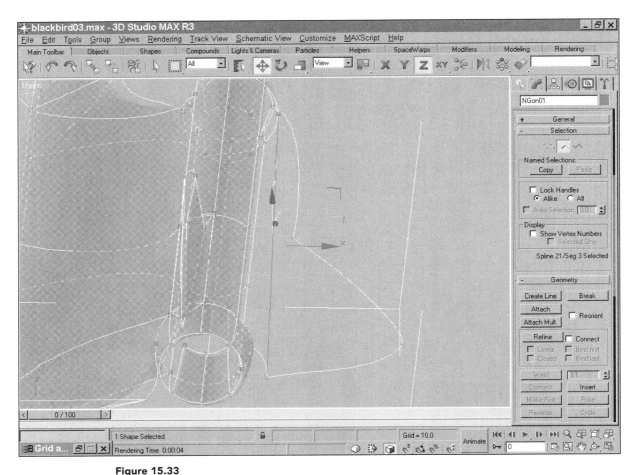

Figure 15.33

The new line for the wingtip.

4. In the Top viewport, click on the Refine button and add two vertices to the spline created in the last step. Add the first one about halfway between the mid-engine circumference spline and the middle vertex on the outer edge of the wingtip spline. Add the second vertex close to the last vertex on the wingtip spline (which has been snapped to the center vertex of the lower-engine circumference spline) and the vertex of the wingtip spline that's furthest from the engine (the actual tip itself).

5. Turn on the Create Line button again (with 3D Snap Toggle still active) and create two new lines from the engine to the outer edge of the wingtip, across the vertices you just created. The result should look like Figure 15.34. You may wish to move the vertices in the middle of the lines a bit toward the top of the aircraft (only a few units at most) to create a more rounded look.

6. Repeat Steps 3 through 5 to create the solid geometry on the underside of the wingtip.

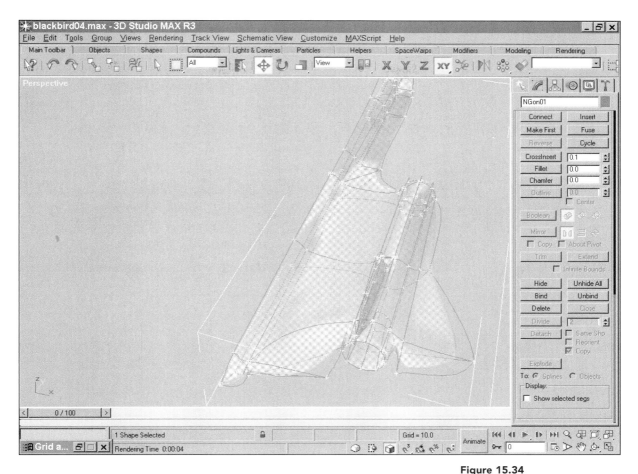

Figure 15.34
The final lines for the top of
the wingtip.

Okay...one last piece to build, and I've saved the easiest for last; you've
already created similar cones twice before.

Creating The Engine Cone

To create the engine cone, follow these steps:

1. In a User or Perspective viewport, rotate and pan the view until you
   can easily see down the front of the engine. Go into the Spline Sub-
   Object mode and select the circular spline inside the engine. Find the
   Detach button in the Sub-Object panel, place a checkmark in the
   box labeled Copy, and click on the Detach button to create a copy of
   this spline.

2. Turn off the Sub-Object button and select the newly detached spline
   object. With the 3D Snap Toggle still on, click on the Create Line button
   and create a straight line between any two vertices on opposite sides of
   the circle, effectively bisecting the circle with the new line. Switch to
   Segment Sub-Object mode and select the line you just created. Click on
   the Divide button to place a vertex in the middle of this spline.

3. Click on the Create Line button one last time and start creating new "pie section" lines from the edge vertices of the circle to the middle vertex of the new line and then out to the corresponding edge vertex. When you're done, turn off the Snap Toggle (press the S key), go to Vertex Sub-Object mode, and select the vertex in the very middle of the pie sections. Move it out toward the front of the aircraft to create the cone. You may also wish to change this vertex to Smooth, Bezier, or Bezier Corner to create more roundness at the tip.

4. Go into Spline Sub-Object mode, select the original circular spline in this shape, and delete it. Then, turn off the Sub-Object button and select the main aircraft spline model. Click on the Attach button and select the cone splines to attach them. New solid cone geometry should appear in the reference model, as seen in Figure 15.35.

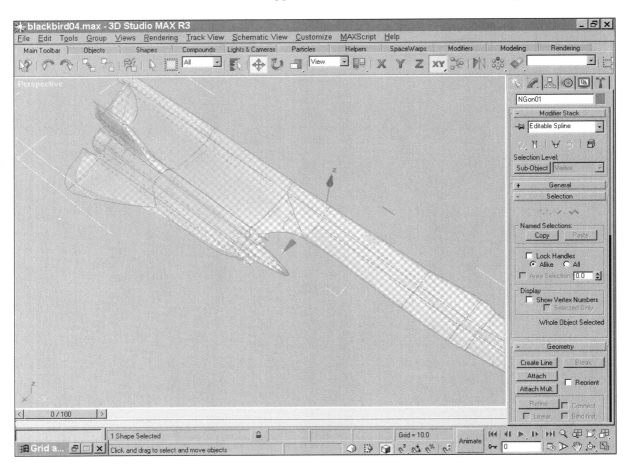

Figure 15.35
The attached engine cone.

Creating The Mirrored Half To Finish The Aircraft

All that's left now is to create a Mirror copy of the spline model and attach it to the original model so you have both halves put together:

1. Select the spline model. In a Front viewport, click on the Mirror button from the Top toolbar. Create a mirror copy along the Viewport X-axis, and for the Clone selection options, select Copy.

2. Select the new object and go into Segment Sub-Object mode. Carefully select all of the segments that lie down the middle of the model *only.* Delete them, turn off the Sub-Object button, and select the original aircraft spline model. Click on the Attach button and select the Mirror copy. If you've done everything properly, the Mirror copy should have new geometry appear beneath the splines, creating a fully shaded and complete aircraft model. Rotate the view to make sure no holes have appeared due to bad vertex alignment or an unintentionally deleted segment in the last step. The final model should resemble Figure 15.36.

Figure 15.36
The completed Blackbird SR71-B model.

MIRROR, MIRROR

One problem that generally plagues Surface Tools modelers is getting a good Mirror copy to attach to the original half-model. Vertices can be out of alignment, or you might have to move the mirrored object to the correct position. An easy fix to this is to create a plane or grid object that can represent where you want the center of your mirror to be.

1. Move the object to the desired center of your Surface Tools model, then select your spline object. Go into the Vertex Sub-Object mode, and in an orthographic viewport (Top or Front seems to work best), make a careful selection of all the vertices down the center of the model.

2. Click on the Align tool button (in the Top toolbar) and press the H key to bring up a menu of objects to align to. Select your plane or grid object, and in the Alignment tool pop-up menu, align the selected vertices to the X-axis *only!* This will give you a good clean line of vertices at the center of your mirror.

3. Go to the Hierarchy panel and click on the Pivot tab. Click on the Affect Pivot Only button to bring up the pivot point display. Repeat the alignment procedure you performed with the vertices previously.

Voila! You now have a clean line of vertices exactly matched up with the point about which your model will be mirrored, so that the mirror copy's vertices will match up precisely with the original.

Note: A completed version of this model is saved in the \CHAP_15 directory as BLACKBIRD_FINAL.MAX.

At this point, you can save the model to your \3DSMAX3\SCENES directory and begin the process of texturing, lighting, and rendering it.

Constructing An Alien Head

So, feeling all warmed up and ready to tackle more? Glad to hear it! Because now you're going to move on to the type of model that made Surface Tools famous: a character head. And, of course, this being a book with the letters "f/x" in the title, we have to have our token space alien. This particular alien is the cute and friendly type, the type of ET that you could bring home to mother. So without further ado, let's begin:

1. From the \CHAP_15 directory of this book's companion CD-ROM, open the file WORM_GUY_TEMPLATE.MAX. In it, you'll find two planes with front and side views of the alien head you're going to create, as shown in Figure 15.37. Start the head model by going into the Front viewport, clicking on the Create tab, and then clicking on the Shapes|Spline|Line button. Create an outline around the left half of the profile in the Front view in two splines, the first starting at the crown of the head and moving to the top of the eyelid and the second going from the bottom of the lower eyelid to the base of the neck. Leave out the eyelids and eyes. Try to be frugal with the number of vertices you use in these splines. It's better to use fewer vertices and add more later than to use too many and then have to delete them later.

2. Switch to the Left viewport and create an outline of the side profile in two splines—one from the back bottom of the neck ending at the upper lip and the other from the lower lip to the front of the bottom

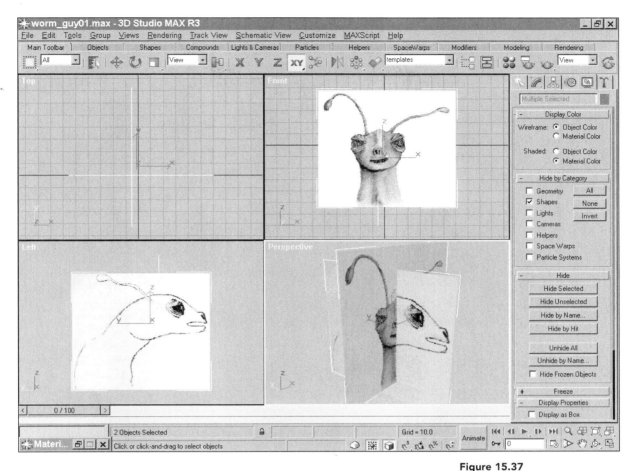

Figure 15.37
The alien head templates.

neckline. Leave the mouth open. Add an Edit Spline modifier to the last spline, then click on the Attach button and attach all of the other spline to this one.

3. Go into Vertex Sub-Object mode, and in the Front viewport, select the bottom vertex of the front profile spline. In the Left viewport, move this vertex to the bottom of the neck on the template, at the middle of the neck. Continue this process of selecting a vertex in the Front viewport and moving it along to the middle of the neckline in the Left view. Then, at the upper part of this spline, start moving the vertices to line up along the lower jawline. The tricky area will be on the jawline, where in order to create the bulge of the jawbone itself, the outline will actually have to lower to the bottom of the jaw and then loop back up before going into the neckline. A finished outline is shown in Figure 15.38. Don't worry if the upper end of the spline doesn't come completely back up to where it started. You can correct this when you start connecting the splines for surfacing.

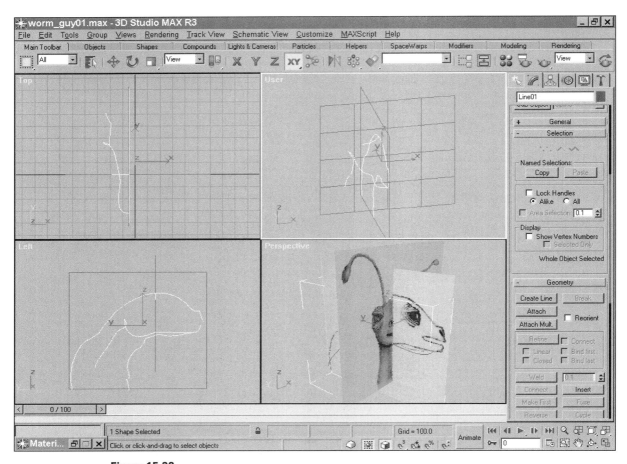

Figure 15.38

The profile splines.

4. Go to the Left viewport, and click on the Create Line button in the Edit Spline modifier. Create a line tracing the inside of the mouth starting and ending at the center profile spline. Turn on the Vertex Sub-Object mode, select the vertex at the corner of the mouth, then go to the Front view and move this vertex to the left (along the Viewport X-axis), aligning it above the corner of the mouth in this view. Continue adjusting the mouth vertices this way until you have a mouth spline curving in both the Left and Front viewports. When you get to the end vertices of the spline, turn on the 3D Snap Toggle and snap the end vertices to their proper positions on the side profile splines. The completed mouth spline is shown in Figure 15.39.

Now that you have the basic structure, you can start adding the features of the face. When building a head, it's best to work almost opposite to the way in which you created the Blackbird. With the Blackbird, you created a basic structure, then added features to it. With a head, you create the basic outline splines, then start creating the features (nose, mouth, eyes), and then "stitch" the features to the outlines and to each other. These

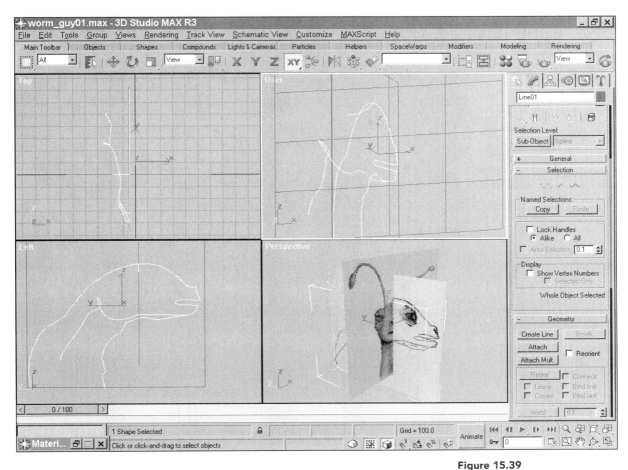

Figure 15.39
The mouth added to
profile splines.

stitches become the broader surfaces of the head, flowing between the
features. So let's dive in to the first feature on the face: the nose.

Creating The Nose

To create the nose, follow these steps:

1. In the Left viewport, locate the notch in the profile spline that repre-
    sents the nose. Click on the Create Line button and create a line that
    represents the area where the nose would meet the face, from the top
    vertex of the nose bulge in the profile spline to the bottom vertex of
    the nose in the side profile. (Make sure you don't overdo the number
    of vertices.) Switch to the Front view and move the vertices of this
    new line to represent where the nose base would appear from the
    Front. A completed line is shown in Figure 15.40.

2. Go into Segment Sub-Object mode and select all of the segments of
    this new line and the segments in the side profile line that represent
    the nose bulge. Click on Scale|Non-Uniform Scale, then go to the
    Front viewport, and holding down the Shift key, create a clone by

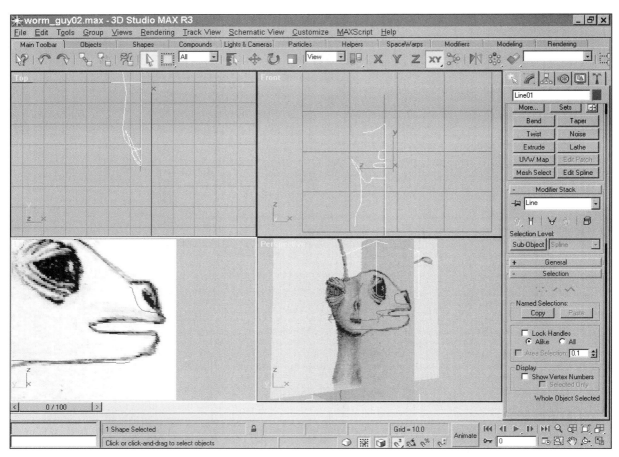

Figure 15.40

The nose outline.

scaling these segments down nonuniformly along the View XY coordinates until the new shape is about the same size as the nostril in the template. Switch to Vertex Sub-Object mode and start moving the vertices of the nostril spline to match the nostril drawing in the front and left views.

3. Turn on your 3D Snap Toggle (with Snap Priority set to Vertices *only*), turn on the Create Line button, and begin creating lines between the vertices of the nostril and the corresponding vertices on the nose outline and the nose bulge in the side profile spline. A completed version of this is shown in Figure 15.41.

4. Now that you have some geometry that you can surface successfully, it's time to make your Reference clone so you can have a solid geometry object beneath your splines. Turn off Sub-Object mode and clone this object by holding down the Shift key and clicking on the head splines, but *not* moving them. In the Clone options dialog box, select Reference. Then, select the Reference object and apply a Surface

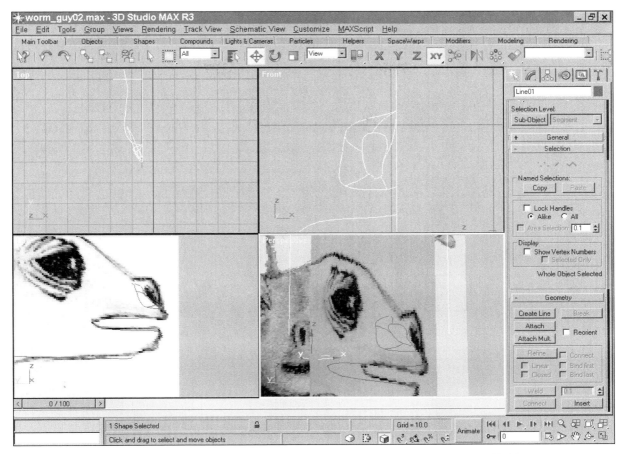

Figure 15.41
The nose splines.

modifier to it (with all default settings and a checkmark placed in the box marked Remove Interior Patches). You should now have a solid ring of geometry around the nostril. Then, apply a Relax modifier to the Reference object with a Relax Value of 1.0 and Iterations set to 7.

5. Go back and select the original head spline model and go into Vertex Sub-Object mode. To flesh out the model a bit, click on the Create Line button and toggle the 3D Snap button on. In the Front viewport, create a new line from the bottom-left vertex of the nose to the corner of the mouth. New geometry should appear in the reference model, effectively creating the upper lip, as shown in Figure 15.42.

6. Now, you need to create the interior of the nostril. Switch to Segment Sub-Object mode and select all of the segments of the nostril outline. Find the Detach button in the Edit Spline modifier panel, place a checkmark in the box marked Copy, and click on the Detach button.

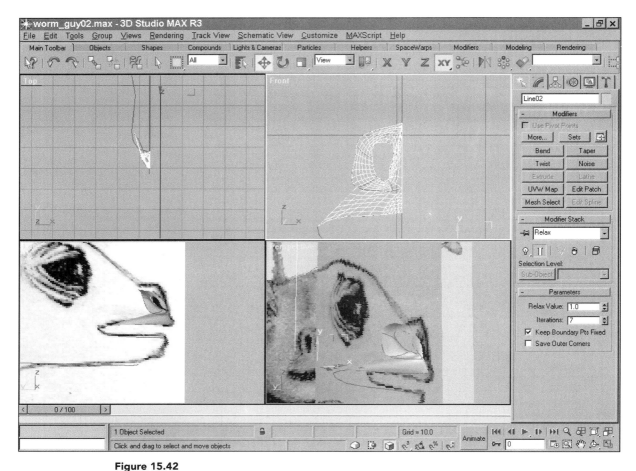

Figure 15.42

The surfaced nose and upper lip.

7. Turn off the Sub-Object button and select the shape you just created. Go into Vertex Sub-Object mode, select all of the vertices of this spline, and click on the Weld button (just to make sure you are only dealing with a single spline for correct Cross-Section placement). Switch to Spline Sub-Object mode and select this spline. In the Left viewport, create a clone of this spline by holding down the Shift key and moving the spline back toward the back of the head (along the Viewport X-axis) about 23 units. In the Front viewport, scale this spline down to about 70 percent.

8. Apply a Cross-Section modifier to this object, then add an Edit Spline modifier. Go into the Spline Sub-Object mode, select the spline that represents the outside of the nostril (the spline detached from the head model), and delete it. Turn on the Create Line button and toggle on the 3D Snap button. Then, on the spline that represents

the back of the nostril, create a new line that runs from one of the vertices on the top of the spline to one of the vertices on the bottom of the spline. This is needed to create areas enclosed by only three or four vertices so the area will be surfaced. Count the vertices on these areas and add more lines if needed.

9. Turn off the Sub-Object button and select the original head splines model. Click on the Attach button and select the nostril splines. If you've completed everything correctly in the preceding step, new solid geometry should appear for the inside and back of the nostril, as shown in Figure 15.43.

Now that you have one interior surface created, let's create the other major surface in this area of the head: the interior of the mouth.

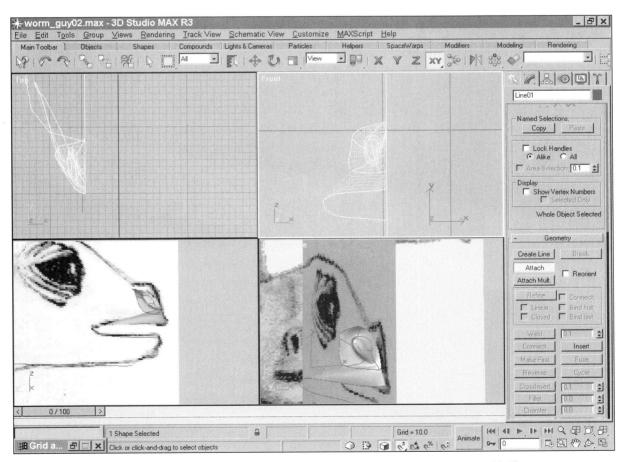

Figure 15.43

The surfaced nostril splines.

Creating The Mouth Interior

To create the interior of the mouth, follow these steps:

1. Go into Spline Sub-Object mode and select the mouth spline. Find the Detach button in the Edit Spline panel, put a checkmark in the box marked Copy, and detach a Copy of the mouth spline to a new object.

2. Turn off the Sub-Object button and select the new shape. Go into Spline Sub-Object mode and select the mouth spline. In the Left viewport, clone this spline by holding down the Shift key and moving the spline to the left (toward the back of the head) along the Viewport X-axis about 25 units. This spline will add thickness to the lips.

3. Select this new spline and create another clone, moving about the same distance toward the back of the head. This time, however, scale up the clone nonuniformly along the Viewport Y-axis about 300 percent. This will be the beginning of the mouth cavity itself. Create another clone of this spline by moving it toward the back of the head again, about 50 units this time.

4. Create one more clone of the last spline created, holding down the Shift key and moving the spline (in the Left view) back along the Viewport X-axis another 50 units. Scale the new spline down along the Viewport Y-axis only, to about 50 percent. The last spline will be the solid back of the mouth cavity. You may also wish to adjust the vertices of this last spline to lie more along a straight line rather than keeping the complex curvature of the other splines, but it isn't necessary to do so. A completed set of mouth interior splines is shown in Figure 15.44.

5. Turn off the Sub-Object button and apply a Cross-Section modifier to this object. Then, apply an Edit Spline modifier, go into Spline Sub-Object mode, and select the original mouth spline that you copied from the head splines. Delete this spline. Click on the Create Line button and toggle on the 3D Snap button. In the Front viewport, find the spline that represents the back of the mouth cavity. Create a line from the open vertex on the top of this line to the bottom, effectively creating a line down the middle of the head at the back of the mouth. Create one more line from the first vertex you chose in the preceding step (the upper vertex in the middle of the head) to the bottom left vertex on the same spline. This will ensure that the back of the mouth cavity gets solid geometry placed over it.

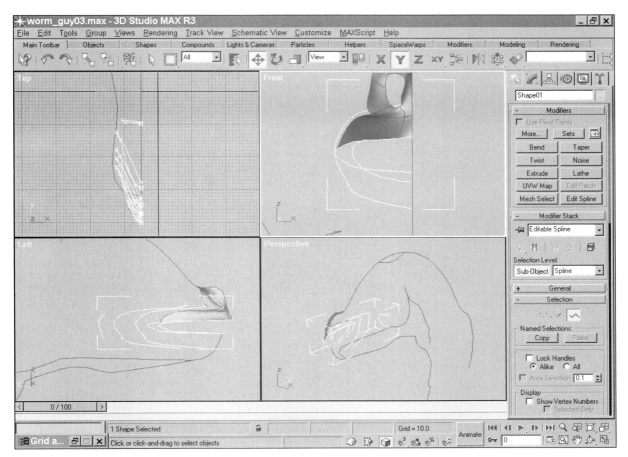

Figure 15.44
The interior mouth splines.

6. Turn off the Sub-Object button and select the original head spline model. Click on the Attach button and select the mouth cavity splines. If you've done everything correctly in the last four steps, new solid geometry will appear in the reference model completing the mouth interior area, as shown in Figure 15.45.

Now on to the next major feature: the eye socket. You will build this, then start stitching geometry together for a more solid model. The antennae and eyelids will come later.

Creating The Eye Socket

To create the eye socket, follow these steps:

1. Begin by going to the Create panel and clicking on the Geometry tab. Click on the Standard Primitives|Geosphere button and create a geosphere in the Front viewport that matches the position of the eye in the template. You'll use this as your eyeball, and it will be a useful reference object as you sculpt the eyelids later on. Position the geosphere to align with the eye in both the Front and Left views.

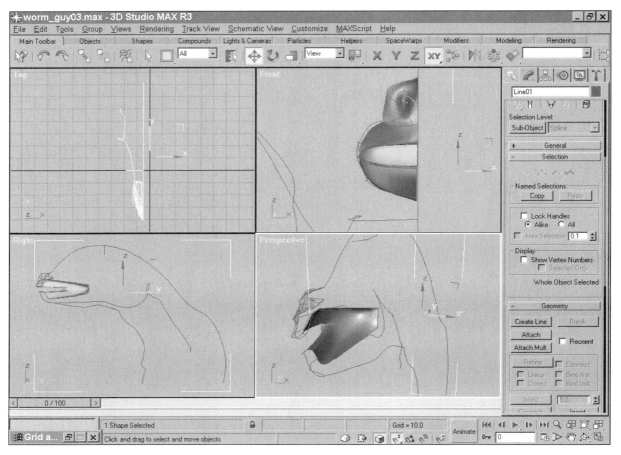

Figure 15.45

The completed and attached mouth interior.

2. In the Create tab, click on the Shapes icon, go to the Left viewport, and click on the NGon button. Create a 10-sided circular NGon roughly in the same position as the eye socket on the template drawings. Remember, this is the eye socket, not the eyelids, so create the NGon shape to fit around the outside of the eyelids. Select the original head spline model, click on the Attach button, and attach the NGon you just created.

3. Go into the Vertex Sub-Object mode and start positioning the vertices of the eye socket to match up with the Front and Left views on the templates. A finished example is shown in Figure 15.46.

Stitching It All Together

Now, we're ready for the meat and potatoes of the model...stitching it together:

1. Turn on the 3D Snap Toggle and click on the Create Line button. Go into a User or Perspective view and hide the template objects.

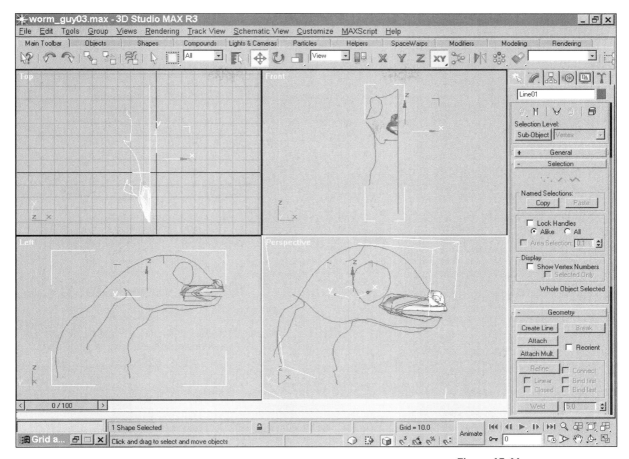

Figure 15.46
The eye socket spline in place
and adjusted.

2. Now comes the fun part. Start creating lines between the vertices
    of the features and the outlines, creating four-sided areas where
    patches will automatically appear in the reference object under-
    neath. Try to avoid three-sided areas whenever possible. You will
    find that you have to refine creation segments to create more
    vertices, and you may find that you need to delete vertices in
    places where a particular vertex doesn't contribute to the desired
    detail. Although it would be nice to break this down to a hard
    science and make every line segment logical and easily explain-
    able, doing so would be impossible. Just keep in mind where
    detail needs to be according to the template drawings (like the
    crest across the head) and an idea of the muscle structure under-
    neath the skin you are creating.

3. With the reference model popping up new patches underneath,
    you'll never have to guess whether you have created a proper surfac-
    ing area; you'll automatically know, and in a very short time you'll

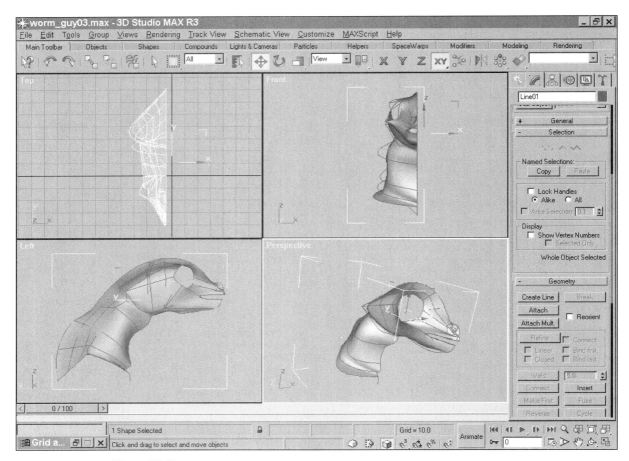

Figure 15.47
The stitched features and profiles.

have a Surfaced model similar to Figure 15.47. Feel free to adjust the Beziers on the vertices to get more roundness and organic structure to the model.

Two more features, and then you're ready to mirror!

Creating The Antennae

The next step is to create the antennae:

1. Go into Segment Sub-Object mode. Find a square area of segments just behind and above the eye socket. A suggested area is shown in Figure 15.48. Select these segments, find the Detach button in the Edit Spline modifier panel, place a checkmark in the box marked Copy, and click on the Detach button to create a new spline object from these segments.

2. Turn off the Sub-Object button and select the new spline object you just created. Go into the Vertex Sub-Object mode, select all of the vertices, and click on the Weld button in the Edit Spline modifier panel. Switch to Spline Sub-Object mode and select this spline.

Note: There's a new feature in the Edit Spline Modifier that's useful for doing massive "stitching" operations on spline models: Cross Insert. When you click on the button and set a unit threshold, the feature will place a vertex on overlapping segments when you place your cursor over them and click (as long as the segments are within the unit threshold you set). Note that you will still have to select the vertices and snap them to one another.

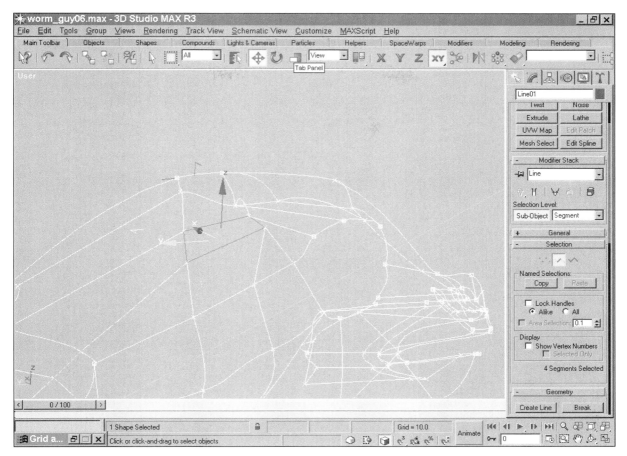

Figure 15.48
Suggested area for the antennae placement.

3. Go to the Front viewport and create a clone of this spline by holding down the Shift key and moving the spline up and to the right until it's just visible over the eye socket. Switch to Vertex Sub-Object mode and select all of the vertices on this new spline. Right-click over one of the selected vertices and change the vertex type to Smooth.

4. Switch back to Spline Sub-Object mode and select the spline you just created. In the Top viewport, uniformly scale this spline down to about 15 percent on both the Viewport X- and Y-axes. Create two more clones of this spline now, moving each upward about 30 units and to the left about 10 units.

5. Select the last spline created in the preceding step and make another clone of it, moving it up and to the left (only about 10 units on each axis this time). In the Top viewport, scale this spline uniformly up to about 220 percent. Create one more clone of this scaled-up spline, and in the Front viewport, move it up and to the left (about 10 units each again). The completed set of antennae splines is shown in Figure 15.49.

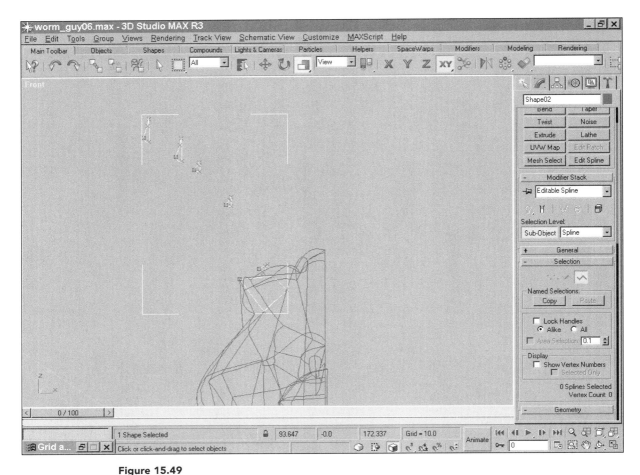

Figure 15.49

The antennae splines.

6. Apply a Cross-Section modifier to this object, then apply an Edit Spline modifier. Select the first spline you started with (the spline on the head at the base of the antennae, and the only one that's still square) and delete it. In a User or Perspective viewport, rotate the view until you can clearly see the topmost round spline of the antennae. Toggle the 3D Snap button on and click on the Create Line button.

7. Create a line bisecting this circle, from one vertex on one side to the corresponding vertex on the other side. Turn off the Create Line button and go into the Vertex Sub-Object mode. Click on the Refine button and add a vertex right in the middle of the bisecting line you just created. Then, turn on the Create Line button again and create a new line from the other vertices on the circular shape on the end to the middle vertex you just created. Turn off the 3D Snap Toggle and select this middle vertex. In the Front viewport, move this vertex up and to the left, creating the cone shape shown in Figure 15.50.

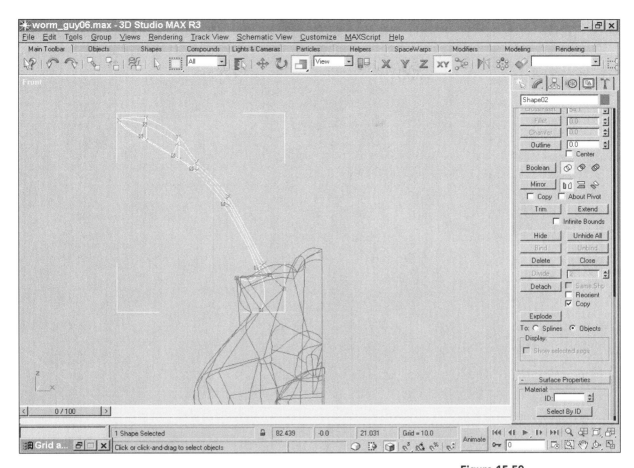

Figure 15.50
The completed antennae splines.

8. Select the original head spline object and click on the Attach button. Select the antennae splines to add the antennae to the head; the solid antennae geometry should appear automatically in the Reference model.

And now for the final part...the eyelids!

Creating The Eyelids

To create the eyelids, follow these steps:

1. Go into the Spline Sub-Object mode and select the eye socket spline. Find the Detach button in the Edit Spline modifier, place a checkmark in the box marked Copy, then click on the Detach button to make a new spline object from the eye socket spline.

2. Turn off the Spline Sub-Object button and select the new spline object created in the preceding step. Go into Spline Sub-Object mode and select the spline. Go to the Front viewport and create a clone of this object by moving it to the left (only a few units), lining it up to the first ridge in the eyelid on the template drawing.

3. Switch to Vertex Sub-Object mode and begin moving the vertices on this spline so that they fall more in line with the eyelid, using the eyeball geosphere as a reference. Switch back to Spline Sub-Object mode and repeat this process three more times, adjusting the vertices after each cloning operation.

4. Switch to Spline Sub-Object mode once again and make one more clone of the last spline created, this time moving it back inside of the eyelids toward the head about 10 units. This will give the eyelid thickness as it rides over the surface of the eye. The eyelid splines are shown in Figure 15.51.

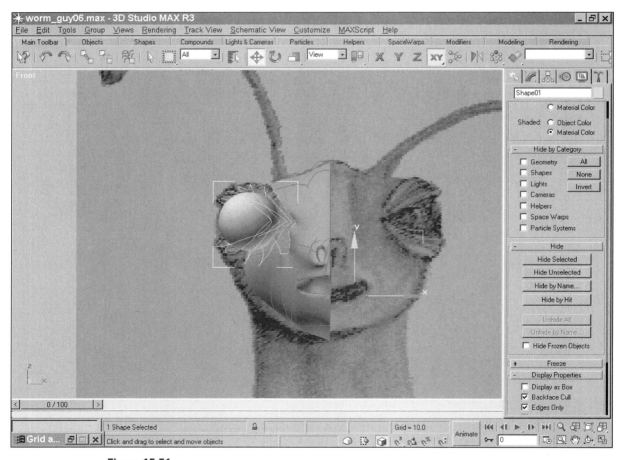

Figure 15.51

The eyelid splines.

5. Turn off the Sub-Object button and apply a Cross-Section modifier to this object (with the Bezier Corner button checked in the Spline Options menu). Next, apply an Edit Spline modifier, go into Spline Sub-Object mode, select the eye socket spline detached from the original model, and delete it. Then, select each of the clones you made in the preceding step and hide them with the Hide button in the Edit Spline modifier panel.

6. Switch to Vertex Sub-Object mode and select all of the vertices on the splines that the Cross-Section modifier created. Begin adjusting them so that they have a distinct ridge running down from each vertex to create the ridge pattern in the eyelids. Leave the vertices at the corners of the eyelids as they are. When this is finished, click on the Unhide All button in the Edit Spline modifier panel to unhide all of the splines. The result is shown in Figure 15.52.

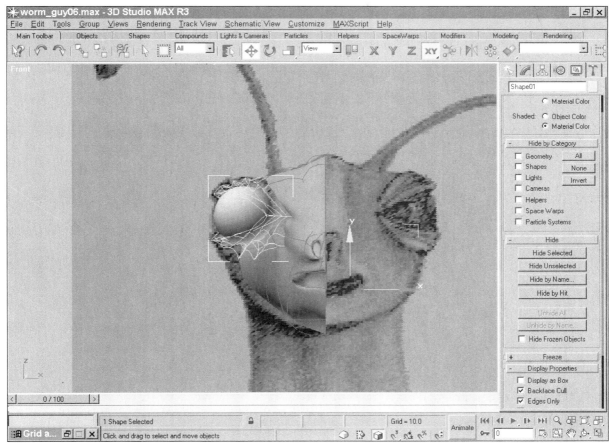

7. Turn off the Sub-Object button, select the original head spline model, click on the Attach button, and select the eyelid splines. The eyelids should now be attached to the head, with solid geometry for them showing in the reference model.

Figure 15.52
The completed eyelid splines.

All that's left now is to mirror the splines and attach them to the original. If your Mirror copy gives you unexpected results, remember to use the vertex/pivot point alignment operation described at the end of the Blackbird project. The final alien head is shown in Figure 15.53.

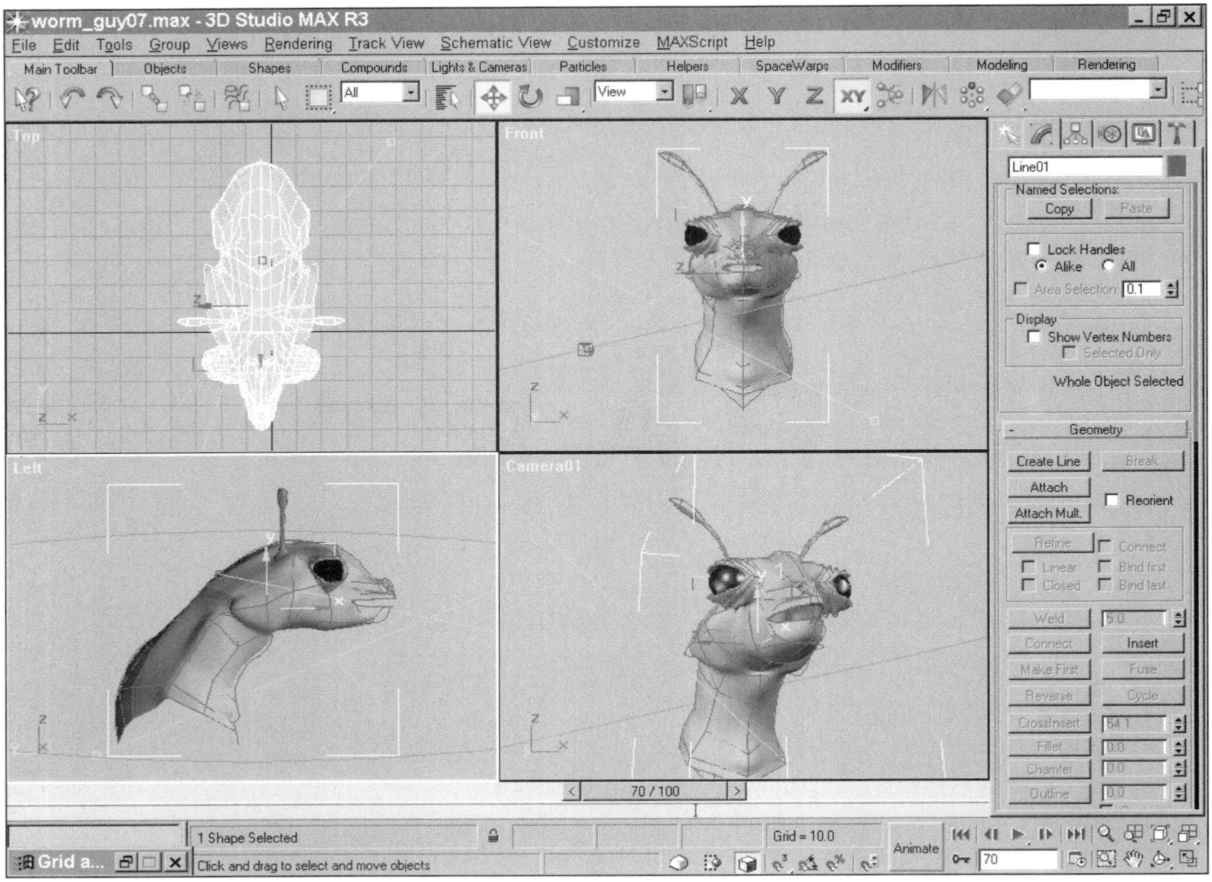

Figure 15.53

The final alien head.

Note: A completed version of this model is saved in the \CHAP_15 directory as WORMGUY_FINAL.MAX.

As with the Blackbird model, you can save the alien head to your \3DSMAX3\ SCENES directory and begin the process of texturing, lighting, and rendering it.

Moving On

Surface Tools has long been a favorite plug-in package for many MAX artists. As you become proficient with it, think about combining it with some of the other features of MAX, such as the Morpher modifier described in Chapter 14. Also, note that spline-based models work well with MAX Release 3's new Flex modifier (for soft body dynamics) and with the Skin modifier (note that both of these are covered in Chapter 13).

Now that you've finished the modeling and animation section of the book, you'll move on to technical stuff. In the next two chapters, contributor Scot Tumlin will show you more fun with MAXScript.

PART IV

MAXSCRIPT AND PLUG-INS

16

AN INTRODUCTION TO MAXSCRIPT RELEASE 3

*The first half of this chapter provides a
refresher course for MAXScript users and
introduces MAXScript to artists new to scripting.
The second half shows how to create script
interfaces that you can dock with the Command
panel and float over the viewports.*

BY SCOT TUMLIN

The Return Of MAXScript

MAXScript is one of the most powerful features in 3D Studio MAX Release 3. It's such an important feature that other 3D applications have followed suit and are either introducing scripting systems of their own or beefing up their existing functionality. MAXScript provides access to the nuts and bolts of 3D Studio MAX. With MAXScript you can automate modeling, animation, materials, and rendering tasks. You can also build custom import/export tools. This comes in handy for exporting MAX data to video game consoles and to other 3D applications.

This chapter is separated into two sections. The first section provides an introduction for artists new to scripting and a refresher course for artists familiar with MAXScript. The second section covers more advanced topics. In the second section, you'll create scripts with utility interfaces and floating interfaces. You'll also create code that transforms objects and switches objects between the five sub-object modes.

The MAXScript Utility

The MAXScript module appears as a button on the Utility tab of the Command panel. Clicking on the Utility tab displays the Utility panel. Clicking on the MAXScript button in the Utility panel reveals a series of buttons, as shown in Figure 16.1.

Let's quickly review the functions of each button:

- The Open Listener button opens the Listener window. The Listener window displays the results from your scripts for debugging purposes.

- The New Script button opens a new text window for code entry. Once your script is written, you can save it from the text window to your MAX \SCRIPTS directory.

- The Open Script button loads a previously saved script from your \SCRIPTS directory into a text window. You can continue to edit and run the loaded script.

- The Run Script button executes a previously saved script. Unlike the Open Script button, the Run Script button doesn't load your script into a window. As you get proficient with scripting, you'll want easy access to your scripts. The Utility field at the bottom of the panel serves this purpose. A folder named \STARTUP appears within your \SCRIPTS folder. Scripts placed in the \STARTUP folder are loaded whenever 3D Studio MAX is started.

- The Close button closes the MAXScript utility rollout.

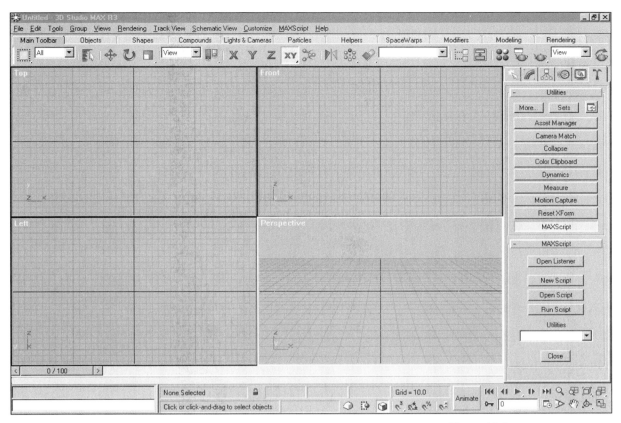

Figure 16.1
The Utility panel expanded,
revealing the MAXScript buttons.

Using MAXScript To Create A Box, Sphere, And Cone

Way back in Chapter 1, we created a tab panel that included tools for creating boxes, spheres, and cones. We also created a macro that duplicated the three construction tools. Now, let's create a script that also creates a box, sphere, and cone:

1. If necessary, click on the Utility tab to display the Utility panel.

2. Click on the MAXScript button to expand the MAXScript utility rollout.

3. Click on the New Script button; a text window appears, as shown in Figure 16.2.

4. Type the following code to create a box, sphere, and cone:

```
b = box length: 50 height: 50 width: 50
s = sphere radius: 25 segs: 16
c = cone radius1: 20 radius2: 0 height: 50 heightsegs: 5
```

Note: Some code lines have been modified to fit within this book's margins. Refer to actual script files on this book's companion CD-ROM.

LOADING THE PRIMITIVES SCRIPT

If you get into trouble or want to save time, you can load this script from the \CHAP_16 directory of the companion CD-ROM. The file is called BSC.MS.

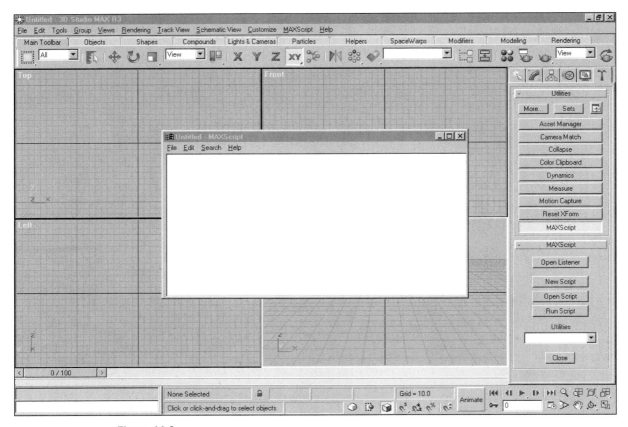

Figure 16.2

A blank script window, ready for your code.

THE EVALUATE ALL KEYBOARD SHORTCUT

Instead of selecting Evaluate All from the File menu, you can press Ctrl+E.

5. In the MAXScript window, select Evaluate All from the File menu. The script is executed and Box, Sphere, and Cone objects appear in the viewports, as shown in Figure 16.3.

6. Move the Box and Cone objects away from the origin (the world coordinate center) to reveal the Sphere object.

7. Select Save from the Script window's File menu, and save the file as TEST.MS.

Let's examine the code. All three lines follow a similar format. They each start with a variable: *b*, *s*, and *c*. Each line also contains a series of parameters, such as length and radius. The first line creates a box with a length, height, and width of 50 units. The box is stored in the variable *b*. The second line creates a sphere with a radius of 25 and 16 segments. The sphere is stored in the variable *s*. The last line creates a cone with a base of 20 units, height of 50 units, and 5 segments. The radius2 parameter determines the top radius of the cone; a 0 value creates the pointed tip.

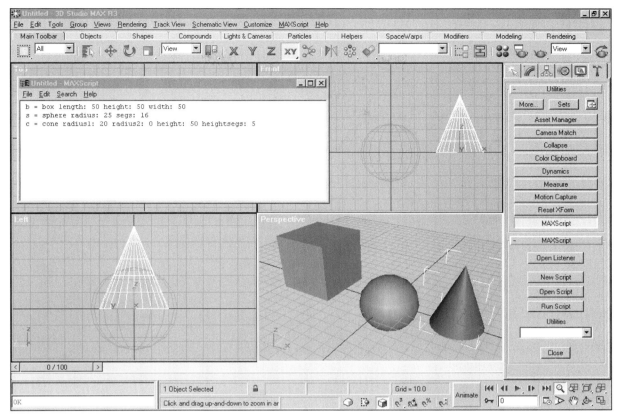

Figure 16.3
Your script creates a box, sphere, and cone.

Applying Transforms To The Box, Sphere, And Cone

The code in the preceding section stores each object in a variable. For example, the Box object is stored in variable *b*. If you wanted to rename, scale, or move the box, you would reference the *b* variable. Let's add code that moves the box and cone away from the origin:

1. Add the highlighted code in the following code snippet to your script:

```
clearlistener()
max select all
max delete
b = box length: 50 height: 50 width: 50
s = sphere radius: 25 segs: 16
c = cone radius1: 20 radius2: 0 height: 50 heightsegs: 5
b.pos.x = -75
c.pos.x = 75
```

Let's take a look at the code you just added to your script. The first line, **clearlistener( )**, clears the Listener window. When you execute a script, the Listener window displays the results of your code.

2. Try it now—open the Listener window and execute the script. Note the information about the box, sphere, and cone added to the Listener window. As you execute code, the Listener window appends the new information. This can get a bit overwhelming when you try to debug your code. Using the **clearlistener( )** command makes debugging code a lot easier.

   Your script will create a new box, sphere, and cone each time it's executed. To keep copies from piling up, you need to delete any objects already in the scene. The second line, **max select all**, selects all the objects in the scene. The third line, **max delete**, deletes the selected objects. Once all the objects in the scene are deleted, a new box, sphere, and cone are created.

   The last two lines move the box and cone. Note how each line starts with a variable. The *b* in **b.pos.x** tells MAXScript to move the variable *b*, which contains the box. The *pos* in **b.pos.x** tells MAXScript to change the position of the Box object. The *x* in **b.pos.x** tells MAXScript to move the object on the X-axis. Finally, the **–75** moves the box negative 75 units on the X-axis. The last line moves the Cone object positive 75 units on the X-axis.

3. Now, run the script. The Listener window is cleared. Next, any previous objects are deleted. The box, sphere, and cone are created and the box and cone are moved, as shown in Figure 16.4.

Now For Something More Advanced

Quick-and-dirty scripts often don't need interfaces; you use them a few times and throw them away. For scripts that you're going to reuse often, it makes sense to create an interface that gives you control over the script parameters.

For example, in the preceding script, you moved the box negative 75 units. If you add a spinner field to the script, the user could "dial in" a specific distance to move the box.

Creating The Transform Script

Let's create a script that moves, rotates, and scales a selected object or objects. The script will include radio buttons to select a transform mode and spinner fields to dial in numerical values. You'll start with the code necessary to create an interface for the Utility panel:

1. If necessary select New from the File menu to clear the scene. Then, click on the Utility tab and click on the MAXScript button to start MAXScript.

LOADING THE TRANSFORM SCRIPT

If you get into trouble or want to save time, you can load this script from the \CHAP_16 directory of this book's companion CD-ROM. The file is called TRANS.MS.

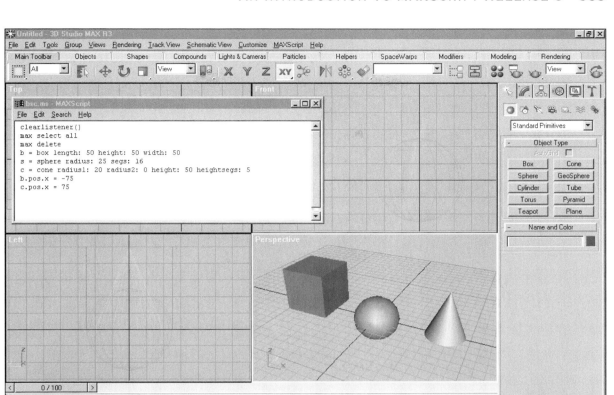

Figure 16.4

The script creates and moves the objects.

2. Click on the New Script button to open a blank script window. Type in the following code, which creates an interface for the script:

```
-- transform script
-- this script moves, rotates and scales selected object(s).

utility trans "Transform"
(

)
```

3. When you're finished, save the script as TRANS.MS.

4. Next, press Ctrl+E to execute the script. The word "Transform" appears in the Utility field of the Utility panel.

5. Click on the transform item in the Utility field. The Utility panel expands with a simple interface for the script, as shown in Figure 16.5.

6. Click on the Close button. The Utility panel contracts, hiding the Transform script.

The first line, -- **transform script**, is a remark. A line that starts with the character -- is ignored by MAXScript. A remark line is a note to

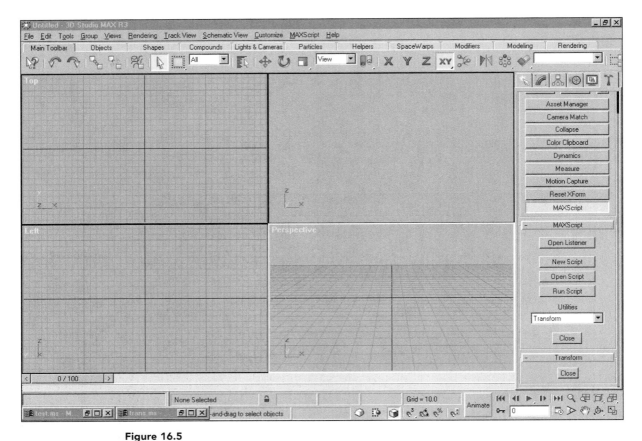

Figure 16.5

The initial interface of the Transform script appears in the Utility panel.

the programmer, or in our case, to the artist. The first line simply announces the title of this script. The second line is another remark, announcing the purpose of the script.

The **utility trans "transform"** line tells MAXScript to place the interface on the Utility panel. The **trans** portion of this line is the name of the script. The **"transform"** portion is the text that appears in the Utility field in the Utility panel. The next line is an open parenthesis. Each open parenthesis has a matching closed parenthesis. Note the closed parenthesis on the last line of the script. Note how the open parenthesis and the closed parenthesis are lined up in the same column. The closed parenthesis denotes the end of the script.

7. Now you need a radio button that selects move, rotation, or scale. Add the highlighted code in the following code snippet:

```
-- transform script
-- this script moves, rotates and scales selected object(s).

utility trans "Transform"
(
```

```
group "Select Transform"
(
    radiobuttons tm labels:#("M:","R:","S:") default: 1
)
)
```

8. Save the script, then press Ctrl+E to execute it.

9. Select Transform from the Utility field; the TRANS script expands and the new radio button appears, as shown in Figure 16.6.

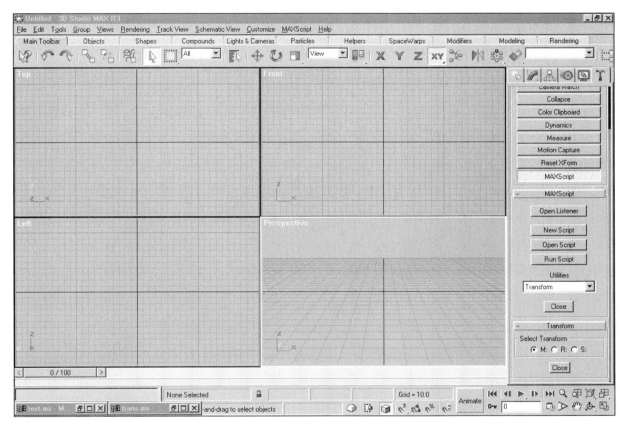

Figure 16.6
You now have a radio button.

So what does the highlighted code do? The first line, **group "Select Transform"**, tells MAXScript to start an interface group. When you ran the script, the new radio button appeared within an embossed rectangle. The embossed rectangle visually denotes an interface group. The group command creates the rectangle and gives the group a title. The **"Select Transform"** portion of the line defines the group's title. When you ran the script, the phrase "Select Transform" appeared over the embossed rectangle.

The line **radiobuttons tm labels:#("M:","R:","S:") default: 1** creates
the radio button. The **tm** portion of the line is the variable that
stores the radio button. Interrogating this variable tells you which of
the three buttons was pressed. The **labels:#("M:","R","S")** portion of
the line creates the labels for each button. Finally, the **default: 1**
portion of the line selects the first button as the default or starting
state of the radio button. In this case M: is the first button.

Let's add a few more buttons to our interface.

10. Add the highlighted code in the following code snippet (the code
     adds a second radio button and spinner):

```
-- transform script
-- this script moves, rotates and scales selected object(s).

utility trans "Transform"
(
    group "Select Transform"
    (
        radiobuttons tm labels:#("M:","R:","S:") default: 1
        radiobuttons ta labels:#("X:","Y:","Z:") default: 1
        spinner tv "Amt: " range:[-10000,10000,0] type: #float
    )
)
```

11. Save the script and press Ctrl+E to execute it.

12. Select Transform from the Utility field. The TRANS script expands
     and a second radio button and spinner field are added to the script
     (shown in Figure 16.7).

The new code adds a second radio button and a spinner field to the
script. The first highlighted line creates a radio button with the variable name *ta*. The labels **X:**, **Y:**, and **Z:** indicate on which axis to
transform. The second highlighted line adds a spinner field to the
interface. The **tv** portion of the line stores the spinner's value in the
variable *tv*. The "**Amt:**" portion of the line creates the spinner's label. The **range:[-10000,10000,0]** defines the lowest value, highest
value, and initial value of the spinner, respectively.

Finally, the **#float** portion of the line defines the *tv* variable as a
floating-point number. A floating-point number contains a decimal
value, whereas an integer variable cannot. You want precision, so a
floating-point variable makes sense.

This concludes the interface portion of the script. Now, you can create the code that actually transforms a selected object or objects.

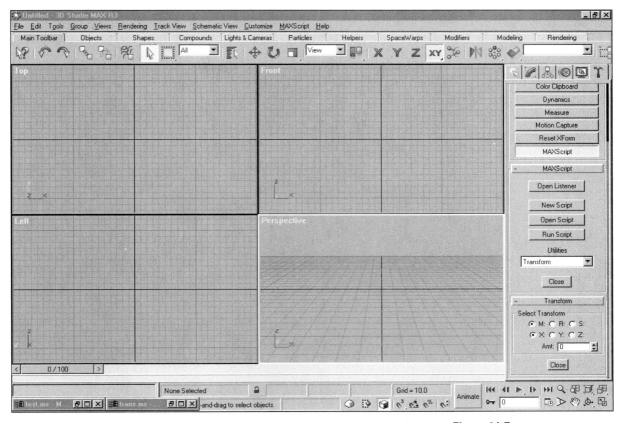

Figure 16.7
The interface is complete.

13. Add the highlighted code shown in Listing 16.1. When you're fin-
    ished, save the revised script.

Listing 16.1   The highlighted code moves the selected object(s).

```
-- transform script
-- this script moves, rotates and scales selected object(s).

utility trans "Transform"
(
    group "Select Transform"
    (
        radiobuttons tm labels:#("M:","R:","S:") default: 1
        radiobuttons ta labels:#("X:","Y:","Z:") default: 1
        spinner tv "Amt: " range:[-10000,10000,0] type: #float
    )

    on tv changed value do
    (
        sobj = selection as array
        if sobj.count > 0 then
        (
            for i = 1 to sobj.count do
            (
```

```
if tm.state == 1 and ta.state == 1 then sobj[i].pos.x = tv.value
if tm.state == 1 and ta.state == 2 then sobj[i].pos.y = tv.value
if tm.state == 1 and ta.state == 3 then sobj[i].pos.z = tv.value
            )
        )
    )
)
```

A Look At Subroutines

Before you run the script, let's go over the new lines of code and their functions. The line **on tv changed value do** tells MAXScript to continue only when the user changes the tv spinner's value. The next line is an open parenthesis; note the matching closed parenthesis toward the end of the code. The matching set of parentheses form a subroutine. Any code placed between these parentheses will execute when the spinner value is changed.

Normally, scripts execute each line in order, starting with the first line of code. This was the case with the first script in this chapter. However, you may want some commands to execute only when certain conditions are met. Subroutines serve this purpose. The first line of a subroutine checks for a condition (for example, **on tv changed value do**). The next line is an open parenthesis. A series of commands follow the open parenthesis. Finally, a matching closed parenthesis ends the subroutine. If the condition is met, the commands within the matching parentheses are executed.

The next line, **sobj = selection as array**, stores the selected object(s) in an array. An array is a variable that stores a series of items (it's similar to a database that holds a series of records). In this case, any selected objects are stored in the array called **sobj**. If you select three objects before running this script, the array **sobj** would contain the three objects.

The next line, **if sobj.count > 0 then**, is an if/then command. An if/then command checks for a condition. What happens next is based on the result of that condition. The **sobj.count** portion of the line gets the number of items in the **sobj** array. The **> 0** portion of the line checks to see if the number of items in the **sobj** array is greater then 0. Basically, the line checks to see if the user selected at least one object. If no objects were selected, the script would do nothing. Again, note the matching parentheses that make this line the beginning of a subroutine. Code that appears between these parentheses would execute only if one or more objects were selected.

At this point, the user selected one or more objects, the tv spinner has been changed, and the **sobj** array contains the selected objects. Now, you have to transform each object in the **sobj** array. The line **for i = 1 to sobj.count do** serves this purpose. This line is a for/loop command. A for/loop command increments through a range of numbers, executing commands with each increment. The **for i = 1** portion of the script stores the value 1 in the variable *i*. The **to sobj.count** portion of the script ends with the total number of objects in the array. If the user selected three objects, the for/loop command would start with 1 and end with 3. Each increment is stored in the variable *i*. Another set of parentheses follows the for/loop command. Code within these parentheses would execute as the for/loop increments.

The line **if tm.state == 1 and ta.state == 1 then sobj[i].pos.x = tv.value** is another if/then statement. Here, you check for two conditions. The **if tm.state == 1** portion of the line checks for the first condition: Did the user select Move from the **tm** radio button? The **ta.state == 1** portion of the script checks for the second condition: Did the user select the X-axis from the **ta** radio button. The **and** portion of this script requires that both conditions be true. If both conditions are true, the **sobj[i].pos.x = tv.value** portion of the line is executed.

Remember how the for/loop command stored a value in *i*? Well, here's where the *i* variable comes in handy. An array can store a number of items. Let's say the user selected three objects before running this script. The **sobj** array would contain the three objects. To access one of the objects in the array, add brackets containing the position in the array variable. For example, to access the first object in the **sobj** array, you would type "sobj[1]". The 1 tells MAXScript to get the first item in the array. To access the third item in the **sobj** array, you would type "sobj[3]". Now you see the purpose of the for/loop. The *i* variable starts as 1, becomes 2, becomes 3, and so on. When the *i* variable is placed between the brackets, each selected object is chosen one at a time. Each selected object is then moved on the X-axis to the value in the tv spinner.

The line **if tm.state == 1 and ta.state == 2 then sobj[i].pos.y = tv.value** checks to see if the user selected M and Y. If both conditions are true, each selected object is moved on the Y-axis to the value on the tv spinner. The line **if tm.state == 1 and ta.state == 3 then sobj[i].pos.z = tv.value** checks to see if the user selected Move on the Z-axis. If both conditions are true, each selected object is moved on the Z-axis to the value on the tv spinner. To check out the subroutine functions, do this:

1. Press Ctrl+E to execute the script and, if necessary, create a few objects.

2. Select one or more objects, select M and X, and change the spinner value. The selected objects move to the value in the spinner.

3. Next, let's add the code needed to rotate and scale selected object(s). Add the highlighted code in Listing 16.2.

Listing 16.2   The code needed to rotate and scale
selected object(s).

```
-- transform script
-- this script moves, rotates and scales selected object(s).

utility trans "Transform"
(
    group "Select Transform"
    (
        radiobuttons tm labels:#("M:","R:","S:") default: 1
        radiobuttons ta labels:#("X:","Y:","Z:") default: 1
        spinner tv "Amt: " range:[-10000,10000,0] type: #float
    )

    on tv changed value do
    (
        sobj = selection as array
        if sobj.count > 0 then
        (
            for i = 1 to sobj.count do
            (
if tm.state == 1 and ta.state == 1 then sobj[i].pos.x = tv.value
if tm.state == 1 and ta.state == 2 then sobj[i].pos.y = tv.value
if tm.state == 1 and ta.state == 3 then sobj[i].pos.z = tv.value

if tm.state == 2 and ta.state == 1 then
sobj[i].rotation.x_rotation = tv.value
if tm.state == 2 and ta.state == 2 then
sobj[i].rotation.y_rotation = tv.value
if tm.state == 2 and ta.state == 3 then
sobj[i].rotation.z_rotation = tv.value

if tm.state == 3 and ta.state == 1 then
sobj[i].scale.x = tv.value
if tm.state == 3 and ta.state == 2 then
sobj[i].scale.y = tv.value
if tm.state == 3 and ta.state == 3 then
sobj[i].scale.z = tv.value
            )
        )
    )
)
```

4. Save the script and press Crtl+E to execute it.

5. Select one or more objects, then try the Rotate and Scale tools. Note how your selected objects change once the spinner value changes.

The line **if tm.state == 2 and ta.state == 1 then sobj[i].rotation.x_rotation = tv.value** checks to see if the user selected R and X. If these two conditions are met, the selected objects are rotated the value in the tv spinner on the X-axis. The next two lines do the same for the Y- and Z-axes.

The line **if tm.state == 3 and ta.state == 1 then sobj[i].scale.x = tv.value** checks to see if the user selected S and X. If these two conditions are met, the selected objects are scaled the value in the tv spinner on the X-axis. Again, the next two lines do the same for the Y- and Z-axes.

This completes the Transform utility script. On your own, try to add the functionality to switch between absolute and relative modes.

Creating The Sub-Object Selector With A Floating Interface

The next tutorial creates a script for a floating menu with a Pick button and radio button listing the five sub-object modes (vertex, edge, face, polygon, element). Once you pick an object, the floating menu switches to one of five sub-object modes based on the radio button's status. The floating interface allows the user to place it anywhere on the screen for easy access.

Let's start with the code needed to create a floating interface:

1. If necessary, reset 3D Studio MAX Release 3, then create three Box objects in your Top viewport. (Their relative sizes don't matter that much; make them about the same size.)

2. Select the Utility panel and click on the New Script button. A blank script window appears.

3. Enter the following code:

```
-- polyedit.ms
-- this script creates a floater with sub-obj selector
clearlistener()    --clear the listener for debug purposes
Rollout first "Sub-Obj Selector"    -- create a rollout
(

)
nf = newrolloutfloater "SOS" 150 225
-- define the title and size
addRollout first nf    -- build/display the floater
```

4. Save the script and press Ctrl+E to execute it. A floater with the title SOS appears, as shown in Figure 16.8.

   Let's take a look at the code. As with our last script, the first two lines are remarks. The next line, **clearlistener( )**, clears the MAXScript Listener window for debugging the script. The fourth line, **Rollout first "Sub-Obj Selector"**, starts a rollout subroutine. The **first** portion of the line is the variable name of this rollout.

   The **"Sub-Obj Selector"** portion of the line defines the title of the rollout. The next two lines contain the matching set of parentheses

LOADING THE POLYEDIT SCRIPT

If you get into trouble or want to save time, you can load the POLYEDIT script from the CHAP_16 directory of the companion CD-ROM. The file is called POLYEDIT.MS.

Figure 16.8

The floating interface for our sub-object selector script.

that contain the rollout's interface elements. Later you will place the buttons for the script between the two parentheses. The line **nf = newrolloutfloater "SOS" 150 225** calls the **newRolloutFloater** function. This function creates and opens a floating window of a given width and height. The **nf = newrolloutfloater** portion of the line stores the floater in the variable *nf*. The **"SOS"** portion of the line defines the title of the new window.

The **150 225** portion of the line defines the width and height of the window. The next line, **addRollout first nf**, places the "SOS" rollout in the floating window. The preceding code displays a floating window with a rollout panel.

Now, let's add a Pick button and a radio button to the rollout panel.

5. If necessary, close the floating window. Then add the highlighted code in the following code snippet to your script.

```
-- polyedit.ms
-- this script creates a floater with sub-obj selector
clearlistener()   --clear the listener for debug purposes
Rollout first "Sub-Obj Selector"   -- create a rollout
(
    group "Sub Obj Mode"       -- create the first ui group
    (
        pickbutton pobj "Pick Object"
        -- create a pick button
        label pname    -- create a label field
        radiobuttons m
        labels:#("Vert","Edge","Face","Poly","Edge")
    )
)
nf = newrolloutfloater "SOS" 150 225
-- define the title and size
addRollout first nf   -- build/display the floater
```

Figure 16.9
Now your script has a Pick button and a radio button.

6. Save the script and press Ctrl+E to execute it. A floating window appears with a Pick button and radio button listing the five sub-object modes (Figure 16.9).

The line **group "Sub Obj Mode"** should look familiar. As with the preceding script, this line creates an interface group in the "SOS" rollout. A matching set of parentheses follows. The line **pickbutton pobj "Pick Object"** creates a Pick button assigned to the variable *pobj*. The **"Pick Object"** portion of the line defines the text that appears within the Pick button. The line **label pname** creates a label field that appears below the Pick button. Later, you'll add code that displays the name of the object that is picked in the label field.

The **pname** portion of the line is the variable that stores the information displayed by the label. The next line, **radiobuttons m labels:#("Vert","Edge","Face","Poly","Edge")**, creates a radio button with five options. The five options match the five sub-object modes available in the modifier tab. Selections made in the radio button are stored in the variable *m*. With the interface complete, you need code to switch between the five sub-object modes.

7. If necessary, close the floating window. Then, add the highlighted code in Listing 16.3 to your script.

Listing 16.3   The code needed to pick an object and change it's sub-object mode via the radio button.

```
-- polyedit.ms
-- this script creates a floater with sub-obj selector
clearlistener()   --clear the listener for debug purposes
Rollout first "Sub-Obj Selector"   -- create a rollout
(
    group "Sub Obj Mode"   -- create the first ui group
    (
        pickbutton pobj "Pick Object"   -- create a pick button
        label pname   -- create a label field
        radiobuttons m
        labels:#("Vert","Edge","Face","Poly","Edge")
    )

    on pobj picked obj do   -- an object was picked
    (
        p = obj; pname.text = p.name
        max modify mode   -- open the modifier panel
        converttomesh(p)
        -- convert the picked obj to an edit mesh
        select p   -- select the picked object
        subObjectLevel = m.state   -- default to vertex mode
    )

    on m changed state do   -- a sub object mode was selected
    (
        subObjectLevel = m.state
        -- set subobj level to radio button
        update(p)                 -- refresh the mesh
    )
)

nf = newrolloutfloater "SOS" 150 225
-- define the title and size
addRollout first nf   -- build/display the floater
```

8. Save the script and press Ctrl+E to execute it. A floating window appears with a Pick button and radio button. Click on the Pick button.

9. Click on one of the boxes you created earlier; a number of events occur. First, the name of the picked object appears under the Pick button. Next, the Command panel switches to the Modify panel. Finally, the picked object switches to the sub-object mode highlighted in the radio button.

10. Select another sub-object mode. The picked object switches to the selected sub-object mode.

11. Click on the Pick button and click on another box. The label under the Pick button changes to the name of the picked object.

12. Again, select another sub-object mode. The picked object switches to the selected sub-object mode.

Okay, let's take a look at the new code. The line **on pobj picked obj do** starts a new subroutine. When the user picks an object, this line is triggered and code within the subroutine is executed. The line **p = obj; pname.text = p.name** stores the picked object's name in the variable *p*. Also, the name of the object is stored in the label's text field. This causes the label to display the name of the picked object. The line **max modify mode** tells the Command panel to display the Modifier tab. The next line, **converttomesh(p)**, converts the data stored in the variable *p* into an editable mesh object. At this point in the code, the *p* variable holds the picked object; thus, the picked object is converted into an editable mesh. This has to happen before sub-object manipulation can occur. The line **select p** highlights the picked object. The next line, **subObjectLevel = m.state**, sets **subObjectLevel** to the current value of the radio button. Therefore, if the radio button is set to vertex, **subObjectLevel** is set to vertex sub-object mode.

The next subroutine starts with the line **on m changed state do**. This line waits for the radio button to change. When the radio button changes, the code within the subroutine executes. The line **subObjectLevel = m.state** also appears in this subroutine. Both lines are exactly the same, but they occur within different events. Within this subroutine, **subObjectLevel** is set when the user changes the radio button. In the preceding subroutine, the same command executes when a new object is picked. This ensures that the radio button and sub-object mode of the picked object always match.

Finally, the line **update(p)** updates or refreshes the picked object. This is important when you add or delete vertices, and perform other actions.

Take a moment and play with the SOS script. Combining this script with the new transform indicators provides an effective workflow for artists who like to work in MAX's Perspective viewport. The new transform indicators can lock to an axis, removing the need for the orthographic views. The SOS script also provides an easy way to quickly switch between the five sub-object modes.

On your own, try to add Modify tools such as Attach, Delete, and Weld to the SOS script.

Moving On

In this chapter, you took a brief, introductory look at MAXScript. You also created interfaces for the Utility panel and floating windows and examined the MAXScript code for if/then and for/loop statements, arrays, and subroutines.

In the next chapter, you'll see how to use a number of MAXScript utilities to speed up your work flow.

A MAXSCRIPT
GRAB BAG

17

This chapter is chock-full of cool and useful utility scripts for 3D Studio MAX Release 3. Need to solve a problem and you don't know where to start? A script in this chapter might be able to help you.

BY SCOT TUMLIN

THE INCLUDED SCRIPTS

Note that all the scripts in this chapter can be found on this book's companion CD-ROM in the \CHAP_17 directory.

Day-To-Day Problem Solving

There are so many uses for MAXScript, it's tough to decide what to write about. However, as I sat down to write this chapter, I reflected on the numerous utility scripts I've written over the last year or so and thought about how they've helped me complete various tasks.

So, here's a grab bag of some of my most useful scripts. The scripts presented in this chapter were chosen both for their utility and for their ability (hey, it rhymes!) to show off MAXScript features. With luck, these scripts can help you solve some of the artistic and production challenges you face as a MAX 3D artist. As you work through these scripts, you may find that some will form the foundation for your own, customized scripts, and others might become invaluable tools that you use every day.

Using Modifiers: The Flip Normals Script

The Flip Normals script (FLIP NORMALS.MS) applies the Normal modifier to one or more selected objects. This script starts by storing the selected objects in an array called **o**. A for/loop is used to move through the array, one object at a time. Each time the for/loop moves through the array, four commands are executed for each selected object. First, **converttomesh o[i]** converts the current object into an Editable Mesh object. Most modifiers work at the face, vertex, or edge level. Thus, your objects must be editable meshes.

Next, the **addmodifier o[i] (normalmodifier( ))** line adds the Normal modifier to the current object. This is the MAXScript equivalent to manually applying the Normal modifier via the Modify panel. The **o[i].normal.flip = true** line flips the current object's normals. Finally, the **update o[i]** line refreshes the current object, updates the screen, and so on. The script is shown in Listing 17.1.

Note: Some code lines have been modified to fit within this book's margins. Refer to actual script files on this book's companion CD-ROM.

Listing 17.1   The Flip Normals script.

```
-- this script flips the normals of selected objects
-- TO USE:   Open the listener window to track progress
-- (optional)
--           select 1 or more objects
--           run the script

clearlistener()   -- clear the listener
o = selection as array   -- places selected objects in an array
                         -- called o

for i = 1 to o.count do   -- repeat these commands for each
                          -- selected object
(
```

```
    -- print status
    format "Flipping the normals of %\" o[i].name
    -- convert the object to an editable mesh
    converttomesh o[i]
    -- add the normal modifier
    addmodifier o[i] (normalmodifier())
    o[i].normal.flip = true   -- flip the normals
    update o[i]   -- update/refresh the object
)
format "done\n"    -- tell me when you're done
```

The Unify Normals Script

The Unify Normals script (UNIFY NORMALS.MS) is a subtle variant of the Flip Normals script. This script uses the same Normal modifier, but the modifier is used to unify, not flip, the face normals.

The **o[i].normal.unify = true** line unifies the normals of the current object. The Flip Normals and Unify Normals scripts form the foundation for applying modifiers to your objects. Now, it's no big deal to apply a modifier to a series of objects; you can do that with a few simple mouse clicks. However, by using these scripts, you can apply multiple modifiers to a series of objects, which can be a great time-saver in an intense production environment. (The script following Unify Normals, Multi Mod, demonstrates this technique.) The Unify Normals script is shown in Listing 17.2.

Listing 17.2   The Unify Normals script.

```
-- this script unifies the normals of selected objects
-- TO USE:  Open the listener window to track progress
-- (optional)
--                 select 1 or more objects
--                 run the script

clearlistener()    -- clear the listener
-- places selected objects in an array called o
o = selection as array

-- repeat these commands for each selected object
for i = 1 to o.count do
(
    -- print status
    format "Unifying the normals of %\n" o[i].name
    -- convert the object to an editable mesh
    converttomesh o[i]
    -- add the normal modifier
    addmodifier o[i] (normalmodifier())
    o[i].normal.unify = true   -- unify the normals
    update o[i]   -- update/refresh the object
)
format "done\n"    -- tell me when you're done
```

The Multi Mod Script

The Multi Mod script (MULTI MOD.MS) applies the Bend, Twist, and Taper modifiers to one or more selected objects. The core of the script uses the **addmodifier** line to apply the Bend, Twist, and Taper modifiers to the array of objects. Once the three modifiers are applied, parameters for them are called.

The **o[i].bend.angle = 60** line bends the current object 60 degrees. Note how the periods separate the object and its parameters. For example, the first period tells us that **bend** is a parameter of **o[i]**. The second period tells us that **angle** is a parameter of **bend**. In the line **$box01.pos.x**, **x** is a parameter of **pos**, and **pos** is a parameter of **$box01**. The **o[i].bend.direction = 90** line sets the direction parameter. The **o[i].bend.axis = 0** line bends the object on the X-axis. The Twist and Taper modifiers are applied in the same fashion. This script is shown in Listing 17.3.

Listing 17.3   The Multi Mod script.

```
-- this script applies the bend, twist and taper modifier to the
-- selected objects
-- TO USE:    Open the listener window to track progress
-- (optional)
--         select 1 or more objects
--         run the script

clearlistener()    -- clear the listener
-- places selected objects in an array called o
o = selection as array

for i = 1 to o.count do    -- repeat these commands for each
                           -- selected object
(
    format "Processing object %\n" o[i].name    -- print status
    -- convert the object to an editable mesh
    converttomesh o[i]
    addmodifier o[i] (bend())       -- add the bend modifier
    o[i].bend.angle = 60            -- bend this obj 60 deg
    o[i].bend.direction = 90        -- bend this obj dir 90
    o[i].bend.axis = 0              -- bend this obj on X
    addmodifier o[i] (twist())      -- add twist mod
    o[i].twist.angle = 120          -- twist this obj 120 deg
    o[i].twist.axis = 2             -- twist this obj on Z
    addmodifier o[i] (taper())      -- add taper mod
    o[i].taper.amount = 4           -- taper this obj 4 units
    update o[i]    -- update/refresh the object
)
format "done\n"    -- tell me when you're done
```

Getting Information From Your Scenes

In the next section, you'll see how you can use MAXScript to derive important information about your MAX scene objects and their properties.

The List Objects Script

The List Objects script (LIST OBJECTS.MS) reports information about the polygon objects in your scene. Yes, you can use summary info for the entire scene, or you can use the Polygon Counter utility, but the latter reports selected and total face counts. This script lists each object in your scene and its face and vertex count. For 3D artists working on real-time, low-polygon-count video game projects, this script tells you where you need to trim the face count.

The script begins by storing all geometry in the scene in an array called **o**. A for/loop is used to move through the array, one object at a time. The **n = o[i].name** line stores the name of the current object in the variable *n*. The **v = o[i].numverts** line stores the vertex count of the current object in the variable *v*. Finally, the **f = o[i].numfaces** line stores the face count of the current object in the variable *f*. The Format command is used to display this information in the Listener window. This script is shown in Listing 17.4.

Listing 17.4   The List Objects script.

```
-- this script lists all the (polygon) objects in your scene with
-- face/vert counts
-- TO USE:    Open the listener window to track progress
-- (optional)
--       run the script

clearlistener()            -- clear the listener
-- places all geometry in an array called o
o = geometry as array
format "This scene contains the following objects..."
for i = 1 to o.count do    -- repeat these commands for
                           -- each selected object
(
   converttomesh o[i]      -- convert the obj to a mesh
   n = o[i].name           -- store the name of the obj in n
   v = o[i].numverts       -- store # of vertices in v
   f = o[i].numfaces       -- store the # of faces in f
   -- print results
   format "Object: % Vertices: % Faces: %\n" n v f
)
format "done\n"    -- tell me when you're done
```

The Camera Info Script

The Camera Info script (CAMERA INFO.MS) displays the settings of each camera in the scene. As your 3D Studio MAX scenes get more complex, retrieving information from them can become more and more tedious. This is especially true if you're using multiple cameras to create multiple setups and "takes" of the same animation. Trying to track down all the parameters of a camera in such a scene can take more time than you really want to allow.

This script starts by storing all cameras in the scene in an array called **c**. A for/loop is used to move through the array of cameras, one at a time. The array stores cameras and camera targets. The **dot = findstring cams[i].name "."** line looks for a period in the name of the camera or camera target. The camera target names contain periods, whereas the camera names do not.

If the current item in the array is a target, the position of the period is stored in the variable *dot*. If the current item in the array is a camera, then *dot* remains undefined. The next line, **if dot == undefined** then checks to see if the variable *dot* is undefined. If it is, the camera is interrogated. If the *dot* variable is not undefined, the target is skipped. The core area of the script uses the Format command to display the current camera's settings in the Listener window. This script is shown in Listing 17.5.

Listing 17.5   The Camera Info script.

```
-- this script lists the settings of all the cameras in the scene
-- TO USE:    Open the listener window to see results
--                 run the script
--                 the settings appear in the listener window
-- NOTE: This script will not work with free cameras.

clearlistener()          -- clear the listener
c = cameras as array     -- store all the cams in an array
for i = 1 to c.count do   -- repeat for each camera
                         -- in the scene
(
    -- is this a camera or camera target?
    dot = findstring cams[i].name "."
    -- if a camera, then continue
    if dot == undefined then
    (
        -- print out each cameras settings
        format "camera name %\n" c[i].name
        format "camera pos is % \n" c[i].pos
        format "camera target pos is % \n" c[i].target.pos
        format "camera fov % \n" c[i].fov
        if c[i].orthoprojection then state = "on"
        else state = "off"
        format "camera orthoProjection [on/off] %\n" state
        format "camera near range % \n" c[i].nearrange
```

```
        format "camera far range % \n" c[i].farrange
        format "camera near clip % \n" c[i].nearclip
        format "camera far clip % \n" c[i].farclip
        format "target distance % \n" c[i].targetdistance
        format "\n"
    )
)
```

The Light Info Script

The Light Info script (LIGHT INFO.MS) displays the settings of all the lights in your scene. This script uses the same commands the Camera Info script uses.

The script starts by storing all lights in the scene in the array **L**. Again, a for/loop is used to move through the array, one light at a time. The **findstring** command is used to determine if the current item is a light or light target. The core area of the script uses the Format command, again, to display each light's settings. A number of if/then commands are used to determine the current light's type (some settings apply only to certain light types). This script is shown in Listing 17.6.

Listing 17.6   The Light Info script.

```
-- this script lists the settings of all the lights in the scene
-- TO USE:    Open the listener window to see results
--                  run the script
--                  the settings appear in the listener window

clearlistener()         -- clear the listener
L = lights as array     -- store all the lights in an array
for i = 1 to L.count do  -- repeat for each light in the scene
(
   -- is this a light or a (light) target, targets have a .target
   -- extension, this line looks for a period/dot in the name.
   -- if it does not exist then "undefined" is returned.
   dot = findstring L[i].name "."
   -- if undefined is returned then go ahead and process this
   -- light, else skip it.
   if dot == undefined then
   (
      -- print out each lights settings
      -- these are general settings for all lights
      format "GENERAL PARAMETERS\n"  -- header for general param.
      format "name %\n" L[i].name     -- name
      format "type %\n" L[i].type     -- type
      format "pos % \n" L[i].pos       -- pos
      -- if a light with a target, print out target pos
      if L[i].type == #targetspot or
      L[i].type == #targetdirect then
      (
         format "tpos % \n" L[i].target.pos
      )
```

```
-- now print out parameters for each light type
-- if this is not an omni light
if L[i].type != #omni then
(
    format "aspect %\n" L[i].aspect
    format "falloff %\n" L[i].falloff
    format "hotspot %\n" L[i].hotspot
    -- convert true/false to on/off
    if L[i].overshoot then s = "on" else s = "off"
    -- overshoot on/off
    format "overshoot [on/off] %\n" s
    format "cone shape %\n" L[i].coneshape
)

-- convert true/false to on/off
if L[i].enabled then s = "on" else s = "off"
format "light [on/off] %\n" s     -- light on/off
format "rgb %\n" L[i].rgb    -- rgb
format "elist %\n" L[i].excludelist
format "ilist %\n" L[i].includelist
-- convert true/false to on/off
if L[i].castshadows then s = "on" else s = "off"
-- shadows on/off
format "cast shadows [on/off] %\n" s
format "multiplier %\n" L[i].multiplier
format "contrast %\n" L[i].contrast
format "soft diff edge %\n" L[i].softendiffuseedge
-- convert true/false to on/off
if L[i].affectdiffuse then s = "on" else s = "off"
format "Diffuse [on/off] %\n" s     -- diffuse on/off
-- convert true/false to on/off
if L[i].affectspecular then s = "on" else s = "off"
-- specular on/off
format "Specular [on/off] %\n" s
-- convert true/false to on/off
if L[i].ambientonly then s = "on" else s = "off"
-- ambient on/off
format "Ambient Only [on/off] %\n" s
-- convert true/false to on/off
if L[i].projector then
(
    format "PROJECTOR PARAMETERS\n"
    -- projector on/off
    format "projector [on/off] on\n"
    format "projmap %\n" L[i].projectormap
    -- convert true/false to on/off
    if L[i].usenearatten then s = "on" else s = "off"
    -- near atten
    format "use near attenuation [on/off] %\n" s
    format "near attenuation start %\n"
    L[i].nearattenstart
    format "near attenuation end %\n"
    L[i].nearattenend
```

```
    -- convert true/false to on/off
    if L[i].usefaratten then s = "on" else s = "off"
    -- far atten
    format "use far attenuation [on/off] %\n" s
    format "far attenuation start %\n"
    L[i].farattenstart
    format "far attenuation end %\n" L[i].farattenend
    case L[i].attendecay of
    (
        1: ad = "none"
        2: ad = "inverse"
        3: ad = "inverse square"
    )
    format "attenuation decay %\n" ad
    format "decay radius %\n" L[i].decayradius
)
else
(
    format "PROJECTOR PARAMETERS\n"
    -- projector on/off
    format "projector [on/off] off\n"
)

format "SHADOW PARAMETERS\n"
-- at the time of this writing, shadow
-- on/off was not supported
-- convert true/false to on/off
if L[i].raytracedshadows then s = "ray traced"
else s = "shadow map"
format "shadow type %\n" s      -- shadow type
-- convert true/false to on/off
if L[i].useglobalshadowsettings then s = "on"
else s = "off"
-- use global
format "use global settings [on/off] %\n" s
format "shadow color %\n" L[i].shadowcolor
format "shadow density %\n" L[i].shadowmultiplier
format "shad projmap %\n" L[i].shadowprojectormap
-- convert true/false to on/off
if L[i].lightaffectsshadow then s = "on" else s = "off"
-- use affect shadows
format "light affects shadows [on/off] %\n" s
-- convert true/false to on/off
if L[i].atmosshadows then s = "on" else s = "off"
-- atmos shad
format "atmosphere shadows [on/off] %\n" s
format "Opacity %\n" L[i].atmosopacity
format "color amt %\n" L[i].atmoscoloramt
-- using rt shadows show these stats
if L[i].raytracedshadows then
(
    format "RT bias %\n" L[i].raytracebias
    format "RT max depth %\n" L[i].maxdepth
)
```

GETTING LIGHT
INFORMATION OVER TIME

The LIGHT INFO2.MS script in
the \CHAP_17 directory of this
book's companion CD-ROM
will generate a list of light
settings over time.

```
    else -- show these stats
    (
        if L[i].type != #omni then
        (
            format "SM Bias %\n" L[i].map_bias
            format "SM Size %\n" L[i].mapsize
            format "SM sample range %\n" L[i].samplerange
        )
    )
    format "\n"
)
)
```

Rendering: The ScotRend Script

The ScotRend script (SCOTREND.MS) renders each camera in the MAX files
located in the selected folder. I created this script for rendering a large number of MAX files overnight. (In some cases, it may be more convenient or
customizable to use a custom batch-rendering script than to use MAX's
Network rendering or Release 3's new Batch rendering features.)

The script starts with a number of variables set to their default values. These
variables are used in the user interface that appears when the script is started.
Once parameters are set, the **for f in getFiles fullstring do** line opens each
file in the selected folder in sequence. The cameras in each file are stored in
an array. The for/loop command is used to process each camera, one at a
time. The Render command generates sequential still or animation files to
your hard drive. This process repeats for each camera in each MAX file.
This script is shown in Listing 17.7.

Listing 17.7   The ScotRend batch rendering script.

```
-- camera renderer script
-- this script opens a series of max files (in a directory)
-- and renders for EACH camera
-- in EACH max file
-- TO USE:  run the script, the utility appears in the
--          MAXScript Panel

-- default values for ui
fmin = 0
fmax = 9999
fsdef = 0
fedef = 1
dby = 1
dwidth = 320
dheight = 240
rezmin = 0
rezmax = 9999
```

```
utility scotrend "Scot-Rend"
(
    group "Parameters for ALL files"
    (
      label linea "Use" -- add use text to ui
      -- ask the user to select the animation range
      radiobuttons rnge labels:#("rnge fm file", "rnge below")
      -- get start and end frame values from user
      spinner sf "Start:" range:[fmin,fmax,fsdef] type: #integer
      spinner ef "End: " range:[fmin,fmax,fedef] type: #integer
      -- add a blank line
      label line1 " "
      -- get the by frame and res for the rendered frames
      spinner bf "By Frame: " range:[fmin,fmax,dby] type: #integer
      spinner w "Width: " range:[rezmin, rezmax,dwidth]
      type: #integer
      spinner h "Height: " range:[rezmin, rezmax,dheight]
      type: #integer
      -- where should the finished files go
      edittext outdir "Dest: " fieldwidth: 105 text: "C:\\temp"
      -- what format to use
      radiobuttons outfmt labels:#("avi","mov","tif","tga")
      -- click this button to start the script
      button do_it "Do It!"
    )

    on do_it pressed do
    (
      clearlistener()    -- clear the listener
      -- get the folder
      foldpath = getSavePath caption: "Sel fldr W/Max files"
      foldstring = foldpath as string
      fullstring = foldstring + "\*.max" as string
      -- repeat this commands for every max file in the folder
      for f in getFiles fullstring do
      (
          max delete   -- start with a new file
          found = loadMaxFile f   -- load a max file
          format "\n"
          -- load okay?
          format "Processing File % Result %\n" f found
          -- store all cameras in the scene in an array
          cams = cameras as array
          -- repeat for EACH camera in THIS scene
          for i = 1 to cams.count do
            (
                -- create the filename to save
                infile = getfilenamefile f
                out = case outfmt.state of
                (
                   1: outfile = outdir.text + "\\" + infile + "_"
                      + cams[i].name + ".avi"
```

```
            2: outfile = outdir.text + "\\" + infile + "_"
               + cams[i].name + ".mov"
            3: outfile = outdir.text + "\\" + infile + "_"
               + cams[i].name + ".tif"
            4: outfile = outdir.text + "\\" + infile + "_"
               + cams[i].name + ".tga"
         )

         -- is this a camera or a target, targets have a
         -- cameraname.target extension, this line looks
         -- for a period/dot in the name. if it does
         -- not exist then "undefined" is returned.
         dot = findstring cams[i].name "."

         -- if undefined is returned then go ahead
         -- and render this camera, else skip it.
         if dot == undefined then
            (
              this_cam = execute ("$" + cams[i].name)
              format "using camera % -- " this_cam.name
              -- use the render command to render out
              -- the sequence
              if rnge.state == 2 then
              render camera: this_cam
              vfb: off fromframe: sf.value
              toframe: ef.value nthframe: bf.value
              outputwidth: w.value outputheight: h.value
              outputfile: outfile
              if rnge.state == 1 then
              render camera: this_cam vfb: off
              framerange: animationRange
              nthframe: bf.value outputwidth: w.value
              outputheight: h.value outputfile: outfile
              format "Render job % finished \n" outfile
            )
         )
      )
      max delete
      format "Done...\n"
   )
)
```

Game Data Export

The following scripts are helpful for MAX users working in the computer games industry, specifically low-polygon, real-time games.

The PolyExport Script

The PolyExport script (POLYEXPORT.MS) saves polygon data to a file you specify. This data can be helpful for game and Web developers who need to integrate their MAX content into a game platform or Web application.

The script starts with the construction of the user interface. Once parameters are set, the line **f = createFile fname.text** creates a new text file. The new file is stored in the variable *f*. Next, the script stores the selected objects in an array. Each object's information is displayed using the Format command. However, each Format command ends with **to: f**. The additional code sends the output to the file, not to the MAXScript Listener window.

This script also generates vertex information over time. The line **for t in start.value to end.value by 1 do at time t** uses a for/loop to move through each frame of animation. The current object's vertex information, at that moment in time, is also output to the file. This script is shown in Listing 17.8.

Listing 17.8   The PolyExport script.

```
-- this script exports poly data to a file
-- TO USE:    Open the listener window to see
-- results (optional)
--          run this script, it will not execute immediately
--          it will appear in the MAXScript utility
-- panel rollout
--          select 1 or more objects to export
--          enter your parameters in the script's ui
--          click on the do it button to start.
--          your data will be saved in the path/file
-- you specify


utility bound "Export Poly Data"    -- start the utility
(
    group "Export"    -- ui group
    (
        spinner start "start:" range:[1,999,1] type:#integer
        spinner end "end:" range:[1,999,100] type:#integer
        -- where should the file go, note the
        -- double // slashes = / in a path
        edittext fname "Dest:" fieldwidth: 105
        text: "C:\\temp\\poly.txt"
        button do_it "Do It!"
    )
    -- execute this when the do it button is pressed
    on do_it pressed do
    (
        clearlistener()
        -- delete this file if it exists
        deleteFile fname.text
        f = createFile fname.text -- create the file
        -- store the selected objects in an array
        o = selection as array
        -- repeat for each selected object
        for i = 1 to o.count do
        (
```

```
-- convert this object to a mesh
converttomesh o[i]
-- output this object's name
format "N %\n" o[i].name to: f
-- output    # of vertices
format "# verts %\n" o[i].numverts to: f
-- # of faces
format "# faces %\n" o[i].numfaces to: f
-- # of texture vertices
format "# t verts %\n" o[i].numtverts to: f
-- # of cpv verts
format "# cpv verts %\n" o[i].numcpvverts to: f
format "Vertices\n" to: f
-- loop thru all verts THIS obj
for j = 1 to o[i].numverts do
(
    -- store current vert pos in v
    v = getvert o[i] j
-- print the current vert pos
format "% \n" v to: f
)

format "Faces\n" to: f
-- loop thru all faces THIS obj
for k = 1 to o[i].numfaces do
(
    -- store the current face info
    gf = getface o[i] k
    -- print the current vert info
    format "% \n" gf to: f
)

format "Face Normals\n" to: f
-- loop thru all faces again
for L = 1 to o[i].numfaces do
(
    -- this time get the face normals
    fnorm = getfacenormal o[i] L
    format "%\n" fnorm to: f
    -- print the face normals info
)

format "anim data start\n" to: f
-- repeat for each frame
for t in start.value to end.value by 1
do at time t
(
    -- print the frame #
    format "F %\n" t to: f
    -- repeat for each vertices
    for u = 1 to o[i].numverts do
    (
```

```
            -- get the vert of THIS obj THIS frame
            this_v = getvert o[i] u
            -- print the results
            format "V %\n" this_v to: f
        )
        format "\n" to: f
        )
        format "anim data end\n" to: f
        close f   -- close the file
        )
    )
)
```

The SRTexport Script

The SRTexport script (SRTEXPORT.MS) exports scale, rotation, and translation information to a file. This script is similar to the PolyExport script, but the SRTexport script exports overall scale, rotation, and translation changes over time.

The script starts by constructing a user interface. Once parameters are set, the script creates a new file for storing object information. Next, the selected objects are stored in an array. A for/loop is used to move through the list of objects. A second for/loop moves through each frame for the current object. The object's scale, rotation, and translation data is exported to the file. A series of if/then statements determine which information is exported. This script is shown in Listing 17.9.

Listing 17.9   The SRTexport script.
```
-- SRT script
-- this script exports the scale, rotation and translation of
-- selected objects in your scene
-- TO USE:    Open the listener window to see results
-- (optional)
--          run this script, it will not execute immediately
--          it will appear in the MAXScript utility panel
--          rollout
--          select 1 or more objects to export
--          enter your parameters in the script's ui
--          click on the do it button to start.
--          your data will be saved in the path/file
--          you specify

utility srt "Srt tool"   -- build the ui
(
    group "Frame Range"
    (
        -- start frame
        spinner start "start:" range:[1,999,1] type:#integer
        -- end frame
        spinner end "end:" range:[1,999,100] type:#integer
    )
```

```
group "Export Options"
(
    -- which should get exported
    radiobuttons shows "Display Scale" labels:#("Yes","No")
    radiobuttons showr "Display Rotation"
    labels:#("Yes","No")
    radiobuttons showt "Display Translation"
    labels:#("Yes","No") 1
    -- where should the file go, note the
    -- double // slashes = / in a path
    edittext fname "Dest:" fieldwidth: 105
    text: "C:\\temp\\srt.txt"
)

group "Click Do It when ready"
(
    button do_it "Do it!"
)
-- wait until the do it button is pressed
on do_it pressed do
(
    -- delete this file if it exists
    deleteFile fname.text
    f = createFile fname.text -- create the file

    clearlistener()
    -- store the selected objects in an array
    sel_obj = selection as array
    -- how many files are getting processed
    format "# of objects %\n" sel_obj.count

    -- repeat for each frame
    for t in start.value to end.value by 1 do at time t
    (
        -- note the to: f at the end of each format line
        -- this sends output to a file,
        -- not the listener window
        -- send a blank line to the file
        format "\n" to: f
        -- each line starts with a frame number
        format "F %\n" t to: f
        -- repeat for each object
        for i = 1 to sel_obj.count do
        (
            -- store the scale x y and z in sx,
            -- sy and sz
            sx = sel_obj[i].scale.x
            sy = sel_obj[i].scale.y
            sz = sel_obj[i].scale.z
            -- store the translation x y and z in tx,
            -- ty and tz
```

```
            tx = sel_obj[i].pos.x
            ty = sel_obj[i].pos.y
            tz = sel_obj[i].pos.z
            -- store the rotation x y and z in the rx,
            -- ry and rz
            rx = sel_obj[i].rotation.x_rotation
            ry = sel_obj[i].rotation.y_rotation
            rz = sel_obj[i].rotation.z_rotation
            -- send the name of this object
            format "N % " sel_obj[i].name to: f
            -- output s, r and t based
            -- on the radio buttons in the ui
        if shows.state == 1 then format "% % % "  sx sy sz
        to: f
        if showr.state == 1 then format "% % % "  rx ry rz
        to: f
        if showt.state == 1 then format "% % % "  tx ty tz
        to: f
            format "\n" to: f
        )
    )
    close f   -- close the file
    format "done...\n"   -- tell me when you're done
  )
)
```

Moving On

In this chapter, you looked at a number of scripts: scripts that use modifiers, scripts that retrieve scene information, scripts for batch rendering, and scripts for exporting game data. These scripts focus on the day-to-day tasks in many 3D production environments.

These are the environments where the power of MAXScript really shines. I hope these scripts come in handy and reduce your production time, as well as help to spark MAXScript ideas of your own.

In the next (and final) chapter, you'll take a look at some fun 3D Studio MAX Release 3 plug-ins included on this book's CD-ROM. You'll see how to use Johnny Ow's Blur and Terrain plug-ins to create interesting optical effects and landscape textures, respectively. Then, an old favorite from the book *3D Studio MAX R2.5 f/x and design* makes a reappearance: Greeble, version 1.5—new and improved for MAX Release 3!

18

Fun With Plug-Ins: Blur, Terrain, and Greeble 1.5

By Jon A. Bell
And Michael
Spaw

Plug-Ins By
Tom Hudson
And Johnny Ow

In this chapter, you'll look at some fun plug-ins for 3D Studio MAX Release 3. First, you'll examine a returning favorite: Tom Hudson's Greeble 1.5, which he's updated with a few new features. Then, you'll see how to use Johnny Ow's Blur and Terrain plug-ins.

The Power Of The Plug-In Market

One of the most exciting aspects of 3D Studio MAX's first year was seeing the enormous number of plug-ins released for the software. MAX's open architecture and the inclusion of the software development kit (SDK) with each copy of the software helped ensure that both fledgling hackers and professional software developers could enhance the core code. In addition, approximately one-third of the MAX source code was available in the SDK, which helped developers build their plug-ins more quickly and easily.

This experiment showed the power of the free market in software development—if a MAX user needed it, a programmer would write it and, in many cases, simply give it away. As of mid-1999, Discreet estimated there were more than 400 plug-ins available; half of them are freeware or shareware and are on the developers' Web pages or at other MAX-specific Internet sites.

Another source for plug-ins is the book that you're now reading. In the \PLUGINS directory of this book's companion CD-ROM are three free 3D Studio MAX Release 3 plug-ins developed by Tom Hudson and Johnny Ow. Tom Hudson is one of the codevelopers of 3D Studio/DOS and MAX, and his original Greeble plug-in made its debut appearance in *3D Studio MAX R2.5 f/x and Design*. Greeble is a nifty object modifier that's perfect for adding complex detail to your objects. For this book, Tom has recompiled Greeble for 3D Studio MAX Release 3 and added several new features.

Johnny Ow is well-known in the MAX community as the developer of several shareware plug-ins, including the two included with this book: Blur and Terrain. The Blur plug-in is a simple yet powerful Video Post filter; with it, you can create such effects as heat distortion and underwater turbulence. Terrain is a MAX material type that enables you to create realistic-looking landscapes.

In this chapter, you'll get a quick look at each plug-in, and experiment with several tutorial files. Please note that these plug-ins are provided on an as-is basis, with only the basic documentation included in this chapter.

Installing The Plug-Ins

The following free plug-ins are in the \PLUGINS directory of this book's companion CD-ROM:

- Blur

- Greeble

- Terrain

Blur is a Video Post filter, Greeble is an object modifier, and Terrain is a material (note that the Terrain material is different from the Terrain modifier that comes with MAX).

The installation process for the plug-ins is quick and easy. Here's how:

1. Make sure you don't have a MAX Release 3 session currently active. If you do, the plug-ins won't appear in the program until you quit or until you load a second session.

2. Place the companion CD-ROM in your CD-ROM drive, then open Windows Explorer.

3. In your 3DSMAX3\PLUGINS directory, create a new folder called FX3, then copy the files GREEBLE.DLM, BLUR.FLT, and TERRAIN.FLT from the CD-ROM's \PLUGINS directory to your \3DSMAX3\ PLUGINS\FX3 directory.

4. Start MAX Release 3. Select Customize|Configure Paths|Plug-Ins, then use the Add feature and the Choose Directory for New Entry browser menu to add the \FX3 subdirectory to your plug-ins paths.

5. Next, quit MAX and restart it. You'll see the Greeble plug-in appear in the Modify panel (when you click on the More button); the Blur filter will appear in the Filters menu of Video Post. The Terrain material will appear in the Material Editor when you open the Material/ Map Browser.

You're now ready to use the plug-ins. First, you'll take a look at Tom Hudson's Greeble; you'll then see how to use Johnny Ow's Blur and Terrain plug-ins.

What's A Greeble?

In the classic science-fiction films of the 1950s, most spacecraft were depicted as smooth-skinned objects. If they were earthly vessels, they were streamlined, cigar-shaped rockets with swept-back fins, designed for launching from an atmosphere. If they were alien ships, they were usually sleek flying saucers or variants, such as the manta-ray ships of George Pal's 1953 film *The War of the Worlds*.

However, as everyone knows, there's no air in space; a ship designed for deep space travel doesn't need streamlining, so it can be of almost any external configuration necessary. Consequently, a spaceship doesn't need a smooth skin; it can have access panels, antennas, piping, and other gross mechanical details scattered across its surface.

An outgrowth of this design aesthetic started taking hold in the 1960s. TV programs such as Gerry Anderson's *Thunderbirds* and (most especially) films like *2001: A Space Odyssey* presented futuristic vehicles with complex surface details. To depict the vehicles' complicated exteriors, the modelmakers on these productions turned to *kit-bashing*—taking pieces from various commercial model kits and applying them to the surfaces of their original designs.

Kit pieces from World War II tank models, railroad cars, battleships, and so on, provided the illusion of intricate hatches, vents, and the like. Subsequent science-fiction films and TV shows, such as the *Alien*, *Star Wars*, and *Star Trek* productions, have continued this approach.

This process must be done artistically, however, with the parts' original intent camouflaged. When done correctly, the application of tiny details helps sell the apparent scale of these vehicles as enormous spacecraft rather than models a few feet long, as shown in Figure 18.1. Done incorrectly, the model simply looks like a brick covered in glue and rolled in model parts, as shown in Figure 18.2.

Figure 18.1
A good example of "greeble" detailing—model kit parts and styrene sheet plastic details applied to a wooden framework.

Figure 18.2
An amazingly bad example of "greeble" detailing—blocky styrene shapes covered with actual model part trees!

Since the advent of kit-bashing, effects artists have given a name to these model kit detail parts. British modelmakers such as Martin Bower and Bill Pearson refer to them as "wiggets"; in the United States, such parts are known as "nernies," "greeblies," or "greebles." After consulting our friend Bill George, a special effects supervisor at Industrial Light + Magic, 3D Studio MAX developer Tom Hudson and I settled on the term *Greeble* for this book's first plug-in.

Tom's Hudson's Greeble modifier plug-in creates procedural surface details on your MAX mesh objects and/or selected faces. With it, you can dress up an area of your model with random details or even create an entire landscape, such as the surface of the *Star Wars Deathstar* or the industrial wasteland at the beginning of *Bladerunner*.

The Greeble Modifier

If you've already installed the Greeble plug-in, you're ready to play:

1. In 3D Studio MAX, select File|Open and load GREEBLE1.MAX from the \CHAP_18 directory of this book's companion CD-ROM. Your screen should look like Figure 18.3.

Figure 18.3
The GREEBLE1.MAX scene file.

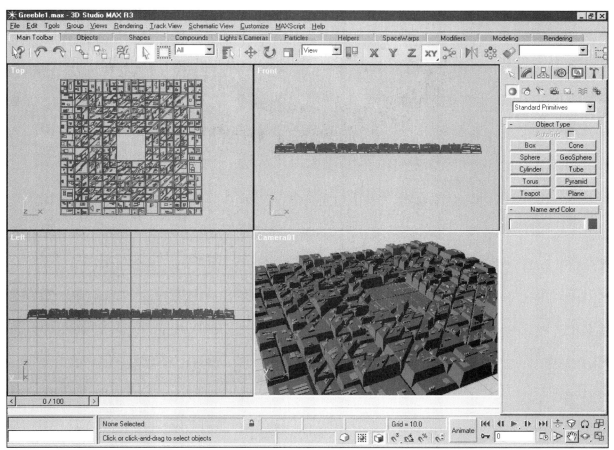

GREEBLE1.MAX shows how the Greeble plug-in creates panels from the source object. This is the top of a Box object with some of the grids made into explicit triangles. The center has had several edges turned off, so it's not a simple quad or triangle; Greeble ignores those faces. The triangular faces are outside this area and are modified. The outer perimeter are the original quads and are also modified.

2. Activate the Camera01 viewport and render the scene. Your rendering should look like Figure 18.4.

Figure 18.4
The Greeble Blend 3 material applied to the object.

To produce this texture effect, I created custom materials that key off the Material ID numbers of the Greeble panels and *widgets*, or plate details.

3. Open the Material Editor and take a look at the Greeble Green 3 material. This is a Multi/Sub-Object material that combines three sets of Blend materials, each using small custom bitmaps. Note that the second material in each Blend type is a face-mapped material, and the mask for each material is also a custom grayscale bitmap (GREEBLE5.JPG). These Blend materials tend to outline and highlight the edges of the Greeble details and make them stand out.

4. Next, load GREEBLE2.MAX from the \CHAP_18 directory. Your screen should look like Figure 18.5.

5. GREEBLE2.MAX shows Greeble applied to various primitives. If you want, render the scene; I've applied the Greeble Green 3 material to these objects as well, as shown in Figure 18.6.

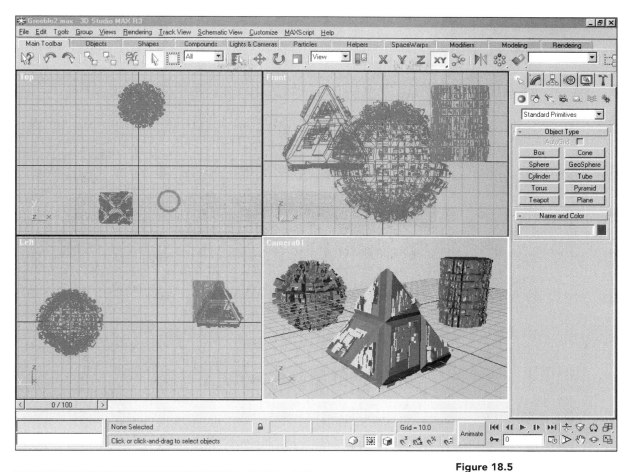

Figure 18.5
The GREEBLE2.MAX scene file.

Figure 18.6
The Greeble Green 3 material
applied to the primitives.

Greeble Controls

The following sections explain the controls for the Greeble plug-in.

Parameters

There are three controls under the Parameters section:

- *Generate From Quads/Triangles*—If checked and the source object has quadrilaterals, triangles, or both defined, they are modified.

- *Generate From Triangles*—If checked and the source object has triangular faces defined, they are modified.

- *Seed*—Specifies the initial random number generator value. Change to get different details.

In GREEBLE2.MAX, select the sphere and uncheck Triangles. You'll see the poles return to normal. Turn off Quadrilaterals and the rest of the sphere will no longer be affected.

Panels

The following controls are in the Panels section:

- *Generate*—If checked, generates extruded panels from the source geometry. If unchecked, no panels will be extruded.

- *Min. Height and Max. Height (animatable)*—Specifies the height range of the panels in units.

- *Taper (animatable)*—Controls the amount of beveling on the panels, shown as a percent value. Tapering 100 percent will make little pyramids. A taper of 0 will make simple extruded blocks.

- *Materials*—A list of comma-separated numbers indicating which sub-object material IDs to use for panel generation. The values entered are used at random when generating the panels, and at least one number should be entered.

  For example, if the field contains only one number (such as 1), only sub-object material ID 1 will be used for the panels. If the field contains two numbers (such as 1,2), the Greeble plug-in will randomly generate panels that use sub-object material numbers 1 and 2, in approximately equal numbers. By using the same number more than once in the material list, you can make a certain sub-object material appear more often. For example, entering "1,1,1,2" will create panels that are Material 1 approximately 75 percent of the time and Material 2 approximately 25 percent of the time.

- *Keep Original Geometry*—If checked, the faces that the panels were generated from will remain. (This is wasteful, but it may come in handy if you collapse the stack and need to extract the original geometry as an element.) Normally this is unchecked, which means the original triangular or quadrilateral geometry is removed when the panels are generated.

- *Select Tops and Select Sides*—If checked, these features, new to Greeble 1.5, enable you to select either the tops or sides of the beveled Panel faces for secondary Greeble application. To see how this works, apply a Greeble 1.5 modifier to your object (or selected sub-object faces) and check Select Sides. Then, apply a second Greeble modifier on top of the first one. You'll see that the beveled side faces of the original "Greebled" object get an additional set of "Greebled" faces. (Note that you may have to adjust the Panel and Widget heights so that this new geometry doesn't poke through the first Greeble-modified faces.)

Widgets

These are the detail bits (you might call them "sub-greebles") that are created on top of the panels. If panels are turned off, the widgets are generated on the original geometry. The controls under Widgets are as follows:

- *Generate*—If checked, generates widgets.

- *Widget Type icons*—These new icons specify the type of widgets that are created. By checking or unchecking them as needed, you can customize the types of details on your objects.

- *Min. Size and Max. Size*—Specifies the size of the widgets, shown as a percentage of the panel size.

- *Max. Height*—Specifies the maximum height of the widgets in world units. The widget generator bases the widget height on its size. The longer or wider a widget is, the shorter it is and vice versa.

- *Density*—Specifies the number of widgets to generate on each panel or source face.

- *Materials*—The same as the Materials control under Panels.

Performance

The Modify For Render Only checkbox enables you to increase the Density setting of your final Greeble Widget details at render time only. Checking it before you increase the Density setting will speed up your viewport redrawing time.

Texture Mapping

The Greeble plug-in creates mapping coordinates for all generated elements automatically. If the sub-object materials assigned to the various generated panels or widgets use mapping, the proper mapping coordinates will appear on the modified object.

The Blur Plug-In

The next plug-in we'll look at is Johnny Ow's Blur plug-in. Blur is a simple Video Post filter that enables you to blur elements of your scene based either on Material ID or Object ID numbers.

If you've placed the Blur filter in your 3DSMAX3\PLUGINS directory, it should be present when you load Video Post. To see, do the following:

1. Load 3D Studio MAX, or save your current work and reset the program.

2. Click on Rendering|Video Post, and when the Video Post menu appears, click on the Add Image Filter Event icon. When the Image Filter Event menu appears, click on the Down arrow, select Blur from the drop-down list, and then click on Setup. The Blur Control menu should appear, as shown in Figure 18.7.

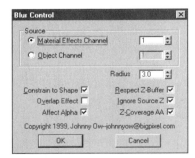

Figure 18.7
The Blur Control menu.

The controls are pretty straightforward and self-explanatory:

- *Source*—Determines which channel the Blur effect will key from, either the Material Effects channel (0 to 255) or the Object channel (1 to 10,000+).

- *Radius*—Sets the radius of the Blur filter (0 to 128). The default is 3. Note that values above 10 will take a long time to render.

- *Constrain To Shape*—Determines whether the Blur effect is uniform or constrained to the actual object shape (such as a particle).

- *Overlap Effect*—Determines whether one level of Blur is applied across the selected objects or whether the effect is cumulative.

- *Affect Alpha*—Determines if the Blur effect shows up in the Alpha channel or not.

- *Respect Z-buffer*—Determines if the Blur effect becomes more or less blurry, depending on the source's distance from the camera.

- *Ignore Source Z*—Determines if the effect should respect or ignore given Z-axis source information.

- *Z-Coverage AA*—Determines if the antialiasing is determined by the Z-axis channel of the source or not.

The Volcano Scene

An interesting way to see the effect of the Blur filter is to examine its effects when applied to a series of MAX particle systems. To test this effect, you'll load a MAX scene of a volcano and then see how the Blur filter alters the appearance of various particle systems in it. To start, do the following:

1. From the \CHAP_18 directory of this book's companion CD-ROM, load the file VOLCANO1.MAX. The file loads, and your screen should look like Figure 18.8.

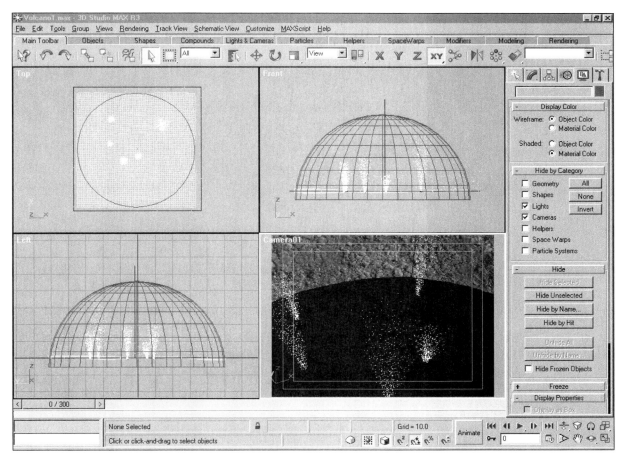

Figure 18.8
The VOLCANO1.MAX test scene.

This scene depicts the inside of a volcanic crater, or a lava dome, and it consists of some fairly simple elements. A high-density QuadPatch object, with an animated Noise, serves as a gently undulating lava surface. A hemisphere (with inverted face normals) creates the domed "roof" over the scene. Meanwhile, several particle systems create both plumes of "smoke" and an overall heat distortion effect, as you'll see in a moment.

2. Open the Material Editor and take a look at the materials in the scene. In the first Material Editor slot, you'll see a Blend material called Blend Lava. It consists of a Lava Top material, depicting a rocky surface, and a Lava Bottom, which depicts actual glowing magma. A bitmap, called VOLCRACK8.TIF, is loaded in the Mask slot to mask the rocky surface from the glowing lava beneath.

3. If you open the Material #2: Lava Bottom component, you'll see that the Material Effects Channel is set to 1. This enables the lava component to glow only when rendered with the Lens Effects Glow filter in Video Post. When you're finished looking at this material, click on the Go To Parent icon and examine the other materials in the Material Editor.

4. In the second Material Editor slot is a material called Heat Blur; its Material Effects Channel is set to 2. This is a completely transparent material that's applied to the large Heat Distortion particle system in the scene; this particle system lies below the "lava" QuadPatch and points directly upward. It's also large enough to encompass the entire scene. As you'll see in a moment, the Blur filter will key off the Material Effects Channel 2 and will create the effect of heat distortion, or waves, radiating upward from the lava surface.

5. In Material Editor Slot #3, you'll see a material called Lava Dome. If you go down to the Maps rollout and open it, you'll see a bitmap called CRAKMUD1.JPG loaded into the Displacement map slot. As you saw in Chapter 8, the Lava Dome object is using 3D Studio MAX Release 3's new render-time Displacement, via the Surface Properties: Sub-Division Displacement settings in the Modify panel.

6. Finally, in Slot # 4 and Slot # 5, you'll see a gradient environment background (not visible unless you hide the dome) and a material called Smoke Particles. This material is used on the smoke "plume" systems visible in the scene, and like the Lava Bottom material, it also has Material Effects Channel 1 set (this will provide a glowing smoke effect when rendered).

7. Okay, that's enough background information—let's take a look at an actual rendering. Close the Material Editor and then click on Render|Video Post. The Video Post menu appears.

8. As you examine the Video Post queue, you'll see that there are several entries in it after the requisite Camera. First, there's a Lens Effects Glow filter; as mentioned earlier, this provides a glowing effect to both the lava and the smoke plumes. (You can examine its settings by selecting it in the queue, clicking the Edit Current Event icon, and then clicking Setup.) You'll see that the Glow size is set to 2.5, the Glow is produced from the Pixel Color, and the Intensity value is set to 75.0.

9. Close your Lens Effects Glow preview screen if it's open, and select the Blur (Heat) item in the queue. Then, click on Edit Current Event and Setup. The Blur filter appears. As mentioned earlier, this Blur filter is keying off of Material Effects Channel 2. The Radius is set to the default of 3.0 pixels, and only Overlap Effect is checked below.

10. Click on Okay, and then click on Okay again to close this menu and return to the Video Post menu. Open and examine the Blur (Smoke) queue item. The settings are identical to the Blur (Heat) filter, although Material Effects Channel 1 is selected. This will apply a Blur effect "on top of" the Lens Effects Glow filter, which is also keying off of Material Effects Channel 1. Close this Blur filter menu when you're finished.

11. All right, enough theory—let's see what this actually looks like when rendered. In the Video Post menu, click on the Execute Sequence icon. When the Execute Video Post menu appears, under Time Output, make sure Single is selected and set to frame 0. Then, click on the Render button to render a 640-by-480 version of this scene.

12. After a few minutes, the rendering should appear, but as it's processing, take a close look at the effects the various filters are having on the image as it renders. First, the overall lava scene renders, and you can see how the Displacement map on the inside of the lava dome creates craggy details on the circular walls. Then, the Glow effect gets added to the lava and the smoke plumes. Next, the first Blur (Heat) filter is applied, and you see a subtle fuzziness appear across your field of view. (This effect is more apparent when the scene is animated, as you'll see in a bit.) Finally, the second Blur (Smoke) filter is applied, and you'll see the glowing smoke further blurred and smeared. Your final rendering should resemble Figure 18.9.

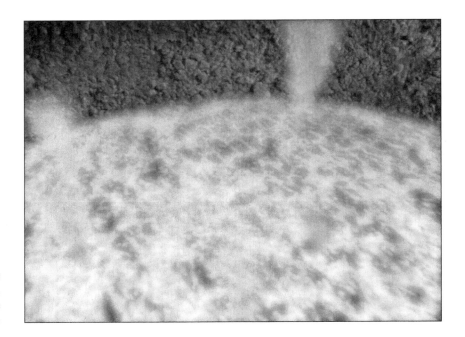

Figure 18.9

The lava dome scene rendered in Video Post with the Lens Effects Glow and Blur filters applied.

13. Although this is an interesting rendering, it might be easier to see the effects of the Blur filter on the Heat Distortion particle system by looking at an animation of this scene. Select File|View File, and from the \CHAP_18 directory of this book's companion CD-ROM, select the file VOLCANO.AVI and view it. This is a low-resolution, 320-by-240 animation of this volcano scene; the camera describes a slow arc down to the right, over the lava field. As you watch the animation, you should be able to see how the Blur filter is causing a slight, intermittent fuzziness or distortion in the atmosphere. (Note that this effect is much more noticeable at higher resolutions, especially when rendered and played back at video resolution.)

Note how the Blur filter doesn't need to key off a specific color; although it blurs the smoke plumes, it also creates a blurring effect on the heat particles that, by themselves, are invisible.

So, what other effects could you use the Blur filter for? Well, when you couple the Blur filter with particle systems, you could create other atmospheric distortion effects. The exhaust from a jet (particularly a vertical takeoff and landing vehicle such as a Harrier jump jet) or even underwater turbulence (such as the wake from a passing submarine or torpedo) are obvious possibilities. In the case of the latter, you could simply parent a particle system to your vessel's propellers, make the particles completely transparent, and then adjust the Blur filter's settings as necessary to create the proper "wake" effect.

The Terrain Plug-In

For the final plug-in, we're going to take a brief look at Johnny Ow's Terrain material. Terrain is an enhanced version of MAX's Top/Bottom material, and it enables you to create realistic-looking landscapes. You can see an example of it here:

1. From the \CHAP_18 directory of this book's companion CD-ROM, load the file TERRAIN.MAX. The file loads, and your screen should look like Figure 18.10.

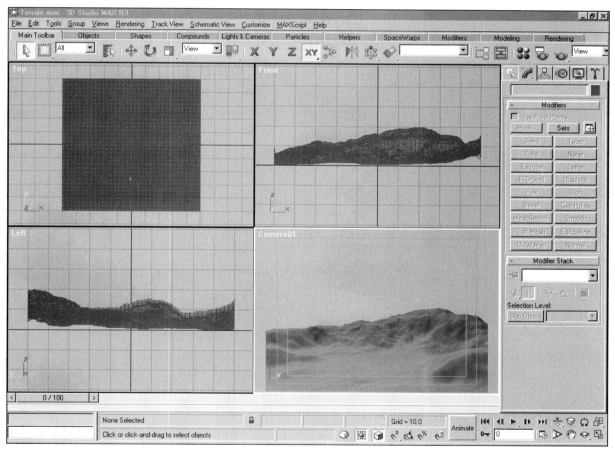

Figure 18.10
The TERRAIN.MAX example scene.

The TERRAIN.MAX scene (courtesy of contributor Michael Spaw) consists of a high-resolution Planar object with a Displace modifier (not the sub-division surfaces Displace map) applied to the object. A grayscale bitmap serves to distort the surface of the object into a rolling landscape. In addition, Combustion atmospheric apparatus and a Cylindrical Volumetric Fog apparatus provide clouds and ground haze, respectively. (Note that these objects are currently hidden in your scene. You can unhide them by unchecking Helpers from the Hide By Category section of the Display panel.)

2. Click on the Terrain object to select it, then go to the Modify panel. At the top level of the stack should be the Displace modifier. As you can see under Parameters, Strength is set to 250, producing the overall topology. Under Image: Bitmap, you'll see a file called TERRAIN.JPG loaded. Click on this button, and when the Select Displacement Image menu appears, click on View to view the image, shown in Figure 18.11. This 512-by-512-resolution grayscale "noise" image distorts the Planar object into a reasonable-looking landscape.

Figure 18.11
The TERRAIN.JPG Displacement bitmap.

3. When you're finished viewing the bitmap, close the Displacement Image menu and open the Material Editor. In the top map slots, you'll see the following: In Slot #1, you'll see MAX Release 3's new Gradient Ramp, used as a Screen Environment background to produce the sky. Then, in Slot #2, you'll see the actual Land Terrain material itself. Activate it, then take a look at the parameters, as shown in Figure 18.12.

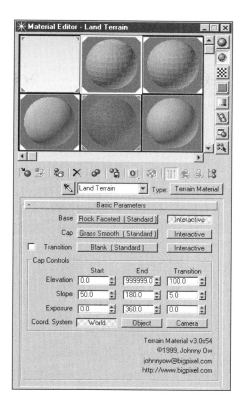

Figure 18.12
The Terrain Material menu, shown in the Material Editor.

4. Under Basic Parameters, you have three sub-material slots: Base, Cap, and Transition (which in this case, is unchecked.) The Base material provides the initial ground cover; here, it's a brownish turf. The Cap material provides a "top layer" material, which in this scene is bright green grass (the overall feeling might be that of a verdant hillside in the British Isles, say). A whitish material used in this slot would provide the (perhaps expected) choice of snow-capped peaks.

5. Open the Base: Rock Faceted material. Here, you'll see an unusual setting: Under Shader Basic Parameters, Faceted is checked. Ordinarily, you don't check Faceted; you usually want a smoothed appearance to your 3D models. It's rare that you specifically want a harsh, polygonal computer-graphics look in your scene. However, in this example, the Faceted checkbox, when coupled with a high-density mesh, creates a hard-edged, granite effect.

6. If you go down to the Maps rollout and open the Diffuse Color slot, you'll see a grayish-beige Noise map loaded. The extremely useful Cellular material, in the Bump slot, provides the rest of the rocky texture.

7. Click on the Go To Parent icon and open the Cap: Grass Smooth material. As the name suggests, the Cap: Grass Smooth material isn't Faceted, so blending between the Base and Cap materials creates an interesting contrast. Again, the Diffuse Color slot of this material contains a Noise map, colored two-tone green to create the grassy patches. (Also, you'll note that this Smooth Cap sub-material doesn't use a Bump map of any kind.)

8. Click on the Go To Parent icon again when you're finished viewing this material. Below these two material slots is a Transition sub-material, which is not used in this example. By loading another material here, you could create a three-layered Terrain effect, blending between the Base and the Cap.

9. Below these sub-material slots is the Cap Controls section. The controls in this section determine how the upper Cap material "sits on" the lower Base material. Essentially, the Elevation, Slope, and Exposure controls determine how much of the Cap material lies on face normals that rotate "away" from the ground plane. In this example, the Slope angle is 50 degrees; the green grass Cap will begin to appear on object faces that are equal to or greater than 50 degrees from horizontal.

10. The Coordinate system in this example is set to World; depending on your scene (and how you've transformed your geometry), you might want to key specific Terrain transition effects from the XYZ coordinates of the specified object or the camera.

11. As with the Greeble and Blur plug-ins described earlier in this chapter, the best way to see how Terrain works is to simply tweak the settings and render to examine the results. So, you should do that now. Activate your Camera01 viewport and render the scene; after a few minutes, it should appear and look like Figure 18.13.

Again, practice makes perfect (or perhaps at least better results than before).

Now, here's an interesting challenge: Can you combine each of the plug-ins described in this chapter in the same scene? What if you used the Greeble plug-in on a vast QuadPatch to create a *Bladerunner*-style industrial landscape? You then might be able to use the Terrain plug-in to place rust and grime on the top surfaces of the "Greebled" objects and other metallic materials along their sides. (Go back and revisit Chapters 5 and 6 in this book for additional material ideas.)

Figure 18.13

An example of the Terrain material used on the Planar object.

Finally, you could create several particle systems, set them as transparent or to any desired color, then apply a Lens Effects Glow and the Blur to create fire, smoke, or heat distortion. The possibilities, even with this handful of plug-ins, are virtually unlimited.

Moving On...For The Last Time

Well, here we are again—the end of yet another 3D Studio MAX f/x book. In a three-and-a-half-year period (from early 1996 to mid-1999), I've written three consecutive 3D Studio MAX special effects books. Although it's been a lot of work, I've had the enjoyment of hearing from numerous 3D Studio MAX users who seem to be benefiting from the hours of MAX experimentation (my wife calls it "playing") that I do on a daily basis.

So, as I wrap up this, yet another MAX book, I don't have a great deal of witty thoughts or banter with which to leave you, other than it's been fun, and I appreciate your comments and questions. I try to respond to every email that I get, so feel free to drop me a line at **joanjon@sirius.com**.

Thanks for your support. Be seeing you....

APPENDIX A:
ABOUT THE
CD-ROM

BY JON A. BELL

This book includes a PC-readable CD-ROM (burned with the Joliet long file-name system), located in a sleeve inside the back cover. The CD-ROM contains all of the example animations and images contained in the book, as well as scene files, models, material libraries, and plug-ins. It also includes more than 300MB of original texture maps, distributed royalty free and available immediately for your personal use.

Demonstration animations for the chapter tutorials are on the CD-ROM as AVI files rendered at 320 by 240 resolution. Various figures (rendered as lossless JPG files) from each chapter are included in the \FIGURES subdirectories within each chapter's directory. As you follow along with the instructions in each chapter, you will be either viewing or loading pertinent images and mesh and/or scene files from the CD-ROM.

Important: You do *not* need to install the MAX files from the companion CD-ROM onto your hard drive. If you load the MAX files directly into 3D Studio MAX, the program will automatically add the proper CD-ROM directories to the MAX Map Paths list. Because of the size of the demo animation files, however, you may want to copy them into your \3DSMAX3\IMAGES directory and play them back from your hard drive to get better playback speed.

Setting Up Your Map Paths

Most of the maps you need for the tutorials are contained in their respective chapter directories and in the \MAPS directory of your companion CD-ROM.

To make sure you have access to all the maps on the CD-ROM, load 3D Studio MAX, select Customize|Configure Paths, and manually add the companion CD-ROM \MAPS directory to your map paths. If you get a "Missing Map" error message when trying to load or render one of the CD-ROM's MAX files, make sure you've got your map paths set up correctly.

The Figures

All the tutorial screen shots presented in this book use the 3D Studio MAX defaults, which are present when you first install the program. If you have altered your keyboard hotkey assignments or other user-customizable features of the user interface, you may find that some of the instructions presented here do not correspond precisely with your 3D Studio MAX desktop layout.

If you wish, you can change most of your default screen settings back to their defaults by using the Customize|Preferences panel. Please see your MAX manuals for further information on configuring your program layout.

The Directories

The companion CD-ROM contains the following directories:

- \ARTBEATS contains 53 digitized explosion images, courtesy of Artbeats Software.

- \CHAP_01 through \CHAP_18 correspond to the tutorials presented in Chapters 1 through 18. They contain the MAX scene files, textures, and other files required for each chapter's tutorials.

- \COLOR GALLERY contains lossless JPG images of all the figures (with the exclusion of four transparencies from Matte World Digital) used in this book's color studio.

- \FX1 contains various scene files from the book *3D Studio MAX f/x: Creating Hollywood-Style Special Effects* (now out of print).

- \FX2 contains various scene files from the previous book, *3D Studio MAX R2.5 f/x and Design*. By the time you read this, the R2.5 f/x book will be out of print, although you may still be able to find copies at your local bookstore or through the Web.

- \FX3 Extras contains bonus MAX scene files and maps not covered in the book's tutorials.

- \MAPS contains all the texture maps used in the book, along with many extra maps.

- \MATLIBS contains the custom *3D Studio MAX R3 f/x and Design* material library, featuring all the materials used on the various MAX scene files throughout this book.

- \PLUGINS contains Tom Hudson's Greeble 1.5 and Johnny Ow's Blur and Terrain plug-ins. (These plug-ins are also included in the \CHAP_18 directory.)

- \UI contains custom UI files for 3D Studio MAX Release 3, which you can load or customize to make your modeling and animating tasks easier.

If you have any questions about this book or the CD-ROM contents, feel free to email me at **joanjon@sirius.com**.

System Requirements

For Release 3 of MAX, Discreet (formerly Kinetix) recommends the following:

- Microsoft Windows NT 4 or Windows 98. Service Pack 4 is required by Windows NT for Year 2000 compliance. Network rendering is not supported on Windows 98.

- Intel-compatible processor at 200MHz minimum (full SMP support, dual Pentium III system recommended).

- 128MB RAM and 250MB swap space minimum (actual amount depends upon scene complexity).

- Graphics card supporting 1024×768×16-bit colors minimum (1280×1024×24-bit recommended). OpenGL and Direct3D hardware acceleration supported.

- Windows-compliant pointing device (specific optimization for Microsoft Intellimouse).

- CD-ROM drive for installation and tutorials.

- Optional hardware include 3D hardware graphics acceleration, network cabling (for network rendering), video input and output devices, three-button mouse, sound card and speakers, joystick and MIDI instruments (for motion capture).

APPENDIX B:
3D STUDIO MAX
RESOURCES

BY JON A. BELL

Since the release of 3D Studio MAX R1 in April 1996, the MAX world has expanded tremendously, and the best source for up-to-date information on MAX-related books, plug-ins, training videos, MAX-compliant hardware, and the like, is through the extensive network of online MAX resources. By following only a few of the URLs listed here, you can link to dozens—perhaps hundreds—of Internet sites (both Web pages and newsgroups) that offer a wealth of MAX information. (If you have trouble locating a specific newsgroup or Web page, use a search engine such as AltaVista or Yahoo!, and type "3D Studio MAX" to see what's out there.) The newsgroups feature ongoing discussion and debate about their particular topics and can be a good resource if you have questions about 3D Studio/DOS, 3D Studio MAX, and related software and hardware.

The number-one place to find MAX information on the Internet is Discreet's own Web site at **http://support.ktx.com**. You should follow the links to the MAX Support forum; there, you can get answers to technical questions, useful tips and tricks on MAX and related software, and just plain gossip.

Other excellent sources of information include:

- **www.digimation.com**—The Web site for Digimation, Discreet's preferred MAX plug-in publisher and distributor.

- **www.3Dartist.com**—The Web site for *3D Artist Magazine*; also features links to many MAX-related hardware and software vendors as well as The MAX Page, a MAX-specific resources page. Note that this URL provides links to a huge number of companies that provide MAX-related software and hardware.

- **www.3Dcafe.com**—Another excellent source for 3D models and plug-ins.

- **www.3Dsite.com**—A great source for 3D models and freeware and shareware plug-ins.

- **www.max3D.com**—News, MAX-related URL links, tutorials, and plug-in information.

- **www.amazon.com**—Billed as "the world's largest bookstore," Amazon offers secure online purchases of a huge variety of books, numbering in the millions. Use its Web site's search features to look for books on 3D Studio MAX and other computer graphics topics.

APPENDIX C: SPECIAL EFFECTS, ANIMATION, AND FILMMAKING RESOURCES

BY JON A. BELL

The following books, magazines, and Web sites may be useful to 3D Studio MAX graphics artists, animators, and filmmakers.

Books

Animals in Motion
Eadweard Muybridge
Hardcover, $24.95
Dover Publications, 1989
ISBN 0486202038

The Muybridge books have long been considered indispensable reference works for artists and animators studying motion. Muybridge's photographic motion studies, done in the late 1880s, are still invaluable today.

Animation, A Reference Guide
Thomas W. Hoffer
Hardcover, $59.95
Greenwood Publications Group, 1982
ISBN 0313210950

Animation: From Script to Screen
Shamus Culhane
Reprint Edition
Paperback, $14.95
St. Martin's Press, 1990
ISBN 0312050526
An ex-Disney animator describes the animation process.

The Complete Book of Scriptwriting
J. Michael Straczynski
Revised
Hardcover, $19.95
Writer's Digest Books, 1996
ISBN 0898795125

Contemporary Animator
John Halas
Hardcover, $54.95
Focal Press, 1991
ISBN 0240512804

Experimental Animation: Origins of a New Art
Robert Russet and Cecile Starr
Reprint Edition
Hardcover, $14.95
Da Capo Press, 1988
ISBN 0306803143

The Grammar of the Film Language
Daniel Arijon
Reprint Edition
Paperback, $24.95
Samuel French Trade, 1991
ISBN 187950507X

The Human Figure in Motion
Eadweard Muybridge
Hardcover, $24.95
Dover Publications, 1989
ISBN 0486202046

The Illusion of Life: Disney Animation
Frank Thomas and Ollie Johnston
Revised
Hardcover, $60
Hyperion, 1995
ISBN 0786860707

Many people regard this as the definitive work on classical animation; computer animators should also study it.

Magazines

American Cinematographer
ASC Holding Corporation
1782 N. Orange Drive, Hollywood, CA 90028
800-448-0145
$5 per issue, subscription $35/year, monthly

American Cinematographer often has articles on special visual effects for both film and TV.

Animation
30101 Agoura Court, Suite 110
Agoura Hills, CA 91301
818-991-2884
$4.95 per issue, subscription $58/year, monthly

Cinefantastique
7240 W. Roosevelt Road., Forest Park, IL 60130
708-366-5566
$5.95 per issue, subscription $48/year, monthly

This science fiction media magazine often features articles on special effects in film and TV.

Cinefex

Box 20027, Riverside, CA 92516

$8.50 per issue, subscription $26/year, quarterly

The definitive resource for the special effects aficionado. Although it's expensive, it's worth every penny—and it's one of the few magazines in which I read every word of every issue. It should be required reading for anyone interested in the visual effects field and computer graphics.

Cinescape

Cinescape Group, Inc.

1920 Highland Avenue, Suite 222

Lombard, IL 60148

708-268-2498

$4.99 per issue, $29.95/year, monthly

Starlog

Starlog Group

475 Park Avenue South

New York, NY 10016

800-877-5549

$4.99 per issue, $39.97/year, monthly

Web Sites

www.3Dcafe.com

3D Café, source for 3D models and textures.

www.aint-it-cool-news

Ain't It Cool News; a movie gossip Web site.

www.darkhorizons.com

A movie gossip Web site.

www.cinescape.com

A movie gossip Web site.

www.filmscoremonthly.com

A Web site for film music, a favorite of the author.

www.bftr.com

Banned From The Ranch, a special effects house in Santa Monica, California.

www.bio-vision.com

Biovision motion capture.

www.blur.com

Blur Studios, a special effects house in Santa Monica, California; Blur creates its effects using 3D Studio MAX.

www.digitaldirectory.com/animation.html

The Digital Directory.

www.dd.com
Digital Domain.

www.disney.com
Walt Disney Pictures.

www.ktx.com
Kinetix, now Discreet.

www.rga.com
R/GA Digital Studios.

www.rhythm.com
Rhythm & Hues Studios.

www.vfxpro.com
A site specializing in special visual effects news.

www.viewpoint.com
Viewpoint DataLabs.

www.viewpoint.com/avalon
Viewpoint DataLabs: Avalon public domain 3D models and textures site.

From start to finish, The Coriolis Group designed *3D Studio MAX R3 f/x and Design* with the creative professional in mind.

The cover was produced on a Power Macintosh using QuarkXPress 3.3 for layout compositing. Text imported from Microsoft Word was restyled using the Futura and Trajan font families from the Adobe font library. It was printed using four-color process and spot UV coating, on 12-point Silverado matte cover.

Select images from the book's color studio were combined to form the color montage art strip that is unique for each Creative Professionals cover. Adobe Photoshop 5 was used in conjunction with filters to create the individual special effects.

The color studio was assembled using Adobe Pagemaker 6.5 on a G3 Macintosh system. Images in TIFF format were color corrected and sized in Adobe Photoshop 5. It was printed using four-color process.

The interior layout was built in Adobe Pagemaker 6.5 on a Power Macintosh. Adobe fonts used include Stone Informal for body, Avenir Black for heads, and Copperplate 31ab for chapter titles. Adobe Photoshop 5 was used to process grayscale art files. The text originated in Microsoft Word.

Imagesetting and manufacturing were completed by Courier, Stoughton, Mass.

WHAT'S ON THE CD-ROM

The *3D Studio MAX R3 f/x and Design* companion CD-ROM contains elements specifically selected to enhance the usefulness of this book, including:

- All MAX scene files used in the book's tutorials—more than 70 different scenes
- Bonus MAX scene files, such as a full-body cartoon dragon, two underwater scenes (one with a photorealistic spotlight effect), and a deep-space galaxy
- A dozen useful MAXScripts—learn how to get camera and light information from your scenes
- Tom Hudson's popular Greeble plug-in—recompiled and updated with new features
- Johnny Ow's Blur Video Post plug-in and Terrain material
- 800 texture maps—including custom metals, rock and stone images, sci-fi spaceship hull textures, and a zero-gravity explosion courtesy of Artbeats Software
- All of the book's figures—full-screen color images for you to examine

System Requirements

For Release 3 of MAX, Discreet (formerly Kinetix) recommends the following:

- Microsoft Windows NT 4 or Windows 98. Service Pack 4 is required by Windows NT for year 2000 compliance. Network rendering is not supported on Windows 98.
- Intel-compatible processor at 200MHz minimum (full SMP support and dual Pentium III system recommended).
- 128MB RAM and 250MB swap space minimum (actual amount depends on scene complexity).
- Graphics card supporting 1024x768x16-bit colors minimum (1280x1024x24-bit recommended). OpenGL and Direct3D hardware acceleration supported.
- Windows-compliant pointing device (specific optimization for Microsoft Intellimouse).
- CD-ROM drive for installation and tutorials.
- Optional: 3D hardware graphics acceleration, network cabling (for network rendering), video input and output devices, a three-button mouse, a sound card and speakers, a joystick and MIDI instruments (for motion capture).